HITLER: A Study in Tyranny,

is the first full account of the career of Adolph Hitler to appear in any language. This Bantam abridgment contains all the fantastic, violent and almost unbelievable incidents in the rise and fall of one of history's most monstrous figures, eliminating only the details of the more obscure and confused political circumstances and maneuvers.

Here are the strokes of fortune as well as the malignant genius which enabled Hitler to capture the German nation and become the terror of the world.

For this special Bantam edition, Mr. Bullock has completely revised and brought up to date his account of Hitler's early days, adding new and significant revelations which have only recently become available.

HITLER: A Study in Tyranny,

is one of the most important books of our time.

HITLER
A STUDY IN TYRANNY

by

ALAN BULLOCK

Censor of St. Catherine's, and
formerly Fellow of New College, Oxford

Authorized Abridgment

Bantam Books • New York

HITLER

*A Bantam Book / published by arrangement with
Harper and Brothers*

PRINTING HISTORY

Harper edition published January 1953
2nd printing.....February 1955
3rd printing.....February 1956
Biography Book Club, March 1953
Bantam edition published November 1958
2nd printing
3rd printing
4th printing
5th printing
6th printing

Library of Congress Catalog Card Number: 58-11780

*Bantam Books are published by Bantam Books, Inc. Its
trade-mark, consisting of the words "Bantam Books"
and the portrayal of a bantam, is registered in the
U. S. Patent Office and in other countries. Marca
Registrada. Printed in the United States of America.
Bantam Books, Inc., 25 W. 45th St., New York 36, N. Y.*

To my
Mother and Father

"Men do not become tyrants in order to keep out the cold."

ARISTOTLE, *Politics*

PREFACE

I began this book with two questions in mind. The first, suggested by much that was said at the Nuremberg Trials, was to discover how great a part Hitler played in the history of the Third Reich and whether Goering and the other defendants were exaggerating when they claimed that under the Nazi régime the will of one man, and of one man alone, was decisive. This led to the second and larger question: if the picture of Hitler given at Nuremberg was substantially accurate, what were the gifts Hitler possessed which enabled him first to secure and then to maintain such power. I determined to reconstruct, so far as I was able, the course of his life from his birth in 1889 to his death in 1945, in the hope that this would enable me to offer an account of one of the most puzzling and remarkable careers in modern history.

The book is cast, therefore, in the form of an historical narrative, interrupted only at one point by a chapter in which I have tried to present a portrait of Hitler on the eve of his greatest triumphs (Chapter Seven). I have not attempted to write a history of Germany, nor a study of government and society under the Nazi régime. My theme is not dictatorship, but the dictator, the personal power of one man, although it may be added that for most of the years between 1933 and 1945 this is identical with the most important part of the history of the Third Reich. Up to 1934 the interest lies in the means by which Hitler secured power in Germany. After 1934 the emphasis shifts to foreign policy and ultimately to war, the means by which Hitler sought to extend his power outside Germany. If at times, especially between 1938 and 1945, the figure of the man is submerged beneath the complicated narrative of politics and war, this corresponds to Hitler's own sacrifice of his private life (which was meagre and uninteresting at the best of times) to the demands of the position he had created for himself. In the last year of his life, however, as his empire begins to crumble, the true nature of the man is revealed again in all its naked ugliness.

In the normal course of events it is a long time before the historian can secure access to the sort of evidence which chance has made available within a few years of the overthrow of the Third Reich. At the end of the war the German State ceased to exist, and a great part of its secret archives fell into the hands of the victorious Allies, a unique event in the history of a Great Power. Moreover, the trial of the surviving German leaders before the International Tribunal at Nuremberg brought to light the most important items of evidence much more quickly than could be expected from the systematic publication of the archives which has now begun but must necessarily take time. Chance has also favoured the historian in unexpected windfalls, such as the discovery of the Ciano and Goebbels diaries, of the records of Ciano's diplomatic conferences, and of many of the letters exchanged between Hitler and Mussolini.

The limitations of this material need to be borne in mind. It is incomplete and patchy. It throws a flood of light on two periods of Hitler's career, the years 1930-1934 and the years 1938-1945, but adds much less to our knowledge of the earlier years or of the period 1934-1938. It is much fuller on foreign policy than on the internal organization of the Nazi dictatorship, and it can be misleading unless due allowance is made for what is still missing. Thus the chance which has preserved the records of Hitler's naval conferences intact can produce a distorted picture of Hitler's strategy, unless careful attention is paid to the records of his military conferences, which are unfortunately fragmentary but appear to tell a very different story.

Despite these difficulties which are inherent in the historical study of any period, it can be claimed that the material already available for the study of this period in German history is richer than that which exists for the history of any other Great Power in this period and possibly a good deal earlier.

I have supplemented the records which have become available since the end of the war by a careful re-reading of *Mein Kampf*, of Hitler's speeches, of much Nazi propaganda material and of evidence published before 1945. The recent memoirs of such men as Dr. Schacht, General Guderian, Dr. Schmidt and others have proved another valuable source of information. Herr von Papen's *Memoirs* appeared too late for me to use, but I have taken account of the evidence which he gave at Nuremberg. I have derived much help from the work of those who have written about Hitler before me, notably Dr. Konrad Heiden, Miss Elizabeth Wiskemann, Mr. H. R. Trevor-Roper and the editor of *The Speeches of Adolf Hitler*, Professor Norman Baynes. Two interesting sources, not normally available to the historian, on which I have been able to draw are the German news-reels of these years and the gramophone recordings of Hitler's speeches.

No man can sit down to write about the history of his own times—or perhaps of any time—without bringing to the task the preconceptions which spring out of his own character and experience. This is the inescapable condition of the historian's work, and the present study is no more exempt from these limitations than any other account of the events of the recent past. Nevertheless, I have written this book without any particular axe to grind or case to argue. I have no simple formula to offer in explanation of the events I have described; few major historical events appear to me to be susceptible of simple explanations. Nor has it been my purpose either to rehabilitate or to indict Adolf Hitler. If I cannot claim the impartiality of a judge, I have not cast myself for the role of prosecuting counsel, still less for that of counsel for the defence. However disputable some of my interpretations may be, there is a solid substratum of fact—and the facts are eloquent enough.

I should like to express my thanks to Mr. A. L. Rowse, who first suggested to me that I should write a life of Hitler, and to the directors of Odhams Press, who commissioned the work and have borne patiently with the difficulties involved in writing it. I am also indebted to members of the staff of Odhams Press Book Department for much good advice. The work of typing a long and illegible manuscript has been done by Miss J. E. Gore, Mrs. Joan Wilson and Miss B. A. Tonkin, to all of whom I am grateful. The Librarian and Staff of the Royal Institute of International Affairs, and of the Wiener Library, have been most helpful in meeting my requests.

To my father I owe, besides much else, the good advice which led me to scrap a first draft and start again. My friend John Wheeler-Bennett has generously allowed me not only to make use of his unique private collection of books on Germany and to draw on his great knowledge of the period, but to read the manuscripts of his forthcoming study of the German Army in politics, *The Nemesis of Power*. I have benefited immensely from this privilege, and owe to him, and to the Warden of St. Antony's College, my warmest thanks for their encouragement. My friend Stanley Hyland has undertaken the intricate task of preparing the index and I am most grateful to him for the skill and patience he has given to the task.

My last and greatest debt is to my wife, not only for her encouragement, but for invaluable help in planning and writing the book and for her critical judgment in revising the manuscript.

The work has been written while I have held a full-time tutorial Fellowship at New College, Oxford, and it is with a sense of sadness as well as of gratitude that I date this preface at the beginning of my last term as a member of that society. I hope that the Warden and Fellows of New College will not look too much askance at the fruit of my years as a Fellow of that ancient foundation.

ALAN BULLOCK

New College, Oxford.
26 April, 1952.

ACKNOWLEDGEMENTS

I wish to acknowledge the permission of the Controller, H.M. Stationery Office to quote from publications issued by the British Government. I wish to express my gratitude to the authors, editors, publishers and agents concerned for permission to quote from the following books: *Mein Kampf* (translated by James Murphy), and *My Part in Germany's Fight*—Hurst & Blackett, Ltd. *The Speeches of Adolf Hitler* (ed. Norman H. Baynes); *Documents on International Affairs*, 1936 and 1939-1946—Oxford University Press and Royal Institute of International Affairs. *Hitler Directs His War* (ed. F. Gilbert)—Oxford University Press, Inc., New York. *The French Yellow Book; The Polish White Book; The Last Attempt*, by B. Dahlerus, and *My War Memories*, by Gen. Ludendorff—Hutchinson & Co. (Publishers), Ltd. *Failure of a Mission*, by Sir N. Henderson—Raymond Savage, Ltd. *I Paid Hitler*, by Fritz Thyssen—Hodder & Stoughton, Ltd. *Hitler Speaks*, by Herman Rauschning, and *The Royal Family of Bayreuth*, by F. Wagner—Eyre & Spottiswoode (Publishers), Ltd. *Hitler as War-Lord*, by Franz Halder—Putnam & Co., Ltd. *Ciano's Diary, 1939-43*—Wm. Heinemann, Ltd. *Ciano's Diplomatic Papers*—Odhams Press, Ltd. *Der Fuehrer*, by K. Heiden—Victor Gollancz, Ltd., and the Houghton Mifflin Co. *A History of National Socialism*, by K. Heiden—Methuen & Co., Ltd. *The Goebbels Diaries*, and *Berlin Diary*, by W. L. Shirer—Hamish Hamilton, Ltd. *The Last Days of Hitler*, by H. R. Trevor-Roper, and *The Life of Neville Chamberlain*, by K. Feiling—Macmillan & Co., Ltd. *Hitler and I*, by Otto Strasser—International Press Alliance Corporation. *Hitlers Tischgespräche* and *Statist auf diplomatischer Bühne*, by Paul Schmidt—Athenäum Verlag. *The Second World War*, vol. I, by Winston S. Churchill—Cassell & Co., Ltd., and the Houghton Mifflin Co.; *Farewell Austria*, by K. von Schuschnigg, and *The Other Side of the Hill*, by B. H. Liddell-Hart—Cassell & Co., Ltd. *Defeat in the West*, by Milton Shulman, and *Hitler and His Admirals*, by A. Martiennsen—Secker & Warburg, Ltd. *To the Bitter End*, by H. B. Gisevius—Jonathan Cape, Ltd., and the Houghton Mifflin Co. *Hitler the Pawn*, by R. Olden—Victor Gollancz, Ltd. *The Fateful Years*, by A. François-Poncet—Victor Gollancz, Ltd., and Harcourt, Brace & Co., Inc. *The Memoirs of Ernst von Weizsäcker*—Victor Gollancz, Ltd., and the Henry Regnery Co. *Panzer Leader*, by Heinz Guderian—Michael Joseph, Ltd. *Hitler*, by K. Heiden —Constable & Co., Ltd. *Account Settled*, by H. Schacht— Weidenfeld & Nicolson, Ltd. *The Errant Diplomat*, by O. Dutch—Arnold & Co. *The Fall of the German Republic*— Allen & Unwin, Ltd. *The Curtain Falls*, by Count Bernadotte —Alfred Knopf, Inc. *The Struggle for Europe*, by Chester Wilmot, and *Rommel*, by Desmond Young—Collins, Sons and Co., Ltd. *Hegel's Lectures on the Philosophy of History*— G. Bell & Sons, Ltd. *Die Deutsche Katastrophe*, by Fr. Meinecke—Eberhard Brockhaus Verlag. *Rätsel um Deutschland*, by B. Schwertfeger—Carl Winter Universitätsverlag. *Les Lettres Secrètes échangées par Hitler et Mussolini*—Editions du Pavois. *Hitler Privat*, by A. Zoller—Droste Verlag. *Austrian Requiem*, by K. von Schuschnigg—Victor Gollancz, Ltd., and G. P. Putnam's Sons. *Blue Print of the Nazi Underground*, by R. W. M. Kempner—Research Studies of the State College of Washington. *Von Schleicher, von Papen et L'Avènement de Hitler*, by G. Castellan—Cahiers d'Histoire de la Guerre, Paris. *Reichswehr and National Socialism*, by Gordon A. Craig—Political Science Quarterly, N.Y. *My New Order* (ed. Count Roussy de Sales)—Harcourt, Brace & Co., Inc., *Der letze Monat*, by Karl Koller—Norbert Wohlgemuth Verlag. *Die letzen 30 Tage*, by Joachim Schultz—Steingrüben Verlag. *Rosenberg's Memoirs*—Ziff-Davis Publishing Co. *I Knew Hitler*, by K. Ludecke—Jarrolds, Publishers (London), Ltd., and *Hitler's Words* by Gordon W. Prange—Public Affairs Press, Washington.

Quotations have been made from a number of other books which lack of space prevents me from acknowledging individually, but I am grateful to all those who have granted me permission to quote. In some cases it has proved impossible to locate sources of copyright property. If, therefore, any quotations have been incorrectly acknowledged I hope the persons concerned will accept my apologies.

CHAPTER ONE

THE FORMATIVE YEARS

1889—1918

I

Adolf Hitler was born at half past six P.M. 20 April, 1889, in the *Gasthof zum Pommer,* an inn in the small town of Braunau on the River Inn which forms the frontier between Austria and Bavaria.

The three republics Hitler was to destroy, the Austria of the Treaty of St. Germain, Czechoslovakia and Poland, were not yet in existence. Four great empires—the Hapsburg, the Hohenzollern, the Romanov and the Ottoman—ruled over Central and Eastern Europe. The Bolshevik Revolution and the Soviet Union were not yet imagined: Russia was still the Holy Russia of the Tsars. In the summer of this same year, 1889, Lenin was a student of nineteen in trouble with the authorities. Stalin was a poor cobbler's son in Tiflis, Mussolini the six-year-old child of a blacksmith in the bleak Romagna.

Hitler's family, on both sides, came from the Waldviertel, a poor, remote country district, lying on the north side of the Danube, some fifty miles north-west of Vienna. In this countryside of hills and woods, with few towns or railways, lived a peasant population cut off from the main arteries of Austrian life. It was from this country stock, with its frequent intermarriages, that Hitler sprang .

The family name, possibly Czech in origin and spelled in a variety of ways, first appears in the Waldviertel in the first half of the fifteenth century. The grandfather of the future Chancellor, Johann Georg Hiedler, seems to have been a wanderer who never settled down, but followed the trade of a miller in several places in Lower Austria. In the course of these wanderings he picked up with a peasant girl from the village of Strones, Maria Anna Schicklgruber, whom he married at Döllersheim in May, 1842.

Five years earlier, in 1837, Maria had given birth to an illegitimate child, who was known by the name of Alois and who may have been the child of Johann Georg Hiedler. Although Johann Georg married Maria in 1842, he did not bother to legitimise the child, who continued to be known by his mother's maiden name of Schicklgruber until he was nearly forty and who was brought up at Spital in the house of his father's brother, Johann Nepomuk Hiedler.

In 1876 Johann Nepomuk took steps to legitimise the young man who had grown up in his house. He called on the parish priest at Döllersheim and persuaded him to cross out the word 'illegitimate' in the register and to append a statement signed by three witnesses that his brother Johann Georg Hiedler had accepted the paternity of the child Alois. This is by no means conclusive evidence, and, in all probability, we shall never know who Adolf Hitler's grandfather, the father of Alois, really was. It has been suggested that he may have been a Jew, without definite proof one way or the other. However this may be, from the beginning of 1877, twelve years before Adolf was born, his father called himself Hitler and his son was never known by any other name until his opponents dug up this long-forgotten village scandal and tried, without justification, to label him with his grandmother's name of Schicklgruber.

Alois left his uncle's home at the age of thirteen to serve as a cobbler's apprentice in Vienna. But he did not take to a trade and by the time he was eighteen he had joined the Imperial Customs Service. From 1855 to 1895 Alois served as a customs officer in Braunau and other towns of Upper Austria. He earned the normal promotion and as a minor state official he had certainly moved up several steps in the social scale from his peasant origins.

As an official in the resplendent imperial uniform of the Hapsburg Service Alois Hitler appeared the image of respectability. But his private life belied appearances.

In 1864 he married Anna Glasl, the daughter of another customs collector. The marriage was not a success. There were no children and, after a separation, Alois' wife, who was considerably older and had long been ailing, died in 1883. A month later Alois married a young hotel servant, Franziska Matzelsberger, who had already borne him a son out of wedlock and who gave birth to a daughter, Angela, three months after their marriage.

Alois had no better luck with his second marriage. Within a year of her daughter's birth, Franziska was dead of tuberculosis. This time he waited half a year before marrying again. His third wife, Klara Pölzl, twenty-three years younger than himself, came from the village of Spital, where the Hitlers had originated. The two families were already related by marriage, and Klara herself was the granddaughter of that Johann Nepomuk Hiedler in whose house Alois had been brought up as a child. She had even lived with Alois and his first wife for a time at Braunau. An episcopal dispensation had to be secured for such a marriage between second cousins, but finally, on 7 January, 1885, Alois Hitler married his third wife, and on 17 May of the same year their first child, Gustav, was born at Braunau.

Adolf was the third child of Alois Hitler's third marriage; only his younger sister, Paula, born in 1896, lived to grow up. There were also, however, the two children of the second marriage with Franziska, Adolf Hitler's half-brother Alois, and his half-sister Angela. Angela was the only one of his relations with whom Hitler maintained any sort of friendship. She kept house for him at Berchtesgaden for a time, and it was her daughter, Geli Raubal, with whom Hitler fell in love.

When Adolf Hitler was born his father was over fifty and his mother was under thirty. Alois Hitler was not only very much older than Klara and her children, but hard, unsympathetic and short-tempered. His domestic life—three wives, one fourteen years older than himself, one twenty-three years younger; a separation, and seven children, including one illegitimate child and two others born shortly after the wedding—suggest a difficult and passionate temperament. Towards the end of his life Alois Hitler seems to have become bitter over some disappointment, perhaps connected with another inheritance. He retired in 1895 at the age of fifty-eight, and stayed in Upper Austria. The family finally settled at Leonding, a village just outside Linz, overlooking the confluence of the Traun and the Danube. Here the retired customs official spent his remaining years, from 1899 to 1903, in a small house with a garden.

Hitler attempted to represent himself in *Mein Kampf* as the child of poverty and privation. In fact, his father had a perfectly adequate pension and gave the boy the chance of a good education. After five years in primary schools, the eleven year old Adolf entered the Linz Realschule in September 1900. This was a secondary school designed to train boys for a technical and commercial career. At the beginning of 1903 Alois Hitler died, but his widow continued to draw a pension and was not left in need. Adolf left the Linz Realschule in 1904 not because his mother was too poor to pay the fees, but because his record at school was so poor that he had to accept a transfer to another school at Steyr, where he finished his education at the age of sixteen.

In *Mein Kampf* Hitler makes much of a dramatic conflict

between himself and his father over his ambition to become an artist. There is no doubt that he did not get on well with his father, but it is highly unlikely that his ambition to become an artist (he was not fourteen when his father died) had much to do with it. A more probable explanation is that his father was dissatisfied with his school reports and made his dissatisfaction plain. Hitler glossed over his poor performance at school which he left without securing the customary Leaving Certificate. He found every possible excuse for himself, from illness and his father's tyranny to artistic ambition and political prejudice. It was a failure which rankled for a long time and found frequent expression in sneers at the "educated gentlemen" with their diplomas and doctorates.

When her son finally left school, in 1905, Frau Hitler sold the house at Leonding and moved to a small flat in Linz, the capital of Upper Austria. She had little control over her self-willed son who refused to settle down to earn his living and spent the next two years indulging in dreams of becoming an artist or architect, living at home, filling his sketch book with entirely unoriginal drawings and elaborating grandiose plans for the rebuilding of Linz. His one friend was August Kubizek, the son of a Linz upholsterer, eight months younger than Hitler, who provided a willing and awe-struck audience for the ambitions and enthusiasms which Hitler poured out in their walks round Linz. Together they visited the theatre where Hitler acquired a life-long passion for Wagner's operas. Wagnerian romanticism and vast dreams of his own success as an artist and Kubizek's as a musician filled his mind. He lived in a world of his own, content to let his mother provide for his needs, scornfully refusing to concern himself with such petty mundane affairs as money or a job.

A visit to Vienna in May and June 1906 fired him with enthusiasm for the splendour of its buildings, its art-galleries and Opera. On his return to Linz, he was less inclined than ever to find a job for himself. His ambition now was to go back to Vienna and enter the Academy of Fine Arts. His mother was anxious and uneasy but finally capitulated. In the autumn of 1907 he set off for Vienna a second time with high hopes for the future.

His first attempt to enter the Academy in October 1907 was unsuccessful. The Academy's Classification List contains the entry:

"The following took the test with insufficient results or were not admitted. . . .
Adolf Hitler, Braunau a.Inn, 20 April 1889.
German. Catholic. Father, civil servant. 4 classes in Realschule. Few heads. Test drawing unsatisfactory."

The result, he says in *Mein Kampf;* came as a bitter shock. The Director advised him to try his talents in the direction of architecture: he was not cut out to be a painter. But Hitler refused to admit defeat. Even his mother's illness (she was dying of cancer) did not bring him back to Linz. He returned only after her death (21 December 1907) in time for the funeral, and in February 1908 went back to Vienna, to resume his life as an "art student".

He was entitled to draw an orphan's pension and had the small savings left by his mother to fall back on. He was soon joined by his friend Kubizek whom he had prevailed upon to follow his example and seek a place at the Vienna Conservatoire. The two shared a room in which there was hardly space for Kubizek's piano and Hitler's table.

Apart from Kubizek, Hitler lived a solitary life. He had no other friends. Women were attracted to him, but he showed complete indifference to them. Much of the time he spent dreaming or brooding. His moods alternated between moody preoccupation and outbursts of excited talk. He wandered for hours through the streets and parks, staring at buildings which he admired, or suddenly disappearing into the public library in pursuit of some new enthusiasm. Again and again, the two young men visited the Opera and the Burgtheater. But while Kubizek pursued his studies at the Conservatoire, Hitler was incapable of any disciplined or systematic work. He drew little, wrote more and even attempted to compose a music drama on the theme of Wieland the Smith. He had the artist's temperament without either talent, training, or creative energy.

In July 1908, Kubizek went back to Linz for the summer. A month later Hitler set out to visit two of his aunts in Spital. When they said goodbye, both young men expected to meet again in Vienna in the autumn. But when Kubizek returned to the capital, he could find no trace of his friend.

In mid-September Hitler had again applied for admission to the Academy of Art. This time, he was not even admitted to the examination. The director advised him to apply to the School of Architecture, but there entry was barred by his lack of a School Leaving Certificate. Perhaps it was wounded pride that led him to avoid Kubizek. Whatever the reason, for the next five years he chose to bury himself in obscurity.

II

Vienna, at the beginning of 1909, was still an imperial city, capital of an Empire of fifty million souls stretching from the Rhine to the Dniester, from Saxony to Montenegro. The monumental buildings erected on the Ringstrasse in the last quarter of the nineteenth century reflected the prosperity and self-confidence of the Viennese middle class; the factories and poorer streets of the outer districts, the rise of an industrial working class. It must have appeared a callous and unfriendly city: Vienna was no place to be without money or a job. His next four years there, from 1909 to 1913, Hitler says, were the unhappiest of his life. They were also in many ways the most important, in which his character and opinions were given definite shape.

Mein Kampf, which was written as a work of political propaganda, is evasive and misleading in the little information it gives about such material questions as the way in which Hitler earned his living, or where he lived. Hitler speaks of his stay in Vienna as "five years in which I had to earn my daily bread, first as a casual labourer, then as a painter of little trifles." Among the jobs he took was one in the building trade, where he quarrelled with the other workmen and was soon forced to leave because he disagreed with their politics. He writes with feeling of the poor boy from the country who discovers himself out of work. "He loiters about and is hungry. Often he pawns or sells the last of his belongings. His clothes begin to get shabby—with the increasing poverty of his outward appearance he descends to a lower social level."

A little further on, Hitler gives another picture of his Vienna days. "In the years 1909-1910 I had so far improved my position that I no longer had to earn my daily bread as a manual labourer. I was now working independently as a draughtsman and painter in water-colours." Hitler explains that he made very little money at this, but that he was master of his own time and felt that he was getting nearer to the profession he wanted to take up, that of an architect.

This is a very highly coloured account compared with the evidence of those who knew him then. Meagre though this is, it is enough to make nonsense of Hitler's picture of himself as a man who had once earned his living by his hands and then by hard work turned himself into an art student.

According to Konrad Heiden, who was the first man to piece together the scraps of independent evidence, in 1909, Hitler was obliged to give up the furnished room in which he had been living in the Simon Denk Gasse for lack of funds. In the summer he could sleep out, but with the coming of autumn he found a bed in a doss-house behind Meidling Station. At the end of the year, Hitler moved to a hostel for men at 27 Meldemannstrasse, in the 20th district of Vienna, over on the other side of the city, close to the Danube. Here he lived, for the remaining three years of his stay in Vienna, from 1910 to 1913.

A few who knew Hitler at this time have been traced and questioned, amongst them a certain Reinhold Hanisch, a tramp from German Bohemia, who for a time knew Hitler well. Hanisch's testimony is partly confirmed by one of the few pieces of documentary evidence discovered for the early years. For in 1910, after a quarrel, Hitler sued Hanisch for cheating him of a small sum of money, and the records of the Vienna police court have been published.

Hanisch describes his first meeting with Hitler in the doss-house in Meidling in 1909. "On the very first day there sat next to the bed that had been allotted to me a man who had nothing on except an old torn pair of trousers—Hitler. His clothes were being cleaned of lice, since for days he had been wandering about without a roof. . . ."

Hanisch and Hitler joined forces in looking for work; they beat carpets, carried bags outside the West Station, and did casual labouring jobs, sometimes shovelling snow off the streets. As Hitler had no overcoat, he felt the cold badly. Then Hanisch had a better idea. He asked Hitler one day what trade he had learned. " 'I am a painter,' was the answer. Thinking that he was a house decorator, I said that it would surely be easy to make money at this trade. He was offended and answered that he was not that sort of painter, but an academician and an artist." When the two moved to the Meldemannstrasse, "we had to think out better ways of making money. Hitler proposed that we should fake pictures. He told me that already in Linz he had painted small landscapes in oil, had roasted them in an oven until they had become quite brown and had several times been successful in selling these pictures to traders as valuable old masters." This sounds highly improbable, but in any case Hanisch, who had registered as Fritz Walter, was afraid of the police. "So I suggested to Hitler that it would be better to stay in an honest trade and paint postcards. I myself was to sell the painted cards, we decided to work together and share the money we earned."

Hitler had enough money to buy a few cards, ink and paints. With these he produced little copies of views of Vienna, which Hanisch peddled in taverns and fairs, or to small traders who wanted something to fill their empty picture frames. In this way they made enough to keep them until in the summer of 1910, Hanisch sold a copy which Hitler had made of a drawing of the Vienna Parliament Building for ten crowns. Hitler, who was sure it was worth far more—he valued it at fifty in his statement to the police—was convinced he had been cheated. When Hanisch failed to return to the hostel, Hitler brought a lawsuit against him which ended in Hanisch spending a week in prison and the break-up of their partnership.

This was in August 1910. For the remaining four years before the First World War, first in Vienna, later in Munich, Hitler continued to eke out a living in the same way. Some of his drawings, mostly stiff, lifeless copies of buildings in which his attempts to add human figures are a failure, were still to be found in Vienna in the 1930's, when they had acquired the value of collectors' pieces. More often he drew posters and crude advertisements for small shops—Teddy Perspiration Powder, Santa Claus selling coloured candles, or St. Stefan's spire rising over a mountain of soap, with the signature "A. Hitler" in the corner. Hitler himself later described these as years of great loneliness, in which his only contacts with other human beings were in the hostel where, according to Hanisch, "only tramps, drunkards and such spent any time."

After their quarrel Hanisch lost sight of Hitler, but he gives a description of Hitler as he knew him in 1910 at the age of twenty-one. He wore an ancient black overcoat, which had been given him by an old-clothes dealer in the hostel, a Hungarian Jew named Neumann, and which reached down over his knees. From under a greasy black derby hat, his hair hung long over his coat collar. His thin and hungry face was covered with a black beard above which his large staring eyes were the one prominent feature. Altogether, Hanisch adds, "an apparition such as rarely occurs among Christians."

From time to time Hitler had received financial help from his aunt in Linz, Johanna Pölzl and, when she died in March 1911, it seems likely that he was left some small legacy. In May of that year his orphan's pension was stopped, but he still avoided any regular work.

Hanisch depicts him as lazy and moody, two characteristics which were often to reappear. If he earned a few crowns, he refused to draw for days and went off to a cafe to eat cream cakes and read newspapers. He had none of the common vices. He neither smoked nor drank and, according to Hanisch, was too shy and awkward to have any success with women. His passions were reading newspapers and talking politics. "Over and over again," Hanisch recalls, "there were days on which he simply refused to work. Then he would hang around night shelters, living on the bread and soup that he got there, and discussing politics, often getting involved in heated controversies."

When he became excited in argument he would shout and wave his arms, until the others in the room cursed him for disturbing them, or the porter came in to stop the noise. Sometimes people laughed at him, at other times they were oddly impressed. "One evening," Hanisch relates, "Hitler went to a cinema where Kellermann's *Tunnel* was being shown. In this piece an agitator appears who rouses the working masses by his speeches. Hitler almost went crazy. . . . For days afterwards he spoke of nothing except the power of the spoken word." These outbursts of violent argument and denunciation alternated with moods of despondency.

Everyone who knew him was struck by the combination of ambition, energy and indolence in Hitler. He was not only desperately anxious to impress people but was full of ideas for making his fortune and fame—from water-divining to designing an aeroplane. In this mood he would begin to spend the fortune he was to make in anticipation, but he was incapable of the application and hard work needed to carry out his projects. He would relapse into moodiness and disappear until he began to hare off after some new trick or short cut to success. His intellectual interests followed the same pattern. He spent much time in the public library, but his reading was indiscriminate and unsystematic. Ancient Rome, the Eastern religions, Yoga, Occultism, Hypnotism, Astrology, Protestantism, each in turn excited his interest for a moment. He started a score of jobs but failed to make anything of them and relapsed into the old hand-to-mouth existence, living by expedients and little spurts of activity.

As time passed these habits became ingrained, and he became more eccentric, more turned in on himself. He struck people as unbalanced. He gave rein to his hatreds—against the Jews, the priests, the Social Democrats, the Hapsburgs—without restraint. The few people with whom he had been friendly became tired of his strange behaviour and wild talk. Neumann, the Jew who had befriended him, was offended by the violence of his anti-Semitism; Kanya, who kept the hostel for men, thought him one of the oddest customers with whom he had had to deal. Yet these Vienna days stamped an indelible impression on his character and mind. "During these years a view of life and a definite outlook on the world took shape in my mind. These became the granite basis of my conduct at that time. Since then I have extended that foundation very little, I have changed nothing in it . . . Vienna was a hard school for me, but it taught me the most profound lessons of my life." However pretentiously expressed, this is true. It is time to examine what these lessons were.

III

The idea of struggle is as old as life itself, for life is only preserved because other living things perish through struggle. . . .
In this struggle, the stronger, the more able win, while the less
able, the weak lose. Struggle is the father of all things. . . . It
is not by the principles of humanity that man lives or is able
to preserve himself above the animal world, but solely by means
of the most brutal struggle. . . . If you do not fight for life, then
life will never be won.

This is the natural philosophy of the doss-house. In this struggle any trick or ruse, however unscrupulous; the use of any
weapon or opportunity, however treacherous, are permissible.
To quote another typical sentence from Hitler's speeches:
"Whatever goal man has reached is due to his originality
plus his brutality." Astuteness; the ability to lie, twist, cheat
and flatter; the elimination of sentimentality or loyalty in favour of ruthlessness, these were the qualities which enabled
men to rise above all, strength of will. Such were the principles which Hitler drew from his years in Vienna. Hitler
never trusted anyone; he never committed himself to anyone,
never admitted any loyalty. His lack of scruple later took
by surprise even those who prided themselves on their unscrupulousness. He learned to lie with conviction and dis-
semble with candour. To the end he refused to admit defeat
and still held to the belief that by the power of will alone he
could transform events.

Distrust was matched by contempt. Men were moved by
fear, greed, lust for power, envy, often by mean and petty
motives. Politics, Hitler was later to conclude, is the art of
knowing how to use these weaknesses for one's own ends.
Already in Vienna Hitler admired Karl Lueger, the famous
Burgomaster of Vienna and leader of the Christian Social
Party, because "he had a rare gift of insight into human nature and was very careful not to take men as something
better than they were in reality." He felt particular contempt
for the masses—"everybody who properly estimates the political intelligence of the masses can easily see that this is not
sufficiently developed to enable them to form general political
judgments on their own account." Here again was material to
be manipulated by a skilful politician although as yet Hitler
had no idea of making a political career.

Hitler writes in *Mein Kampf* of the misery in which the
Vienna working class lived at this time, but it is evident from
every line of his account that these conditions produced no

feeling of sympathy in him. "I do not know which appalled me most at that time: the economic misery of those who were then my companions, their crude customs and morals, or the low level of their intellectual culture." Least of all did he feel any sympathy with the attempts of the poor and the exploited to improve their position by their own efforts. Hitler's hatred was directed not so much against the rogues, beggars, bankrupt business men and *déclassé* "gentlemen" drifting in and out of the hostel in the Meldemannstrasse, as against the working men who belonged to organizations like the Social Democratic Party and the trade unions and who preached equality and the solidarity of the working classes. It was these, much more than the former, who threatened his claim to superiority. He passionately refused to join a trade union, or in any way to admit that he accepted the status of a working man.

The whole ideology of the working-class movement was alien and hateful to him:

All that I heard had the effect of arousing the strongest antagonism in me. Everything was disparaged—the nation because it was held to be an invention of the capitalist class (how often I had to listen to that phrase!); the Fatherland, because it was held to be an instrument in the hand of the *bourgeoisie* for the exploitation of the working masses; the authority of the law, because this was a means of holding down the proletariat; religion, as a means of doping the people, so as to exploit them afterwards; morality, as a badge of stupid and sheepish docility. There was nothing that they did not drag in the mud. . . . Then I asked myself: are these men worthy to belong to a great people? The question was profoundly disturbing; for if the answer were "Yes," then the struggle to defend one's nationality is no longer worth all the trouble and sacrifice we demand of our best elements if it be in the interest of such a rabble. On the other hand, if the answer had to be "No," then our nation is poor indeed in men. During these days of mental anguish and deep meditation I saw before my mind the ever-increasing and menacing army of people who could no longer be reckoned as belonging to their own nation.

Hitler found the solution of his dilemma in the "discovery" that the working men were the victims of a deliberate system for corrupting and poisoning the popular mind, organized by the Social Democratic Party's leaders, who cynically exploited the distress of the masses for their own ends. Then came the crowning revelation: "I discovered the relations existing between this destructive teaching and the specific character of a people, who up to that time had been almost unknown to me. Knowledge of the Jews is the only key whereby one may understand the inner nature and the real aims of Social Democracy."

There was nothing new in Hitler's anti-Semitism; it was endemic in Vienna, and everything he ever said or wrote about the Jews is only a reflection of the anti-Semitic periodicals and pamphlets he read in Vienna before 1914. In Linz there had been very few Jews—"I do not remember ever having heard the word at home during my father's lifetime." Even in Vienna Hitler had at first been repelled by the violence of the anti-Semitic Press. Then, "one day, when passing through the Inner City, I suddenly encountered a phenomenon in a long caftan and wearing black sidelocks. My first thought was: is this a Jew? They certainly did not have this appearance in Linz. I watched the man stealthily and cautiously, but the longer I gazed at this strange countenance and examined it section by section, the more the question shaped itself in my brain: is this a German? I turned to books for help in removing my doubts. For the first time in my life I bought myself some anti-Semitic pamphlets for a few pence."

The language in which Hitler describes his discovery has the obscene taint of most anti-Semitic literature: "Was there any shady undertaking, any form of foulness, especially in cultural life, in which at least one Jew did not participate? On putting the probing knife carefully to that kind of abscess one immediately discovered, like a maggot in a putrescent body, a little Jew who was often blinded by the sudden light."

Characteristic of Viennese anti-Semitism was its sexuality. "The black-haired Jewish youth lies in wait . . . satanically glaring and spying on the unsuspicious girl whom he plans to seduce, adulterating her blood and removing her from the bosom of her own people. . . . The Jews were responsible for bringing negroes into the Rhineland with the ultimate idea of bastardizing the white race which they hate and thus lowering its cultural and political level so that the Jew might dominate." Elsewhere Hitler writes of "the nightmare vision of the seduction of hundreds of thousands of girls by repulsive, crooked-legged Jew bastards." More than one writer has suggested that some sexual experience—possibly the contraction of venereal disease—is at the back of Hitler's anti-Semitism.

In all the pages which Hitler devotes to the Jews in *Mein Kampf* he does not bring forward a single fact to support his wild assertions. This was entirely right, for Hitler's anti-Semitism bore no relation to facts, it was pure fantasy: to read these pages is to enter the world of the insane, a world peopled by hideous and distorted shadows. The Jew is no longer a human being, he has become a grimacing, leering devil, the incarnation of evil, into which Hitler projects all that he hates and fears—and desires. Like all obsessions, the Jew is not a partial, but a total explanation. The Jew is everywhere, responsible for everything—the Modernism in art and music Hitler disliked; pornography and prostitution; the anti-national criticism of the Press; the exploitation of the masses by Capitalism, and its reverse, the exploitation of the masses by Socialism; not least for his own failure to get on. "Thus I finally discovered who were the evil spirits leading our people astray. . . . My love for my own people increased correspondingly. Considering the satanic skill which these evil counsellors displayed, how could their unfortunate victims be blamed? . . . The more I came to know the Jew, the easier it was to excuse the workers."

Behind all this, Hitler soon convinced himself, lay a Jewish world conspiracy to destroy and subdue the Aryan peoples, as an act of revenge for their own inferiority. Their purpose was to weaken the nation by fomenting social divisions and class conflict, and by attacking the values of race, heroism, struggle, and authoritarian rule in favour of the false internationalist, humanitarian, pacifist, materialist ideals of democracy. "The Jewish doctrine of Marxism repudiates the aristocratic principle of nature and substitutes for it and the eternal privilege of force and energy, numerical mass and its dead weight. Thus it denies the individual worth of the human personality, impugns the teaching that nationhood and race have a primary significance, and by doing this takes away the very foundations of human existence and human civilization."

In Hitler's eyes the inequality of individuals and of races was one of the laws of Nature. This poor wretch, often half-starved, without a job, family or home, clung obstinately to any belief that would bolster up the claim of his own superiority over the labourers, the tramps, the Jews and the Slavs with whom he rubbed shoulders in the streets.

Hitler had no use for any democratic institution: free speech, free press or parliament. During the earlier part of his time in Vienna he had sometimes attended the sessions of the Reichsrat, the representative assembly of the Austrian half of the Empire, and he devotes fifteen pages of *Mein Kampf* to expressing his scorn for what he saw. "The majority represents not only ignorance but cowardice. . . . The majority can never replace the man."

All his life Hitler was irritated by discussion. In the arguments into which he was drawn in the Hostel for Men or in cafés he showed no self-control in face of contradictions or debate. He began to shout and shower abuse on his opponents, with an hysterical note in his voice. It was precisely the same pattern of uncontrolled behaviour he displayed when he came to supreme power and found himself crossed or contradicted.

Belief in equality between races was an even greater offence in Hitler's eyes than belief in equality between individuals. He had already become a passionate German nationalist. In Austria-Hungary this meant even more than it meant in Germany, and the fanatical quality of Hitler's nationalism reflects his Austrian origin.

For several hundred years the Germans of Austria played the leading part in the politics and cultural life of Central Europe. Until 1871 there had been no single unified German state. Germans had lived under the rule of a score of different states loosely grouped together in the Holy Roman Empire, and then, after 1815, in the German Federation. In the middle of the nineteenth century it was still Vienna, not Berlin, which ranked as the first of German cities. Moreover, the Hapsburgs not only enjoyed a pre-eminent position among the German states, but also ruled over many different peoples.

On both counts the Germans of the Austrian lands, who identified themselves with the Hapsburgs, looked on themselves as an imperial race of political privilege and boasting of a cultural tradition which few other peoples in Europe could equal. From the middle of the nineteenth century, however, this position was first challenged and then undermined.

Prussia defeated Austria at Sadowa in 1866, and thereafter the new German Empire with its capital at Berlin took the place hitherto occupied by Austria and Vienna as the premier German state.

At the same time the pre-eminence of the Germans within the Hapsburg Empire itself was challenged, first by the Italians, who secured their independence in the 1860s; then by the Magyars of Hungary, to whom equality had to be conceded in 1867; finally by the Slav peoples. Especially in Bohemia and Moravia, where the most advanced of the Slav peoples, the Czechs, lived, it was bitterly resented by the Germans and fiercely resisted. This conflict of the nationalities dominated Austrian politics from 1870 to the break-up of the Empire in 1918.

In this conflict Hitler had no patience with concessions. The Germans should rule the Empire, at least the Austrian half of it, with an authoritarian and centralized administration; there should be only one official language—German—

and the schools and universities should be used "to inculcate a feeling of common citizenship," an ambiguous expression for Germanization. The representative assembly of the Reichsrat, in which the Germans (only thirty-five per cent of the population of Austria) were permanently outnumbered, should be suppressed. Here was a special reason for hatred of the Social Democratic Party, which refused to follow the nationalist lead of the Pan-Germans, and instead fostered class conflicts at the expense of national unity.

In September, 1938, at the time of the Sudeten crisis, Hitler said in a newspaper interview: "The Czechs have none of the characteristics of a nation, whether from the standpoint of ethnology, strategy, economics, or language. To set an intellectually inferior handful of Czechs to rule over minorities belonging to races like the Germans, Poles, Hungarians, with a thousand years of culture behind them, was a work of folly and ignorance." This was a view which Hitler first learned in Austria before 1914, and indeed the whole Czech crisis of 1938-1939 was part of an old quarrel rooted deep in the history of the Hapsburg Empire from which Hitler came.

When Hitler returned to Vienna after the Anschluss had been carried out and the dream of a Greater Germany which Bismarck had rejected had at last been fulfilled, he said with a touch of genuine exultation: "I believe that it was God's will to send a boy from here into the Reich, to let him grow up and to raise him to be the leader of the nation so that he could lead back his homeland into the Reich." In March, 1938, the Austrian-born Chancellor of Germany reversed the decision which Bismarck, a Prussian-born Chancellor, had made in the 1860s when he excluded the German Austrians from the new German Reich.

IV

The political ideas and programme which Hitler picked up in Vienna were entirely unoriginal. They were the clichés of Radical and Pan-German gutter politics, the stock-in-trade of the anti-Semitic and nationalist Press. The originality was to appear in Hitler's grasp of how to create a mass-movement and secure power on the basis of these ideas.

The three parties which interested Hitler were the Austrian Social Democrats, Georg von Schoenerer's Pan-German Nationalists and Karl Lueger's Christian Social Party.

From the Social Democrats Hitler derived the idea of a

mass party and mass propaganda. In *Mein Kampf* he describes the impression made on him when "I gazed on the interminable ranks, four abreast, of Viennese workmen parading at a mass demonstration. I stood dumbfounded for almost two hours, watching this enormous human dragon which slowly uncoiled itself before me."

Studying the Social Democratic Press and Party speeches, Hitler reached the conclusion that: "the psyche of the broad masses is accessible only to what is strong and uncompromising. . . . The masses of the people prefer the ruler to the suppliant and are filled with a stronger sense of mental security by a teaching that brooks no rival than by a teaching which offers them a liberal choice. They have very little idea of how to make such a choice and thus are prone to feel that they have been abandoned. Whereas they feel very little shame at being terrorized intellectually and are scarcely conscious of the fact that their freedom as human beings is impudently abused. . . . I also came to understand that physical intimidation has its significance for the mass as well as the individual. . . . For the successes which are thus obtained are taken by the adherents as a triumphant symbol of the righteousness of their own cause; while the beaten opponent very often loses faith in the effectiveness of any further resistance."

From Georg Ritter von Schoenerer, who founded the Pan-German movement in Austria, Hitler took his extreme German Nationalism, his anti-Socialism, his anti-Semitism, his hatred of the Hapsburgs and his programme of reunion with Germany. But Schoenerer, Hitler believed, made three cardinal errors.

The Nationalists failed to grasp the importance of the social problem, directing their attention to the middle classes and neglecting the masses. They wasted their energy in a parliamentary struggle and failed to establish themselves as the leaders of a great movement. Finally they made the mistake of attacking the Catholic Church and split their forces instead of concentrating them. "The art of leadership," Hitler wrote, "consists of consolidating the attention of the people against a single adversary and taking care that nothing will split up this attention. . . . The leader of genius must have the ability to make different opponents appear as if they belonged to one category."

It was in the third party, the Christian Socialists, and their remarkable leader, Karl Lueger, that Hitler found brilliantly displayed that grasp of political tactics, the lack of which hampered the success of the Nationalists. Lueger had made himself Burgomaster of Vienna—in many ways the most important elective post in Austria—and by 1907 the Christian Socialists under his leadership had become the strongest party in the Austrian parliament. Hitler saw much to criticize in Lueger's programme. His anti-Semitism was based on religious and economic, not on racial, grounds ("I decide who is a Jew," Lueger once said), and he rejected the intransigent nationalism of the Pan-Germans, seeking to preserve and strengthen the Hapsburg State with its mixture of nationalities. But Hitler was prepared to overlook even this in his admiration for Lueger's leadership.

The strength of Lueger's following lay in the lower middle class of Vienna, the small shopkeepers, business men and artisans, the petty officials and municipal employees. "He devoted the greatest part of his political activity," Hitler noted, "to the task of winning over those sections of the population whose existence was in danger."

Years later Hitler was to show a brilliant appreciation of the importance of these same classes in German politics. From the beginning Lueger understood the importance both of social problems and of appealing to the masses.

Finally, instead of quarrelling with the Church, Lueger made it his ally and used to the full the traditional loyalty to crown and altar. Again pointing to his later career, Hitler remarks: "He was quick to adopt all available means for winning the support of long-established institutions, so as to be able to derive the greatest possible advantage for his movement from those old sources of power."

It would be an exaggeration to suppose that Hitler had already formulated clearly the ideas he set out in *Mein Kamp* in the middle of the 1920s. None the less the greater part of the experience on which he drew was already complete when he left Vienna, and to the end Hitler bore the stamp of his Austrian origins.

v

Hitler left Vienna for good in the spring of 1913. He was then twenty-four years old, awkward, moody and reserved, yet nursing a passion of hatred and fanaticism which from time to time broke out in a torrent of excited words. Years of failure had laid up a deep store of resentment in him, but had failed to weaken the conviction of his own superiority.

In *Mein Kampf* Hitler speaks of leaving Vienna in the spring of 1912, but the Vienna police records report him as

living there until May, 1913. Hitler is so careless about dates
and facts in his book that the later date seems more likely
to be correct. Hitler is equally evasive about the reasons
which led him to leave. He writes in general terms of his
dislike of Vienna and the state of affairs in Austria:

My inner aversion to the Hapsburg State was increasing daily.
. . . This motley of Czechs, Poles, Hungarians, Ruthenians,
Serbs and Croats, and always that bacillus which is the solvent
of human society, the Jew, here and there and everywhere—
the whole spectacle was repugnant to me. . . . The longer I
lived in that city the stronger became my hatred for the pro-
miscuous swarm of foreign peoples which had begun to
batten on that old nursery ground of German culture. All these
considerations intensified my yearning to depart for that country for which my heart had been secretly longing since the
days of my youth. I hoped that one day I might be able to
make my mark as an architect and that I could devote my
talents to the service of my country. A final reason was that I
hoped to be among those who lived and worked in that land
from which the movement should be launched, the object of
which would be . . . the reunion of the country in which I
was born with our common fatherland, the German Empire.

All this, we may be sure, is true enough, but it gives no
specific reason why, on one day rather than another, Hitler
decided to go to the station, buy a ticket and at last leave the
city he had come to detest.

A possible explanation is that Hitler was anxious to escape
military service, for which he had failed to report each year
since 1910. Enquiries were being made by the police, and he
may have found it necessary to slip over the frontier. Eventually he was located in Munich and ordered to present
himself for examination at Linz. The correspondence between
Hitler and the authorities at Linz has been published. Hitler's
explanation, with its half truths, lies, evasions and its characteristic mixture of the brazen and the sly, ranks as the first of
a long series of similar "explanations" with which the world
was to become only too familiar. Hitler denied that he had
left Vienna to avoid conscription, and asked, on account of
his lack of means, to be allowed to report at Salzburg, which
was nearer to Munich than Linz. His request was agreed to,
and he duly presented himself for examination at Salzburg on
5 February 1914. He was rejected for military or auxiliary
service on the grounds of poor health, and the incident was
closed. But after the Germans marched into Austria in 1938
a very thorough search was made in Linz for the records connected with Hitler's military service and Hitler was furious
when the Gestapo failed to discover them.

It was in the May of 1913 that Hitler moved to Munich, across the German frontier. He found lodgings with a tailor's family, by the name of Popp, which lived in the Schleissheimerstrasse, a poor quarter near the barracks. In retrospect, Hitler described this as "by far the happiest time of my life. . . . I came to love that city more than any other place known to me. A German city! How different from Vienna."

It may be doubted if this represented Hitler's feelings at the time. His life followed much the same pattern as before. His dislike of hard work and regular employment had by now hardened into a habit. He made a precarious living by drawing advertisements and posters, or peddling sketches to dealers. He was perpetually short of money. Despite his enthusiasm for the architecture and paintings of Munich, he was not a step nearer making a career than he had been on the day when he was turned down by the Vienna Academy.

The shadowy picture that emerges from the reminiscences of the few people who knew him in Munich is once again of a man living in his own world of fantasy. He gives the same impression of eccentricity and lack of balance, brooding and muttering to himself over his extravagant theories of race, anti-Semitism and anti-Marxism, then bursting out in wild, sarcastic diatribes. He spent much time in cafés and beer-cellars, devouring the newspapers and arguing about politics. Frau Popp, his landlady, speaks of him as a voracious reader, an impression Hitler more than once tries to create in *Mein Kampf.* Yet nowhere is there any indication of the works he read. Hitler's own comment on reading is illuminating. "Reading had probably a different significance for me from that which it has for the average run of our so-called 'intellectuals.' I know people who read interminably, book after book, from page to page. . . . Of course they 'know' an immense amount, but . . . they have not the faculty of distinguishing between what is useful and useless in a book; so that they may retain the former in their minds and if possible skip over the latter. . . . Reading is not an end in itself, but a means to an end. . . . One who has cultivated the art of reading will instantly discern, in a book or journal or pamphlet, what ought to be remembered because it meets one's personal needs or is of value as general knowledge."

This is a picture of a man with a closed mind, reading only to confirm what he already believes, ignoring what does not fit in with his preconceived scheme. Hitler was speaking the truth when he said: "Since then [i.e., since his days in Vienna] I have extended that foundation very little, and I have changed nothing in it."

Hitler was indignant at the ingorance and indifference of people in Munich to the situation of the Germans in Austria. Since 1879 the two states, the German Empire and the Hapsburg Monarchy, had been bound together by a military alliance, which remained the foundation of German foreign policy up to the defeat of 1918. Hitler felt that this predisposed most Germans to refuse to listen to the exaggerated accounts he gave of the "desperate" position of the German Austrians in the conflict of nationalities within the Monarchy.

Hitler's objection to the alliance of Germany and Austria was twofold. It crippled the Austrians in their resistance to what he regarded as the deliberate anti-German policy of the Hapsburgs. At the same time, for Germany herself it represented a dangerous commitment to the support of a state which, he was convinced, was on the verge of disintegration. Hitler would have agreed with the view expressed by Ludendorff in his memoirs: "A Jew in Radom once said to one of my officers that he could not understand why so strong and vital a body as Germany should ally itself with a corpse. He was right."

When Franz Ferdinand was assassinated by Serbian students at Sarajevo on 28 June, 1914, Hitler's first reaction was confused. For, in his eyes, it was Franz Ferdinand, the heir to the Hapsburg throne, who had been more responsible than anyone else for that policy of concessions to the Slav peoples which roused the anger of the German nationalists. But, as events moved towards a general European war, Hitler brushed aside his doubts. At least Austria would be compelled to fight, and could not, as he had always feared, betray her ally Germany. "I believed that it was not a case of Austria fighting to get satisfaction from Serbia, but rather a case of Germany fighting for her own existence . . . for its freedom and for its future. . . . For me, as for every other German, the most memorable period of my life now began. Face to face with that mighty struggle, all the past fell away into oblivion."

There were other, deeper and more personal reasons for his satisfaction. War meant to Hitler the opportunity to slough off the frustration, failure and resentment of the past six years. Here was an escape from the tension and dissatisfaction of a lonely individuality into the excitement and warmth of a close, disciplined collective life, in which he could identify himself with the power and purpose of a great organization. "The war of 1914," he wrote in *Mein Kampf*, "was certainly not forced on the masses; it was even desired by the whole people"—a remark which illustrates at least this man's state of mind.

On 1 August Hitler was in the cheering, singing crowd which gathered on the Odeons Platz to listen to the proclamation declaring war. In a chance photograph that has been preserved his face is clearly recognizable, his eyes excited and exultant; it is the face of a man who has come home at last. Two days later he addressed a formal petition to King Ludwig III of Bavaria, asking to be allowed to volunteer, although of Austrian nationality, for a Bavarian regiment. The reply granted his request. "I opened the document with trembling hands; no words of mine can describe the satisfaction I felt. . . ."

Together with a large number of other volunteers he was enrolled in the 1st Company of the 16th Bavarian Reserve Infantry Regiment, known from its original commander as the List Regiment. Another volunteer in the same regiment was Rudolf Hess; the regimental clerk was a Sergeant-major Max Amann, later to become business manager of the Nazi Party's paper and of the Party publishing house. After a period of initial training, on 21 October, 1914, they entrained for the Front.

After two days' journey they reached Lille and were sent up into the line as reinforcements for the 6th Bavarian Division of the Bavarian Crown Prince Rupprecht's VIth Army. Hitler's first experience of fighting was in one of the fiercest and most critical engagements of the war, the First Battle of Ypres, when the British succeeded in stemming an all-out effort by the Germans to burst through to the Channel coast. For four days and nights the List Regiment was in the thick of the fighting with the British round Becelaere and Gheluvelt. In a letter to his old Munich landlord, the tailor Herr Popp, Hitler reported that when they were pulled out of the line and sent into rest billets at Werwick the regiment had been reduced in four days from three thousand five hundred to six hundred men; only thirty officers were left and four companies had to be broken up.

Throughout the war Hitler served as a *Meldeganger*, a runner whose job was to carry messages between Company and Regimental H.Q. A close comrade was Ernst Schmidt— one of the sources for this period of his life. Although Hitler was not actually in the trenches, there is little doubt that his was a dangerous enough job, and for the greater part of four years he was at the Front or not far in the rear.

In 1916 they took part in the heavy fighting on the Somme, and near Bapaume, on 7 October Hitler was wounded in the leg, and was sent back to Germany for the first time for two years.

After a period in hospital at Beelitz, near Berlin, and at Munich with the Reserve battalion of his regiment, he returned to the Front at the beginning of March, 1917, now promoted to lance-corporal. He was in time to take part in the latter stages of the Battle of Arras and in the Third Battle of Ypres in the summer. With the rest of the regiment Hitler went forward in the last great German offensive in the spring of 1918.

During the night of 13-14 October the British opened a gas attack. Hitler was caught on a hill south of Werwick and his eyes were affected. By the time he got back to Rear H.Q. he could no longer see. On the morning of 14 October he collapsed and was sent back to a military hospital at Pasewalk, not far from Stettin. He was still there, recovering from the injury to his eyes, when the war ended, 11 November.

VI

What sort of a soldier was Hitler? As early as December, 1914, he had been awarded the Iron Cross, Second Class, and when Hitler in March, 1932, brought a lawsuit against a newspaper which had accused him of cowardice, his former commanding officer, Lieutenant-Colonel Engelhardt, testified to his bravery in the fighting of November, 1914, when the regiment had first gone into action. Much more interesting is the Iron Cross, First Class, an uncommon decoration for a corporal, which Hitler was awarded in 1918. The most varied and improbable accounts have been given of the action for which he won this. The date on which he received the award was 4 August, 1918, but dates ranging over a period from the autumn of 1915 to the summer of 1918 have been suggested for the exploit for which it was given. According to one witness, single-handed he took prisoner fifteen (others say ten or twelve) Frenchmen; according to another they were Englishmen. The official history of the List Regiment says nothing at all. Whatever the occasion, it was certainly a decoration of which Hitler was proud and which he habitually wore after he had become Chancellor.

In view of his long service and the shortage of officers in the German Army in the last months of the war, the fact that Hitler never rose above the rank of corporal aroused curiosity in the German Press before 1933. There is no evidence that Hitler ever applied or was eager for promotion.

It is probable, also, that the impression of eccentricity which he continued to give was no recommendation. Hans Mend, another of Hitler's fellow-soldiers in the List Regiment, wrote of him as "a peculiar fellow. He sat in the corner of our mess holding his head between his hands, in deep contemplation. Suddenly he would leap up, and, running about excitedly, say that in spite of our big guns victory would be denied us, for the invisible foes of the German people were a greater danger than the biggest cannon of the enemy." This led to violent attacks on the Marxists and Jews, in the old style of the Vienna Hostel for Men. On other occasions, Mend recalls, "he sat in a corner, with his helmet on his head, buried deep in thought, and none of us was able to rouse him from his listlessness."

While not unpopular with his comrades, they felt that he did not share their interests or attitude to the war. He received no letters, no parcels from home. He did not care about leave or women. He was silent when the others grumbled about the time they had to spend in the trenches or the hardships. Konrad Heiden states in his book *Der Fuehrer*, "We all cursed him and found him intolerable. There was this white crow among us that didn't go along with us when we damned the war."

The few photographs of this time seem to bear this out—a solemn pale face, prematurely old, with staring eyes. He took the war seriously, feeling personally responsible for what happened, and identifying himself with the failure or success of German arms. These were not endearing qualities, but they do not detract from Hitler's good record as a soldier, at least as brave as the next man and a good deal more conscientious.

Many years afterwards Hitler would still refer to "the stupendous impression produced upon me by the war—the greatest of all experiences. For, that individual interest—the interest of one's own ego—could be subordinated to the common interest. . . ." Like many other Germans, Hitler regarded the comradeship, discipline and excitement of life at the Front as vastly more attractive than the obscurity, aimlessness and dull placidity of peace. This was particularly true of Hitler, for he had neither family, wife, job nor future to which to return. This was his world: here he had a secure place such as he had never found in Vienna or Munich. In the years after the war it was from ex-servicemen like this who could never settle down into monotonous peace-time routine that the Freikorps, the Nazis, and a score of extremist parties recruited their members. The war, and the impact of war upon the individual lives of millions of Germans, were among the essential conditions for the rise of Hitler and the Nazi Party.

It is surprising, in view of his later pretensions as a strategist in the Second World War, that Hitler has nothing to say in *Mein Kampf* about the conduct of the military operations. At the time he wrote his book he was still too anxious to secure the favour of the Army leaders to indulge in the attitude of contempt he later adopted towards the generals. In any case, Hitler followed the conventional nationalist line of argument: the German Army had never been defeated, the war had been lost by the treachery and cowardice of the leaders at home, the capitulation of November, 1918, was a failure of political not military leadership.

At the time of his stay in hospital at Beelitz and his visit to Munich (October, 1916-March, 1917) Hitler became indignant at the contrast between the spirit of the Army at the Front and the poor morale and lack of discipline at home. There he encountered shirkers who boasted of dodging military service, grumbling, profiteering, the black market, and other familiar accompaniments of wartime civilian life; it was with relief that he returned to the Front. In *Mein Kampf* his contempt for parliamentary deputies and journalists is lavish: "All decent men who had anything to say, said it point-blank in the enemy's face; or, failing this, kept their mouths shut and did their duty elsewhere. Uncompromising military measures should have been adopted to root out the evil. Parties should have been abolished and the Reichstag brought to its senses at the point of the bayonet, if necessary. It would have been still better if the Reichstag had been dissolved immediately."

This is no more than the common talk of any one of the ex-servicemen's (*Frontkämpfer*) associations which sprang up after the war and comforted their wounded pride by blaming Socialist agitators, Jews, profiteers and democratic politicians for the "shameful treachery" of the "Stab in the Back." But Hitler adds a characteristic twist which shows once more the originality of his ideas as soon as he was faced with a question of political leadership. It was not enough, he concluded, to use force to suppress the Socialist and anti-national agitation to which he attributed the sapping of Germany's will to go on fighting. "If force be used to combat a spiritual power, that force remains a defensive measure only, so long as the wielders of it are not the standard bearers and apostles of a new spiritual doctrine . . . It is only in the struggle between *Weltanschauugen* [world views] that physical force, consistently and ruthlessly applied, will eventually turn the scale in its own favour." This was the reason for the failure of every attempt to combat Marxism hitherto, including the failure of Bismarck's anti-socialist legislation—"it lacked the basis of a new *Weltanschauung*."

Out of this grew the idea of creating a new movement which would fight Social Democracy with its own weapons. For power lay with the masses, and if the hold of the Jew-ridden Marxist parties on their allegiance was to be broken, a substitute had to be found. The key, Hitler became convinced, lay in propaganda, and the lesson Hitler had already drawn from the Social Democrats and Lueger's Christian Socialists in Vienna was completed by his observation of the success of English propaganda during the war, by contrast with the failure of German attempts.

There were two themes on which Hitler constantly played in the years that followed the war: Man of the People, and Unknown Soldier of the First World War. When he spoke to the first Congress of German Workers in Berlin on 10 May, 1933, he assured them: "Fate, in a moment of caprice or perhaps fulfilling the designs of Providence, cast me into the great mass of the people, amongst common folk. I myself was a labouring man for years in the building trade and had to earn my own bread. And for a second time I took my place once again as an ordinary soldier amongst the masses." These were the twin foundations of his demagogy and, in however garbled a fashion, they correspond to the two formative experiences of his life, the years in Vienna and Munich, and the years at the Front.

Those years between the end of 1908 and the end of 1918 had hardened him, taught him to be self-reliant, confirmed his belief in himself, toughened the power of his will. From them he emerged with a stock of fixed ideas and prejudices which were to alter little in the rest of his life: hatred of the Jews; contempt for the ideals of democracy, internationalism, equality and peace; a preference for authoritarian forms of government; an intolerant nationalism; a rooted belief in the inequality of race and individuals, and in the heroic virtues of war. Most important of all, in the experiences of those years he had already hit upon a conception of how political power was to be secured and exercised which, when fully developed, was to open the way to a career without parallel in history. Much of what he had learned remained to be formulated even in his own mind, and had still to be crystallized into the decision to become a politician. It required only a sudden shock to precipitate it. That shock was supplied by the end of the war, the capitulation of Germany and the overthrow of the Empire.

CHAPTER TWO

THE YEARS OF STRUGGLE

1919 — 1924

When the war ended Hitler was still in hospital at Pasewalk. The acknowledgement of Germany's defeat and the establishment of a democratic Republic were both intolerable to him. Everything with which he had identified himself seemed to be defeated, swept aside in a torrent of events which had been released, as he had no doubt, by the same Jews who had always desired the humiliation of Germany.

Like many others among the mob of demobilized men, he had little prospect of finding a job. The old problem of how to make a living, conveniently shelved for four years, reappeared. Characteristically, Hitler turned his back on it. "I was forced now to scoff at the thought of any personal future, which hitherto had been the cause of so much worry to me. . . ." He was not interested in finding a steady job; he never had been. After all, what had he to lose in the break-up of a world in which he had never found a place? But with a sure instinct, he saw in the distress of Germany the opportunity he had been looking for but had so far failed to find.

"At that juncture innumerable plans took shape in my mind. . . . Unfortunately, every project had to give way before the hard fact that I was quite unknown and therefore did not have even the first prerequisite necessary for effective action." None the less, he did not despair. With considerable naivety, he wrote in *Mein Kampf*: "Generally speaking, a man should not take part in politics before he has reached the age of thirty." Hitler was now in his thirtieth year, the time was ripe and the decision was taken: "I resolved that I would take up political work."

But how? Uncertain as yet of the answer, Hitler made his way through a disorganized country back to Munich. He was still in uniform and still drew his rations and pay from the Army.

Few towns in the Reich were as sensitive to the mood of

unrest as Munich: its political atmosphere was unstable and exaggerated towards one extreme or the other. During the war Hitler himself had remarked that bad morale and war-weariness were more pronounced in Munich than in the north. The revolution of 1918 broke out in Munich before Berlin, and the Wittelsbach King of Bavaria was the first to abdicate. Bavaria became a natural centre for all those who were eager to get rid of the republican régime in Germany, and the Bavarian Government turned a blind eye to the treason and conspiracy against the legal government of the Reich which were being planned on its doorstep in Munich. It was in Bavaria that the irreconcilable elements of the Freikorps gathered, armed bands of volunteers formed under the pa-tronage of the Reichswehr at the end of the war to maintain order and protect the eastern frontiers of Germany, but now just as willing to turn their guns against the Republic. The Freikorps were the training schools for the political murder and terrorism which disfigured German life up to 1924, and again after 1929.

Among the regular Army officers stationed in Munich were men like Major-General Ritter von Epp and his assist-ant, Major Ernst Roehm. In the Freikorps and in the innu-merable defence leagues, and ex-servicemen's associations which sprang up in Bavaria, they saw the nucleus of that army which should one day revenge the humiliations of 1918. When that day would come no one knew, but in the mean-time it was essential to keep together the men who had been the backbone of the old German Army, now reduced by the terms of the Treaty to a mere hundred thousand.

Poehner, the Police President of Munich, gave the famous reply, when asked if he knew there were political murder gangs in Bavaria: "Yes, but not enough of them." Wilhelm Frick, later Hitler's Minister of the Interior, was Poehner's assistant; one of his colleagues in the Bavarian Ministry of Justice was Franz Gürtner, later Hitler's Minister of Justice.

At the back of the minds of such men was the dream which bewitched the German Right for twenty years: over-throwing the Republic, restoring Germany as the greatest Power of Europe and restoring the Army to its rightful position. Such was the promising setting in which Hitler began his career.

Hitler lived through the exciting days of April and May, 1919, in Munich itself. According to *Mein Kampf*, he was to have been put under arrest, but drove off with his rifle the three men who came to arrest him. Once the Communists had been overthrown, he gave information before the military

Commission of Enquiry which tried and shot those reported active on the other side. He then got a job in the Army Political Department, a centre for the activities of such men as Roehm. After attending a course of "political instruction" for the troops, Hitler was himself given the task of inoculating the men against contagion by socialist, pacifist or democratic ideas. This was the first recognition of the fact that he had any political ability at all. Then, in September, he was instructed to investigate a small group meeting, the German Workers' Party, which might be of interest to the Army.

The German Workers' Party was originally set up by a locksmith, Anton Drexler, whose idea was a party which would be both working class and nationalist. He saw what Hitler had also seen, that a middle-class movement like the Fatherland Front was hopelessly out of touch with the masses, and that these were coming increasingly under the influence of anti-national and anti-militarist propaganda. It can scarcely have been a very impressive scene when, on the evening of 12 September, 1919, Hitler attended his first meeting in a Munich beer-cellar in which twenty-five people had gathered. One of the speakers was Gottfried Feder, an economic crank well known in Munich, who had already impressed Hitler at one of the political courses arranged for the Army. A few days later Hitler received a postcard inviting him to attend a committee meeting of the German Workers' Party.

After some hesitation Hitler went. The committee met in an obscure beer-house, the *Alte Rosenbad*, in the Herrn-strasse. "I went through the badly lighted guest-room, where not a single guest was to be seen, and searched for the door which led to the side room; and there I was face to face with the Committee. Under the dim light shed by a grimy gas-lamp I could see four people sitting round a table."

As Hitler frankly acknowledges, this very obscurity was an attraction. It was only in a Party which, like himself, was beginning at the bottom that he had any prospect of imposing his ideas. After a few days he joined the Committee as its seventh member.

Slowly and painfully he prodded his cautious and unimaginative colleagues on the committee into bolder methods. Invitations were multigraphed, a small advertisement inserted in the local paper, a larger hall secured. When Hitler himself spoke for the first time the result was only to confirm the chairman, Karl Harrer, in his belief that Hitler had no talent for public speaking. But Hitler persisted and at the beginning of 1920 he was put in charge of the Party's propaganda. By the use of clever advertising he got nearly two thousand people into the *Festsaal* of the *Hofbräuhaus*. The principal speaker was overshadowed by Hitler who was forcing the pace, much to the dislike of Harrer, who resigned as chairman. On 1 April, Hitler left the Army and devoted all his time to the Party.

Hitler's and Drexler's group was not the only National Socialist party. In Bavaria itself there were rival groups, while across the frontier in Austria and in the Sudetenland the pre-war German Social Workers' Party had been reorganized as the German National Socialists Workers' Party—and began to use the Hakenkreuz, the swastika, as its symbol. Up to August, 1923, there were fairly frequent contacts between these different National Socialist groups, but little came of them. Hitler was too jealous of his independence to submit to interference from outside.

Much more important to Hitler was the support he received from Roehm, a man of ability and character, however unpleasant, who exercised considerable influence in the shadowy world of the Freikorps. He had actually joined the German Workers' Party before Hitler, for, like Hitler, any party which could recapture the working classes for a nationalist and militarist allegiance interested him. He admired the toughness of the Communists, who fought for what they believed in; he wanted working-class organizations with the same qualities on his own side.

When Hitler began to build up the German Workers' Party, Roehm pushed in ex-Freikorps men to swell the Party's membership. From these elements the first "strong-arm" squads were formed, the nucleus of the S.A. Above all, Roehm was the indispensable link in securing for Hitler the protection, or at least the tolerance, of the Army and of the Bavarian Government. Without the unique power and influence of the Army Hitler would never have been able to exercise his methods of incitement, violence and intimidation. At every step from 1914 to 1945 Hitler's varying relationship to the Army was of the greatest importance to him: never more so than in these early years in Munich. Before his death the Army was to learn the full measure of his ingratitude.

Yet however important this help from outside, the foundation of Hitler's success was his own energy and ability as a political leader. Without this, the help would never have been forthcoming. Hitler's genius lay in his unequalled grasp of what could be done by propaganda, and his flair for seeing how to do it. He had to learn in a hard school, on his feet night after night, arguing his case in every kind of hall, often, in the early days, in the face of opposition, indifference or amused contempt; learning to hold his audience's attention, to win them over; most important of all, learning to read the minds of his audiences, finding the sensitive spots on which to hammer. "He could play like a virtuoso on the well-tempered piano of lower middle-class hearts," says Dr. Schacht. Behind that virtuosity lay years of experience as an agitator and mob orator. Hitler came to know Germany and the German people at first hand as few of Germany's other leaders ever had. Here was one great advantage Hitler had over nearly all the politicians with whom he had to deal, his immense practical experience of politics in the street, the level at which any politician must be effective if he is to carry a mass vote.

Hitler was the greatest demagogue in history. Those who add "only a demagogue" fail to appreciate the nature of political power in an age of mass politics. As he himself said: "To be a leader, means to be able to move masses."

The lessons which Hitler drew from the activities of the Austrian Social Democrats and Lueger's Christian Socialists were now tried out in Munich. Success was far from being automatic. Hitler made mistakes and had much to learn before he could persuade people to take him seriously, and the end of 1923 saw the collapse of his movement in a fiasco. But Hitler learned from his mistakes, and by the time he came to write *Mein Kampf* in the middle of the 1920s he was able to set down the conditions of success. The pages where he discusses the technique of mass propaganda stand out in brilliant contrast with the turgid attempts to explain his entirely unoriginal political ideas.

The first and most important principle for political action laid down by Hitler is: Go to the masses. He is quite open in explaining how this is to be achieved. "The receptive powers of the masses are very restricted, and their understanding is feeble. On the other hand, they quickly forget. Such being the case, all effective propaganda must be confined to a few bare necessities and then must be expressed in a few stereotyped formulas." Hitler had nothing but scorn for the intellectuals who are always looking for something new. "Only constant repetition will finally succeed in imprinting an idea on the memory of a crowd." For the same reason it is better to stick to a programme even when certain points in it become out of date: "As soon as one point is removed from the sphere of dogmatic certainty, the discussion may easily lead to endless debates and general confusion."

When you lie, tell big lies. This is what the Jews do, working on the principle, "which is quite true in itself, that in the big lie there is always a certain force of credibility;

because the broad masses of a nation are always more easily corrupted in the deeper strata of their emotional nature than consciously or voluntarily, and thus in the primitive simplicity of their minds they more readily fall victims to the big lie than the small lie, since they themselves often tell small lies in little matters, but would be ashamed to resort to large-scale falsehoods. . . . The grossly impudent lie always leaves traces behind it, even after it has been nailed down."

Above all, never hesitate, never qualify what you say, never concede an inch to the other side, paint all your contrasts in black and white. This is the "very first condition which has to be fulfilled in every kind of propaganda: a systematically one-sided attitude towards every problem that has to be dealt with. . . .

Vehemence, passion, fanaticism, these are "the great magnetic forces which alone attract the great masses; for these masses always respond to the compelling force which emanates from absolute faith in the ideas put forward, combined with an indomitable zest to fight for and defend them. . . . The doom of a nation can be averted only by a storm of glowing passion; but only those who are passionate themselves can arouse passion in others."

Hitler showed a marked preference for the spoken over the written word. "The force which ever set in motion the great historical avalanches of religious and political movements is the magic power of the spoken word." The employment of verbal violence, the repetition of such words as "smash," "force," "ruthless," "hatred," was deliberate. Hitler's gestures and the emotional character of his speaking, lashing himself up to a pitch of near-hysteria in which he would scream and spit out his resentment, had the same effect on an audience, so that men groaned or hissed and women sobbed involuntarily, caught up in the spell of hatred and exaltation, from which all restraint had been removed. The orator will always follow the lead of the great mass in such a way that from the living emotion of his hearers the apt word which he needs will be suggested to him and in its turn this will go straight to the hearts of his hearers."

Propaganda was not confined to the spoken word. There were the red posters to provoke the Left; the flag, with its black swastika in a white circle on a red background, a design to which Hitler devoted the utmost care; the salute, the uniform and the hierarchy of ranks. Mass meetings and demonstrations were another device which Hitler borrowed from the Austrian Social Democrats. The essential purpose of such meetings was to create a sense of power, of belonging to a movement whose success was irresistible. Hitler here hit upon a psychological fact which was to prove of great importance in the history of the Nazi movement: that violence and terror have their own propaganda value, and that the display of physical force attracts as many as it repels. "When our political meetings first started," Hitler writes, "I made it a special point to organize a suitable defence squad. . . . who had been trained and brought up to realize that only terror is capable of smashing terror." Defence is an ambiguous word to describe such activities, for, as Hitler adds, "the best means of defence is attack, and the reputation of our hall-guard squads stamped us as a political fighting force and not as a debating society."

From the first these men were used to provoke disturbance and to beat-up political opponents as part of a deliberate campaign of intimidation. In September, 1921, Hitler personally led his followers in storming the platform of a federalist meeting. When examined by the police commission which enquired into the incident, Hitler replied: "It's all right. We got what we wanted. Ballerstedt did not speak."

Hitler gave his use of violence the widest possible publicity so that people were forced to pay attention to what he was doing even against their will. No government of any determination would have tolerated such methods, but Berlin had virtually no authority in Bavaria, and the Bavarian State showed remarkable complacence towards political terrorism, provided it was against the Left.

The "strong-arm" squads were first formed in the summer of 1920, but their definitive organization dates from 3 August, 1921, when a so-called "Gymnastic and Sports Division" was set up inside the Party. "It is intended," said the Party proclamation, "to serve as a means for bringing our youthful members together in a powerful organization for the purpose of utilizing their strength as an offensive force at the disposal of the movement." After 5 October, it changed its name to *Sturmabteilung* (the S.A., or Storm Section of the Party) and was largely composed of ex-Freikorps men.

Next year, in August, S.A. formations paraded with swastika flags flying in a demonstration of the Patriotic Associations on the Munich Königsplatz, and a month later eight "Hundreds" (*Hundertschaften*) were organized. In October, Hitler took his stormtroopers to Coburg for a nationalist demonstration, defied the police ban on marching and fought a pitched battle in the streets with the Socialists and Communists. A special medal was later designed for those who had taken part in Coburg Day.

Inevitably, Hitler's propaganda methods, his attempt to

turn the Party into a mass following for himself and to ride roughshod over the other members of the committee, produced resentment. In the early summer of 1921 Hitler spent some time in Berlin, where he got in touch with certain of the nationalist groups in the north. While he was away from Munich the other members of the committee tried to recapture the direction of the party. Hitler returned immediately to Munich, and countered by offering his own resignation. This put the rest of the committee in an awkward position, for there was no doubt who found the Party funds as well as the publicity. The last thing they could afford was to let Hitler resign. Hitler, however, demanded dictatorial powers if he was to remain, together with the retirement of the committee and a ban on Party negotiations for six years. In a leaflet defending themselves, Drexler and the rest of the committee wrote:

> A lust for power and personal ambition have caused Herr Adolf Hitler to return to his post after his six weeks' absence in Berlin . . . bringing dissension and schism into our ranks by means of shadowy people behind him, and thus furthering the interests of the Jews and their friends. It grows more and more clear that his purpose is simply to use the National Socialist Party as a springboard for his own immoral purposes. . . .

Drexler was obliged to repudiate the leaflet after Hitler had brought a libel suit, and at two extraordinary meetings in July, 1921, Hitler was not only made President, but the statutes were altered to give him unlimited power. Drexler was kicked upstairs as Honorary President.

The split between Hitler and the committee went deeper than personal antipathy and mistrust. Drexler and Harrer had always thought of the Party as a workers' and lower-middle-class Party, radical and anti-capitalist as well as nationalist. These ideas were expressed in the programme, with its Twenty-five Points (drawn up by Drexler, Hitler and Feder, and adopted in February, 1920), which was nationalist and anti-Semitic in character, but at the same time strongly against Capitalism, the trusts, the big industrialists and the big landowners.

There is no doubt that on Drexler's and Feder's part this represented a genuine programme to which they always adhered. All programmes to Hitler, however, were means to an end, to be taken up or dropped as they were needed. "Any idea," he says in *Mein Kampf,* "may be a source of danger if it be looked upon as an end in itself." Hitler's own programme was much simpler: power, power for himself, for the Party and the nation with which he identified himself. Hitler was as much interested in the working class and the lower middle class as Drexler, but he was interested in them as material for political manipulation. Their grievances and discontents were the raw stuff of politics, a means, but never an end.

All forms of discontent were grist to his mill; there was as much room in his Party for the unemployed ex-officer like Goering and Hess, or the embittered intellectual like Rosenberg and Goebbels, as for the working man who refused to join a trade union or the small shopkeeper who wanted to smash the windows of the big Jewish department stores. Ambition, resentment, envy, avidity for power and wealth—in every class—these were the powerful motive forces Hitler sought to harness. He was prepared to be all things to all men, because to him all men represented only one thing, a means to power. The character of Hitler's following no less than his methods shocked the prim, old-fashioned prejudices of Drexler and his friends, but they had no weapons with which to fight against his combination of energy and unscrupulousness, backed by the argument of success.

Hitler put in Max Amann, the ex-sergeant-major of the List Regiment, to run the business side of the Party, and Dietrich Eckart as editor of its paper, *Völkischer Beobachter*. The power of making all big decisions he kept in his own hands. He was working as he had never worked before; it was only sheer hard work that could create the illusion of success. But it was work which suited him: his hours were irregular, he was his own master, his life was spent in talking, he lived in a whirl of self-dramatization, and the gap between his private dream-world and his outer life had been narrowed, however slightly.

Until the end of his life Hitler looked back to these early years as the heroic period of the Party's struggle, the *Kampfzeit*. In January, 1932, he said:

> I cast my eyes back to the time when with six other unknown men I founded this association, when I spoke before eleven, twelve, thirteen, fourteen, twenty, thirty, fifty persons. When I recall how after a year I had won sixty-four members for the movement, I must confess that that which has today been created, when a stream of millions is flowing into our movement, represents something unique in German history. The bourgeois parties have had seventy years to work in. Where is the organization which in seventy years has achieved what we have achieved in barely twelve?

This was the "miracle" of National Socialism. "A people

is shattered and then a small company of men arises and begins an Odyssey of wanderings, which begins in fanaticism, which in fanaticism pursues its course."

Who were the men with whom Hitler began his "Odyssey" in Munich? One of the most important was Ernst Roehm, a man for whom soldiering was his whole life and who had little but contempt for anything outside it. Roehm had too much the unruly temper of a soldier of fortune to fit into the rigid pattern of the Reichswehr: he had finally to resign his commission in 1923. None the less he provided an invaluable link with the Army authorities, even after his resignation, and more than any other man it was he who created the S.A.

Another ex-officer may be mentioned with Roehm: Hermann Goering, the last commander of the crack Richthofen Fighter Squadron and holder of Germany's highest decoration for bravery under fire, the *Pour le Mérite*. Four years younger than Hitler, he had come to Munich in 1921 with no very clear purpose, but nominally to study at the University. In the autumn of 1922 he too heard Hitler speak, was attracted to the movement, and shortly became commander of the S.A.

Like Roehm, Gottfried Feder and Dietrich Eckart had joined the German Workers' Party before Hitler. Eckart was considerably older than Hitler, a not very successful journalist, poet and playwright, fond of beer, food and talk, a friend of Roehm, with violent nationalist, anti-democratic and anti-clerical opinions, a racist with an enthusiasm for Nordic folk-lore and a taste for Jew-baiting. He talked well even when he was fuddled with beer, and undoubtedly had a big influence on the younger and still very raw Hitler. He lent him books, corrected his style of expression in speaking and writing, and first introduced him to Berchtesgaden. Eckart had a wide circle of friends, amongst them the wealthy piano manufacturers, the Bechsteins. Frau Hélène Bechstein took a great liking to Hitler, gave parties for people to meet the new prophet, found money for the Party and later visited him in prison. It was through Eckart again that Hitler met Hess and Rosenberg.

Alfred Rosenberg had been trained as an architect in Moscow, but had fled to escape the Revolution. Through Rosenberg, Hitler came into touch with a group of passionately anti-Bolshevik and anti-Semitic Russian *émigrés*.

The fact that Rosenberg had been trained as an architect impressed the man who had failed to get into the Vienna Academy, while his pedantic and laborious discussion of questions of race and culture led Hitler to see in him the heir to the mantle of Houston Stewart Chamberlain and the great prophet of the new racist *Weltanschauung*. In the summer of 1923, Hitler visited *Haus Wahnfried,* the home of the Wagner family in Bayreuth. For Hitler this was holy ground. He impressed Winnifried Wagner and captivated the aged Houston Stewart Chamberlain, who had married one of Wagner's daughters.

Two years after the *Völkischer Beobachter* had been bought for him, Hitler made it into a daily. This required money. Most of it was provided by Frau Gertrud von Seidlitz, a Baltic lady who had shares in Finnish paper mills, while Putzi Hanfstaengl, a son of the rich Munich family of art publishers, advanced a loan of a thousand dollars. Hanfstaengl, who had been educated at Harvard, not only took Hitler into his own home—where he delighted him by his piano-playing, but introduced him to a number of other well-to-do Munich families.

Ill at ease on any formal social occasion, Hitler cleverly exploited his own awkwardness. A description of him by a fellow guest at a party in 1923 is quoted by Konrad Heiden:

Hitler had sent word to his hostess that he had to attend an important meeting and would not arrive until late: I think it was about eleven o'clock. He came, none the less, in a very decent blue suit and with an extravagantly large bouquet of roses, which he presented to his hostess as he kissed her hand. While he was being introduced, he wore the expression of a public prosecutor at an execution. I remember being struck by his voice when he thanked the lady of the house for tea or cakes, of which, incidentally, he ate an amazing quantity. It was a remarkably emotional voice, and yet it made no impression of conviviality or intimacy but rather of harshness. However, he said hardly anything but sat there in silence for about an hour; apparently he was tired. Not until the hostess was so incautious as to let fall a remark about the Jews, whom she defended in a jesting tone, did he begin to speak and then he spoke without ceasing. After a while he thrust back his chair and stood up, still speaking, or rather yelling, in such a powerful penetrating voice as I have never heard from anyone else. In the next room a child woke up and began to cry. After he had for more than half an hour delivered a quite witty but very one-sided oration on the Jews, he suddenly broke off, went up to his hostess, begged to be excused and kissed her hand as he took his leave. The rest of the company, who apparently had not pleased him, were only vouchsafed a curt bow from the doorway.

As Heiden remarks, no one at that party ever forgot Adolf Hitler.

There were other less reputable or less presentable companions: Heinrich Hoffmann, who was to become the one man allowed to photograph Hitler; Max Amann, Hitler's tough, rude, but reliable business manager and publisher; Christian Weber, a former horse-trader, of great physical strength, who had worked as a "chucker-out" at "Donisl's," a disreputable Munich dive, and whose social life consisted in drinking endless *seidels* of beer; Roehm, whose homosexuality was later to become notorious; Julius Streicher, an elementary-school teacher in Nuremberg, who excelled in a violent and crude anti-Semitism. In 1923 Streicher founded *Der Stürmer* (The Stormtrooper), in which he published fantastic accounts of Jewish ritual murders, of the Jewish world conspiracy revealed in the so-called "Protocols of the Elders of Zion," and of Jewish sexual crimes. Hitler's success in persuading Streicher to join the Nazis with his Nuremberg following was a minor triumph. These were the men with whom the "miracle" of National Socialism was accomplished.

How Hitler managed to make a living at this time is far from clear. In the leaflet which was drawn up by the dissident members of the Committee in July, 1921, this was one of the principal points of accusation: "If any member asks him how he lives and what was his former profession, he always becomes angry and excited. . . . So his conscience cannot be clear, especially as his excessive intercourse with ladies, to whom he often describes himself as the King of Munich, costs a great deal of money."

During the libel action to which this led, Hitler was asked to tell the court exactly how he lived. Did he, for instance, receive money for his speeches? "If I speak for the National Socialist Party," Hitler replied, "I take no money for myself. But I also speak for other organizations, such as the German National Defence and Offensive League, and then, of course, I accept a fee. . . ." The probable answer is that Hitler was as careless about money as he had been in Vienna, that he lived from hand to mouth and bothered very little about who was going to pay for the next meal. Up to 1929 he continued to occupy one or two rooms in a poorish street near the River Isar (No. 41 Thierschstrasse). He habitually wore an old and dirty trench-coat, or a cheap raincoat, and troubled little about his personal appearance or comforts.

Undoubtedly Hitler received contributions from those who sympathized with the aims of his Party, but their amount and importance have been exaggerated. Not until considerably later did Hitler succeed in touching the big political funds of the German industrialists in the Ruhr and the Rhineland: in fact, the Nazi Party was launched on very slender resources.

Nazism was a phenomenon which throve only in conditions of disorder and insecurity. While these had been endemic in Germany ever since the defeat of 1918, two new factors made their appearance in 1923 which brought the most highly industrialized country of continental Europe to the verge of economic and political disintegration: the occupation of the Ruhr and the collapse of the mark.

By the autumn of 1922 the German Government professed itself unable to continue paying reparations and requested a moratorium. The French Government of Poincaré used the technical excuse of a German default in deliveries of timber to move French troops into the industrial district of the Ruhr on 11 January, 1923. To cut off eighty per cent of steel and pig-iron production and more than eighty per cent of her coal from the rest of Germany, as the French proceeded to do, was to bring the economic life of the whole country to a standstill.

The result of the French occupation was to unite the German people as they had never been united since the early days of the war. The German Government called for a campaign of passive resistance, which became a state of undeclared war with the weapons on one side strikes, sabotage and guerilla warfare, and on the other arrests, deportations and economic blockade.

The occupation of the Ruhr gave the final touch to the deterioration of the mark. The savings of the middle classes and working classes were wiped out at a single blow with a ruthlessness which no revolution could ever equal. Even if a man worked till he dropped, it was impossible to buy enough clothes for his family—and work, in any case, was not to be found. The violence of Hitler's denunciations of the corrupt, Jew-ridden system which had allowed all this to happen, the bitterness of his attacks on the Versailles settlement and on the Republican Government which had accepted it, found an echo in the misery and despair of large classes of the German nation.

Hitler saw the opportunity clearly enough, but it was more difficult to see how to take advantage of it and turn the situation to his own profit. The National Socialists might overthrow the Republic only if Hitler succeeded in uniting all the nationalist and anti-republican groups in Bavaria, and if he secured the patronage of more powerful forces—of which the most obvious was the Bavarian Government and the District Command of the Army—for a march on Berlin.

Hitler devoted his energies throughout 1923 to achieving these two objectives.

In the early months of 1923 he was afraid lest the French occupation of the Ruhr might unite Germany behind the Government. In the *Völkischer Beobachter* he wrote: "So long as a nation does not do away with the assassins within its borders, no external successes can be possible. . . . the real deadly enemy of the German people lurks within the walls of the nation. . . . Down with the November criminals, with all their nonsense about a United Front."

With the tide of national feeling running high against the French, and in support of the Government's call for resistance, this was an unpopular line to take. To make people listen to him, Hitler summoned five thousand of the S.A. Stormtroopers to Munich for a demonstration at the end of January, 1923. The authorities promptly banned it. Hitler began to rave: the S.A. would march even if the police opened fire. The Bavarian Government retorted by issuing an additional ban on twelve meetings which Hitler was to address after the demonstration. At last, only after General von Lossow had satisfied himself that his officers could be relied on to fire on the National Socialists if necessary—a significant change of attitude—were Roehm and Epp able to secure his co-operation. The ban was lifted and Hitler held his demonstration.

In his speech at this first Party Day Hitler made no secret of his hope that the Berlin Government would fail to unite the nation in resistance to the French.

Whoever wants this fire [of enthusiasm for the glory of the Fatherland] to consume every single German must realize that first of all the arch-enemies of German freedom, namely, the betrayers of the German Fatherland, must be done away with. . . . And here the great mission of our movement begins. In all this prattle about a "united front" and the like, we must not forget that between us and those betrayers of the people [i.e., the Republican Government in Berlin] . . . there are two million dead. . . . We must always remember that in any new conflict in the field of foreign affairs the German Siegfried will again be stabbed in the back."

Hitler had no use for talk of a new war of liberation which could only strengthen the position of the Government. The time to deal with the French would come when the Republic had been overthrown. Here Hitler's essentially political outlook differed sharply from that of the Army and ex-Freikorps officers like Roehm, who thought of a war of revenge against France.

This conflict had been present from the beginning in the very different views Hitler and Roehm took of the S.A. For Roehm, as for the other officers and ex-officers who helped to train the S.A., the first object was to build up in secret the armed forces forbidden by the Treaty of Versailles. With the outbreak of undeclared war with France, the Army leaders believed that this might well prove the prelude to a general war. In order to strengthen the Army it was planned to draw on the para-military formations like the S.A. and Roehm flung himself into his task with such effect that by autumn the S.A. numbered fifteen thousand men.

For Hitler, on the other hand, the S.A. was not just a disguised Army reserve; these were to be *political* troops used for political purposes. With shrewder insight than Roehm and his friends, Hitler saw that to rebuild Germany's national and military power, and to reverse the decision of the war, it was necessary to begin by capturing political power in the State, and the S.A. were to be used for that purpose. Once that had been secured, the rest would follow—as it did after 1933.

Hitler's hatred was still directed, not against the French, but against the Republic, which he depicted as a corrupt racket run by the Jews at the expense of the national interests. No accusation against the Jews was too wild for him, but his most bitter scorn was reserved for the "respectable" parties of the Right who hesitated to act.

But Hitler's speeches were not even reported in the Press.

The French occupation of the Ruhr still continued, but by fall, 1923, the initial mood of national unity on the German side had gone. The value of the mark continued to fall. There were widespread strikes and riots under Communist leadership in many working-class districts. Trains and trucks were raided for food by the half-starving population of the cities.

Encouraged by the growing disorder and the increasingly strained relations between Munich and Berlin, Hitler renewed his agitation in August. The fact that Stresemann, the new Chancellor, was known to be anxious to end the exhausting campaign of passive resistance in the Ruhr and Rhineland enabled Hitler to change front. He now adopted the more popular line of attacking the Berlin Government for the betrayal of the national resistance to the French, as well as for allowing the inflation to continue.

On 2 September, the anniversary of the German defeat of France at Sedan in 1870, a huge demonstration, celebrated German Day at Nuremberg amidst scenes of great enthusiasm. All the Patriotic Associations took part. During the parade Hitler stood beside Ludendorff, and afterwards flayed the Government in a violent speech.

Ludendorff's presence was important. His reputation as the greatest military figure of the war and an unremitting opponent of the Republic made him the hero of the Right-wing extremists, while he still enjoyed considerable prestige in the Army. There was no one better placed to preside over a union of the quarrelsome and jealous patriotic leagues, and Hitler had carefully maintained close relations with the old man for some time past. Ludendorff in politics was invincibly stupid as well as tactless. He disliked Bavarians, was on the worst possible terms with Crown Prince Rupprecht, the Bavarian Pretender, and constantly attacked the Church in the most Catholic part of Germany. But at least he was reliable on the question of Bavarian separatism, and his political stupidity was an asset for, skilfully managed, he could bring a great name to Hitler's support without entrenching on the control of policy which Hitler was determined to keep in his own hands.

The demonstration at Nuremberg had immediate practical consequences. The same day a new German Fighting Union (*Deutscher Kampfbund*) was set up and a manifesto issued over the old signatures of Friedrich Weber (*Bund Oberland*), Heiss (*Reichsflagge*) and Adolf Hitler. The object of this renewed alliance was declared to be the overthrow of the November Republic and of the *Diktat* of Versailles.

The crisis came to a head on 26 September when Stresemann announced the decision of the Reich Government to call off the campaign of passive resistance in the Ruhr unconditionally, and to lift the ban on reparation deliveries to France and Belgium. This was a courageous and wise decision, intended as the preliminary to negotiations for a peaceful settlement. But it was also the signal the Nationalists had been waiting for to stir up a renewed agitation against the Government. "The Republic, by God," Hitler had declared on 12 September, "is worthy of its fathers. . . . Subserviency towards the enemy, surrender of the human dignity of the German, pacifist cowardice, tolerance of every indignity, readiness to agree to everything until nothing remains."

On 25 September the leaders of the *Kampfbund*—Hitler, Goering, Roehm, Kriebel, Heiss and Weber—had already met. For two and a half hours Hitler put his point of view and asked for the political leadership of the alliance. So strong was the impression he made that both Heiss and

Weber agreed, while Roehm, convinced that they were on the edge of big events, next day resigned his commission and finally threw in his lot with Hitler.

Hitler's first step was to put his own fifteen thousand S.A. men in a state of readiness and announce fourteen immediate mass meetings in Munich alone. Whether he intended to try a *coup d'état* is not clear, but Knilling, the Bavarian Minister President, was thoroughly alarmed. On 26 September the Bavarian Cabinet proclaimed a state of emergency and appointed Gustav von Kahr, a Right-wing politician with strong monarchist and particularist leanings, as State Commissioner with dictatorial powers. Kahr promptly banned Hitler's meetings and refused to give way when Hitler, beside himself with rage, screamed that he would answer him with bloody revolution.

In the confused events that led up to the unsuccessful *putsch* of 8-9 November, the position of two of the three parties is tolerably clear. Hitler consistently demanded a move on Berlin to be backed by the political and military authorities in Bavaria, but aiming at the substitution of a new régime for the whole of Germany. Hitler's hesitations arose from recognition of the fact that he could not carry such a plan through with his own resources, and must, somehow or other, persuade Kahr, the State Commissioner, and General Lossow to join him.

The Central Government in Berlin had to face the threat of civil war from several directions: from Bavaria, where Hitler was openly calling for revolt, and where Kahr, the State Commissioner, began a course of action counter to the policy of Berlin; from Saxony, increasingly under the influence of the Communists, who were also aiming at a seizure of power; from the industrial centres, like Hamburg and the Ruhr, where Communist influence was strong; from the Rhineland, where the Separatists were still active, and from the nationalist extremists of the north.

The Stresemann Government's chances of mastering this critical situation depended upon the attitude of the Army. The High Command could be relied upon to use force to suppress any attempt at revolution from the Left, but its attitude towards a similar move from the Right might well be uncertain. In the years since the war, the protection of the Army had been invoked again and again by those like Hitler who were patently disloyal to the Republic and scheming to accomplish its overthrow.

Nothing could more clearly illustrate the unique position of the Army in German politics, a position fully appreciated by the Commander-in-Chief, General von Seeckt and the

Army High Command. Seeckt, one of the most remarkable men in the long history of the German Army, had the insight to see that it was in the long-term interests of Germany, and of the Army, to uphold the authority even of a Republican government, and so to preserve the unity of the Reich, rather than allow the country to be plunged into civil war.

Seeckt's attitude allowed the political and military authorities in Berlin to speak with one voice, and on 26 September President Ebert conferred emergency powers upon the Minister of Defence, Gessler, and Seeckt. This meant that the Army assumed the executive functions of the government and undertook the responsibility of safeguarding both the security of the Reich and the inviolability of the Republican Constitution. An attempt by Hitler—or anyone else—to march on Berlin would be met by the Army on the side of the Government.

But there was a third party to be taken into account, the civil and military authority in Bavaria represented by Kahr and Lossow. It was the existence of this third factor, and the uncertainty of the policy Kahr and Lossow would adopt, which gave Hitler a chance of success.

Although the Bavarian Government had now appointed Kahr to keep Hitler in check, relations between Munich and Berlin were strained. It was the action of the Bavarian Government in conferring dictatorial powers on Kahr which had led the Reich to declare a state of emergency itself, and Kahr's intentions were suspect in Berlin.

Kahr's aims are still far from clear: probably they were never entirely clear to him at the time. Kahr, however, was attracted by the idea of overthrowing the Republican régime and putting in a conservative government which would give Bavaria back her old monarchy. At other times he played with the possibility of breaking away with the Reich altogether and establishing an independent South German State. Such ideas were anathema to Hitler. None the less he saw that if Kahr could only be persuaded to help overthrow the Republican régime in Berlin, he could have every hope of double-crossing his Bavarian allies once he was in power. It was equally possible for Kahr to use Hitler and the forces of the *Kampfbund*. An uneasy alliance developed between Kahr and the Nazis, each trying to exploit the other's support. Once again the critical decision lay with the Army, this time with the local commander in Bavaria, Lossow. Like Kahr, however, Lossow never quite succeeded in making up his mind until events decided for him.

In October, 1923, the quarrel between Munich and Berlin flared up, under direct provocation from Hitler. When the

Nazi *Völkischer Beobachter* printed scurrilous attacks on Seeckt, Stresemann and Gessler, the Minister of Defence used his emergency powers to demand the suppression of the paper. Kahr refused. When the Minister of Defence went over his head and ordered General von Lossow to execute the ban, Lossow let himself be persuaded by Kahr into disobeying his orders. The next step was Berlin's removal of Lossow from his post on 20 October, but Kahr announced that Lossow would remain in command of the Army in Bavaria, and exacted a special oath of allegiance to the Bavarian Government from both officers and men, an open breach of the constitution. On 27 October Kahr rejected an appeal from President Ebert, demanded the resignation of the Reich Government and ordered the armed bands which supported him to concentrate on the borders of Bavaria and Thuringia.

All this suited Hitler admirably. Power in Bavaria was concentrated in the hands of a triumvirate consisting of Kahr, Lossow and Colonel Seisser, the head of the State police. It was now, Hitler argued, only a question of whether Berlin marched on Munich, or Munich on Berlin. The situation in Saxony and Thuringia, on the northern borders of Bavaria, offered a splendid pretext for Kahr and Lossow to act. For there the Social Democratic cabinets had brought the Communists in as partners, thereby providing the Communists with a spring-board for their own seizure of power. Action by Bavaria to suppress this threat would undoubtedly command wide support, and, once at Dresden, Hitler reckoned, they would soon be in Berlin.

Hitler and Roehm suspected that behind the façade of German Nationalism, with its cry of *"Auf nach Berlin"* (On to Berlin!), which Kahr kept up to satisfy the *Kampfbund,* he was playing with Bavarian separatist ideas under the very different banner of *"Los von Berlin"* (Away from Berlin!). Each side watched the other with growing suspicion.

Meanwhile Berlin was beginning to master its difficulties. By the end of October the threat of a Communist revolution had been broken and the offending governments in Saxony and Thuringia turned out, thus depriving the Bavarian conspirators of their best pretext for intervention outside their own frontiers. Colonel Seisser, the third of the Bavarian triumvirate, was sent to Berlin to size up the situation.

For Hitler, however, there could be no drawing back. He had worked his supporters up to such a pitch that a failure to act now must mean the collapse of the Nazi Party and the total discredit of its leader. Lieutenant Wilhelm Brückner later gave evidence that he had begged Hitler to strike soon, since "the day is coming when I won't be able to hold the men back. If nothing happens now, they'll run away from us." By November, Roehm says, the preparations for action were complete, and the state of tension in Munich was such that the crisis had to find an immediate solution.

Seisser's report from Berlin was far from encouraging. Kahr and Lossow, who had no wish to become involved in an enterprise that was bound to fail, insisted that they alone should decide the time to act and that they should not be hustled. Hitler was by now convinced that the only way to get Kahr and Lossow to do what he wanted was to present them with a *fait accompli*, otherwise, they might carry out their own *coup* without him.

The original plan, proposed by Scheubner-Richter and Rosenberg, was to take advantage of the presence of Kahr, Lossow, and Seisser as well as the Crown Prince Rupprecht, at the parade to be held in Munich on 4 November, *Toten-gedenktag*, the Day of Homage to the Dead. Armed Storm-troopers were to surround them just before the parade and persuade them at the point of the pistol to lead the national revolution which Hitler would then proclaim. This plan fell through, but its essential features were kept and put into oper-ation on 8 November when it was announced that a big meeting would be held in the *Bürgerbräu Keller* at which Kahr was to speak. Lossow and Seisser, together with most of the other Bavarian political leaders, were all expected to be present. Kahr refused to see Hitler on the morning of the 8th, and Hitler was soon convinced that this meeting was to be the prelude to the proclamation of Bavarian independ-ence and the restoration of the Wittelsbach monarchy on the 12th. Whether this was in fact Kahr's intention remains un-certain, but on the spur of the moment Hitler decided to forestall Kahr.

Shortly after Kahr had begun to speak on the evening of 8 November the hall was surrounded by the S.A. and Hitler burst in at the head of a group of armed men. Carrying a pistol in his hand, he leapt on to a table and fired at the ceiling to secure attention. Before anyone had grasped what was happening, Hitler pushed his way on the platform and shouted out: "The National Revolution has begun. This hall is occupied by six hundred heavily armed men. No one may leave the hall. The Bavarian and Reich Governments have been removed and a provisional National Government formed. The Army and police barracks have been occupied, troops and police are marching on the city under the swastika ban-ner." This was a bold piece of bluff, but no one could be certain that it was just bluff. There were six hundred S.A.

men outside, and a machine-gun in the vestibule. Leaving Goering to keep order in the hall, Hitler pushed Kahr, Lossow and Seisser into a side room. Meanwhile Scheubner-Richter was driving through the night to Ludwigshöhe to fetch General Ludendorff, whom Hitler wanted as the figurehead of his revolution.

Hitler, who was wildly excited, began the interview with Kahr and his companions in melodramatic style: "No one leaves this room alive without my permission." He announced that he had formed a new government with Ludendorff. (This, too, was untrue; Ludendorff knew nothing of what was happening.) They had only one choice: to join him. Waving his gun, and looking as if he was half out of his mind, he shouted: "I have four shots in my pistol. Three for my collaborators if they abandon me. The last is for myself." Setting the revolver to his head, he declared: "If I am not victorious by tomorrow afternoon, I shall be a dead man."

The three men were less impressed than they should have been. They found it difficult to take Hitler's raving at all seriously, despite the gun and the armed guards at the windows.

So far Hitler had made little progress. Now, leaving the room without a word, he dashed into the hall and announced that the three men had agreed to join him in forming a new German government:

> . . . I propose that, until accounts have been finally settled with the November criminals, the direction of policy in the National Government be taken over by me. Ludendorff will take over the leadership of the German National Army. Lossow will be German Reichswehr Minister, Seisser Reich Police Minister. The task of the provisional German National Government is to organize the march on that sinful Babel, Berlin, and save the German people. . . .Tomorrow will see either a National Government in Germany or us dead.

This was a clever move. The announcement that agreement had been reached completely changed the mood of the crowd in the hall, which shouted its approval: the sound of the cheering impressed the three men who were still held under guard in the side room.

No sooner had Hitler returned to them than Ludendorff appeared. He was thoroughly angry with Hitler for springing a surprise on him, and furious at the distribution of offices which made Hitler, not Ludendorff, the dictator of Germany, and left him with the command of an army which did not exist. But he kept himself under control: this was a great national event, he said, and he could only advise the others to collaborate. Hitler added: "We can no longer turn back; our action is already inscribed on the pages of world history."

In apparent unity they all filed back into the hall. While the audience climbed on to the seats and cheered in enthusiasm, each made a brief speech, swore loyalty and shook hands on the platform. Barely had this touching scene of reconciliation been completed than Hitler was called out to settle a quarrel which had started when Stormtroopers of the *Bund Oberland* tried to occupy the Engineers' barracks. By a bad error of judgment he left the hall without taking precautions. As soon as Hitler had gone, and the audience began to pour out of the exits, Lossow excused himself on the grounds that he must go to his office to issue orders, and left unobtrusively, followed by Kahr and Seisser. It was the last that was seen of General von Lossow or von Kahr that night.

Hitler already had several hundred Stormtroopers of the S.A. and *Kampfbund* at his command. By morning these had grown to some three thousand men, for considerable forces continued to come in during the night. While his own bodyguard occupied the offices of the Social Democratic *Münchener Post* and smashed the machines, the *Reichskriegsflagge*, under Roehm's leadership, seized the Army H.Q. in the War Ministry on Schönfeldstrasse, and set up barbed-wire and machine guns. Hitler, whose main forces were kept on the other side of the Isar, came over to Roehm before midnight and held a council of war with Ludendorff, Kriebel and Weber. As time passed, however, they became concerned at the absence of any news from Lossow or Kahr, and were at a loss what to do next. Messages to Lossow at the 19th Infantry Regiment's barracks produced no answer; nor did the messengers return. The night was allowed to pass without the seizure of a single key position, apart from Roehm's occupation of the Army headquarters. This was partly due to the *Kampfbund* leaders' ignorance of what was happening and unwillingness to recognize that they had been deceived; even more, however, to the improvised character of the whole affair. Finally, Poehner and Major Hühnlein were dispatched to occupy the police headquarters, but were promptly arrested instead, together with Frick.

As General von Lossow returned from the *Bürgerbräu Keller* Seeckt telegraphed from Berlin that, if the Army in Bavaria did not suppress the *putsch*, he would do it himself. There was considerable sympathy with Hitler and Roehm among the junior officers from the rank of major downwards, but the senior officers were indignant at the insolence of this ex-corporal, and in the end discipline held. From the

infantry barracks on the *Oberwiesenfeld* orders were sent out
to bring in reinforcements from outlying garrisons. Meanwhile Kahr issued a proclamation denouncing the promises
extorted in the *Bürgerbräu Keller* and dissolving the Nazi
Party and the *Kampfbund*. From Crown Prince Rupprecht
came a brief but pointed recommendation to crush the *putsch*
at all costs. Rupprecht had no use for a movement which
had Ludendorff as one of its leaders.

By the morning of 9 November it was clear that the attempt
had miscarried. At dawn Hitler, Ludendorff and the other
leaders returned to the *Bürgerbräu*, leaving Roehm to hold
out in the War Ministry. Meantime, Ludendorff, who was
convinced that the Army would never fire on the legendary
figure of the First World War, had persuaded Hitler, against
his better judgment, that they must take the offensive and try
to restore the position by marching on Lossow's headquarters. Once he stood face to face with the officers and men
of the Army, Ludendorff was convinced that they would
obey him and not Lossow.

While these anxious discussions were being held in the
Bürgerbräu Keller, troops of the Regular Army had surrounded Roehm and his men in the centre of the city. Both
sides were reluctant to open fire—there were many old comrades among Roehm's Stormtroopers. All that Roehm could
do was to sit tight.

Shortly after eleven o'clock in the morning a column of
two or three thousand men left the *Bürgerbräu Keller* and
headed for the Ludwig Bridge leading to the centre of the
city. During the night a number of hostages had been taken,
and with the threat of shooting these Goering persuaded the
police at the bridge to let them pass. At the head of the
column fluttered the swastika flag and the banner of the
Bund Oberland. In the first row marched Hitler, between
Ludendorff, Scheubner-Richter and Ulrich Graf on one side,
Dr. Weber, Feder and Kriebel on the other. Most of the
men carried arms, and Hitler himself had a pistol in his hand.
Crowds thronged the streets and there was an atmosphere
of excitement and expectation. Julius Streicher, who had
been haranguing the crowd in the Marienplatz, climbed down
to take his place in the second rank. Rosenberg and Albrecht
von Graefe, the sole representative of the North German
Nationalists, who had arrived that morning at Ludendorff's
urgent summons, trudged unhappily along with the rest.

The column swung down the narrow Residenzstrasse, singing as it went. Beyond lay the old War Ministry, where
Roehm was besieged.

The police, armed with carbines, were drawn up in a cordon across the end of the street to prevent the column debouching on to the broad Odeonsplatz. The Stormtroopers completely outnumbered the police—there were no troops present—but the narrowness of the street prevented them bringing their superior numbers to bear. Who fired first has never been settled. One of the National Socialists—Ulrich Graf—ran forward and shouted to the police officer: "Don't fire, Ludendorff and Hitler are coming," while Hitler cried out: "Surrender!" At this moment a shot rang out and a hail of bullets swept the street. The first man to fall was Scheubner-Richter, with whom Hitler had been marching arm-in-arm. Hitler fell, either pulled down or seeking cover. The shooting lasted only a minute, but sixteen Nazis and three police lay dead or dying in the street. Goering, badly wounded, was carried into a house. Weber, the leader of the *Bund Oberland,* stood against the wall weeping hysterically. All was confusion, neither side being at all sure what to do next. One man alone kept his head. Erect and unperturbed, General Ludendorff, with his adjutant, Major Streck, by his side, marched steadily on, pushed through the line of police and reached the Platz beyond.

The situation might still have been saved, but not a single man followed him. Hitler at the critical moment lost his nerve. According to two eye-witnesses, Hitler was the first to scramble to his feet and, stumbling back to the end of the procession, allowed himself to be pushed by Schulz into a yellow motorcar on the Max Josef Platz. He was undoubtedly in great pain from a dislocated shoulder, and probably believed himself wounded. But there was no denying that under fire the Nazi leaders had broken and fled, Hitler the first. Only two among them had been killed or badly wounded, Scheubner-Richter and Goering; the other killed and wounded were all in the following ranks, exposed to the fire by the action of their leaders in taking cover.

Two hours later Roehm was persuaded to capitulate and was taken into custody. Goering was smuggled across the Austrian frontier by his wife. On 11 November Hitler was arrested at Uffing, where he was being nursed by Hanfstaengl's mother and sister.

In many ways the attempt of 8-9 November was a remarkable achievement for a man like Hitler who had started from nothing only a few years before. In less than a couple of hours on the night of 8 November he had transformed the political situation in Bavaria and made a revolution by sheer bluff; evidence of political talent of an unusual kind.

But the mistakes had been gross. Worst of all, from Hit-

ler's point of view, was the contrast between his own behaviour under fire—the first to get to his feet and make his
escape by car, leaving the wounded, the dead and the rest
of his followers to fend for themselves—and that of Ludendorff, who, in the sight of all, had marched steadily forward
and brushed aside the police carbines with contemptuous
ease.

The truth is, however, that Hitler had never intended to
use force; from the beginning his conception had been that
of a revolution in agreement with the political and military
authorities. "We never thought to carry through a revolt
against the Army: it was *with it* that we believed we should
succeed." This explains why no adequate preparations had
been made for a seizure of power by arms. The *coup* was to
be limited to forcing Kahr and Lossow into acting with him,
in the belief that it was only hesitation, not opposition, that
held them back. Again and again Hitler had told his men
that when the moment came they need not worry, neither
the Army nor the police would fire on them. The shots on
the Odeonsplatz represented the final collapse of the premises upon which the whole attempt had been constructed.
From the moment it became certain that Lossow and Kahr
had taken sides against him, Hitler knew that the attempt
had failed. There was a slender chance that a show of force
might still swing the Army back to his side, and so he agreed
to march. But the last thing Hitler wanted, or was prepared
for, was to shoot it out with the Army.

Never was Hitler's political ability more clearly shown than
in the way he recovered from this set-back. For the man who,
on 9 November, 1923, appeared to be broken and finished
as a political leader—and had himself believed this—succeeded by April, 1924, in turning his trial for treason into a
political triumph.

The trial was held in Munich, and it was a trial for a conspiracy in which the chief witnesses for the prosecution—
Kahr, Lossow and Seisser—had been almost as deeply involved as the accused. The full story was one which most of
the political leaders of Bavaria were only too anxious to avoid
being made public. Hitler exploited this situation to the full.

The trial began before a special court on 26 February,
1924. It lasted for twenty-four days. For the whole of this
period it was front-page news in every German newspaper,
and a large group of foreign correspondents attended the
trial. For the first time Hitler had an audience outside the
frontiers of Bavaria.

From the first day Hitler's object was to recover the political initiative, and virtually put the chief witnesses for the

prosecution in the dock. He did this by the simple device of assuming full responsibility for the attempt to overthrow the Republic, and, instead of apologizing for this crime, indignantly reproaching Lossow, Kahr and Seisser with the responsibility for its failure. This was a highly effective way of appealing to nationalist opinion, and turning the tables on the prosecution. Hitler declared: "One thing was certain . . . If our enterprise was actually high treason, then during this whole period Lossow, Kahr and Seisser must have been committing high treason along with us, for during all these weeks we talked of nothing but the aims of which we now stand accused."

This was perfectly true, as everybody in the court knew, and Hitler pressed his advantage. "I alone bear the responsibility," he concluded, "but. . . . there is no such thing as high treason against the traitors of 1918. It is impossible for me to have committed high treason, for the treason would not consist in the events of 8 November, but in all our activities and our state of mind in the preceding months—and then I wonder why those who did exactly the same are not sitting here with me. . . . I feel myself the best of Germans who wanted the best for the German people."

Neither Kahr nor Seisser had the skill to withstand such tactics, while the judges sat placidly through Hitler's mounting attack on the Republic whose authority they represented. One man alone stood up to Hitler, and this surprisingly enough, was General von Lossow.

Von Lossow was an angry man. His career had ended abruptly as a result of the November affair, and he had to listen in silence while his reputation was torn to shreds in the court, and he was represented as a coward, who had lacked the courage to declare either for or against the conspiracy. Now he had his chance to reply, and he expressed all the contempt of the officer caste for this jumped-up, ill-educated, loud-mouthed agitator who had never risen above the rank of corporal and now tried to dictate to the Army the policy it should pursue. Lossow dealt bluntly with Hitler's own ambitions: "He thought himself the German Mussolini . . . and his followers, who had entered on the heritage of the Byzantine monarchy, regarded him as the German Messiah." For his own part he looked upon Hitler as fitted to play no more than the role of a political drummer.

But Hitler, in his final speech, established a complete mastery over the court. Lossow had said he was fit only to be "the drummer" and had accused him of ambition.

How petty are the thoughts of small men (Hitler retorted).

Believe me, I do not regard the acquisition of a Minister's portfolio as a thing worth striving for. I do not hold it worthy of a great man to endeavour to go down in history just by becoming a Minister. One might be in danger of being buried beside other Ministers. I aimed from the first at something a thousand times higher than a Minister. I wanted to become the destroyer of Marxism. I am going to achieve this task, and if I do, the title of Minister will be an absurdity as far as I am concerned. . . .

Hitler not only took the responsibility for what had happened and left to those who had refused to march with him the odium of abandoning the national cause; he deliberately built up the failure of 8 and 9 November into one of the great propaganda legends of the movement.

When the bodies of the sixteen dead of 1923 were reinterred in 1935 in a new memorial, Hitler said: "They now pass into the German immortality. . . . Here they lie as true witnesses to our movement." These were the men whom twelve years before Hitler had left dying in the street while he fled. By skilful propaganda he had turned the fiasco of 1923 and his own failure as a leader into retrospective triumph.

But the unsuccessful *putsch* of 1923 has a still more important place in the history of the Nazi movement for the lessons which Hitler drew from it. In 1936, three years after he became Chancellor, he summed them up: "We recognized that it is not enough to overthrow the old State, but that the new State must previously have been built up and be practically ready to one's hand. Later you lived through another revolution. But what a difference between them! In 1933 it was no longer a question of overthrowing a state by an act of violence; meanwhile the new State had been built up and all that there remained to do was to destroy the last remnants of the old State—and that took but a few hours."

The failure of 1923 strengthened his hand. "This evening and this day (8-9 November) made it possible for us afterwards to fight a battle for ten years by legal means; for, make no mistake, if we had not acted then I should never have been able to found a revolutionary movement, and yet all the time maintain legality. One could have said to me with justice: You talk like all the others and you will act just as little as all the others."

Hitler had already laid the foundations of this policy at the trial of 1924. In his closing speech, he went out of his way to avoid recrimination and renew the old offer of alliance with the Army. "I believe that the hour will come when the masses, who today stand in the street with our swastika banner, will unite with those who fired upon them. . . .

When I learned that it was the police who fired, I was happy that . . . the Reichswehr stands as untarnished as before. One day the hour will come when the Reichswehr will stand at our side, officers and men."

It took Hitler nine years to convince the Army that he was right. Meanwhile, Ludendorff was acquitted, and Hitler was given the minimum sentence of five years' imprisonment. Despite the attempts of the police to get him deported, Hitler was in fact released from prison after serving less than nine months—and promptly resumed his agitation against the Republic. Such were the penalties of high treason in a State where disloyalty to the régime was the surest recommendation to mercy.

CHAPTER THREE

THE YEARS OF WAITING

1924 — 1931

Fifty miles west of Munich lies the small town of Landsberg where Hitler served his term with some forty other National Socialists and they had an easy and comfortable life. They ate well—Hitler became quite fat in prison—had as many visitors as they wished, and spent much of their time out of doors in the garden, where, like the rest, Hitler habitually wore leather shorts with a Tyrolean jacket. On his thirty-fifth birthday, which fell shortly after the trial, the parcels and flowers he received filled several rooms. He had a large correspondence in addition to his visitors, and as many newspapers and books as he wished. Hitler presided at the midday meal, claiming and receiving the respect due to him as leader of the Party: much of the time, however, from July onwards he shut himself up in his room to dictate *Mein Kampf*, which was begun in prison and taken down by Emil Maurice and Rudolph Hess.

Max Amann, who was to publish the book, had hoped for sensational revelations of the November *putsch*. But Hitler was too canny for that; there were to be no recriminations. His own title for the book was *Four and a Half Years of Struggle against Lies, Stupidity and Cowardice*, reduced by Amann to *Mein Kampf—My Struggle*. Even then Amann was to be disappointed. For the book contains very little autobiography, but is filled with page after page of turgid discussion of Hitler's ideas, written in a verbose style which is both difficult and dull to read.

Dietrich Eckart, Feder, and Rosenberg had all published books or pamphlets and Hitler was eager to prove that he too, even though he had left school without a certificate, had read and thought deeply, acquiring his own *Weltanschauung*. It is this desire to make people take him seriously as an original thinker, which accounts for his pretentious style, the use of long words and constant repetitions, all the tricks of a half-educated man seeking to give weight to his words.

Before his arrest Hitler had managed to send a pencilled note to Rosenberg with the brief message: "Dear Rosenberg, from now on you will lead the movement." As Rosenberg himself admits in his memoirs, this was a surprising choice. As a leader he was ineffective, finding it difficult either to make up his mind or to assert his authority. It was precisely the lack of these qualities which attracted Hitler: Rosenberg as his deputy would represent no danger to his own position.

What was to be done now that the Party had been dissolved and Hitler was in prison? Hitler's answer, however camouflaged, was simple: Nothing. He had no wish to see the Party revive its fortunes without him.

There were long and sometimes bitter arguments between Hitler and his visitors at Landsberg on the issues of combining with other similar movements in 1924. Hitler was both suspicious and evasive. He tried by every means to delay decisions until he was released.

A further cause of disagreement was the S.A. Roehm had at once set to work to weld together again the disbanded forces of the *Kampfbund*. The *Frontbann*, as it was now called, grew rapidly, for Roehm was an able organizer, possessed untiring energy and soon had some thirty thousand men enrolled.

But the greater Roehm's success, the more uneasy Hitler became. His activities threatened Hitler's chances of leaving prison. The Bavarian Government arrested some of the subordinate leaders of the *Frontbann*, and Hitler's release on parole, which he had expected six months after sentence had been passed, was delayed. "Hitler, Kriebel and Weber in their cell," Roehm wrote later ". . . felt that their approaching freedom was endangered and laid the blame, not on the enemy, but on the friends who were fighting for them."

Hitler was no less worried by the character Roehm was giving to the new organization which had replaced and absorbed the old S.A. The two men had never agreed about the function of the Stormtroops. For Hitler the S.A. were to be instruments of political intimidation and propaganda subordinate to the Party. On 15 October, however, Roehm wrote to Ludendorff, as leader of the *Völkisch* bloc in the Reichstag:

> . . . that the defence organizations should be given appropriate representation in the parliamentary group and that they should not be hindered in their special work. . . .

Hitler flatly disagreed with such a view. In December, when new elections for the Reichstag were held, Roehm did not find a place on the Nazi list.

By the end of Hitler's year in prison these quarrels and disagreements had reached such a pitch that it appeared possible to write off the former Nazi Party as a serious force in German or Bavarian politics. Yet, Hitler had already remarked to Hess: "I shall need five years before the movement is on top again."

Much of the blame for this state of affairs fell on Hitler—with considerable justice. "Hitler," Ludecke writes, "was the one man with power to set things straight; yet he was deliberately fostering the schism in order to keep the whip-hand over the party." And he succeeded. The plans for a united *Völkisch* Front came to nothing. Ludendorff and Roehm left in disgust. The price of this disunity was heavy, but for Hitler it was worth paying. By the time he came out of prison the Party had broken up almost completely—but it had not found an alternative leader, there was no rival to oust.

Hitler's first move on leaving prison was to call on the Minister-President of Bavaria and leader of the strongly Catholic and particularist Bavarian People's Party, Dr. Heinrich Held. The *putsch*, Hitler admitted, had been a mistake; his one object was to assist the Government in fighting Marxism; he had no use for Ludendorff's and the North Germans' attacks on the Catholic Church, and he had every intention of respecting the authority of the State. Held's attitude was one of scepticism tinged with contempt, but he agreed—with a little prompting from Gürtner, still Minister of Justice, and Held's friend as well as Hitler's—to raise the ban on the Party and its newspaper.

On 27 February, Hitler gathered the few who remained faithful for a mass meeting in the *Bürgerbräu Keller*. Max Amann conducted the meeting. Strasser, Roehm and Rosenberg stayed away. Besides Amann, Hitler's only prominent supporters were Streicher and Esser, Gottfried Feder and Frick.

Hitler had not lost his gifts as an orator. When he finished speaking at the end of two hours there was loud cheering from the four thousand who filled the hall. He was perfectly frank in his claims.

> If anyone comes and wants to impose conditions on me, I shall say to him: "Just wait, my young friend, and see what conditions I impose on you. I am not contending for the favour of the masses. At the end of a year you shall judge, my comrades. If I have acted rightly, well and good. If I have acted wrongly, I shall resign my office into your hands. Until then, however, I alone lead the movement, and no one can impose conditions on me so long as I personally bear the responsibility. And I once more bear the whole responsibility for everything that occurs in the movement. . . . To this struggle of ours there are only two possible issues: either the enemy pass over our bodies or we pass over theirs, and it is my desire that, if in the struggle I should fall, the Swastika banner shall be my winding sheet."

With the re-founding of the Nazi Party in February, 1925, Hitler set himself two objectives. The first was to establish his own absol ᵗᵒ control over the Party by driving out those who were not prepared to accept his leadership without question. The second was to build up the Party and make it a force in German politics within the framework of the constitution. Ludecke reports a conversation with Hitler in Landsberg prison: ". . . Instead of working to achieve power by an armed *coup*, we shall have to hold our noses and enter the Reichstag against the Catholic and Marxist deputies. If out-voting them takes longer than out-shooting them, at least the result will be guaranteed by their own Constitution. Any lawful process is slow. . . . Sooner or later we shall have a majority—and after that, Germany."

Hitler's speech on 27 February had laid great stress on the need to concentrate opposition against a single enemy—Marxism and the Jew. But he had added, in an aside which delighted his audience: "If necessary, by one enemy many can be meant." In other words, under cover of fighting Marxism and the Jew, the old fight against the State would be resumed. The authorities were alarmed and immediately afterwards prohibited him from speaking in public in Bavaria and other German states as well. It was a severe handicap for a leader whose greatest asset was his ability as a speaker. Hitler, however, had no option but to obey.

An even more serious handicap was the improvement in the position of the country, which began while Hitler was in prison. Dr. Schacht, as special commissioner to restore the German currency, had succeeded by the summer of 1924 and the inflation was at an end. Stresemann's hopes of a settlement with the allied Powers had not proved vain. A new reparations agreement—the Dawes Plan—was negotiated, and this was followed in turn by the evacuation of the Ruhr; the Locarno Pact, guaranteeing the inviolability of the Franco-German and Belgian-German frontiers: the withdrawal of allied troops from the first zone of the demilitarized Rhineland, and Germany's entry into the League of Nations by unanimous vote of the Assembly on 8 September, 1926. In the second presidential election held in April the Nazis supported Field-Marshal von Hindenburg, who had been brought in at the last minute by the Nationalists. Hindenburg won by a narrow margin, but the Nazis had little cause for congratulation. For Hindenburg, the greatest figure of the old Army, a devoted Monarchist, a Conservative and a Nationalist, to be at the head of the State reconciled conservative Germans to the Republic régime.

Such success as the Nazis had at this time was due less to Hitler than to Gregor Strasser, who was threatening to take Hitler's place as the effective leader of the Party and was breaking new ground in the north of Germany and the Rhineland, where the Party had hitherto failed to penetrate. A powerfully built man with a strong personality, Strasser was an able speaker and an enthusiast of radical views who laid as much stress on the anti-capitalist points in the Nazi programme as on its nationalism. He was critical of Hitler's attitude and little disposed to submit to his demands for unlimited authority in the Party.

Given Party leadership in North Germany, with the help of his brother, Otto Strasser, he rapidly built up an organization which, while nominally acknowledging Hitler as leader, soon began to develop into a separate party. Gregor Strasser, who was a Reichstag deputy founded the *Berliner Arbeitszeitung*, edited by Otto Strasser, and a fortnightly periodical, *Nationalsozialistische Briefe*, intended for Party officials. As editor of the *Briefe* and Gregor's private secretary, the Strassers secured a young Rhinelander, then still under thirty, a man who had attended a number of universities, and written novels and film scripts which no one would accept. His name was Paul Josef Goebbels.

Hitler had little sympathy with the Strassers' anti-capitalism and their demand for the breaking up of big estates, which embarrassed him in his search for backers among the industrialists and landowners. But while Hitler spent his time in Berchtesgaden, Gregor and Otto Strasser were actively at work extending their influence in the movement.

On 22 November, 1925, the Strassers called together a meeting of the North German district leaders in Hanover.

Hitler was represented by Gottfried Feder, but it was only by a bare majority that Feder was admitted to the meeting at all, after Goebbels had demanded his ejection.

The split between the Strassers and Hitler crystallized round a question which excited much feeling in Germany in 1925-1926, whether the possessions of the former German royal houses should be regarded as their own private property or as the public property of the different states. On this issue Gregor and Otto Strasser sided with working-class opinion against the princes, while Hitler supported the propertied classes. At this time he was receiving fifteen hundred marks a month (three-quarters of his income) from the divorced Duchess of Sachsen-Anhalt, and he denounced the agitation as a Jewish swindle. The Hanover meeting voted to follow the Strasser line, only Ley and Feder supporting Hitler. When Feder protested in Hitler's name, Goebbels jumped to his feet: "In these circumstances I demand that the petty bourgeois Adolf Hitler be expelled from the National Socialist Party." More important still, the Hanover meeting accepted the Strassers' programme and resolved to substitute it for the Twenty-five Points of the official programme adopted in February, 1920. This was open revolt.

Hitler took time to meet the challenge, but when he did move he showed his skill in the way he outmanoeuvred Strasser without splitting the Party. On 14 February, 1926, he summoned a conference in his turn, this time in the South German town of Bamberg. Hitler deliberately avoided a Sunday, when the North German leaders would have been free to attend in strength. As a result the Strasser wing of the Party was represented only by Gregor Strasser and Goebbels. In the south Hitler had made the position of District Leader (*Gauleiter*) a salaried office, a step which left the gauleiters free to attend solely to Party business and made them much more dependent upon himself. He could thus be sure of a comfortable majority in the meeting at Bamberg.

Strasser was outnumbered from the beginning, and Hitler added to his triumph by the capture of Goebbels, hitherto one of the Strassers' strongest supporters. Halfway through the meeting Goebbels stood up and declared that, after listening to Hitler, he was convinced that Strasser and he had been wrong, and that the only course was to admit their mistake and come over to Hitler. Having won his point, Hitler did all he could to keep Strasser in the Party. In the middle of the debate he put his arm round his shoulders and said: "Listen, Strasser, you really musn't go on living like a wretched official. Sell your pharmacy, draw on the Party funds and set yourself up properly as a man of your worth should." Hitler's conciliatory tactics proved successful. The Strasser programme was abandoned, a truce patched up and the unity of the Party preserved. This was not the end of the Strasser episode, but Hitler had handled his most dangerous rival with skill and papered over the breach between himself and the radical wing of the Party.

Hitler had still to face other difficulties in the Party. There was persistent criticism and grumbling at the amount of money the Leader and his friends took out of Party funds for their expenses, and at the time he spent away from headquarters in Berchtesgaden or driving around the countryside with his niece, the blonde Geli, in a large motorcar at the Party's expense. Quarrelling, slander and intrigue over the most petty and squalid issues seemed to be endemic in the Party.

To keep these quarrels within bounds, Hitler set up a Party court in 1926, the *Uschla* (Committee for Investigation and Settlement) which became an effective instrument for Hitler's tighter control over the Party.

In July, 1926, Hitler felt strong enough to hold a mass rally of the Party at Weimar, in Thuringia, one of the few States in which he was still allowed to speak. Five thousand men took part in the march past, with Hitler standing in his car and returning their salute, for the first time, with outstretched arm. Hoffman's photographs made it all look highly impressive, and a hundred thousand copies of the *Völkischer Beobachter* were distributed throughout the country. It was the first of the *Reichsparteitage* later to be staged, year after year, at Nuremberg.

Goebbels was now wholeheartedly Hitler's man. In November Hitler appointed him as gauleiter of "Red" Berlin, an assignment which was to stretch to the full his remarkable powers as an agitator. By doing this Hitler not only strengthened the movement in a key position, but provided another check against the independence of the Strasser group. The Strasser brothers had kept their own press and publishing house in Berlin, and Goebbels, whose desertion to Hitler the Strassers regarded as rank treachery, employed every means in his power to reduce their influence and following. In 1927 he founded *Der Angriff* as a rival to the Strassers' paper, and used the S.A. to beat up their most loyal supporters. Appeals to Hitler by Gregor and Otto Strasser produced no effect: he declared he had no control over what Goebbels did. None the less it was Hitler's game that Goebbels was playing for him.

The old trouble with the S.A. reappeared. In November, 1926, Hitler reformed the S.A. and found a new commander in Captain Pfeffer von Salomon, but the ex-officers still thought only in military terms. Both the Berlin and Munich S.A. leadership had to be purged. The Munich S.A. had become notorious for the homosexual habits of Lieutenant Edmund Heines and his friends: it was not for his morals, however, or his record as a murderer, that Hitler threw him out in May, 1927, but for his lack of discipline and insubordination. Such was the *élite* of the new Germany.

Whatever steps Hitler took, however, the S.A. continued to follow its own independent course, and Pfeffer refused to admit Hitler's right to give orders to his Stormtroops who were not interested in politics; what they lived for was precisely this "playing at soldiers" Hitler condemned. In time Hitler was to find an answer in the black-shirted S.S., a hand-picked *corps d'élite* (sworn to absolute obedience) very different from the ill-disciplined S.A. mob of camp followers. But it was not until 1929 that Hitler found the right man in Heinrich Himmler, who had been Gregor Strasser's adjutant at Landshut and later his secretary. It took Himmler some years before he could provide Hitler with what he wanted, an instrument of complete reliability with which to exercise his domination over the Party and eventually over the German nation.

By 1928 the Party organization was divided into two main branches: one directed by Gregor Strasser and devoted to attacking the existing régime, the other directed by Constantin Hierl and concerned with building up in advance the cadres of the new State.

Propaganda was a separate department, the director of which worked directly under Hitler and in November, 1928, he put in Goebbels as his propaganda chief. At the end of 1927 another familiar figure, Hermann Goering, returned to Germany from Sweden. Goering established himself in Berlin, living by his wits and his social connections. Hitler, looking for just such contacts in upper-class Berlin, soon renewed his association with Goering. In May, 1928, as their reward Goering and Goebbels were both elected to the Reichstag on the short Nazi list of twelve deputies, together with Strasser, Frick and General von Epp.

But the fact which overshadowed all Hitler's efforts in these years was the continued success of the Republican régime. By 1927 the despised Government of the "November criminals," the Jew-ridden "Republic of Betrayal," had succeeded in restoring order, stabilizing the currency, negotiating a settlement of reparations, ending the occupation of the Ruhr and securing Germany's entry into the League of Nations. These and other political successes were matched by an economic recovery which touched every man and woman in the country. The basis of this recovery was the huge amount of foreign money lent to Germany, especially by American investors, after the Dawes Plan and the re-establishment of the currency seemed to have made her a sound financial risk again.

Not only the German Government, but the States, the big cities, even the Churches, as well as industry and business, borrowed at high rates and short notice, spending extravagantly without much thought of how the loans were to be repaid except by borrowing more. In this way Germany made her reparation payments promptly, financed the re-equipment of her industry, and saw a steady rise in the standard of living of all classes.

Against more food, more money, more jobs, and more security, all Hitler's and Goebbels' skill as agitators made little headway. Hitler's instinct was right. The foundations of this sudden prosperity were exceedingly shaky, and Hitler's prophecies of disaster, although he was wrong in predicting a new inflation, were to be proved right. But, in 1927 and 1928, few in Germany wanted to listen to such gloomy threats.

In September, 1928, Hitler called a meeting of the Party leaders in Munich and talked to them frankly. Much of his speech was taken up with attempting to belittle Stresemann's achievement in foreign policy, but he did not disguise the difficulties which lay ahead. Above all, they had to strengthen the individual Party comrade's confidence in the victory of the movement. It is the one striking quality of his leadership in these years, the fact that he never let go, never lost faith in himself and was able to communicate this, to keep the faith of others alive, in the belief that some time a crack would come and the tide at last begin to flow in his favour.

Hitler's first chance came in 1929, a prelude to the great crisis of 1930-1933, and it came in the direction Hitler had foreseen, that of foreign policy.

The occasion was the renewal of negotiations for a final settlement of reparations. At the Hague in August, 1929, Stresemann succeeded in linking the two questions of reparations and evacuation, and in persuading the French to agree that the withdrawal of the occupying forces should begin in September, five years ahead of time, and be completed by the end of June, 1930.

Before Stresemann died on 3 October, 1929, he had overcome the opposition of the French, but the Germans still remained to be convinced. On 9 July, 1929, a national committee had been formed to organize a campaign for a plebiscite rejecting the new reparations settlement and the "lie" of Germany's war-guilt which represented the legal basis of the Allies' claims, and to use the issues of foreign policy and reparations for their ultimate purpose of overthrowing, or at least damaging, the hated Republic. It was by means of this campaign that Hitler first made his appearance on the national stage of German politics.

The leader of the agitation was Alfred Hugenberg, a bigoted German nationalist, a domineering and unscrupulous man of sixty-three, who had made a fortune out of the inflation and with it bought up a whole network of newspapers and news agencies, as well as a controlling interest in the big UFA film trust. These he used not so much to make money as to push his own views. In 1928 he took over the leadership of the German National Party.

Hugenberg could count on the support of the *Stahlhelm*, by far the largest of the German ex-servicemen's organizations, under the leadership of Franz Seldte; of the Pan-German League; and of powerful industrial and financial interests, represented by Dr. Albert Voegler, General Director of the big United Steel, and later by the President of the Reichsbank, Dr. Hjalmar Schacht. What they lacked was mass support, someone to go out and rouse the mob. Through Finanzrat Bang, Hitler and Hugenberg met at a nationalist club in Berlin. Hitler was not easily persuaded to come in, partly because of the opposition to such an alliance with the reactionary Hugenberg which he could expect to meet from the radical Strasser group. But he put his price high: complete independence in waging the campaign in his own way, and a large share of the Committee's resources to enable him to do it. For his representative on the Joint Finance Committee Hitler deliberately chose Gregor Strasser: when others in the Party complained, he laughed and told them to wait until he had finished with his allies.

In September, 1929, Hugenberg and Hitler published a draft "Law against the Enslavement of the German People." After repudiating Germany's responsibility for the war, Section III demanded the end of all reparations and Section IV the punishment of the Chancellor, the Cabinet and their representatives for high treason if they agreed to new financial commitments. Yet after all the violent propaganda about turning Germany into a "Young colony," crippling national survival for two generations, and enslaving the nation to foreign capitalists, this was a sharp failure. On 13 March, 1930, President Hindenburg put his signature to the Young

Plan laws. The fury of the Hugenberg and Nazi Press, and their open attacks on the President ("Is Hindenburg still alive?" Goebbels sneered in *Der Angriff*) revealed the bitterness of their defeat.

But the defeat for Hugenberg and his "Freedon Law" was no defeat for Hitler. In the preceding six months he had succeeded for the first time in breaking into national politics and showing something of his ability as a propagandist. To millions of Germans who had scarcely ever heard of him before, Hitler had now become a familiar figure, thanks to a publicity campaign entirely paid for by Hugenberg's rival party. More important still, he had attracted the attention of those who controlled the political funds of heavy industry and big business to his remarkable gifts as an agitator.

Already, through Otto Dietrich, Hitler had been brought into touch with Emil Kirdorf. Otto Dietrich, soon to become Hitler's Press Chief, was the son-in-law of the owner of the *Rheinisch-Westfälische Zeitung* (the paper of the Ruhr industrialists), and political adviser to the Mining Union. Kirdorf was one of the biggest names in German industry, and the man who controlled the political funds of the so-called Ruhr Treasury (*Ruhrschatz*). At the Nuremberg Party Day of August, 1929, Kirdorf was a guest of honour. From now on Hitler could count upon increasing support from at least some of those who had money to invest in nationalist, anti-democratic and anti-working-class politics.

With this money Hitler took over the Barlow Palace, an old mansion on the Briennerstrasse in Munich, and had it remodelled as the Brown House. A grand staircase led up to a conference chamber, furnished in red leather, and a large corner room in which Hitler received his visitors beneath a portrait of Frederick the Great. Before that, in 1929, Hitler himself had moved to a large nine-roomed flat covering the entire second floor of No. 16, Prinzregentenstrasse, one of Munich's fashionable streets. Hitler himself was now seen more frequently in Munich, occasionally in the company of his favourite niece, Geli Raubal, who had a room in the new flat.

At the Party conference which followed the alliance with Hugenberg Hitler had had to meet a good deal of criticism, voiced by Gregor Strasser, of the dangers of being tarred with the reactionary brush and losing support by too close association with the "old gang," the old ruling class of pre-war Germany, the industrialists, the Junkers, the former generals and higher officials who were the backbone of the National Party. His critics had underestimated Hitler's unscrupulousness, that characteristic duplicity, now first exhibited on this scale. With considerable skill he turned the campaign against the Young Plan, in itself an outright failure, to great political advantage for himself and his Party, then not only dropped the alliance with Hugenberg and the Nationalists as unexpectedly as he had made it, but proceeded to attack them.

Germany's astonishing recovery was abruptly ended in 1930 under the impact of the World Depression. The fact that 1930 was also the year in which Hitler and the Nazi Party for the first time became a major factor in national politics is not fortuitous. Ever since he came out of prison at the end of 1924 Hitler had prophesied disaster, only to see the Republic steadily consolidate itself. Those who ever heard of Adolf Hitler called him a fool. Now, in 1930, disaster cast its shadow over the land again, and the despised prophet entered into his inheritance. Three years later he told a Munich audience: "We are the result of the distress for which the others were responsible." It was the depression which tipped the scales against the Republic and for the first time since 1923 shifted the advantage to Hitler's side.

Hitler neither understood nor was interested in economics, but he was alive to the social and political consequences of events which, like the inflation of 1923, affected the life of every family in Germany. The most familiar index of these social consequences is the figure for unemployment—over six million in 1932 and again in 1933. Translated into terms of men standing hopelessly on the street corners of every industrial town in Germany; of houses without food or warmth; and of boys and girls leaving school without any chance of a job, one may begin to guess some of the incalculable human anxiety and embitterment burned into the minds of millions of ordinary German working men and women. In Germany the effect was more marked than in Great Britain, since it came on top of the defeat and the inflation, through which most of these people had already lived.

The social consequences of the depression affected the middle and the lower middle class sharply. For they—the clerks, shopkeepers, small business men, the less successful lawyers and doctors, the retired people living on their savings—were threatened with the loss not only of their livelihood, but of their respectability. The middle classes had no trade unions or unemployment insurance, and poverty carried a stigma of degradation for them that it did not have for the working class. The small property holder or business man was forced to sell at depreciated values to the big men. As during the inflation, anti-capitalist feeling against the combines, the trusts and department stores spread widely amongst a class which had once owned, or still owned, property itself.

Millions of Germans in industry, commerce, and agriculture as well, saw the apparently solid framework of their existence cracking and crumbling. In such circumstances men are no longer amenable to the arguments of reason. In such circumstances men entertain fantastic fears, extravagant hatreds and extravagant hopes. In such circumstances the extravagant demagogy of Hitler began to attract a mass following as it had never done before.

Although its full force was not to strike Germany until 1931, it was already clear that the economic crisis would produce a political crisis as well—a crisis of the régime. The greatest weakness of the Weimar Republic from the beginning had been its failure to provide a stable party basis for government. The party leaders, absorbed in manoeuvring and bargaining for party advantages—*Kuhhandel*, cattle-trading, is the expressive German word—were not displeased with this situation. Weak governments suited them to the extent that it made those in power more accessible to party pressure and blackmail. But the moment the country was faced with a major crisis, differences on the share of sacrifice each class was to bear—whether unemployment pay and wages were to be cut, taxes raised, a capital levy exacted, tariffs increased, and help given to landowners and farmers —were allowed to become so bitter that the methods of parliamentary government, which in Germany meant the construction of a coalition by a process of political bargaining, become more and more difficult to follow, and were in danger of being completely discredited.

Such a situation was much to the advantage of the Nazis, who had been unremitting in their attacks on the parliamentary republic and democratic methods of government. They had already launched a propaganda campaign especially designed to win support among the first class to feel the depression, the farmers. Hitler was impressed by a German agricultural expert, Walther Darré who had recently written a book on the peasantry as the "Life Source of the Nordic Race," and appointed him as the Party's agricultural adviser with the commission to draw up a peasant programme. This was published over Hitler's name on 6 March, 1930, and was marked not only by practical proposals to give economic aid to the farming population, but also by its insistence upon the peasantry as the most valuable class in the community. In the years ahead the farmers' support richly repaid the work of propaganda and organization they began during 1930.

In the case of agriculture it was simple to play for the support of both the big landowners and the peasants, since these had a common economic interest in the demand for protection and higher prices, and a common grievance in their neglect by parties preoccupied with the urban population. But when it came to industry, business and especially the retail trade, it was not so easy to square the circle, for here there was an open clash of interests between the workers and the employers, no less than between the small trader or shopkeeper and the big companies and department stores. Hitler needed the support of both, of the industrialists and big business interests because they controlled the funds, and of the masses because they had the votes. But in origin the National Socialists had been a radical anti-capitalist party, and this side of the Nazi programme was of increasing importance in a period of economic depression.

The question, how seriously Hitler took the socialist character of National Socialism was to remain one of the main causes of disagreement within the Nazi Party up to the summer of 1934; this was well illustrated in 1930 by the final breach between Hitler and Otto Strasser.

When Gregor Strasser moved to Munich, his brother Otto remained in Berlin, and through his paper, the *Arbeitsblatt* (still the official Nazi journal in the north), and his publishing house maintained an independent radical line which irritated and embarrassed Hitler. In April, 1930, the trade unions in Saxony declared a strike, and Otto Strasser came out in full support of their action. The industrialists made it perfectly plain to Hitler that unless the Party at once repudiated the stand Strasser had taken there would be no more subsidies. Although Hitler enforced an order that no member of the Party was to take part in the strike, he was unable to silence Strasser's papers. Following this, on 21 May Hitler suddenly appeared in Berlin and invited Otto Strasser to meet him for a discussion at his hotel. The only account we possess of it is Otto Strasser's, but there is little doubt that it can be accepted.

Hitler's tactics were a characteristic mixture of bribery, appeals and threats. He offered to take over the *Kampfverlag* on generous terms, and make Otto Strasser his Press Chief for the entire Reich; he appealed to him, with tears in his eyes and in the name of his brother Gregor, as an ex-soldier and a veteran National Socialist; he threatened that if Strasser would not submit to his orders he would drive him and his supporters out of the Party and forbid any member to have anything to do with him or his publications.

After further discussion, Otto Strasser came to what he regarded as the heart of the matter. "You want to strangle the social revolution," he told Hitler, "for the sake of legality and your new collaboration with the bourgeois parties of the Right."

Hitler, rattled by this suggestion, retorted angrily: "I am a Socialist, and a very different kind of Socialist from your rich friend, Reventlow. I was once an ordinary working-man. I would not allow my chauffeur to eat worse than I eat myself. What you understand by Socialism is nothing but Marxism. Now look: the great mass of working-men want only bread and circuses. They have no understanding for ideals . . . and we can never hope to win the workers . . . by an appeal to ideals. We want to make a revolution for the new dominating caste which is not moved, as you are, by the ethic of pity, but is quite clear in its own mind that it has the right to dominate others because it represents a better race: this caste ruthlessly maintains and assures its dominance over the masses . . ."

Strasser had demanded the nationalization of industry. Hitler scorned such a proposal: "Democracy has laid the world in ruins, and nevertheless you want to extend it to the economic sphere. It would be the end of German economy. . . . The capitalists have worked their way to the top through their capacity, and on the basis of this selection, which again only proves their higher race, they have a right to lead. Now you want an incapable Government Council . . . which has no notion of anything, to have a say: no leader in economic life would tolerate it."

When Strasser asked him what he would do with Krupps if he came to power, Hitler replied: "Of course I should leave it alone. Do you think that I should be so mad as to destroy Germany's economy?"

At the end of June Hitler wrote to Goebbels instructing him to drive Otto Strasser and his supporters from the Party. Goebbels obliged with alacrity. Otto Strasser stuck to his Socialist principles, published his talks with Hitler, broke with his brother Gregor (who stayed with Hitler), and set up a party later known as the Black Front. The dispute over the Socialist objectives of National Socialism was to reappear in the next few years—but Hitler had only gained, not lost, by making clear his own attitude. In September, 1930, the Nazi success at the National elections astonished the world. It was Hitler, not Strasser, who captured the mass vote, while the Black Front dwindled into insignificance and its founder sought refuge over the frontier.

In the election campaign, which followed the dissolution in July and led up to polling day on 14 September, the Nazis used every trick of propaganda to attract attention and win votes. In the big towns there was a marked increase in public disorder in which the S.A. took a prominent part. Slogans painted on walls, posters, demonstrations, rallies, mass meetings, crude and unrestrained demagogy, anything that would help to create an impression of energy, determination and success was pressed into use. Hitler's appeal in the towns was especially to the middle-class hit by the depression and the new generation, many who were voting for the first time, responded eagerly to attacks on the "System" which left them without jobs, and to the display of energy, the demand for discipline, sacrifice, action and not talk, which was the theme of Nazi propaganda.

In 1930 the mood of a large section of the German nation was one of resentment. Hitler, with an almost inexhaustible fund of resentment in his own character to draw from, offered them a series of objects on which to lavish all the blame for their misfortunes. It was the Allies, especially the French, who were to blame; the Republic, with its corrupt and self-seeking politicians; the money barons, the bosses of big business, the speculators and the monopolists; the Reds and the Marxists, who fostered class hatred and kept the nation divided; above all, the Jews, who fattened and grew rich on the degradation and weakness of the German people. The old parties and politicians offered no redress; Germany must look to new men, to a new movement to make her strong and feared, to restore to her people the dignity, security and prosperity which were their birthright. . . .

To audiences weighed down with anxiety and a sense of helplessness Hitler cried: If the economic experts say this or that is impossible, to hell with economics. What counts is will, and if our will is hard and ruthless enough we can do anything. . . . It is not your fault that you were defeated in the war and have suffered so much since. It is because you were betrayed in 1918 and have been exploited ever since by those who are envious of you and hate you; because you have been too honest and too patient. Let Germany awake and renew her strength, let her remember her greatness and recover her old position in the world, and for a start let's clear out the old gang in Berlin.

This is a fair summary of the sort of speech Hitler and his lieutenants made at hundreds of meetings in the summer of 1930. It showed a psychological perception of the popluar mood which was wholly lacking from the campaigns of the other parties. Hitler never forgot the principle he had underlined in *Mein Kampf*: go for the masses. Only the Communists could rival Hitler in this sort of agitation, but the

Communists were hampered by rigid doctrinaire beliefs, while Hitler was prepared to adapt or abandon his programme to suit his audience.

In the middle of September thirty million Germans went to the polls, and the results surprised even Hitler. Nazi seats in the Reichstag had increased from 12 to 107. From ninth the Nazis had become the second Party in the State and overnight Hitler had become a politician of European importance. The foreign correspondents flocked to interview him. *The Times* printed his assurances of goodwill at length, while in the *Daily Mail* Lord Rothermere welcomed Hitler's success as a reinforcement of the defences against Bolshevism.

Now that the Nazis had won this great electoral success the question arose, what use were they going to make of it? Hitler gave part of an answer in a speech he made at Munich ten days after the election: "If today our action employs among its different weapons that of Parliament . . . we are a parliamentary Party by compulsion, under constraint, and the Constitution compels us to use this means. . . . It is not for seats in Parliament that we fight, but we win seats in Parliament in order that one day we may be able to liberate the German people."

Almost certainly Hitler meant to have his revolution, but he meant to have it after, not before, he came to power. He was too impressed by the power of the State to risk defeat in the streets, as he had in 1923. The revolutionary romanticism of the barricades was out of date since the invention of the machine-gun. Hitler's aim now—as it had been in 1923 —was a revolution with the power of the State on his side. But revolution was not the means of securing such power; that had to be obtained legally.

Meanwhile the attitude of the average Party member was probably best summed up by Goering when he said: "We are fighting against this State and the present System because we wish to destroy it utterly, but in a legal manner—for the long-eared plain-clothes men. Before we had the Law for the Protection of the Republic we said we hated this State; under this law we say we love it—and still everyone knows what we mean."

Two particular problems were bound up with the question of legality up to 1934, the relations of the Nazi Party and the Army, and the role to be played by the S.A. The two questions are only different sides of the same penny, but it will be easier to deal with them separately.

Since Roehm's resignation the relations between the Nazis and the Army had been bad. In an effort to control the S.A., Hitler had forbidden them to have any connection with the

Army, and the Ministry of Defence had retorted by forbidding the Army to accept National Socialists as recruits or
to employ them in arsenals and supply depots. This was in
1927.

Yet Hitler was very much aware that the Army's support,
or at least its neutrality, was the key to his success. In March,
1929, he delivered a speech at Munich on National Socialism
and the Armed Forces which was both a challenge to the
Army and a bid for its favour. Hitler began by attacking General von Seeckt's guiding principle of the new Army—that the
Army must stand apart from politics. This, Hitler declared,
was simply to put the Army at the service of the Republican
régime, which had stabbed the old Army in the back in 1918
and betrayed Germany to her enemies.

> The victory of one course or the other lies partially in the
> hands of the Army—that is, the victory of the Marxists or of our
> side. Should the Leftists win out through your wonderful un-
> political attitude, you may write over the German Army:
> "The end of the German Army." For then, gentlemen, you
> must definitely become political, then the red cap of the
> Jacobins will be drawn over your heads. . . . You may then
> become hangmen of the régime and political commissars, and,
> if you do not behave, your wife and child will be put behind
> locked doors. And if you still do not behave, you will be thrown
> out and perhaps stood up against a wall, for a human life
> counts little to those who are out to destroy a people.

Hitler's speech was published verbatim in a special Army
issue of the *Völkischer Beobachter,* and Hitler followed it
up by articles in a new Nazi monthly, *the Deutscher Wehrgeist*
(*The German Military Spirit*), in which he argued that by its
attitude of hostility towards nationalist movements like the
Nazis the Army was betraying its own traditions and cutting
the ground away from under its own feet. Hitler's arguments,
which showed again his uncanny skill in penetrating the
minds of those he sought to influence, were not without effect,
especially among the younger officers, who saw little prospect
of promotion in any army limited by the Treaty to a hundred
thousand men, and who were attracted by Hitler's promises
that he would at once expand and restore the Army to its
old position in the State if he came to power.

On 23 September, at the trial of three young officers
charged with spreading Nazi propaganda, before the Supreme
Court at Leipzig, Hitler had become the leader of the second
most powerful Party in the country, and the Army leaders
were extremely interested to discover what his attitude towards
the Army would be. As a witness, Hitler did not miss his

opportunity and every one of his statements was made with an eye to its effect on the Army. He went out of his way to reassure them about the S.A. Stormtroops. "They were set up exclusively for the purpose of protecting the Party in its propaganda, not to fight against the State. I have been a soldier long enough to know that it is impossible for a Party Organization to fight against the disciplined forces of the Army. . . . I did everything I could to prevent the S.A. from assuming any kind of military character. We are none of us interested in replacing the Army; my only wish is that the German State and the German people should be imbued with a new spirit. . . . We will see to it that, when we have come to power, out of the present Reichswehr a great German People's Army shall arise. There are thousands of young men in the Army of the same opinion."

The President of the Court here interrupted to remark that the Nazis could scarcely hope to realize these ideals by legal means. Hitler indignantly denied this. There were no secret directives. "On questions of this kind only my orders are valid and my basic principle is that if a Party regulation conflicts with the law it is not to be carried out. . . . "

There is little doubt that it was Hitler's explicit statement at Leipzig, coming immediately after his success in the elections, which provided the basis for his subsequent negotiations with the Army leaders and their eventual agreement to his assumption of power.

Hitler's talk of legality, however, was only a half-truth, a trick to get power on the cheap, to persuade the generals and the other guardians of the State to hand over power without forcing him to seize it. They were only tactics of legality, for everything about the movement proclaimed its brazen contempt for law. Hitler had therefore to take care that in his preoccupation with tactics he did not so far compromise the revolutionary character of his movement as to rob it of its attractive power.

The danger point was the S.A., which was to become the expression of the Party's revolutionary purpose. One of the favourite S.A. slogans was: "Possession of the streets is the key to power in the State," and from the beginning of 1930 the political struggle in the Reichstag and at elections was supplemented—in part replaced—by the street fights of the Party armies in Berlin and the other big cities.

In the course of one of these gang feuds in February, 1930, a young Berlin S.A. leader, Horst Wessel, was shot by the Communists, and was skilfully built up by Goebbels into the prototype of the martyred Nazi idealist, whose verses provided the S.A. with their marching song, the famous *Horst Wessel*

Lied. In the first six months of 1930 the authorities issued a number of prohibitions to check this growth of public disorder. Outdoor meetings and parades were forbidden in Prussia; a new Law for the Protection of the Republic and for the suppression of political disturbances was passed in March; in June the Prussian Minister of the Interior prohibited the Nazis from wearing uniforms and emblems. But these measures proved ineffective; forbidden to wear their brown shirts, the Nazis paraded in white. By night they and the Communists marched in formation singing down the streets, broke up rival political meetings, beat up opponents and raided each other's "territory." As unemployment rose, the number of recruits mounted. Anything was better than loafing on the street corners, and the S.A. offered a meal and a uniform, companionship and excitement.

The key to this campaign was incessant activity, a sustained effort of propaganda and agitation kept up all the year round. In this the S.A. had an essential part to play, for violence and the display of force had always formed a central part of Nazi propaganda. But it was propaganda that Hitler had in mind; the S.A. were to be the shock troops of a revolution that was never to be made. Hitler's problem was to keep the spirit of the S.A. alive without allowing it to find an outlet in revolutionary action; to use them as a threat, yet never to compromise his plan of coming to power without a head-on collision with the forces of the State, above all with the Army.

In October, Hitler persuaded Ernst Roehm, then serving as an officer in the Bolivian Army, to return to Germany, to take over the reorganization of the S.A. as its Chief of Staff. In Roehm, he hoped, he had found the man to pull the S.A. together and keep it in hand.

As 1930 closed Hitler had considerable cause for satisfaction. In the Reichstag the Nazis—every man in brown uniform—had already shown their strength and their contempt for Parliament by creating such disorder that the sittings had to be frequently suspended. In the streets the S.A. had scored another triumph by forcing the Government to ban the further showing of the anti-militarist film, *All Quiet on the Western Front,* by calculated hooliganism.

Hitler was in no danger of underestimating the opposition to his leadership which still existed in the Party. Success alone would silence criticism. Yet success no longer seemed impossible. In 1930 he had reached the threshold of power.

At the beginning of January, 1931, Roehm took over his new duties as Chief of Staff of the S.A. He immediately set to work to make the S.A. by far the most efficient of the Party armies.

The organization was closely modelled on that of the Army, with its own headquarters and General Staff quite separate from the organization of the Party, and its own training college for S.A. and S.S. leaders opened at Munich. At the time Roehm took over, in January, 1931, the S.A. numbered roughly a hundred thousand men; a year later Hitler could claim three hundred thousand.

The direction of the Party in the years 1931 and 1932 was for all practical purposes in the hands of six men—Hitler himself, Roehm, Gregor Strasser, Goering, Goebbels and Frick. Roehm's importance consisted not only in his brilliant talents as an organizer and his office as Chief of Staff of the S.A., but also in his contacts with the Army. Goering, with his wide range of acquaintances, his good-humoured charm and ease of manner, became in the course of 1931 Hitler's chief political "contact-man" in the capital, with a general commission to negotiate with other parties and groups.

The leader of the Nazi Party in the Reichstag was Dr. Wilhelm Frick. An early and convinced National Socialist, he was useful to Hitler as a good administrator and a man who knew thoroughly the machinery and the mentality of the German civil service. There were others—but none of these held anything like the position of the five men with whom Hitler captured power.

So highly organized a machine must have cost large sums of money to run, yet there is no more difficult question to answer than how Hitler got that money. For unfortunately the evidence is both incomplete and imprecise. A good deal of money, of course, came from the Party itself—from membership dues; from the sale of Party newspapers and literature, which members were always being pressed to buy; from the admission charges and collections at the big meetings. There is no doubt that the Party made heavy demands on its members—even the unemployed S.A. men had to hand over their unemployment-benefit money in return for their food and shelter. Almost certainly the proportion of revenue which was raised by the Party itself has been underestimated. There were also subsidies from interested supporters but how much this produced in hard cash it is impossible to say.

Hitler, however much he received from Kirdorf, Thyssen and the rest, was neither a political puppet created by the capitalists, nor a mere agent of the big industrialists who had lost his independence. Thyssen's and Schacht's accounts are records of the disillusionment of those who thought they had bought Hitler and would call the tune he was to play. They were to discover, like the conservative politicians and the generals, that, contrary to the popular belief, bankers and business men are too innocent for politics when it is played by a man like Hitler.

In speaking of the Nazi movement as a "party" there is a danger of mistaking its true character. For the Nazi Party was no more a party, in the normal democratic sense of that word, than the Communist Party is today; it was an organized conspiracy against the State. The Party's programme was important to win support, and, for psychological reasons, the programme was never allowed to become a subject for discussion. But the leaders' real object was to get their hands on the State. They were the gutter *élite*, avid for power, position and wealth; the sole object of the Party was to secure power by one means or another.

No State could tolerate the threat which such an organization implied, if it was resolved to remain master in its own house. Why then were no effective steps taken by the German Government to arrest the leaders of the Nazi Party and break it up? If the people in authority had been really determined to smash the Nazi movement they would have found the means. The question to be asked is, why they lacked the will and the determination? To this there are several answers.

In the first place, Hitler's tactics of legality were designed to enable him to win the maximum advantage from the democratic constitution of the Weimar Republic. He shrewdly realized he would be the loser, not the gainer, in any attempt to resort to force, whereas so long as he kept within the letter of the law he could fetter the authorities with their own slow-moving legal processes.

In the second place, so long as the challenge to the authority of the State was camouflaged by fair words, there was a strong temptation for any government in Germany in 1931 and 1932 not to add to its difficulties. For throughout the winter of 1930-1931 the economic crisis, far from lifting, bore down more heavily. The measures taken by the Bruening Government, while imposing considerable sacrifices on the people, were insufficient to enable the Government to master the crisis. In such circumstances Hitler found no difficulty in laying the blame for all the economic distress on the Government's policy, particularly as Germany was still saddled with reparation payments. Further, the worsening of the crisis in the summer of 1931 had been partly occasioned by a stinging rebuff in foreign policy, when France, supported by Italy and Czechoslovakia, had taken the German Foreign Minister's proposal to form an Austro-German Customs Union to be a move towards the political and territorial union, expressly forbidden by the Treaties of Versailles and St.

Germain. The measures taken by the French not only helped to precipitate the German financial crisis but forced the German Foreign Minister to announce the project was being abandoned. The result was to inflict a sharp humiliation on the Bruening Government and to inflame national resentment in Germany.

Hitler was not slow to point the lesson: so long as Germany continued to be ruled by the present system she would continue to suffer economic misery at home and contemptuous insults abroad. Two years before Gregor Strasser had written: "Everything that is detrimental to the existing order has our support. . . . We are promoting catastrophic policies—for only . . . the collapse of the liberal system, will clear the way for the new order. . . . " The Nazis were now beginning to garner the harvest of their policy of catastrophe.

Faced with such difficulties, both in domestic and foreign policy, any government was unlikely to add to its problems by the uproar which the suppression of the Nazi Party, the second largest in the Reichstag, would inevitably have entailed, so long as Hitler was clever enough to avoid any flagrant act of illegality. The refusal of the German parties to unite in face of the emergency and jointly assume responsibility for the unpopular measures which had to be taken, drove Bruening into a dangerous dependence on the support of the President and that of the Army. The attitude of both towards the Nazis was equivocal. Here was the third reason for the reluctance to take action against the Nazis.

From the beginning of 1930, General Groener, the Minister of Defence, a man of integrity and experience, had been uneasily conscious that a good many members of the Officer Corps were becoming sympathetic to the Nazis. The nationalist appeal of Nazi propaganda and its promise of a powerful Germany with an expanded Army were beginning to have their effect.

In the autumn of 1931 Dr. Bruening writes: "the two generals (von Schleicher and von Hammerstein) and myself were fully agreed that, if the Nazis imitated Mussolini's March on Rome the Army would make short work of them. . . . We also expected that we would finally get Hindenburg's consent to the immediate suppression of the Nazi Party, if they resorted to open revolt."

But it was not at all certain that the Government would be able to count on the support of the Army if it was a question of suppressing the Nazi Party without the pretext of revolt. Once again the cleverness of Hitler's tactics of legality was demonstrated.

The President, Field-Marshal von Hindenburg, was now

eighty-four and such political judgment as he had ever had was failing. What he cared about most of all was the German Army in which he had spent his life. "The Reichswehr obeyed him, but he listened to it. He absorbed into his mind and spirit everything to which it was sensitive. He was flesh and blood of its flesh and blood, an off-shoot of that Prusso-German militarism which had produced so many first-rate technical and so few politically far-sighted heads." Faithfully reflecting opinion in the Army, Hindenburg too was opposed to the use of force against the Nazis. He would only agree to it if there was some unequivocal act of rebellion on their part.

More important still than the opinion of President Hindenburg was that of Major-General Kurt von Schleicher, who, by 1930-1932, had made himself virtually the authoritative voice of the Army in politics. General Schleicher was that curiosity in the German Army, a General Staff Officer—able, charming and ambitious—who was more interested in politics than in war. Groener had made Schleicher the head of a new department in his Ministry, the *Ministeramt*. This was to handle all matters common to both the Army and Navy and to act as liaison between the armed services and other ministries. Schleicher used the key position created for him to make himself one of the most powerful political figures in Germany. Both Groener and the C. in C. of the Army, General von Hammerstein, were under his influence. Through an old friendship with Hindenburg's son he had an entrée to the old man, who listened and was impressed by what he said.

Schleicher's object was to secure a strong government which, in place of futile coalitions would master the economic and political crisis and prevent the Army being forced to intervene to put down revolution. "The load which constantly weighed on General Schleicher's mind," Bruening writes, "was the fear . . . that Nazi and Communist uprisings might break out simultaneously and thus give foreign powers an opportunity to extend their borders still further at Germany's expense." In particular he feared an attack by Poland, if the German Army should be fully occupied with internal disturbance.

Schleicher, therefore, shared fully—and was partly responsible for—the reluctance of Groener and Hindenburg to take any initiative against the Nazis. But Schleicher went further: impressed by the Nazi success at the elections and by their nationalist programme, he began to play with the idea of winning Hitler's support for Bruening and converting the Nazi movement with its mass following into a prop of the existing government, instead of a battering ram directed against it.

Schleicher made a beginning by removing the ban on the

Army's employment of National Socialists in arsenals and supply depots and of Nazi enlistment in the Army. In return Hitler reaffirmed his adherence to legality by forbidding the S.A. to take part in street-fighting. During the succeeding months Schleicher had several talks with Roehm, eager as always to work with the Army. By the latter half of 1931 he was ready to try to secure Hitler's agreement to Hindenburg's re-election as a first step to drawing the Nazis into support of the Government and taming their revolutionary ardour.

Nothing could have suited Hitler better. He had built up a remarkable organization, the strength of which grew steadily, but the question remained how was he to change his success into the hard coin of political power. One way of adding to the Nazi vote was to combine with Hugenberg's German National Party. On 9 July, 1931, Hitler and Hugenberg met in Berlin and issued a statement to the effect that they would henceforward co-operate for the overthrow of the existing "System." But alliance with the Nationalists, with their strongly upper-class character, was in fact a dubious policy for the Nazis, bound to lead to much discontent in the radical wing of the Party. Although Hitler continued to make intermittent use of the Nationalist alliance, it was only when no other course presented itself.

If Hitler was to carry his policy of legality to success it could only be done in one way, a possibility created by the peculiar system under which Germany was now governed. Neither able to find a stable parliamentary majority nor to win an election, the Chancellors were forced to use the President's emergency powers, upon which they relied to issue decrees, in effect, thus transferring political power in Germany from the nation to the little group of men round the President. If Hitler could persuade these men to take him into partnership and make him Chancellor, with the right to use the President's emergency powers—a presidential, as opposed to a parliamentary, government—then he could dispense with the clear electoral majority which still eluded him and with the risky experiment of a *putsch*.

Neither Schleicher nor the President was at all satisfied with the existing situation. They were looking for a government which, while prepared to take resolute action to deal with the crisis, would also be able to win mass support in the country, and, if possible, secure a majority in the Reichstag. Bruening had failed to win such a majority. Schleicher, therefore, began to look elsewhere for the mass support which he felt to be necessary for the presidential government.

Hitler's six million votes were a promise of the support Hitler could provide, if he was brought in. Also the organized violence of the S.A. was a threat of the revolution he might make if he were left out. Hitler's game, therefore, from 1931 to 1933 was to use the revolution he was unwilling to make and the mass support he was unable to turn into a majority, the first as a threat, the second as a promise, to persuade the President and his advisers to take him into partnership and give him power.

This is the key to the complicated and tortuous political moves of the period between the autumn of 1931 and 30 January, 1933, when the game succeeded and Hindenburg appointed Adolf Hitler as Chancellor—legally. The milestones on the path of the Nazi Party to power between these two dates are the successive negotiations between the little group of men who bore the responsibility for the experiment of presidential government and the Nazi leaders. Hitler did not at the time see this as the only means by which he could come to power legally. He continued to speculate on the possibility of a coalition with the Nationalists—even at one time with the Centre—or, better still, on the chances of winning an outright majority at the next elections. Each time the negotiations broke down he turned again to these alternatives. Yet each time he gives the impression that his eye is always on a resumption of negotiations, and that the measures he takes are designed primarily to put pressure on the other side to begin talks again rather than to bring him into office by other means.

Years ago, in Vienna, Hitler had admired the tactics of Karl Lueger and had summed them up in two sentences in *Mein Kampf*: "In his political activity, Lueger attached the main importance to winning over those classes whose threatened existence tended to stimulate rather than paralyse their will to fight. At the same time he took care to avail himself of all the instruments of authority at his disposal, and to bring powerful existing institutions over to his side, in order to gain from these well-tried sources of power the greatest possible advantage for his own movement." Hitler was well on the way to "winning over those classes whose existence was threatened"; now he faced the task of "bringing powerful existing institutions over to his side," above all the Army and the President. The years of waiting were at an end.

CHAPTER FOUR

THE MONTHS OF OPPORTUNITY

October, 1931 — 30 January, 1933

The first contacts between Hitler and the men who disposed of power in Germany were scarcely auspicious. At the beginning of the autumn of 1931 Schleicher had a meeting with Hitler, arranged with Roehm's help, and subsequently persuaded both the Chancellor and the President to see him.

What Bruening asked for was Hitler's support until the reparations question was settled and Hindenburg re-elected as President. After this had been accomplished he was willing to retire and allow someone else more acceptable to the parties of the Right to take his place. Instead of giving a direct answer, Hitler launched into a monologue, the main point of which was that when he came to power he would not only get rid of Germany's debts but would rearm and, with England and Italy as his allies, force France to her knees. He failed to impress the Chancellor and the meeting ended inconclusively.

The interview with President Hindenburg was the first occasion on which the two men had met. Hitler was nervous and ill-at-ease; his niece, Geli Raubal, with whom he was in love, had committed suicide three weeks before, and he had wired to Goering, who was at the bedside of his dying wife in Sweden, to return and accompany him. Nazi accounts of the meeting are singularly reticent, but Hitler obviously made the mistake of talking too much and trying to impress the old man with his demagogic arts; instead he bored him. Hindenburg is said to have grumbled to Schleicher afterwards that he was a queer fellow who would never make a Chancellor, but, at most, a Minister of Posts.

Altogether it was a bad week for Hitler. The day after his interview with the President he took part in a great demonstration of the Right-wing "National" opposition at Harzburg. Hugenberg, representing the Nationalists; Seldte and Duesterberg, the leaders of the *Stahlhelm*; Dr. Schacht and General von Seeckt; Graf Kalkreuth, the president of the Junkers' Land League, and half a score of figures from the Ruhr and

Rhineland industries, all joined in passing a solemn resolution uniting the parties of the Right. They demanded the immediate resignation of Bruening's Government followed by new elections. Hitler had been reluctant to take part in the Rally and Frick felt obliged to defend the decision to the Nazi contingent with a speech in which he said openly that they were only using the Nationalists as a convenient ladder to office. Hitler felt oppressed by his old lack of self-confidence in face of all these frock-coats, top-hats, Army uniforms and formal titles. To add to his irritation, the *Stahlhelm* arrived in much greater numbers than the S.A., and Hugenberg and Seldte stole the limelight. Hitler read his speech in a perfunctory fashion, and left before the *Stahlhelm* marched past. The united front of the National Opposition had virtually collapsed before it was established.

Hitler went on 17 October to Brunswick, where more than a hundred thousand S.A. and S.S. men tramped past the saluting base for six hours, and the thundering cheers mollified his wounded vanity. Thirty-eight special trains and five thousand lorries brought the Brown Shirts pouring into Brunswick. Hitler presented twenty-four new standards, and at night a great torchlight parade lighted up the countryside. This was a show the like of which neither Hugenberg and the *Stahlhelm* nor the Government could put on: while they continued to talk of the need for popular support, Hitler already had it.

The first attempt to initiate negotiations had broken down, but events continued to flow in Hitler's favour. It was a grim winter in Germany and Bruening's emergency measures were poor comfort to a people suffering from hunger, cold, lack of work and lack of hope. Nor was Bruening, with his aloof and reserved manner, the man to put across a programme of sacrifice and austerity.

By contrast, the Nazis gained steadily in strength. Their membership rose to more than 800,000 at the end of 1931. Following their success in provincial elections at Oldenburg and Hamburg, the Nazis swept the board at the Hessian elections in November. The threat and the promise were gaining in weight.

These facts were not lost on Schleicher, who continued his talks with Hitler in November and December, more and more impressed with the need to bring Hitler into the game and make use of him.

Hitler meanwhile kept up the attack on Bruening as the embodiment of all the evils of the "System" by which Germany had been governed since 1918. His open letter (published 13 December, 1931) to Bruening is interesting for Hitler's frank statement of what he meant by legality. "You refuse, as a 'statesman,' to admit that if we come to power legally we could then break through legality. Herr Chancellor, the fundamental thesis of democracy runs: 'All power issues from the People.' The constitution lays down the way by which a conception, an idea, and therefore an organization, must gain from the people the legitimation for the realization of its aims. But in the last resort it is the People itself which determines its Constitution.

"Herr Chancellor, if the German nation once empowers the National Socialist Movement to introduce a Constitution other than that which we have today, then you cannot stop it. . . ."

Here was a plain enough warning of what Hitler meant to do when he got power, yet Schleicher, Papen and the rest were so sure they could manage this ignorant agitator that they only smiled and took no notice.

Bruening had fewer illusions, but all his plans depended upon being able to hold out until economic conditions improved, or he could secure some success in foreign policy. His ability to do this depended in turn upon the re-election of Hindenburg as President. Old and failing as Hindenburg was, Bruening still believed that he could rely on the President to support him and continue to sign his decrees. The old man reluctantly agreed only when the Chancellor promised to try to secure an agreement with the Reichstag Party leaders to prolong the presidential term without re-election. And so Bruening, too, agreed to further negotiations with Hitler in order to win him over to his plan.

Hitler was in Munich, in the offices of the *Völkischer Beobachter*, when the telegram was brought in to him. He is reported to have crashed his fist down on the telegram in exultation: "Now I have them in my pocket. They have recognized me as a partner in their negotiations."

Bruening's proposal was substantially the same as in the previous autumn: Hitler was asked to agree to a prolongation of Hindenburg's presidency for a year or two, until the country had begun its economic recovery and the issues of reparations and the German claim to equality of rights in armaments had been settled. In return, Bruening renewed his offer to resign as soon as he had settled the question of reparations.

Hitler asked for time to consider his reply and withdrew to the Kaiserhof, opposite the Reich Chancellery. Hugenberg, also consulted by the Chancellor, as leader of the Nationalists, was strongly opposed to prolonging Hindenburg's term of office, arguing that it could only strengthen Bruening's position, and Goebbels took the same view. In his diary he wrote:

" . . . Bruening only wants to stabilize his own position indefinitely. . . . The contest for power, the game of chess, has begun. . . . It will be a fast game, played with intelligence and skill. The main point is that we hold fast. . . . " Roehm as well as Goebbels argued that it would be fatal for the Party to appear to avoid a chance to go to the nation, especially after the recent successes in the provincial elections. Long and anxious debates followed among the Nazi leaders. In the end Roehm's point of view was accepted.

Both Hitler and Hugenberg rejected Bruening's proposal, but Hitler tried to drive a wedge between Chancellor and President. He did this by writing direct to the President over Bruening's head, warning him that the Chancellor's plan was an infringement of the Constitution; adding, however, that he himself was willing to support Hindenburg as the joint presidential candidate of the Nazis and the Nationalists if the old man would agree to dismiss Bruening, form a Right-wing "National" government and hold new elections for the Reichstag and the Prussian Diet. The newly elected Reichstag, in which Hitler was confident of a majority for the Nazi and Nationalist parties, would then proceed to prolong his term of office without an election.

With Hindenburg's refusal, Hitler launched a violent attack on Bruening, and an acrimonious exchange followed. After this any hopes of avoiding an election for the presidency were at an end. For a second time the attempt to make a deal with Hitler had failed. Bruening, who had never had much hopes of its success, threw all his energy into the campaign. Schleicher was equally set on securing the President's re-election, since the position and powers of the Presidency were at the basis of his plans. For that reason he was willing to support Bruening, but after that, General von Schleicher considered, a lot of things might happen. The President himself, nettled by the refusal of the Right-wing parties to support him, finally agreed to stand for re-election. On the Government side, therefore, the breakdown of negotiations had won at least a temporary consolidation of forces in Bruening's favour.

This was far from being the case in the Nazi camp. Now that his attempt to split Hindenburg and Bruening had failed, Hitler had to face an awkward decision. Was he strong enough to risk an open contest with Hindenburg? Hindenburg, or rather the Hindenburg legend, was a formidable opponent. Failure might destroy the growing belief in Nazi invincibility: on the other hand, dare they risk evading the contest?

For a month Hitler hesitated, to the anxiety and worry of

the Nazi leaders, and not until 22 February would Hitler allow Goebbels to announce his candidature to a packed Nazi meeting at the big Berlin *Sportpalast*." . . .a storm of deafening applause rages for nearly ten minutes. Wild ovations for the leader. The audience rises with shouts of joy. They nearly raise the roof. . . . People laugh and cry at the same time." Characteristically, Hitler, after hesitating for a month, now flung himself into the campaign with a whole-hearted conviction of success. Once embarked on a course of action, Hitler was not a man to look back.

Even before Hitler finally broke off the negotiations with Bruening, Goebbels was already at work on the election campaign. On 24 January he noted: "The elections are prepared down to the minutest detail. It will be a struggle such as the world has never before witnessed. . . . We now need only to press the button to set the machine going."

One of Goebbels' greatest anxieties had been the financing of the election campaign. On 5 January he wrote despairingly: "Money is wanting everywhere. . . . Nobody will give us credit." A month later (8 February) he was much more cheerful: "Money affairs improve daily. The financing of the electoral campaign is practically assured." One of the reasons for this sudden change was a visit Hitler had paid to Düsseldorf, the capital of the German steel industry, on 27 January.

At the meeting, arranged by Fritz Thyssen, Hitler spoke to the Industry Club. It was the first time that many of the West German industrialists had met Hitler, and their reception of him was cool and reserved. Yet Hitler, far from being nervous, spoke for two and a half hours without pause, and made one of the best speeches of his life. In it is to be found every one of the stock ideas out of which he built his propaganda, brilliantly dressed up for his audience of business men. For this reason it is worth quoting at some length as an example of his technique.

Hitler began by attacking Bruening's view that the dominant consideration in German politics at this time ought to be the country's foreign relations. "I regard it as of the first importance to break down the view that our destiny is conditioned by world events. . . ." The determining factor in national life was the inner worth of a people and its spirit. In Germany, however, this inner worth had been undermined by setting up the false values of democracy and the supremacy of mere numbers in opposition to the creative principle of individual personality.

Hitler chose his illustrations with skill. Private property, he pointed out, could only be justified on the ground that men's achievements in the economic field were unequal. "But it is absurd to build up economic life on the conceptions of achievement, of the value of personality and on the authority of personality, while in the political sphere you deny this authority and thrust in its place the law of the greatest number—democracy."

Hitler dwelt at length on the threat of Communism, for it was something more, he said, than "a mob storming about in some of our streets in Germany, it is a conception of the world which is in the act of subjecting to itself the entire Asiatic continent." Already, unemployment was driving millions of Germans to look on Communism as the "logical theoretical counterpart of their actual economic situation." This was the heart of the German problem—not the result of foreign conditions, "but of our internal aberration, our internal division, our internal collapse." And this state of affairs was not to be cured by the economic expedients embodied in emergency decrees.

> . . . There is only one fundamental solution—the realization that there can be no flourishing economic life which has not before it and behind it a flourishing, powerful State as its protection. . . . There can be no economic life unless behind this economic life there stands the determined political will of the nation absolutely ready to strike—and to strike hard. . . .

The same, Hitler went on, was true of foreign policy. "The Treaty of Versailles in itself is only the consequence of our own slow inner confusion and aberration of mind. . . . It was no good appealing for national unity and sacrifice . . . when only fifty per cent of a people are ready to fight for the national colours, while fifty per cent have hoisted another flag which stands for a State which is to be found only outside the bounds of their own State."

"Unless Germany can master this internal division in *Weltanschauungen* no measures of the legislature can stop the decline of the German nation. (*Very true!*)" Recognizing this fact, the Nazi movement had set out to create a new outlook which would re-unite and re-vitalize the German people.

> Remember that it means sacrifice when today many hundreds of thousands of S.A. and S.S. men every day have to mount on their lorries, protect meetings, undertake marches, sacrifice themselves night after night and then come back in the grey dawn to workshop and factory, or as unemployed to take the pittance of the dole; it means sacrifice when from the little they possess they have to buy their uniforms, their shirts, their badges, yes, and even pay their own fares. But there is already in all this the force of an ideal—a great ideal! And if the whole German nation today . . . possessed this idealism,

Germany would stand in the eyes of the world otherwise than she stands now!

When Hitler sat down the audience rose and cheered him wildly. Large contributions from heavy industry flowed into the Nazi treasury. As the Army saw in Hitler the man who promised to restore Germany's military power, so the industrialists came to see in him their champion against Communism and the trade unions, giving a free hand to private enterprise and economic exploitation in the name of the principle of "creative individuality."

The election campaign for the Presidency was notable because of the bitterness with which it was fought, because of the extraordinary confusion of parties, but chiefly because of the vigorous character of the Nazi campaign, a masterpiece of organized agitation which attempted to take Germany by storm. Every constituency down to the most remote village was canvassed. The walls of the towns were plastered with screaming Nazi posters; films of Hitler and Goebbels were made and shown everywhere (an innovation in 1932); gramophone records were produced which could be sent through the post, two hundred thousand marks spent on propaganda in one week alone. But, true to Hitler's belief in the superiority of the spoken word, the main Nazi effort went into organizing a chain of mass meetings at which the principal Nazi orators, Hitler, Goebbels, Gregor Strasser, worked their audiences up to hysterical enthusiasm by mob oratory of the most unrestrained kind. Between 22 February and 12 March Goebbels made nineteen speeches in Berlin (including four in the huge *Sportpalast*) and addressed mass meetings in nine other towns as widely separated as Breslau, Dresden, Cologne, Hamburg and Nuremberg, dashing back to Berlin by the night train to supervise the work of the central propaganda organization. Hitler, hurriedly made a German citizen on the eve of the election by Nazi-controlled Brunswick, spoke to sixty thousand people at Breslau; in other places to crowds estimated at one hundred thousand.

The result was baffling. When the polls closed on the evening of 13 March the Nazi vote had been pushed up to just under eleven and a half millions, an increase of eighty-six per cent from September, 1930, giving Hitler nearly one-third of the total votes in Germany. Yet all the Nazi efforts left them more than seven million votes behind Hindenburg. This was outright defeat, and Goebbels was in despair.

By a quirk of chance, however, Hindenburg's vote was

slightly short of the absolute majority required. A second election had therefore to be held. While Goebbels in Berlin threw up his hands, in Munich before morning on 14 March special editions of the *Völkischer Beobachter* were on the streets carrying Hitler's new election manifesto: "The first election campaign is over, the second has begun today. I shall lead it."

It was an uphill fight, with Hitler driving a tired and dispirited Party, but the ingenious mind of Goebbels, once he had recovered his nerve, hit on a novel electioneering device. The leader should cover Germany by plane—"Hitler over Germany." On 3 April the flight began with four mass meetings in Saxony, at which Hitler addressed a quarter of a million people. In all, twenty different towns were covered in a week from East Prussia to Westphalia, from the Baltic to Bavaria. On 8 April, when a violent storm raged over Western Germany and all other air traffic was grounded, the leader flew to Dusseldorf and kept his engagement, with the whole Nazi Press blaring away that here at last was the man with the courage Germany needed.

Defeat was certain, but by his exacting performance Hitler pushed up his vote again on 10 April by more than two millions. The President was safely home with a comfortable 53 per cent, yet by tenacity and boldness Hitler had avoided disaster, capturing votes not only from the Nationalists but also from the Communists, whose vote fell by over a million. The day after the election Goebbels wrote in his diary: "The campaign for the Prussian State elections is prepared. We go on without a breathing-space."

Once again, however, the awkward question presented itself: how was electoral success, which still fell far short of a clear majority, to be turned to political advantage? On 11 March Goebbels noted: "Talked over instructions with the S.A. and S.S. commanders. Deep uneasiness is rife everywhere. The notion of an uprising haunts the air." And again, on 2 April: "The S.A. getting impatient. It is understandable enough that the soldiers begin to lose morale through these long-drawn-out political contests. It has to be stopped, though, at all costs. A premature *putsch* would nullify our whole future." On the other side, Gregor Strasser now renewed his argument that the chances of success for the policy of legality were being thrown away by Hitler's "all-or-nothing" attitude. What was the point of Hitler's virtuoso performance as an agitator, Strasser asked, if it led the Party only into a political cul-de-sac?

For the moment Hitler had no answer either to the impatient S.A. or to the critical Strasser. It was the Government which now took the initiative and used its advantage to move at last against the S.A.

At the end of November, 1931, the State authorities of Hesse had secured certain documents drawn up by the State Party legal adviser, Dr. Werner Best, after secret discussions among a small group of local Nazi leaders. These papers contained a draft of the proclamation to be issued by the S.A. in the event of a Communist rising, and suggestions for emergency decrees to be issued by a provisional Nazi government after the Communists had been defeated. According to the documents arrangements were to be made for the immediate execution of those who resisted the Nazi authorities, who refused to co-operate or who were found in possession of arms. Amongst the measures proposed was the abolition of the right to private property, of the obligation to pay debts, of interest on savings, and of all private incomes.

The discovery of these plans caused a sensation, and seriously embarrassed Hitler, who declared (probably with justice) that he had known nothing of them and, had he known, would have disavowed them. Despite pressure from the Prussian State Government, however, the Reich Government declined to take action against the Nazis. But as evidence of Nazi plans for a seizure of power continued to accumulate, however much Hitler underlined his insistence upon legal methods, the character of the S.A. was such that the idea of a *putsch* was bound to come naturally. On the day of the first presidential election, Prussian police, raiding Nazi headquarters, found copies of Roehm's orders and marked maps which confirmed the report that the S.A. had been prepared to carry out a *coup d'état* if Hitler secured a majority. Near the Polish frontier other orders were captured instructing the local S.A. in Pomerania not to take part in the defence of Germany in the event of a surprise Polish attack.

As a result of these discoveries the State governments, led by Prussia and Bavaria, presented Groener with an ultimatum. Either the Reich Government must act against the S.A. or, they hinted, they would take independent action themselves. Groener felt obliged to act and on 10 April, the day of the second election, a meeting presided over by the Chancellor confirmed Groener's view, and on the 14th a decree dissolved the S.A., the S.S., and all their affiliated organizations.

Roehm for a moment thought of resistance; after all, the S.A. now numbered four hundred thousand men. But Hitler was insistent: the S.A. must obey. His authority held, and overnight the brown shirts disappeared from the streets. But the S.A. organization was left intact to appear as ordinary Party members, Bruening and Groener would get their answer, Hitler declared, at the Prussian elections.

Prussia, by far the largest of the German states, embracing nearly two-thirds of the whole territory of the Reich, with a population of forty out of a total of sixty-five millions, had been the stronghold of German democracy. The Prussian Ministry of the Interior, which controlled by far the biggest police force in Germany had been more active than any other official agency in trying to check Nazi excesses, and was the object of venomous Nazi attacks. To capture a majority in Prussia, therefore, would be a political victory for the Nazis second only in importance to securing a majority in the Reichstag.

The date of the Prussian elections had been fixed for 24 April, at the same time as other State elections. Altogether some four-fifths of Germany would go to the polls. Despite the work of the Nazi propaganda machine, and Hitler's second series of highly publicized flights over Germany, plus the support of the Nationalists, the Nazis were not strong enough to form an administration in Prussia. Elsewhere, in Würt-temberg, Bavaria and Hamburg they were well short of a majority. The deadlock therefore continued. Three times the trumpet had sounded and still the walls refused to fall.

At this moment there appeared a *deus ex machina* in the shape of General von Schleicher, prepared to discuss once again the admission of the Nazis by the back door.

Unknown to Hitler, it had already been agreed between Roehm and Schleicher that, in the event of a war-emergency, the S.A. would come under the command of the Army. Schleicher, however, was still attracted by the idea of bringing Hitler himself into the Government camp. In either case, the prohibition of the S.A. was bound to embarrass his plans. Schleicher went behind Groener's back and per-suaded Hindenburg to write an irritable letter to Groener complaining about the activities of the Social Democratic *Reichsbanner,* with the implication that the prohibition of the S.A. had been one-sided, meanwhile letting Hitler know he did not agree with the ban. The letter had been made public almost before Groener had received it. A malicious whispering campaign against Groener himself preceded, on 10 May, Goering's violent attack on him in the Reichstag. When Groener, a sick man, attempted to reply, he met a storm of abuse and obstruction from the Nazi benches. Scarce-ly had he sat down, exhausted by the effort, when he was blandly informed by Schleicher, the man he regarded almost as his own son, that the Army no longer had confidence in him, and that it would be best for him to resign. Bruening loyally defended Groener, but there was such uproar in the Reichstag that the Chamber had to be cleared by the police. The next day Groener resigned. The Nazis were jubilant.

Schleicher had now made up his mind that the chief obstacle to his plan for a deal with the Nazis was Bruening, the butt of Nazi attacks on the "System." The man he had himself proposed as Chancellor in March, 1930, had outlived his usefulness. With the same cynical disloyalty with which he had stabbed Groener in the back, Schleicher now set about unseating Bruening.

Bruening was not in a strong position to defend himself. He had failed to secure a stable majority in the Reichstag, and had so far failed to restore prosperity to Germany, even though he believed that the next few months would see a gradual easing of the depression. His great hope—the cancellation of reparations and the recognition of Germany's right to equality in armaments—had been frustrated, the first by the postponement of the Reparations Conference until June, 1932, the second by the opposition of the French. Ironically, his one great success, the re-election of the President, weakened rather than strengthened his position. Under the careful coaching of Schleicher and other candid friends, the old man had come to resent the Chancellor as the man whose obstinacy had forced him to endure an election campaign, and to stand as the candidate of the Left against his own friends on the Right.

Moreover, Bruening had made strong enemies who enjoyed great influence with the President, among them the industrialists, and members of the powerful Junker class. Finally, Schleicher, claiming to speak with the legendary authority of the Army, announced that the Army no longer had confidence in the Chancellor. A stronger man was needed and he already had a suitable candidate in Papen. He added the all-important assurance that the Nazis had agreed to support the new Government.

Ostensibly Hitler played no part in the manoeuvres which led to Bruening's dismissal.

What Schleicher offered to Hitler was the overthrow of the Bruening Cabinet, the removal of the ban on the S.A. and S.S., and new elections for the Reichstag. In return for these solid advantages he asked only for tacit support, the "neutrality" of the Nazis towards the new presidential cabinet which Papen was to form. Such a promise cost Hitler nothing. Time would show who was to do the double-crossing, Schleicher or the Nazis. Meanwhile Hitler's agreement provided Schleicher with a winning argument for Hindenburg. Papen would be able to secure what Bruening had failed to get, Hitler's support, without taking him into the Cabinet.

Groener's fall on 13 May raised the hopes of the Nazi leaders high. On the 18th Goebbels wrote in his diary: "Back in Berlin"—he had been to Munich to report to Hitler— "For Bruening alone winter seems to have arrived. He is being secretly undermined and is already completely isolated. He is anxiously looking for collaborators—'My kingdom for a Cabinet Minister!' . . .Our mice are busily at work gnawing through the last supports of Bruening's position." "Rat" would perhaps have been a better word to describe the part played by General von Schleicher.

The President requested the Chancellor's resignation and on 30 May Bruening resigned. It was the end of democratic government in Germany. The key to power over a nation of sixty-five million people now lay in the hands of an aged soldier of eighty-five and the little group of men who determined his views.

That afternoon Hitler and Goering saw the President at four o'clock and the interview lasted only a few minutes. Hindenburg informed them briefly that he intended to appoint von Papen as Chancellor and understood that Hitler had agreed to support him. Was this correct? Hitler answered: "Yes." Back in Berlin, Goebbels commented in his diary: "Von Papen is, it seems, to be appointed Chancellor, but that is neither here nor there. The Poll! The Poll! It's the people we want. We are all entirely satisfied."

Franz von Papen, a man in his fifties, came from a Catholic family of the Westphalian nobility. He had belonged to the right cavalry regiment (he was a celebrated gentleman-rider) and now to the right clubs, the *Herrenklub* and the *Union*. He had great charm, a wide acquaintance in the social world, connections with both German and French industry (he had married the daughter of a wealthy Saar industrialist), and considerable political ambitions. So far these ambitions had not been taken seriously by anyone else. Schleicher, attracted to the improbable choice of Papen as Chancellor by the belief that he would prove a pliant instrument in his hands, seriously underestimated Papen's ambition and tenacity, no less than of his unscrupulousness. The choice startled everyone and pleased few, with the important exception of the President, who was delighted with a Chancellor who could charm and flatter so well that he soon established relations with him such as no other minister had ever had.

Only with great difficulty, and by the exercise of the President's personal authority, had it been possible to collect a Cabinet of men willing to serve under Papen. Of its ten members, seven belonged to the nobility with known Right-wing views, and from the beginning there was not the least chance of Papen avoiding an overwhelming defeat if he met parliament; the power of the "Cabinet of Barons" was openly and unashamedly based upon the support of the President and the Army.

Of the four parties which commanded mass support, the Communists and the Social Democrats were bound to oppose Papen's government; the Centre had excommunicated him; only the fourth, the Nazis, remained in temporary tolerance, bought at the price of the dissolution of the Reichstag and the lifting of the ban on the S. A. The dominant question now was whether this temporary arrangement could be turned into a permanent coalition.

Both sides were willing to consider such a proposal—Hitler because this was the only legal way in which he could come to power if he failed to win an outright majority; Papen and Schleicher, because this offered the only prospect of recruiting popular support and the best chance, as they believed, of taking the wind out of the Nazi sails. The elements of a deal were present all the time; the question was, on whose terms —Hitler's or Papen's? Each side tried to blockade the other. When Papen could not get Nazi support on his terms, he left them to cool their heels, calculating that the strain would force Hitler to reduce his demands. Hitler, on his side, tried to stick it out without capitulating. This is the underlying pattern of events in the latter half of 1932. Superimposed on it is a second pattern created by the fact that both sides became divided on the right tactics to pursue; on one side this is represented by a split between Papen and Schleicher, on the other side by the quarrel between Hitler and Gregor Strasser.

Papen dissolved the Reichstag on 4 June, and fixed the new elections for the last day of July. Even this brief delay aroused Nazi suspicions; and when the lifting of the S.A. ban was postponed until the middle of the month, relations between Hitler and the new Government became strained. On 5 June Gobbels wrote in his diary: "We must disassociate ourselves at the earliest possible moment from the temporary bourgeois Cabinet." Unless the Nazis were to be tarred with the brush of Reaction and to leave to the Left a monopoly of attacking the "Cabinet of Barons," they had to assert their independence.

When the ban on the S.A. was lifted, Thaelmann, the Communist leader, described it as an open provocation to murder. This proved to be literally true, for, in the weeks which followed, murder and violence became everyday occurrences in the streets of the big German cities. The fiercest fighting was between the Nazis and the Communists; of eighty-six people killed in July, 1932, thirty were Communists and thirty-eight Nazis. Provocation was certainly not confined to one side: on an election visit to the Ruhr in July, Goebbels was given a rough reception, and the funerals of S.A. men became the occasion of big Nazi demonstrations. Pitched battles took place on Sunday, 10 July, in which eighteen people were killed. The next Sunday, the 17th, saw the worst riot of the summer, at Altona, near "Red" Hamburg, where the Nazis under police escort staged a march through the working-class districts of the town, and were met by a fusillade of shots from the roofs and windows, which they immediately returned. Nineteen people were reported to have been killed and two hundred and eighty-five wounded on that day alone.

On 20 July, on the flimsy pretext that the Prussian Government could not deal firmly with the Communists, Papen used the President's emergency powers to depose the Prussian Ministers, appointing himself as Reich Commissioner for Prussia. By this action Papen hoped partly to conciliate the Nazis, partly to steal some of the Nazi thunder against "Marxism." To carry out his plan Papen had stretched the constitutional powers of the President to the limit, and the fact that the two largest working-class organizations in Germany, the Social Democratic Party and the trade unions, had not put up even a token resistance in face of Papen's *coup d'état*, was a significant pointer to the lack of opposition which Hitler might expect if he came to power.

The elections were held on the last day of July and Goebbels had been making his preparations since the beginning of May. This fourth campaign in five months found the Nazi organization in top form. The argument that things must change, and the promise that, if the Nazis came to power, they would, proved a powerful attraction to a people driven by two years of economic depression and mass unemployment, made worse by the inability of the Government to relieve the nation's ills. It was the spirit of revolt engendered by these conditions to which Nazism gave expression, unhampered by the doctrinaire teaching and class exclusiveness of Communism.

"Once more eternally on the move," Goebbels complained on 1 July. "Work has to be done standing, walking, driving, flying. The most urgent conferences are held on the stairs, in the hall, at the door, or on the way to the station. It nearly drives one out of one's senses. One is carried by train, motor-car and aeroplane criss-cross through Germany. . . . The audience generally has no idea of what the speaker has already gone through during the day before he makes his speech in the evening. . . . And in the meantime he is struggling with the heat, to find the right word, with the sequence of a thought, with a voice that is growing hoarse, with unfortunate acoustics and with the bad air that reaches him from the tightly packed audience of thousands of people."

The whole familiar apparatus of Nazi ballyhoo was brought into play—placards, Press, sensational charges and counter-charges, mass meetings, demonstrations, S.A. parades. As a simple feat of physical endurance, the speaking programme of men like Hitler and Goebbels was remarkable. Again Hitler took to the skies, and in the third "Flight over Germany" visited and spoke in close on fifty towns in the second half of July. Delayed by bad weather, Hitler reached one of his meetings, near Stralsund, at half past two in the morning. A crowd of thousands waited patiently for him in drenching rain. When he finished speaking they saluted the dawn with the mass-singing of *"Deutschland über Alles."* This was more than clever electioneering. The Nazi campaign could not have succeeded by ingenuity of methods alone, if it had not exerted a powerful appeal to the popular mood.

When the results were announced on the night of 31 July the Nazis had outstripped all their competitors, with 13,745,-000 votes and 230 seats in the Reichstag. They were now by far the largest party in Germany, their nearest rivals, the Social Democrats, polling just under eight million votes, the Communists five and a quarter million.

Although the Nazi vote (37.3 per cent) fell short of a clear majority, from the point of view of a deal with Papen and Schleicher, Hitler felt himself to be in a very strong position. The combined strength of the Nazis and the Communists (230 and 89), added up to more than fifty per cent of the Reichstag, sufficient to make government with parliament impossible, unless the Nazis could be brought to support the Government. With a voting strength of 13,700,000, a party membership of over a million and a private army of 400,000 S.A. and S.S., Hitler was knocking on the doors of the Chancellery at the head of the most powerful political party Germany had ever seen.

Inflamed by the election campaign, and believing that the

long-awaited day was within sight, the S.A. threatened to get out of hand. Goebbels wrote in his diary: "The air is full of presage. . . . The whole party is ready to take over power. . . . The S.A. are closely concentrated round Berlin; the manoeuvre is carried out with imposing precision and discipline." The outbreaks of street-shooting and bomb-throwing flared up, especially in the eastern provinces of Silesia and East Prussia. In the beginning of August a score of incidents was reported every day, culminating on 9 August in the murder at Potempa, a village in Silesia, of a Communist who was brutally kicked to death by five Nazis in front of his mother. The same day Papen's Government announced the death penalty for clashes which led to people being killed. The Nazis at once protested indignantly.

Aware of the highly charged feeling in the Party, Hitler took time before he moved. He held a conference of his leaders at Tegernsee, in Bavaria, on 2 August, but he was in a mood for "all-or-nothing." On 5 August he saw Schleicher and put his demands before him: the Chancellorship for himself, and other Nazis at the head of the Prussian State Government, the Reich and Prussian Ministries of the Interior (which controlled the police). With these were to go the Ministry of Justice and a new Ministry of Popular Enlightenment and Propaganda, which was reserved for Goebbels. An Enabling Bill, giving Hitler full power to govern by decree, would be presented to the Reichstag; if the Chamber refused to pass it, it would be dissolved. Hitler came away in high hopes that Schleicher would use all his influence to secure the Chancellorship for him. He was so pleased that he suggested to Schleicher a tablet should be affixed to the house to commemorate their historic meeting. He then returned to Berchtesgaden to await events.

On 9 August, Strasser and Frick joined him there with disquieting news. The violent behaviour of the S.A. was making people ask if the Nazis were fit to have power. A message from Schacht confirmed this. Business and industrial circles were becoming worried lest Hitler might favor radical economic experiments on the lines Gottfried Feder and Gregor Strasser had often threatened. Still no word from Berlin.

On 11 August Hitler decided to bring matters to a head. Sending messengers ahead to arrange for him to see the Chancellor and the President, he motored north to Berlin, arriving late in the evening of the 12th and drove out to Goebbels' house. Roehm had already visited Papen and Schleicher and had asked bluntly who was to be Chancellor. Had Hitler misunderstood Schleicher? The answer Roehm had been given was none too satisfactory. After Goebbels told him the news, Hitler paced up and down for a long time. A hundred times he must have asked himself whether he was pitching his claims too high. On the other hand, to agree to anything less than full power, was to court trouble with the Party and the S.A. Hitler went to bed late; the decisive meeting with Papen and Schleicher was fixed for the next day at noon.

On the Government side of the fence, Papen was less impressed by Hitler's success than might have been expected. Hitler had failed to win the majority he hoped for, and indeed, Papen saw no reason at all why he should resign in Hitler's favour. He enjoyed the favour of the President as no one ever had before, and the President certainly had no wish to exchange the urbane and charming Papen for a man whom he disliked. Papen, like most other political observers, was convinced that the Nazis had reached their peak and from now on would begin to lose votes. If he did deal with Hitler it must be on his, and not Hitler's, terms.

How Hitler's conversation with Schleicher on 5 August is to be reconciled with this it is impossible to say. Perhaps Schleicher only realized that the Chancellorship for Hitler was out of the question after their meeting on 5 August. Certainly by 13 August, when Hitler met Schleicher and Papen, the most they were prepared to offer him was the Vice-Chancellorship, together with the Prussian Ministry of the Interior for one of his lieutenants. The President, Papen told him, insisted on maintaining a presidential cabinet in power and this could not be headed by a Party leader like Hitler. Hitler lost his temper and began to shout. He must have the whole power, nothing less. He talked wildly of mowing down the Marxists, of a St. Bartholomew's Night, and of three days' freedom of the streets for the S.A. Both Papen and Schleicher were shocked by the raging uncontrolled figure confronting them and were scarcely reassured by his declaration that he wanted neither the Foreign Ministry nor the Ministry of Defence, but only as much power as Mussolini had claimed in 1922. Hitler merely meant by this a coalition government, such as Mussolini had originally formed, but they understood him to be claiming a dictatorship in which he would govern alone without them—and, as the history of Hitler's Chancellorship was to show, they were fundamentally right.

Hitler left in a rage of disappointment, and drove back to Goebbels' flat. When a telephone call came from the President's Palace at three o'clock, Frick or Goebbels answered that there was no point in Hitler coming, as a decision had already been arrived at. But the President insisted. Nothing, it was said, would be finally decided till he had seen Hitler—and Hitler, angry and shaken, went.

The President received him standing up and leaning on his stick. His manner was cold. Hitler's argument that he sought power by legal means, but to obtain his ends must be given full control over government policy, made no impression on the old man. According to Meissner, the President retorted that in the present tense situation he could not take the risk of transferring power to a new Party which did not command a majority and which was intolerant, noisy and undisciplined.

> Hindenburg added that . . . he was ready to accept Hitler and his movement in a coalition government, the precise composition of which could be a subject of negotiation, but that he could not take the responsibility of giving exclusive power to Hitler alone. . . . Hitler, however, was adamant in his refusal to put himself in the position of bargaining with the leaders of the other parties and of facing a coalition government.

Before the interview was over Hindenburg took the chance to remind Hitler of the promise, which he had now broken, to support Papen's Government. For once, the Nazi propaganda machine was caught off its guard, and the Government's damaging version was halfway round the world before the Nazis realized what was happening. It spoke of Hitler's "demand for entire and complete control of the State"; described the President's refusal to hand over power to "a movement which had the intention of using it in a one-sided manner"; referred explicitly to Hitler's disregarded pre-election promises of support and repeated Hindenburg's warning on the way to conduct opposition. Hitler's humiliation in the eyes of the world, and of his own Party, was complete.

If ever Hitler needed confidence in his own judgment, it was now. A false move could destroy his chances of success, and it was easy to make such a move. The policy of legality appeared discredited and bankrupt. Hitler had won such electoral support as no other party had had in Germany since the First World War, he had kept strictly to the letter of the Constitution and knocked on the door of the Chancellery, only to have the door publicly slammed in his face. He was angry and resentful, feeling he had walked into a trap and was being laughed at by the superior people who had made a fool of him. In such a mood there was a great temptation to give the S.A. their head, and let the smug bourgeois politicians see whether he was just a "revolutionary of the big mouth," as Goebbels had once called Strasser.

There was strong pressure from the Party in the same direction. The S.A. had always disliked the policy of legality, and had only been constrained to submit to it with difficulty. Now that legality had led to humiliation they were even more restive. The difficulties with which Hitler was confronted are vividly illustrated by the case of the Potempa murderers. The five S.A. men responsible for the murder of the Communist miner, Pietrzuch, were sentenced to death on 22 August. The S.A. were furious: this was to place the nationally-minded Nazis and the anti-national Communists on the same footing, the very reverse of what Hitler and the Nazis meant by justice. Hitler had therefore to choose between offending public opinion and travestying his own policy of legality if he came out on the side of the murderers, or risking a serious loss of confidence on the part of the S.A. if he failed to intervene on their behalf, thus publicly admitting his inability to defend his own followers. Hitler's answer was to send a telegram to the five murderers: "My comrades: In the face of this most monstrous and bloody sentence I feel myself bound to you in limitless loyalty. . . . To fight against a government which could allow this is our duty." He followed this with a violent manifesto in which he attacked Papen: "German fellow countrymen: whoever among you agrees with our struggle for the honour and liberty of the nation will understand why I refused to take office in this Cabinet. . . . Herr von Papen, I understand your bloody 'objectivity' now. I wish that victory may come to nationalist Germany . . . but I am certainly not fitted to be the executioner of nationalist fighters for the liberty of the German people." A few days after Hitler's telegram their sentences were commuted to imprisonment for life.

There is no doubt that Hitler's action shocked German public opinion, yet this was the price which Hitler had to pay if he meant to keep his movement together. Nor is there any reason to suppose that he felt the least compunction about the murder; kicking a political opponent to death was well within the bounds of what Hitler meant by legality. Although Hitler came out in uncompromising opposition to Papen's Government, he was determined to avoid open conflict with the Army and to come to power legally.

Shortly after the Potempa incident Hermann Rauschning, one of the leaders of the Danzig Senate, visited Hitler at *Haus Wachenfeld* on the Obersalzberg. The Danzig visitors found him moody and preoccupied, sitting on the veranda and staring out over the mountain landscape. His silence was interspersed with excited and violent comments, many of them on the character of the next war. Much of it was prophetic; he laid great stress upon the psychological and subversive preparations for war—if these were carried out with care, peace would be signed before the war had begun. "The place of artillery preparation for frontal attack will in future be taken by revolutionary propaganda, to break down the enemy psychologically before the armies begin to function at all. . . . How to achieve the moral break-down of the enemy before the war has started—that is the problem that interests me. . . . We shall provoke a revolution in France as certainly as we shall *not* have one in Germany. The French will hail me as their deliverer. The little man of the middle class will acclaim us as the bearers of a just social order and eternal peace. None of these people any longer want war or greatness." Only when they came to discuss Danzig did Hitler show any interest. His first question was whether Danzig had an extradition agreement with Germany, and it was soon clear that in his mind was the possibility of having to go underground, if the Government should ban the Party. In that case Danzig, with its independent status under the League, might offer a useful asylum.

In August and September the Nazis made an approach to the Centre Party: together they could command a majority in the Reichstag. One practical result of these talks was the election of Goering to the presidency of the Reichstag by the combined votes of the Nazis, the Centre and the Nationalists on 30 August.

Papen refused to be impressed by the threat of a Nazi-Centre combination against him. He was firmly convinced that, in the threat to dissolve the Reichstag and force a further appeal to the country, he held the ace of trumps, and, if necessary, he was resolved to play it.

The climax of these weeks of intrigue and manoeuvring came on 12 September. Foreseeing trouble, Papen procured a decree for the Chamber's dissolution from the President in advance. The actual course of events, however, took both sides by surprise. When the session opened, before a crowded audience in the diplomatic and public galleries, the Communist deputy Torgler moved a vote of censure on the Government as an amendment to the Order of the Day. It had been agreed amongst the other parties that one of the Nationalist deputies should formally oppose it. When the moment came, however, the Nationalists made no move, and amid a puzzled and embarrassed silence Frick rose to ask for half an hour's delay. At a hurried meeting in the palace of the Reichstag President, Goering, Hitler, Strasser and Frick decided to out-smart the Chancellor and defeat the Government.

Immediately the deputies had taken their seats again: Goering, as President, announced that a vote would be taken at once on the Communist motion of no-confidence. Papen white with anger, then produced the traditional red portfolio which contained the decree of dissolution, and had it placed on Goering's table, while he and the other members of the Government ostentatiously marched out of the Chamber. Still Goering had no eyes for anything but the voting. The Communist vote of no-confidence was carried by 513 votes to 32, and Goering promptly declared the Government overthrown. As for the scrap of paper laid on his desk, which he now found time to read, it was, he declared, obviously worthless since it had been countersigned by a Chancellor who had now been deposed.

Whether—as the Nazis affected to believe—the elaborate farce in the Reichstag, and the almost unanimous vote against him, had really damaged Papen or not, for the moment the Chancellor had the advantage. For Papen insisted that, under the circumstances, the result of the motion was invalid. The Reichstag was dissolved, after sitting for less than a day, and the Nazis faced the fifth major electoral contest of the year.

Privately they were only too well aware that Papen was right and that they must count on a reduced vote. Hitler refused to consider a compromise, and accepted von Papen's challenge, but there was no disguising the fact that this would be the toughest fight of all.

One of the worst difficulties was lack of money. Four elections since March had eaten deep into the Party's resources, and Hitler's arrogant claim for the whole power, his condonation of violence at Potempa, the swing towards Radicalism in the campaign against the "Government of Reaction"—all these factors, combined, no doubt, with strong hints from von Papen to industrial and business circles, had placed the Party in a tight spot.

In these circumstances it was only Hitler's determination and leadership that kept the Party going. His confidence in himself never wavered. When the Gauleiters assembled at Munich early in October he used all his arts to put new life and energy into them. "He is great and surpasses us all," Goebbels wrote enthusiastically. "He raised the Party's spirits out of the blackest depression. With him as leader the movement must succeed."

The fifth election of the year on 6 November found a mood of stubborn apathy growing among the German people, a feeling of indifference and disbelief, against which propaganda and agitation beat in vain. It was precisely on this that Papen had calculated and his calculation was not far wrong. For the first time since 1930 the Nazis lost votes, and their seats in the Reichstag were reduced from 230 out of 608 to 196 out of 584, although they were still the largest party in the Chamber.

Papen, delighted, regarded the results as a moral victory for his government and a heavier defeat for Hitler than the figures actually showed. At first, it looked as if Hitler might be forced to accept von Papen's terms. In this third period, however, it was Papen who overplayed his hand, with un-expected results.

On 9 November Goebbels recorded in his diary: "The Wilhelmstrasse has sent an emissary to the leader. The same conditions are proposed as those suggested on 13 August (i.e., the Vice-Chancellorship), but he remains inexorable." Three days later he wrote: "The leader is keeping away from Berlin. The Wilhelmstrasse waits for him in vain; and that is well. We must not give in as we did on 13 August."

On 13 November Papen wrote officially to Hitler sug-gesting that they should bury their differences and renew negotiations for a concentration of all the nationally minded parties. Hitler's reply ruled out the possibility of any further negotiations between himself and Papen at this stage. Indeed, he had already issued a manifesto immediately after the elections in which he had charged Papen, by his reactionary policy, with driving the masses to Bolshevism. There could be no compromise with such a régime.

Papen, perfectly prepared to plunge the country into still another election to force the Nazis to their knees, unexpect-edly encountered opposition from Schleicher. Not only was Schleicher irritated by Papen's increasing independence and the close relationship he had established with the President, but he began to see in Papen's personal quarrel with Hitler an obstacle to securing that concentration of the "national" forces which was, in Schleicher's view, the only reason for ever having made Papen Chancellor. He was more than ever alarmed at the prospect of a civil war with both the Commu-nists and the Nazis on the other side of the barricade. Papen was becoming more of a hindrance than an asset to his own objective of clearly making a deal with the Nazis.

Schleicher found support for his views in the Cabinet, and Papen was urged to resign to allow the President to consult the Party leaders to find a way out of the deadlock, which appeared to be impossible so long as Papen remained in office. With considerable shrewdness Papen swallowed his anger and agreed; he was confident that negotiations with Hitler and the other party leaders would lead nowhere, and that he would return to office with his hand strengthened. His own influence over the President, who was obviously irritated by the whole affair, saw no reason at all why he should part with Papen, and had become increasingly suspicious of Schleicher, augured well for Papen's success. Accordingly, on 17 November, Papen tendered the resignation of his Cabinet, and the President, on his advice, requested Hitler to call.

Events followed the course Papen had foreseen. On 18 November Hitler arrived in Berlin, conferred with Party leaders, and drove to the Palace. The gist of Hindenburg's offer was contained in three sentences: "You have declared," the President said, "that you will only place your movement at the disposal of a government of which you, the leader of the Party, are the head. If I consider your proposal, I must demand that such a Cabinet should have a majority in the Reichstag. Accordingly, I ask you, as the leader of the largest party, to ascertain if, and on what conditions, you could obtain a secure workable majority in the Reichstag on a definite programme."

On the face of it this was a fair offer, but it was clearly impossible for Hitler to secure a majority in the Reichstag. The Centre Party and Hugenberg's Nationalists would never join a coalition. In any case, Hitler wanted to be made not a parliamentary, but a presidential, Chancellor, with the same sweeping powers as the President had given to Papen. The old man sternly refused. If Germany had to be governed by the emergency powers of a presidential Chancellor, then there was no point in replacing Papen; the only argument in favour of his resignation was that Hitler would be able to provide what Papen had failed to secure—a parliamentary majority. Hindenberg flatly refused to alter his terms, and Hitler could only retort that the negotiations had been foredoomed to fail in view of Hindenburg's resolve to keep Papen, whatever the cost. Once again the policy of legality had led to public humiliation; once again the leader returned from the President's Palace empty-handed and out-manoeuvred.

Schleicher, meanwhile, had not been idle, and through Gregor Strasser he was now sounding out the possibility of the Nazis joining a Cabinet in which Schleicher himself would take the Chancellorship. The offer was communicated to Hitler in Munich. For once the Nazi version seems more probable: Hitler declined to be drawn by Schleicher's move and called a conference of his chief lieutenants at Weimar on 1 December, where Strasser came out strongly in favour of joining a Schleicher Cabinet and found some support from Frick. Goering and Goebbels, however, were opposed, and Hitler accepted their point of view.

· Meanwhile, on the evening of 1 December, Schleicher and Papen saw Hindenburg together, and from the discussion that followed Papen emerged triumphant: the President entrusted him with the formation of a new presidential cabinet. But Schleicher now declared, as the representative of the Army, that the Army no longer had confidence in Papen and was not prepared to take the risk of civil war which Papen's policy of governing by decree and using force to smash any opposition, would entail. At a crucial cabinet meeting on the morning of 1 December, Schleicher developed this argument and produced detailed evidence in its support. Once again the Army had shown itself to be the supreme arbiter in German politics, and Papen was left without a reply.

Von Papen had only two consolations, but they were to prove substantial. At last Schleicher, the man who had used his influence behind the scenes to unseat Groener, Bruening, and now Papen, was forced to come out into the open and assume personal responsibility for the success or failure of his plans. On 2 December General von Schleicher became the last Chancellor of pre-Hitler Germany, and—Papen's second consolation—he took office at a time when his credit with the President, on which he had drawn so lavishly in the past year, was destroyed. The old man, who had tolerated his intrigues neither forgot nor forgave the methods by which Schleicher turned out Papen. Let von Schleicher succeed if he could; but if turned to the President for support, he need expect no more mercy than he had shown his own victims.

Schleicher had now to make good his claim that he could succeed where Papen had failed, and produce that national front, including the Nazis, which had been his consistent aim for two years. For all his love of intrigue and lack of scruple, Schleicher was an intelligent man. Without Papen's class prejudices he had never fallen into the error of supposing that "strong" government by itself was a remedy for the crisis, nor did he underestimate the force which lay behind such extremist movements as the Nazis and the Communists. His aim, repeatedly stated in these years, was to harness one of these movements, the Nazis, to the service of the State.

Schleicher's closest contact in the Nazi Party at this time was Gregor Strasser. To Strasser National Socialism was a real political movement, not, as it was to Hitler, the instrument of his ambition. He took its programme seriously, as

Hitler never had, and he was the leader of the Nazi Left-wing which, to the annoyance of Hitler's industrialist friends, still dreamed of a German Socialism and still won votes for the Party by its anti-capitalist radicalism. But Strasser, as head of the Party Organization, was more in touch with feeling throughout the local branches than anyone else, and more impressed than any of the other leaders by the set-backs of the autumn. He became convinced that the only course to save the Party from going to pieces was to make a compromise and get into power at once, even as part of a coalition. Hitler's attitude he regarded as illogical for he saw the Party's chance to influence government policy and carry out at least a part of its programme being sacrificed to Hitler's ambition and refusal to accept anything less than "the whole power."

The day after Schleicher became Chancellor he sent for Gregor Strasser and made an offer to the Nazis. Having failed to interest Hitler, Schleicher suggested that Strasser himself should enter his Cabinet as Vice-Chancellor and Minister-President of the Prussian State Government. If he accepted, Strasser could take over Schleicher's plans for dealing with unemployment and help to establish co-operation with the Trade Unions. The offer was a clever move on Schleicher's part. Not only was it attractive to Strasser as a way out of the Party's difficulties, but it would almost certainly split the Party leadership. In that case, if Hitler stood out Strasser might agree to come into the Cabinet and carry his following out of the Party. The same day elections in Thuringia showed nearly a forty per cent drop in the Nazi vote.

On 5 December at a conference of the Party leaders, Strasser found support from Frick, the leader of the Nazi group in the Reichstag, whose members were powerfully impressed by the Thuringian results. Goering and Goebbels, however, were hotly opposed, and carried Hitler with them. Hitler laid down terms for discussion with Schleicher, but placed the negotiations with the Chancellor in the hands of Goering and Frick, deliberately excluding Strasser. On 7 December Hitler and Strasser had a further conversation in the Kaiserhof, in the course of which Hitler bitterly accused Strasser of bad faith, of trying to go behind his back and oust him from the leadership of the Party. Strasser angrily retorted that he had been entirely loyal. Back in the Hotel Excelsior, he wrote Hitler a long letter in which he resigned from his position in the Party. He reviewed the whole course of their relationship since 1925, attacked the irresponsibility and inconsistency of Hitler's tactics, and prophesied disaster if he persisted in them.

There is no doubt that Hitler was shaken by Strasser's revolt, as he had never been by an electoral defeat. The threat to his own authority in the Party touched him more closely than the loss of votes or the failure of negotiations had ever done. Goebbels wrote in his diary: ". . . The situation in the Party is getting worse from hour to hour. The leader must immediately return to the Kaiserhof. . . . Treachery, treachery, treachery! For hours the leader paces up and down the room in the hotel. Suddenly he stops and says: 'If the Party once falls to pieces, I shall shoot myself without more ado!' "

But Strasser had always lacked the toughness to challenge Hitler outright, and now, instead of rallying the latent opposition to Hitler in the Party, he cursed the whole business and took his family off for a holiday in Italy.

Strasser's disappearance gave Hitler time to recover. A declaration condemning Strasser in the sharpest terms was submitted to a full meeting of the Party leaders and Gauleiters in the Palace of the President of the Reichstag on 9 December. Hitler used all his skill to appeal to the loyalty of his old comrades and brought tears to their eyes. With a sob in his voice he declared that he would never have believed Strasser guilty of such treachery. At the end of this emotional *tour de force* "the Gauleiters and Deputies," Goebbels records, "burst into a spontaneous ovation for the leader. All shake hands with him, promising to carry on until the very end and not to renounce the great Idea, come what may. Strasser now is completely isolated, a dead man. . . ."

Schleicher continued his talks with the other Party leaders, including representatives of the Trade Unions. The failure to bring in the Nazis at this stage did not unduly depress him. On 15 December he expounded his specific plans to remedy the economic crisis and provide work in a broadcast to the nation. Here, however, he failed to overcome the distrust and hostility of Social Democrats and the Trade Unions, or even of the Centre, which, remembering his part in the overthrow of Bruening, was not converted to his support by his policy not unlike Bruening's own. At the same time the industrialists disliked his conciliatory attitude towards labour; the farmers were furious at his reduction of agricultural protection; the East Elbian landowners denounced his plans for land settlement as "agrarian Bolshevism" with the same uncompromising class spirit they had shown towards Bruening.

Schleicher made the great mistake of underestimating the forces opposed to him, believing that his enemies could not combine against him. So far as the Nazis were concerned there were good grounds for believing them to be a declining force. The most immediate problem was shortage of funds. The Party was filled with thousands of officials who kept on the Party pay-roll often without clearly defined functions, often with duties that were either unnecessary or duplicated by someone else. The hard core of the S.A. consisted of unemployed men who lived in S.A. messes and barracks; it must have cost immense sums, however limited the amount spent on each man. S.A. men were sent into the streets, rattling their boxes and asking passers-by to spare something "for the wicked Nazis."

More serious was the sense of defeatism and demoralization in the Party. Every week-end after the Strasser crisis, Hitler, Goering, Ley and Goebbels visited the different *Gaue* to talk to Party officials, and restore their confidence in the leadership. Despite Goebbels' efforts at whistling in the dark at the end of 1932, two and a half years after the first great election campaign, he wrote in his diary: "This year has brought us eternal ill-luck. . . . The past was sad, and the future looks dark and gloomy; all chances and hopes have quite disappeared."

Then suddenly, at the turn of the year, Hitler's luck changed, and a chance offered itself. The varied antagonisms which Schleicher had aroused found a common broker in the unexpected figure of Franz von Papen, and on 4 January Papen and Hitler met quietly in the house of the Cologne banker, Kurt von Schroeder. The meeting was arranged through Wilhelm Keppler, one of the Nazi "contact-men" with the world of business and industry.

The talk with Papen, which lasted for two hours, was held in Schroeder's study with only the banker present besides the two principals. First, Papen slipped out of the responsibility for Hitler's humiliation by putting all the blame on Schleicher for Hindenburg's refusal to consider Hitler as Chancellor. But what Papen had really come to talk about was the prospect of replacing Schleicher's Government: he suggested the establishment of a Nationalist and Nazi coalition in which he and Hitler would be joint Chancellors. "Then Hitler made a long speech in which he said, if he were made Chancellor, it would be necessary for him to be the head of the Government, but that supporters of Papen's could go into his Government as ministers, if they were willing to go along with him in the policy of changing many things. . . . Papen and Hitler reached agreement in principle so that . . . they could find a way to get together."

Next day, to the embarrassment of both the participants, the meeting was headline news in the Berlin papers, and awkward explanations had to be given. Papen denied that the meeting was in any way directed against Schleicher.

Much hard bargaining lay ahead, and Schleicher's position had still to be more thoroughly undermined. But the two men had found common ground in their dislike of Schleicher and their desire to be revenged on him, each had sounded out the other's willingness for a deal. Hitler, moreover, received the valuable information that Schleicher had not been given the power to dissolve the Reichstag by the President, and arrangements were made to relieve the financial straits of the Nazi Party. Schroeder was one of a group of industrialists and bankers who, in November, 1932, sent a joint letter to Hindenburg urging him to give Hitler the powers to form a presidential cabinet. Now, with Papen's blessing and Schroeder's help, arrangements were made to pay the Nazis' debts, quite possibly facilitated by Hitler's break with Gregor Strasser, the leader of the anti-capitalist wing of the Party. A few days later Goebbels noted: "The financial situation has improved all of a sudden." On 5 January, commenting on the news of the meeting, Goebbels remarked: "The present Government knows that this is the end for them. If we are successful, we cannot be far from power."

If the Nazis could do little to help forward the intrigue against Schleicher which had to be left to von Papen, it was important to remove the impression of their declining strength. For this purpose Hitler decided to concentrate all the Party's resources on winning the elections in the tiny state of Lippe. On 15 January the Nazis were rewarded by an electoral victory and so loud was the noise made by the Nazi propaganda band that, even against their own better judgment, the group round the President were impressed.

The Nazis then proceeded to stage a mass demonstration in front of the Communist headquarters in Berlin, the *Karl Liebknecht Haus*. "We shall stake everything on one throw to win back the streets of Berlin," Goebbels wrote. The Government, after some hesitation, banned the Communists' counter-demonstration, and on 22 January, with a full escort of armed police, ten thousand S.A. men paraded on the Bülowplatz and listened to a ranting speech by Hitler. "The Bülowplatz is ours," Goebbels exulted. "The Communists have suffered a great defeat. . . . This day is a proud and heroic victory for the S.A. and the Party."

By 20 January it was clear that Schleicher's attempt to contruct a broad front representing all but the extremist parties had failed. The Nationalists had been alienated by the Chancellor's schemes for land colonization and they finally broke with Schleicher on 21 January and turned to the Nazis. The final stage of negotiations for a Nazi-Nationalist Coalition opened on the evening of the 22nd in Ribbentrop's house at Dahlem.

On the Nazi side the principal negotiator was Goering, who faced, with Hitler and Frick, that evening Papen, Meissner, the President's State Secretary; and the President's son, Oskar von Hindenburg. One important gain Hitler made that night was to win over Oskar von Hindenburg, with whom he had a private conversation of an hour. It is believed that Hitler secured his support by a mixture of bribes and blackmail, possibly threatening to start proceedings to impeach the President and to disclose Oskar's part in the *Osthilfe* (government subsidy) scandals and tax evasion on the presidential estate. "In the taxi on the way back," Meissner recorded, ". . . the only remark [Oskar] made was that it could not be helped—the Nazis had to be taken into the Government."

On 28 January, Schleicher, recognizing the impossibility of being able to deal with the Reichstag when it met on the 31st, requested the power from the President to dissolve it. Ironically, Schleicher had reached the same position as Papen, when he had forced Papen out because the latter wanted to fight Hitler, and had himself urged the support of the National Socialists. But it was now Papen who was able to offer the President the alternative which Schleicher had advocated in December. With the knowledge that this alternative had been prepared behind Schleicher's back in the last few days, the President refused the powers to override the constitution which the General requested, and left him no option but to resign. At noon on 28 January the President officially entrusted Papen with negotiations to provide a new government.

It was still uncertain whether it would be possible to bring Hitler and Hugenberg into the same coalition, and eager at any cost to prevent a Papen Chancellorship, and still convinced that the only practical course was to bring Hitler into the Government, Schleicher sent the Commander-in-Chief of the Army, General von Hammerstein, to warn Hitler that Papen might still leave them both out in the cold. In that case Schleicher suggested a Hitler-Schleicher coalition to rule with the united support of the Army and the Nazis. Hitler, however, still hoping to hear that agreement had been reached for a full coalition between Papen, Hugenberg and himself, remained non-committal.

Much more alarming to Hitler was the possibility that the Army, under Schleicher and Hammerstein, might at the last moment prevent the formation of the proposed coalition. The keys to the attitude of the Army were held by the President, the old Field-Marshal and embodiment of the military tradition, and by General von Blomberg. Hindenburg had agreed to the formation of a Ministry in which Hitler was to be Chancellor and had nominated Blomberg to serve as Minister of Defence under Hitler. Blomberg had been in touch with Hitler before this, and had been hurriedly recalled from serving as chief military adviser to the German delegation at the Geneva Disarmament Conference, but without Schleicher's or Hammerstein's knowledge. Fortunately for Hitler, Blomberg accepted his new commission from the President, and the threat of a last-minute repudiation by the Army was thereby avoided.

It is possible that fear of what Schleicher might do helped Papen and Hugenberg to compose their remaining differences with the Nazis. At any rate, on the morning of Monday the 30th, after a sleepless night during which he sat up with Goering and Goebbels to be ready for any eventuality, Hitler received the long-awaited summons to the President. The deal which Schleicher had made the object of his policy, and for which Strasser had worked, was accomplished at last, with Schleicher and Strasser left out.

During the morning a silent crowd filled the street between the Kaiserhof and the Chancellery. Shortly after noon a roar went up from the crowd: the leader was coming. He ran down the steps to his car and in a couple of minutes was back in the Kaiserhof. As he entered the room his lieutenants crowded to greet him. The improbable had happened: Adolf Hitler, the petty official's son from Austria, the down-and-out of the hostel for men, the *Meldegänger* of the List Regiment, had become Chancellor of the German Reich.

CHAPTER FIVE

REVOLUTION AFTER POWER

30 JANUARY, 1933—AUGUST, 1934

Nazi propaganda later built up a legend which represented Hitler's coming to power as the upsurge of a great national revival. The truth is more prosaic. Despite the mass support he had won, Hitler came to office in 1933 as the result, not of any irresistible revolutionary or national movement sweeping him into power, nor even of a popular victory at the polls, but as part of a shoddy political deal with the "Old Gang" whom he had been attacking for months past. Hitler did not seize power; he was jobbed into office by a backstairs intrigue.

The German Right wanted to regain its old position in Germany as the ruling class; to destroy the hated republic and restore the monarchy; to put the working classes "in their places"; to rebuild the military power of Germany; to reverse the decision of 1918 and to restore Germany—their Germany—to a dominant position in Europe. Blinded by self-interest and prejudice, the Right forsook a true conservatism, abandoned its own traditions and made the gross mistake of regarding Hitler as a man who would enable them to achieve their ends.

This was the policy put into effect by the Nazi-Right coalition, and based on the belief that Hitler and the Nazis, once they had been brought into the government, could be held in check and tamed. At first sight the terms to which Hitler had agreed appeared to confirm this belief.

He was not even a presidential chancellor; Hindenburg had been persuaded to accept "the Bohemian corporal," on the grounds that this time Hitler would be able to provide a parliamentary majority. No sooner was the Cabinet formed than Hitler started negotiations to bring the Centre Party into the coalition. When these negotiations did not lead to agreement it was Hitler who insisted, against Hugenberg's opposition, that new elections must be held in order to provide a parliamentary basis for the coalition in the form of an electoral majority.

Papen still saw nothing but cause for self-congratulation on his own astuteness. He had levelled scores with General von Schleicher, yet had realized Schleicher's dream to harness the Nazis to the support of the State—and this, not on Hitler's, but on his own terms. For Hitler, Papen assured his friends, was his prisoner, tied hand and foot by the condition he had accepted. True, Hitler had the Chancellorship, but the real power, in Papen's view, rested with the Vice-Chancellor, himself.

It was the Vice-Chancellor, not the Chancellor, who enjoyed the special confidence of the President; it was the Vice-Chancellor who held the key post of Minister-President of Prussia, with control of the Prussian administration and police; and the Vice-Chancellor who had the right, newly established, to be present on all occasions when the Chancellor made his report to the President. Also, only three of the eleven Cabinet posts were held by Nazis, and apart from the Chancellorship both were second-rate positions. . . .

It was with these arguments that Papen overcame Hindenburg's reluctance to make Hitler Chancellor. In this way they would obtain that mass support which the "Cabinet of Barons" had so notoriously lacked. Hitler was to play his old role of barker for a circus with his name at the top of the bill, but in which the real decisions would be taken by those who outnumbered him by eight to three in the Cabinet. This was Papen's *realpolitik* and Papen as he prided himself— knew how to distinguish between the reality and the mere outward show of power.

Rarely has disillusionment been so complete or so swift to follow. Those who, like Papen, believed they had seen through Hitler were to find they had badly underestimated both the leader and his movement. For Hitler's originality lay in his realization that effective revolutions, in modern conditions, are carried out with, and not against, the power of the State: the correct order of events was first to secure access to that power and then begin his revolution. Hitler never abandoned the cloak of legality; then he turned the law inside out and made illegality legal.

In the six months that followed, Hitler was to demonstrate a cynicism and lack of scruple—qualities on which his partners particularly prided themselves—which left Papen and Hugenburg gasping. At the end of those six months they were to discover, like the young lady of Riga, the dangers of going for a ride on a tiger.

At five o'clock on the afternoon of Monday, 30 January, Hitler presided over his first Cabinet meeting. The Cabinet was still committed to seeking a parliamentary majority by securing the support of the Centre Party, and Goering duly reported on the progress of his talks with its leader, Monsignor Kaas. If these failed, then, Hitler suggested, it would be necessary to dissolve the Reichstag and hold new elections. Hugenberg saw the danger of letting Hitler conduct an election campaign with the power of the State at his command, and had Hitler's solemn promise that the composition of the coalition government would not be altered, whatever the results of the elections.

The next day, when Hitler saw Monsignor Kaas, he took good care that the negotiations with the Centre should fail and, on the advice of Papen, Hindenburg agreed once more to sign a decree dissolving the Reichstag "since the formation of a working majority has proved impossible." The Centre Party protested to the President that this was not true but the decree had been signed, the date for the new elections fixed and the first and most difficult of the obstacles to Hitler's success removed. Papen and Hugenberg had allowed themselves to be gently guided into the trap. Goebbels wrote:

"The struggle is a light one now, since we are able to employ all the means of the State. Radio and Press are at our disposal. We shall achieve a masterpiece of propaganda. Even money is not lacking this time."

In order to leave no doubts of the expectations they had, Goering summoned a number of Germany's leading industrialists to his palace on the evening of 20 February. Hitler spoke to them on much the same lines as at Düsseldorf a year before, but Goering was blunter: ". . . The sacrifice asked for is easier to bear if it is realized that the elections will certainly be the last for the next ten years, probably even for the next hundred years." At Schacht's suggestion it was agreed to raise an election fund of three million Reichsmarks to be divided between the partners in the coalition, but there was little doubt that the Nazis would get the lion's share.

Throughout the election campaign Hitler refused to outline any programme for his Government. "In fourteen years the System which has now been overthrown has piled mistake upon mistake, illusion upon illusion." What had the Nazis to put in its place? He was no democratic politician, Hitler virtuously replied, to trick the people into voting for him by a few empty promises. "I ask of you, German people, that after you have given the others fourteen years you should give us four." "What I claim is fair and just: only four years for us and then others shall form their judgment and pass sentence. I will not flee abroad, I will not seek to escape sentence."

Hitler did not rely on the spoken word alone. Although the other parties were still allowed to function, their meetings were broken up, their speakers assaulted and beaten, their posters torn down and their papers continually suppressed. Official figures admitted fifty-one people killed during the campaign and several hundreds injured. This time the Nazis did not mean to be robbed of power by any scruples about fair play or free speech.

Papen believed he had tied Hitler down by restricting the number of Cabinet posts held by the Nazis to a bare minimum, but the real key to power in the State—control of the Prussian police force and of the Prussian State Administration—lay with Goering, as Prussian Minister of the Interior. By the curious system of dual government which existed in Germany, that office administered two-thirds of Germany, and was of much greater importance than the Reich Ministry of the Interior, a head without a body. In the critical period of 1933-1934, no man after Hitler played so important a role in the Nazi revolution as Goering. His energy and ruthlessness together with his control of Prussia, were indispensable to Hitler's success. Goering showed no intention of being restrained by Papen or anybody else; he enforced his will, as if he already held absolute power.

The moment Goering entered office he began a drastic purge of the Prussian State service, paying particular attention to the senior police officers, where he made a clean sweep in favour of his own appointments, many of them S.A. or S.S. leaders. In the middle of February Goering issued an order to show no mercy to the activities of "organizations hostile to the State"—that is to say, the Communists, and Marxists in general—Goering continued: "Police officers who makes use of fire-arms in the execution of their duties will . . . benefit by my protection; those who . . . fail in their duty will be punished. . . ." In other words, when in doubt shoot.

On 22 February Goering published an order establishing an auxiliary police force. Fifty thousand men were called up, among them twenty-five thousand from the S.A. and fifteen thousand from the S.S. All they had to do was to put a white arm-band over their brown shirts or black shirts: they then represented the authority of the State. It was the equivalent of handing over police powers to the razor and cosh gangs. For the citizen to appeal to the police for protection became more dangerous than to suffer assault and robbery in silence. At best, the police turned their backs and looked the other way; more often the auxiliaries helped their S.A. comrades to beat up their victims. This was "legality" in practice.

The day after Hitler became Chancellor, Goebbels noted in his diary: "In a conference with the leader we arrange measures for combating the Red terror. . . . First the Bolshevik attempt at a revolution must burst into flame. At the given moment we shall strike." On 24 February the police raided Communist H.Q. in Berlin. An Official communiqué reported the discovery of plans for a Communist revolution. The publication of the captured documents was promised in the immediate future. They never appeared, and on the night of 27 February the Reichstag building mysteriously went up in flames.

Goering and Goebbels were looking for some pretext to smash the Communist Party. After rejecting various plans—such as an attack on Hitler—they hit on the notion of setting fire to the Reichstag building. An underground passage linked Goering's Palace of the President of the Reichstag with the main building across the street. Through this a small group of S.A. men under the command of Karl Ernst, the leader of the Berlin S.A., entered the deserted building on the evening of the 27th and scattered a chemical preparation with a delayed-action effect over carpets, curtains and chairs. As they were leaving, a half-crazed young Dutchman, picked up by the S.A., after attempting to set fire to other buildings, and carefully groomed for the part of dupe, climbed into the Reichstag and proceeded on his own account to start fires at a number of points. By the time the police and the fire-brigades arrived the fire was out of control and rapidly engulfed the whole building.

Van der Lubbe's arrest in the act of incendiarism, his immediate confession and his Communist associations, added greatly to the plausibility of the official version that the fire was part of a general plan of Communist terrorism. The Reichstag Fire Trial in Leipzig was later to prove a major embarrassment to the Nazi régime, but, long before that, the Reichstag Fire had fully served its political purpose.

The day after the fire, on 28 February, Hitler promulgated a decree signed by the President and described "as a defensive measure against Communist acts of violence." It began by suspending the guarantees of individual liberty under the Weimar Constitution:

Thus, restrictions on personal liberty, on the right of free expression of opinion, including freedom of the Press; on the rights of assembly and association; violations of the privacy of postal, telegraphic and telephonic communications; warrants for house searches; orders for confiscation as well as restrictions on property, are permissible beyond the legal limits otherwise prescribed.

Armed with these all-embracing powers, Hitler and Goering were in a position to take any action they pleased against their opponents. They cleverly postponed the formal proscription of the Communist Party until after the elections, so that the working-class vote should continue to be divided between the rival parties of the Communists and the Social Democrats. But acts of terrorism against the Left-wing parties were now intensified.

Meanwhile, in the last week of the election campaign, the Nazi propaganda machine produced the most hair-raising accounts of Communist preparations for insurrection and a "blood-bath," for which the Reichstag Fire and the arrest of van der Lubbe were used to provide substantiation. Hitler stormed the country in a last hurricane campaign, declaring his determination to stamp out the Left without mercy. For the first time the radio carried his words into every corner of the country.

To leave no doubt of what they meant, Goering assured an audience at Frankfurt on 3 March:

"Fellow Germans, my measures will not be crippled by any judicial thinking. . . . I don't have to worry about Justice, my mission is only to destroy and exterminate, nothing more. This struggle will be a struggle against chaos, and such a struggle I shall not conduct with the power of the police. A bourgeois State might have done that. Certainly, I shall use the power of the State and the police to the utmost, my dear Communists, so don't draw any false conclusions; but the struggle to the death, in which my fist will grasp your necks, I shall lead with those down there—the Brown Shirts."

The campaign reached its climax on Saturday, 4 March, the "Day of the Awakening Nation," when Hitler spoke in Koenigsberg, the ancient coronation town and capital of East Prussia.

As Hitler finished speaking bonfires blazed out on the hilltops, all along the "threatened frontier" of the east. It was the culmination of a month in which the tramping columns of S.A. troops, the torchlight parades, the monster demonstrations, cheering crowds, blaring loudspeakers, and moboratory, the streets hung with swastika flags, the open display of brutality and violence, with the police standing by in silence—all had been used to build up the impression of an irresistible force which would sweep away every obstacle in its path.

In face of all this it is a remarkable fact that still the German people refused to give Hitler the majority he sought but with the proscription of the Communist deputies they would have a clear parliamentary majority themselves, without the need of the Nationalist votes. The chances of Papen, Hugenburg and the Nationalists acting as an effective brake on their partners in the coalition appeared slight.

Hitler's dictatorship rested on the constitutional foundation of a single law: the so-called Enabling Law, *Gesetz zur Behebung der Not von Volk und Reich* (Law for Removing the Distress of People and Reich). As it represented an alteration of the Constitution, a majority of two-thirds of the Reichstag was necessary to pass it, and Hitler's first preoccupation after the elections was to secure this. The Nazis held the whip-hand with the decree of 28 February, and in addition, Hitler was prepared to promise anything at this stage for votes to get his bill through, with the appearances of legality preserved intact.

Hitler's master-stroke of conciliation towards the President, the Army and the Nationalists was the ceremony in the Potsdam Garrison Church, to mark the opening of the

Reichstag. At the same time Hitler established the claim of
the new régime to be the heir of the military traditions of
old Prussia and its Hohenzollern kings.

The date, 21 March, was that on which Bismarck had
opened the first Reichstag of the German Empire in 1871, and
on which Hitler was now to open the first Reichstag of the
Third Reich. The guard of honour of the Army drawn up
on one side, and the S.A. on the other, were the symbols
of the two Germanies, the old and the new, united by the
handshake of President and Chancellor.

In the church one whole gallery was filled with the mar-
shals, generals and admirals of the Imperial régime, all wearing their pre-war uniforms, and headed by Field-Marshal von
Mackensen in the uniform of the Death's Head Hussars.
When ths door was thrown open, the audience rose to its
feet. The members of the Government entered the church.
All eyes were on two men: the Austrian, Adolf Hitler, clad in
formal morning-dress, awkward but respectful, and
beside him the massive figure of the aged President, the
Prussian Field-Marshal who had first stood in this church in
1866 when, as a young lieutenant of the Guards, he had returned from the Austro-Prussian War in which German unity
had been forged. Slowly the old man advanced down the
aisle, leaning on his cane. As he reached the centre, he
turned and solemnly saluted with his Field-Marshal's baton
the empty throne of the Kaiser and the Crown Prince.

Following the President's brief address, Hitler spoke,
with an eye to the representatives of the old régime who
sat before him:

> . . . By a unique upheaval, in the last few weeks our na-
> tional honour has been restored and, thanks to your under-
> standing, *Herr General-Feldmarschal,* the union between the
> symbols of the old greatness and the new strength has been
> celebrated. We pay you homage. A protective Providence
> places you over the new forces of our Nation.

The Chancellor crossed to the old Marshal's chair and,
bending low, grasped his hand: the apostolic succession had
been established.

Alone, the old man descended stiffly into the crypt to the
tomb of Frederick the Great. Outside, in the March sunshine,
the guns roared in salute and, to the crash of trumpets and
drums, the German Army, followed by the S.A. and the
Stahlhelm, paraded before the President, the Chancellor and
the Crown Prince. As night fell a torchlight procession of
ten thousand S.S. troops swept through the Brandenburger

Tor to the cheers of a huge crowd, while at the Opera Furt-wängler conducted a brilliant performance of Wagner's *Die Meistersinger*.

As the French Ambassador later wrote: "After the dazzling pledge made by Hitler at Potsdam, how could Hindenburg and his friends fail to dismiss the apprehension with which they had begun to view the excesses and abuses of his party?"

It was the other face of Nazism that was to be seen when the Reichstag assembled in the temporary quarters of the Kroll Opera House two days later. The Enabling Bill which was laid before the House gave the Government the power for four years to enact laws without the co-operation of the Reichstag, specifically stating that this power should include the right to deviate from the Constitution and to conclude treaties with foreign States. It also provided that laws to be enacted by the Government should be drafted by the Chancellor, and should come into effect on the day after publication.

To reach the doors, the deputies had had to pass through a solid rank of black-shirted S.S. men encircling the building; inside, the corridors and walls were lined with brown-shirted S.A. troops.

Hitler's opening speech was restrained.

The Government [he declared] will only make use of these powers in so far as they are essential for carrying out vitally necessary measures. Neither the existence of the Reichstag nor that of the Reichsrat is menaced. The position and rights of the President remain unaffected. It will always be the foremost task of the Government to act in harmony with his aims. The separate existence of the federal States will not be done away with. . . .

The Government [he concluded] offers to the parties of the Reichstag the opportunity for friendly co-operation. But is is equally prepared to go ahead in face of their refusal and of the hostilities which will result from that refusal. It is for you, gentlemen of the Reichstag, to decide between war and peace.

After a recess it was the turn of the leader of the Social Democrats, Otto Wels, to speak. There was silence as he walked to the tribune, but from outside came the baying of the Stormtroopers chanting: "We want the Bill—or fire and murder." It needed courage to stand up before this packed assembly—most of the Communists and about a dozen of the Social Democrat deputies had already been thrown into prison—and to tell Hitler and the Nazis to their faces that the Social Democratic Party would vote against the Bill. Wels spoke with moderation; to be defenceless, he added, was not to be without honour. But the very suggestion of opposition roused Hitler to a fury. Brushing aside Papen's attempt to restrain him, he mounted the tribune a second time and gave the Reichstag, the Cabinet and the Diplomatic Corps a taste of his real temper, savage, mocking and brutal. "I do not want your votes," he spat at the Social Democrats. "Germany will be free, but not through you. Do not mistake us for bourgeois. The star of Germany is in the ascendant, yours is about to disappear, your death-knell has sounded."

Then came the vote, and excitement mounted. When Goering declared the figures—for the Bill, 441; against, 94— the Nazis leaped to their feet and with arms outstretched in salute sang the Horst Wessel song. Outside in the square the huge crowd roared its approval. The Nazis had every reason to be delighted: with the passage of the Enabling Act, Hitler secured his independence, not only from the Reichstag but also from the President. Now Hitler had for himself full power to set aside the Constitution. The street gangs had seized control of the resources of a great modern State, the gutter had come to power.

In March, 1933, however, Hitler was still not the dictator of Germany. The process of *Gleichschaltung*—"co-ordination"—by which the whole of the organized life of the nation was to be brought under the single control of the Nazi Party, had still to be carried out. Hitler and Frick had not waited for the passage of the Enabling Act to take steps to bring the States governments firmly under their control. Hitler had no intention of allowing such a conflict between Bavaria and the Reich as he had exploited in 1923 to develop again. On the evening of 9 March von Epp, with full authority from Berlin, carried out a *coup d'état* in Munich. The Held Government was turned out, and Nazis appointed to all the principal posts.

Similar action was taken in the other States, and the first week in April Hitler nominated Reich Governors (*Reichstatthälter*) in every State, and gave them the power to appoint and remove State Governments, to dissolve the Diets, to prepare and publish State laws, and to appoint and dismiss State officials. All eighteen of the new Reich Governors were Nazis, usually the local Gauleiters. In Prussia the new law afforded an opportunity to turn out Papen, who "asked to be relieved of his post." Hitler now appointed himself *Reichstatthälter* for Prussia and promptly delegated his powers to Goering as Prussian Minister-President.

On the first anniversary of Hitler's accession to power, 30 January, 1934, a Law for the Reconstruction of the Reich rounded off this work in which all representative self-government from the level of the States downwards through the whole system of local government had been stamped out.

If Hitler meant to destroy Marxism in Germany he had obviously to break the independent power of the huge German trade-union movement, the foundation on which the Social Democratic Party rested. In March and April the S.A. broke into and looted the offices of many local trade-union branches. The Nazis cleverly camouflaged their intentions by declaring May Day a national holiday, and holding an immense workers' rally in Berlin which was addressed by Hitler. On the morning of the next day the trade-union offices all over the country were occupied by S.A. and S.S. troopers. Many union officials were arrested, beaten and thrown into concentration camps. All the unions were then merged into a new German Labour Front under control of Robert Ley, who declared: "Workers! . . . I myself am a poor peasant's son and understand poverty, I myself was seven years in one of the biggest industries in Germany and I know the exploitation of anonymous capitalism. Workers! I swear to you . . . we will build up the protection and rights of the worker even further."

Hitler gave similar assurances to the First Congress of German Workers on 10 May in a speech that again shows his skill in adapting himself to his audience. But the intentions behind Hitler's talk of honouring labour and abolishing the class war were not long concealed. Before the month was out a new law ended collective bargaining and appointed Labour Trustees, under the Government's orders, to settle conditions of work.

The Social Democrats too attempted to carry on loyally for a time. Their efforts proved equally futile. On 10 May Goering ordered the occupation of the Party's buildings and newspaper offices, and the confiscation of the Party's funds, and on 22 June Frick banned the Social Democratic Party as an enemy of people and State.

The remaining parties represented a more delicate problem, but this did not long delay their disappearance; not even Hitler's partners in the coalition, the Nationalists, were spared.

On 14 July the Official Gazette contained the brief announcement, signed by Hitler, Frick and Gürtner:

"The German Government has enacted the following law, which is herewith promulgated:

"Article I: The National Socialist German Workers' Party constitutes the only political Party in Germany.

"Article II: Whoever undertakes to maintain the organizational structure of another political Party or to form a new political Party will be punished with penal servitude up to three years or with imprisonment up to three years, if the action is not subject to a greater penalty according to other regulations."

With the suppression of the parties, the basis of the coalition which had brought Hitler into power disappeared. With the passage of the Enabling Law the need for it had gone. "The reactionary forces," Rauschning reports Hitler saying that after the Reichstag Fire ". . . hope I will achieve my own ruin by mismanagement. But . . . our great opportunity lies in acting before they do. We have no scruples, no bourgeois hesitations. . . . They regard me as an uneducated barbarian. Yes, we are barbarians. We want to be barbarians. It is an honourable title."

As so often later in his foreign policy, Hitler resorted to his favourite tactic of surprise, of doing just the things no one believed he would dare to do, with a bland contempt for convention or tradition. In a few weeks he had banned or dissolved all other political parties, had taken over the *Stahlhelm* and the Trade Unions, and with equal success had ridden rough-shod over the rights of the federal States. The methods of gangsterism applied to politics, the crude and uninhibited use of force in the first, not in the last, resort, produced startling results.

Any opposition in the Cabinet crumpled up before the wave of violence which was eliminating all the political landmarks in the German scene. Papen, shorn of his power as Reich Commissioner in Prussia, was a shrunken figure. Hitler no longer paid attention to the rule that the Vice-Chancellor must always be present when he saw the President; indeed, he rarely bothered to see the President at all, now that he had the power to issue decrees himself. By the summer of 1933 Hitler was complete master of a Government in which Papen only remained on sufferance, and which was independent alike of Reichstag, President and political allies. For Hitler had grasped a truth which eluded Papen, the political dilettante, that the key to power no longer lay in the parliamentary and presidential intrigues by means of which he had got his foot inside the door—and by means of which Papen still hoped to bind him—but, outside, in the masses of the German people. Papen, deceived by Hitler's tactics of legality, had never grasped that the revolutionary character of the Nazi movement would only be revealed after Hitler had come to power, and was now astonished and intimidated by the forces he had released.

For it is a mistake to suppose, as Papen did, that because Hitler came to power by the backstairs there was no genuine revolutionary force in the Nazi Party. The S.A. regarded Hitler's Chancellorship as the signal for that settling of accounts which they had been promised for so long. With the long-drawn-out economic depression and the accompanying political uncertainty and bitterness, the revolutionary impulse of the S.A. was bound to strike echoes in a large section of the German people. This wave of revolutionary excitement which passed across Germany in 1933 took several forms.

Its first and most obvious expression was violence. Violence had been common enough in Germany for many months before 1933, but the violence of the period between the Reichstag Fire and the end of the year was on a different scale from anything that had happened before. The Government itself deliberately employed violence and intimidation as a method of governing, using such agencies as the Gestapo (the Prussian Secret State Police established by Goering), and the concentration camps opened at Oranienburg, Dachau, and other places. At the same time, the open contempt for justice and order shown by the State encouraged the normally suppressed impulses of cruelty, envy and revenge. Men were arrested, beaten and murdered for no more substantial reason than to satisfy a private grudge, to secure a man's job or his apartment, and to gratify a taste for sadism. In Berlin and other big cities local S.A. gangs established "bunkers" in disused warehouses or cellars, to which they carried off anyone to whom they took a dislike, either to maltreat them or hold them to ransom. The normal sanctions of the police and the courts were withdrawn, and common crime from robbery to murder brazenly disguised as "politics." The only measure taken by the Government was to issue amnesties for "penal acts committed in the national revolution."

Yet violence, if it repelled, also attracted many, especially among the younger generation. For 1933, like other revolutionary years, produced a sense of new possibilities, the end of frustration, the beginning of action, a feeling of exhilaration and anticipation after years of hopelessness. Hitler recognized this mood when he told the German people to hold up their heads and rediscover their old pride and self-confidence. It is wrong to lay stress only on the element of coercion, and to ignore the degree to which Hitler commanded a genuine popular support in Germany. To suppose that the huge votes which Hitler secured in his plebiscites were even principally due to the Gestapo and the concentration camps is to miss what Hitler knew so well, the immense attraction to the masses of force plus success.

Side by side with this went the familiar and seamy accompaniment of all revolutionary upheavals, the rush to clamber on the band wagon. The purge of the civil service, the closing of the professions to Jews, the creation of new posts in government and local government service, in industry and business whetted the appetites of the unsuccessful, the ambitious and the envious. Most of the men who now held power in Germany, Hitler himself, Goering, Goebbels, and the thousands of Nazis who had become mayors of cities, government officials and heads of departments, belonged to one or other of these classes. The six million unemployed, who had not disappeared overnight when Hitler came to power, represented a revolutionary pressure that was not easily to be dammed.

It was by harnessing these forces of discontent and revolt that Hitler had created the Nazi movement, and as late as the middle of June, 1933, he was still prepared to tell a gathering of Nazi leaders in Berlin: ". . . The German Revolution will not be complete until the whole German people has been fashioned anew, until it has been organized anew and has been reconstructed."

But there was a point beyond which this revolutionary process could not go without seriously endangering the efficiency of the State and of the German economy. The two dangers to which Hitler had to pay particular attention were the disruption of the economic organization of the country, and attempts to interfere with the inviolability of the Army.

Hitler had never been a Socialist; he was indifferent to economic questions. What he saw, however, was that radical economic experiments at such a time would throw the German economy into a state of confusion, and would prejudice, if not destroy, the chances of cooperation with industry and business to end the Depression and bring down the unemployment figures. Such an argument which directly touched his own power, took precedence over economic panaceas.

On 13 July Hitler summoned the Gauleiters to Berlin and told them: "Political power we had to conquer rapidly and with one blow; in the economic sphere other principles of development must determine our action. Here progress must be made step by step without any radical breaking up of existing conditions which would endanger the foundations of our own life. . . ."

July, 1933, in fact marked a turning point in the development of the revolution. At Leipzig Hitler spoke of the ending of the second phase of the battle for Germany. The task of the new phase Hitler described as "educating the millions who do not yet in their hearts belong to us."

Hitler's own wish to bring the revolution to an end, for the time being at least, and to consolidate its gains, is plain enough. However he was far from convincing all his followers of the necessity of his new policy. Once again opposition found its strongest expression in the S.A. Its leader was Ernst Roehm, the S.A. Chief of Staff, who spoke in the name of the hundreds of thousands of embittered Nazis who had been left out in the cold, and wanted no end to the revolution until they too had been provided for. Goering, in line with the change of policy, announced the dismissal of the S.A. and S.S. auxiliary police; they were no longer needed. On 6 August, before a parade of eighty thousand S.A. men on the Tempelhof Field outside Berlin, Roehm gave his answer: "Anyone who thinks that the tasks of the S.A. have been accomplished will have to get used to the idea that we are here and intend to stay here. . . ."

From the summer of 1933 to the summer of 1934 this quarrel over the Second Revolution was to form the dominant issue in German politics.

Throughout the autumn of 1933 and the spring of 1934 for the next nine months demands to renew and extend the Revolution grew louder and more menacing. Roehm, Goebbels and many of the S.A. leaders made open attacks on *Reaktion*, that comprehensive word which covered everyone the S.A. disliked, from capitalists and stiff-necked generals to the respectable bourgeois citizen with a job. Now, they grumbled, the Nazis had gone respectable, and many who had secured a Party card only the day before were allowed to continue with their jobs while deserving *Altkaempfer* were left out on the streets. In characteristically elegant language they began to talk of clearing out the pig-sty, and driving a few of the greedy swine away from the troughs.

While the S.A., which was a genuine mass movement with strong radical leanings, became restive and eager to perpetuate the revolution, Roehm and the S.A. leadership became involved in a quarrel with the Army. It was the old issue which Roehm had fought over with Hitler in the 1920s. On this subject Hitler was as strongly opposed as ever to Roehm's inveterate desire to turn the S.A. into soldiers and to remodel the Army.

There were particularly strong reasons why Hitler wished to avoid alienating the Army leaders at this time. The willingness of the Army to see Hitler become Chancellor, the benevolent neutrality of the Army during the months following 30 January, in which he successfully crushed all resistance and arrogated more and more power to himself—these were decisive factors in the establishment of the Nazi régime. The steps by which Hitler made sure of the Army's friendly attitude are unfortunately not yet known to us. Two points, however, are tolerably clear: first, that the key figure was General Werner von Blomberg, and second, that Hitler promised to relieve the Army from being forced to intervene in a civil war, thus allowing it to preserve intact its traditions and its independent position in the State.

Hitler's relations with Blomberg became closer as he began to take the first steps in rebuilding the military power of Germany. Hitler was dependent upon the generals for the technical skill necessary to plan and carry out German rearmament. Looking ahead, he recognized the importance of having the Army again on his side, if he was to succeed Hindenburg.

Roehm took a different view. By the end of 1933 the S.A. numbered between two and three million men, and the S.A. leaders, like the gangsters they were, were avid for the prestige, the power and the pickings they would acquire by supplanting the generals. Their motives were as crude as their manners, but undeniably men like Roehm and Heines were tough, possessed ability and commanded powerful forces.

Hitler needed the generals' support, and did not intend to let Roehm and the S.A. spoil his plans. On their side, the generals were adamant in their refusal to accept the S.A. on an equal footing with the Army, and determined to maintain the Army's privileged position in the State. Here was one institution which they were resolved should not be Nazified, and Roehm's pretensions were rejected with contempt.

Although in a number of speeches in the latter half of 1933, Hitler went out of his way to reassure the generals that he remained loyal to his compact with them, the problem of the S.A. remained. If it was not to be incorporated into the Army, as Roehm wanted, what was to become of it? The S.A. was the embarrassing legacy of the years of struggle. As more normal conditions began to return, the S.A., conscious of the unpopularity which their excesses had won for them, began to feel themselves no longer wanted. In a speech to fifteen thousand S.A. officials in the Berlin *Sportpalast* in November, 1933, Roehm gave expression to this mood of frustration in a violent attack on the "reactionaries." "One often hears . . . that the S.A. have lost any reason for existence," he declared. But he would tell these gentlemen that the old bureaucratic spirit must still be changed "in a gentle, or if need be, in an ungentle manner." Roehm's attack was greeted with loud applause.

Thus the issue between the S.A. and the Army became a test case involving the whole question of the so-called Second Revolution—the point at which the revolution was to be halted—and the classic problem of all revolutionary leaders once they have come to power, the liquidation of the Party's disreputable past.

Hitler first attempted to solve this problem by conciliation and compromise. A law promulgated on 1 December, made both Roehm as Chief of Staff of the S.A., and Hess, the deputy leader of the Party, members of the Reich Cabinet. So far as Roehm was concerned, this repaired an omission which had long been a grievance with the S.A.

At the beginning of the New Year Hitler addressed a letter to Roehm of unusual friendliness, employing throughout the intimate form of the second person singular, and ending:

> At the close of the year of the National Socialist Revolution, therefore, I feel compelled to thank you, my dear Ernst Roehm, for the imperishable services which you have rendered to the National Socialist movement and the German people, and to assure you how very grateful I am to Fate that I am able to call such men as you my friends and fellow combatants.
>
> In true friendship and grateful regard,
Your Adolf Hitler.

With Roehm and Hess in the Cabinet more attention was now paid to the needs and grievances of the "old fighters," and members of the Party or S.A. who had suffered sickness or injury in the political struggle for the national movement were to receive State pensions or payments.

Roehm, however, was not to be silenced by such sops. In February he proposed in the Cabinet a plan to use the S.A. as the basis for the expansion of the Army, and that a single Minister should be appointed to take charge of the Armed Forces of the State. The obvious candidate for such a post was Roehm himself. The Army High Command presented a unanimous opposition to such a proposal and appealed to the President, as the guardian of the Army's traditions, to put a stop to Roehm's attempted interference.

Hitler declined to take Roehm's side in the dispute, and although temporarily checked, Roehm kept up his pressure on the Army, and relations between himself and General von Blomberg, the Minister of Defence, grew strained. A few days later, however, the situation was transformed for Hitler when he and von Blomberg were secretly informed that President Hindenburg could not be expected to live very much longer. Within a matter of months, perhaps of weeks, the question of the succession would have to be settled.

So long as the independent position of the President existed alongside his own, so long as the President was Commander-in-Chief of the Armed Forces and so long as the oath of allegiance was taken to the President and not to himself, Hitler's power was something less than absolute. He was determined that when Hindenburg died he and no one else should succeed to the President's position. It was to Adolf Hitler, and not to a possible rival, that the Armed Forces should take the new oath of allegiance. The first and most important step was to make sure of the Army, whose leaders claimed to represent the permanent interests of the nation independently of the rise and fall of governments and parties.

In the second week of April an opportunity presented itself. On 11 April Hitler left Kiel on the cruiser *Deutschland* to take part in naval manoeuvres. He was accompanied by General von Blomberg, the Minister of Defence; Colonel General Frieherr von Fritsch, the Commander-in-Chief of the German Army; and Admiral Raeder, the Commander-in-Chief of the German Navy. It is believed to have been during the course of this short voyage that Hitler came to terms with the generals: the succession for himself, in return for the suppression of Roehm's plans and the continued inviolability of the Army's position as the sole armed force in the State. On the Army side, a conference of senior officers under Fritsch's chairmanship endorsed Blomberg's decision in favour of Hitler after—but only after—the terms of the *Deutschland* Pact had been communicated to them.

Roehm had powerful enemies inside the Party as well as in the Army. Goering, who had been made a general by Hindenburg to his great delight, was on the worst of terms with the Chief of Staff of the S.A. He began to collect a powerful police force "for special service," which he kept ready under his own hand at the Lichterfelde Cadet School near Berlin. On 1 April, 1934, Himmler, already head of the Bavarian police and Reichsfuehrer of the black-shirted S.S., was unexpectedly appointed by Goering as head of the Prussian Gestapo. Goering found in Himmler an ally against a common enemy, for the first obstacle Himmler sought to remove from his path was Ernst Roehm. Himmler and his S.S. were still a part of the S.A. and subordinate to Roehm's command, although the rivalry between the S.A. and S.S. was bitter, and Roehm's relationship with Himmler could hardly have been less cordial. Hess, Bormann and Major Buch (the chairman of the *Uschla*) were collecting complaints and scandals—and there were plenty—about Roehm and the other S.A. leaders.

Roehm's only friends in the Party leadership were Goebbels and—paradoxically enough—the man who was to have him murdered, Hitler. Goebbels was by temperament a radical and maintained a link between the Chief of Staff and Hitler until the middle of June, when he turned against Roehm, as he had betrayed Strasser in 1926. As for Hitler, it was not until the latter part of June that he was persuaded to move against Roehm and the S.A., as Goering and Himmler long had been urging him to do.

Roehm himself and the other S.A. leaders, like the brutal and corrupt Heines, had acquired a bad reputation for the disorder, luxury and perversion of their way of living. By the middle of May, Roehm recognized that the S.A. were on the defensive and ordered his local leaders to keep a record of all complaints and attacks directed against the S.A.

The situation with which Hitler had to deal was produced by the intersection of three problems, that of the Second Revolution, of the S.A. and the Army, and of the succession to Hindenburg. It was the problem of the succession, which introduced a note of urgency by making Hitler's own position vulnerable.

If Hitler was to secure their support for his succession to the Presidency, the Army leadership was determined to exact in return the removal of the S.A. threat to take over the Army and renew the revolution. The alternative, urged by Roehm—for Hitler himself to take the lead in renewing the revolution and, relying on the S.A., to destroy any opposition by force—would create more problems than it would remove.

Driven at last to decide, Hitler chose to stand by his agreement with the Army, but for as long as possible he sought to avoid a decision. When he had made it, he disguised it as action forced on him not by pressure from the Right, but by disloyalty and conspiracy on the Left.

On 4 June Hitler sent for Roehm and had a conversation with him which lasted for five hours. According to Hitler, he warned Roehm against any attempt to start a Second Revolution. At the same time as he assured Roehm that he had no intention of dissolving the S.A., Hitler reproached him with the scandal created by his own behaviour and that of his closest associates in the S.A. leadership. What else was said is not known, but a day or two later Hitler ordered the S.A. to go on leave for the month of July, returning to duty on 1 August, while Roehm announced on 7 June that he himself was about to take a period of sick leave. During their leave the S.A. were forbidden to wear their uniforms or to take part in any demonstrations or exercises.

Hitler agreed to attend a conference of S.A. leaders to discuss the future of the movement at Wiessee, near Munich, on 30 June. It was a rendezvous which Hitler did not fail to keep.

What happened between 8 June and 30 June?

Hitler gave his version in his speech of 13 July. According to this, Roehm had renewed his old relations with General von Schleicher. The two men, according to Hitler, agreed on a concrete programme:

"1. The present régime in Germany could not be supported.

"2. Above all the Army and all national associations must be united in a single band.

"3. The only man who could be considered for such a position was the Chief of Staff, Roehm.

"4. Herr von Papen must be removed, and Schleicher himself would be ready to take the position of Vice-Chancellor, and in addition further important changes must be made in the Reich Cabinet."

Since Roehm was not sure that Hitler would agree, he made preparations to carry out his plan by a *coup*, the main role in which was to be played by the S.A. Staff Guards. To complete the conspiracy, Hitler continued, Schleicher and General von Bredow got in touch with "a foreign Power" (later identified as France). At the same time Gregor Strasser, who had retired into private life after Hitler's Chancellorship, was brought into the plot.

After his talk with Hitler on 4 June, Roehm—still according to Hitler's version—planned to take Hitler captive, hoping to use his authority to call out the S.A. and paralyse the other forces in the State. The action taken at the end of June was directed, Hitler claimed, to forestalling Roehm's *putsch* by only a matter of hours.

Part of this story can with some certainty be rejected as untrue from the beginning. On the very day he was supposed to be storming the Chancellery in Berlin, Roehm was seized in bed at the hotel in Wiessee where he was taking a cure and awaiting Hitler's arrival for their conference. Most of the other S.A. leaders were either on their way to Wiessee or had arrived. Karl Ernst, the S.A. leader in Berlin (whom Hitler represented as one of the most important figures in the plot), was taken prisoner at Bremen, where he was about to leave by boat for a honeymoon in Madeira. The whole story of an imminent *coup d'etat* was a lie, either invented later by Hitler as a pretext for his own action, or possibly made use of at the time by Goering and Himmler to deceive Hitler and force him to move against Roehm. Frick testified after the war that it was Himmler who convinced Hitler that Roehm meant

to start a *putsch*. Roehm certainly had great ambitions for his
S.A. and made no secret of them. He had been in close relations with Schleicher before 30 January, 1933—so had Gregor
Strasser, who was to have been Schleicher's Vice-Chancellor.
Schleicher was an able, ambitious and unscrupulous intriguer.
But the fact that Schleicher and Strasser were both shot in the
same purge as Roehm is open to a very different interpretation. For, if there were two men in Germany who might well
have felt insecure in the event of any purge, two men whom
Hitler was certain to regard as dangerous whatever they did,
they were Gregor Strasser and Kurt von Schleicher. There
were many old scores levelled on the week-end of 30 June,
1934, and the murder of Schleicher and Strasser may well fall
into this category.

It is very likely that Roehm and those who shared his
views discussed how to win Hitler over and force his hand,
but there is no proof at all that such discussions had gone
so far as to merit the name of a conspiracy. The conspirators
of June, 1934, were not Roehm and the S.A., but Goering
and Himmler, the enemies of Roehm; the treachery and disloyalty were not on Roehm's side, but on theirs and Hitler's;
and if ever men died convinced—not without reason—that
they had been "framed," it was the men who were shot on
30 June, 1934.

There is good reason to regard Hitler's account of these
events with suspicion, as the awkward apologia of a murderer
seeking to justify his crime by defaming his victims.

Throughout June, 1934, there was an ominous tension in
Berlin, heightened by rumours and much speculation. At the
end of May both Bruening and Schleicher were warned that,
in the event of a purge, their lives were in danger. Bruening
took the advice seriously and left for Switzerland; Schleicher
went no farther than the Starnbergersee, and returned in time
to be shot.

On 14 June Hitler flew to Venice for his first conversation
with Mussolini. Mussolini, at the height of his reputation and
resplendent with uniform and dagger, patronized the worried
Hitler, who appeared in a raincoat and a soft hat. Mussolini
was not only pressing on the subject of Austria, where Nazi
intrigues were to lead to trouble before the summer was out,
but frankly advised Hitler to put the Left wing of the Party
under restraint, and Hitler returned from Venice depressed
and irritable.

At this stage Hitler was given a sharp reminder of the
realities of the situation from an unexpected quarter. Papen
remained Vice-Chancellor and still enjoyed the special con-

fidence of the old President, and for the last time he made
use of his credit with Hindenburg to stage a public protest
against the recent course, and, even more, against the pro-
spective course, of events in Germany. If Hitler refused to
listen then Papen believed that he would have the support
of Hindenburg, who was equally unhappy about the state of
affairs. In case of need Papen counted on the President's
ordering the Army to intervene.

Papen's protest was made in the course of a speech at the
University of Marburg on 17 June and crystallized the
anxieties and uncertainties of the whole nation. Its outstanding
passages were those which dealt with the talk of a Second
Revolution.

> Whoever toys irresponsibly with such ideas should not forget
> that a second wave of revolution might be followed by a
> third, and that he who threatens to employ the guillotine may
> be its first victim.
>   Nor is it clear where such a second wave is to lead. There
> is much talk of the coming socialization. Have we gone
> through the anti-Marxist revolution in order to carry out a
> Marxist programme? . . . Would the German people be the
> better for it, except perhaps those who scent booty in such a
> pillaging raid? . . . Germany must not embark on an adven-
> ture without a known destination, nobody knowing where it
> will end. History has its own clock. It is not necessary con-
> tinually to urge it on.

The same day that Papen made his speech, Hitler spoke
at Gera and was scathing in his references to "the pygmy
who imagines he can stop with a few phrases the gigantic
renewal of a people's life." But Papen's protest was not so
easily brushed aside. Goebbels took immediate steps to ban
its publication but copies were smuggled out of Germany
and published abroad, creating a sensation which did not fail
to penetrate to Germany. When Papen appeared in public at
Hamburg on 24 June he was loudly cheered. It was evident
that he had spoken for a great part of the nation.

On 20 June Papen went to see Hitler and demand the
removal of the ban on publishing his speech. In a stormy
interview Papen threatened his own and the resignation of the
other conservative ministers in the Cabinet. Hitler saw quite
clearly that he was face to face with a major crisis. When he
flew to Neudeck on 21 June to see the ailing President, he
was met by General von Blomberg, with an uncompromising
message: either the Government must bring about a relaxation of the state of tension or the President would declare
martial law and hand over power to the Army. The Army was
claiming the fulfilment of its bargain, and by now Hitler

must have realized that more was at stake than the succession to the Presidency: the future of the whole régime was involved.

It is impossible to penetrate Hitler's state of mind in the last week of June. Obviously he must have been aware of the preparations which were now rapidly put in hand, yet to the very last day he seems to have hesitated to take the final step. At this stage it was not Hitler, but Goering and Himmler, who gave the orders and prepared to eliminate their rivals in the Party leadership. In the background the Army made its own arrangements. On 25 June the Commander-in-Chief, General von Fritsch, placed the Army in a state of alert, ordering all leave cancelled and the troops confined to barracks. On 28 June the German Officers' League expelled Roehm, and on 29 June the *Völkischer Beobachter* carried a signed article by General von Blomberg, the Minister of Defence, which was a plain statement of the Army's position. The Army leaders were quite content to leave it to Goering and Himmler to carry out the purge, but Blomberg's article left no doubt that whatever was done would be done with their blessing.

Far away from the tension and rumours of Berlin, on the shores of the Tegernsee, Roehm continued to enjoy his sick leave with his usual circle of young men, and to prepare lazily for the S.A. conference at the week-end, at which Hitler was expected. So little was he aware of what was being planned that he had left his Staff Guards in Munich. His carelessness and confidence are astonishing. Yet, even in Berlin, the local S.A. leader, Karl Ernst, who alerted the Berlin S.A. on the afternoon of 29 June, was so far misled as to believe the danger was a *putsch* by the Right directed against Hitler. Ernst never understood what had happened, even after his arrest, and died shouting: *"Heil, Hitler."*

On the 29th Hitler, keeping away from Berlin, made a tour of labour camps in Westphalia, and in the afternoon stopped at Godesberg on the Rhine, where he brought himself to take the final decision. Goebbels, who in the past few days had hurriedly dropped his contacts with Roehm, brought the news that the Berlin S.A., although due to go on leave the next day, had been suddenly ordered to report to their posts. At two o'clock the morning of the 30th Hitler flew to Munich. Before leaving he had telegraphed to Roehm to expect him at Wiessee the next day. "It was at last clear to me that only one man could oppose and must oppose the Chief of Staff."

The purge had already begun in Munich when Hitler landed at the Oberwiesenfeld airfield at four o'clock on the Saturday morning. On the evening of the 29th Major Buch, the chairman of the *Uschla,* a group of men including friends from Hitler's old Munich days, arrested the local S.A. leaders on the pretext that they were about to carry out a *coup d'état.* At the Ministry of the Interior, where the *S.A. Obergruppenfuehrer,* Schneidhuber, and his deputy were held under guard, Hitler who had now worked himself up into a fury tore off their insignia with his own hand and cursed them for their treachery.

In the early morning of the 30th a fast-moving column of cars tore down the road from Munich to Wiessee, where Roehm and Heines were still asleep in their beds at the Hanselbauer Hotel. The accounts of what happened at Wiessee are contradictory. Heines, the *S.A. Obergruppenfuehrer* for Silesia, who was found sleeping with one of Roehm's young men, is said to have been dragged out and shot on the road. Other accounts say he was taken to Munich with Roehm and shot there.

Back in Munich, seven to eight hundred men of Sepp Dietrich's *S.S. Leibstandarte Adolf Hitler* had been brought in from their barracks—the Army providing the transport— and ordered to provide a shooting squad at the Stadelheim Prison. It was there that Roehm was now shot by order of the man who seven months before had written to thank him for his imperishable services.

In Berlin the executions, directed by Goering and Himmler, began on the night of 29-30 June and continued throughout the Saturday and Sunday, and once again the principal victims were the leaders of the S.A. But in Berlin the net was cast more widely. When the bell rang at General von Schleicher's villa and the general went to the door, he was shot down where he stood and his wife with him. His friend, General von Bredow, was shot on his doorstep the same evening. Gregor Strasser, arrested at noon on the Saturday, was executed in the Prinz Albrechtstrasse Prison. Goering would certainly have removed Papen too, if he had not been Vice-Chancellor and under the special protection of the President. Despite this, Papen's office was wrecked, he himself was kept under house arrest for four days, two of his advisers, Bose and Edgar Jung, were shot, and two others arrested.

Late on the Saturday, Hitler returned from Munich. Among those who waited at the Tempelhof was H. B. Gisevius, who has described the scene. Goering, Himmler, Frick and a group of police officers stood watching for the plane. As it dived out of the sky and rolled across the field a guard of honour presented arms. The first to step out was Hitler. "A brown shirt, black bow-tie, dark-brown leather jacket, high black army boots. He wore no hat; his face was pale, unshaven, sleepless, at once gaunt and puffed. Under the forelock pasted against his forehead his eyes stared dully." Without saying a word, Hitler shook hands with the group on the airfield; the silence was broken only by the repeated click of heels. He walked slowly past the guard of honour, and not until he had started to walk towards his car did he begin to talk to Goering and Himmler. "From one of his pockets Himmler took a long, tattered list. Hitler read it through, while Goering and Himmler whispered incessantly into his ear. We could see Hitler's finger moving slowly down the sheet of paper. Now and then it paused for a moment at one of the names. At such times the two conspirators whispered even more excitedly. Suddenly Hitler tossed his head. There was so much violent emotion, so much anger in the gesture, that everyone noticed it. . . . Undoubtedly, we thought, they were now informing him of Strasser's 'suicide'. . . . The bathos of the scene, the woebegone expressions, the combination of violent fantasy and grim reality, the gratuitously blood-red sky, like a scene out of Wagner—it was really too much for me."

The executions went on all day Sunday—while Hitler gave a tea-party in the Chancellery garden—and were not confined to Berlin. Only on Monday morning did the shooting cease, when the German people, shaken and shocked, returned to work, and Hindenburg addressed his thanks to the Chancellor for his "determined action and gallant personal intervention, which have nipped treason in the bud." General von Blomberg had already expressed the devotion and fidelity of the Army in an order of the Day. The Army was very well satisfied with the events of the week-end.

How many were killed has never been settled. According to Gisevius, Goering ordered all the documents relating to the purge to be burned. Little by little, a list of names was pieced together. The *White Book* published in Paris gave a total of four hundred and one, and listed one hundred and sixteen by name.

The largest group of victims belonged to the S.A., but another group included Papen's two assistants, who served as substitutes for Papen himself, von Bose and Edgar Jung. Bose was talking to two industrialists from the Rhineland in the Vice-Chancellery when he was asked to step into the next room and see three S.S. men who has just arrived: shots rang out, and when the door was opened the S.S. men had gone and Bose was lying dead on the floor. A number of other Catholic leaders were shot.

Many of those murdered had little, if any, connection with Roehm or the S.A., and fell victims to private quarrels. Father Bernhard Stempfle, who had once revised the proofs of *Mein Kampf*, was discovered in the woods outside Munich; he had been shot "while trying to escape." In Hirschberg, Silesia, a group of Jews was murdered, for no other apparent reason than to amuse the local S.S. In Munich, on the evening of 30 June, Dr. Willi Schmidt, the music critic of the *Muenchener Neueste Nachrichten*, was playing the 'cello in his flat while his wife made supper and their three children were playing. Suddenly the door bell rang and four armed S.S. men came to take him away without explanation. There never was any explanation, except that the S.S. men were looking for someone else with the same name and shot the wrong man. When Frau Schmidt got her husband's body back, she was warned under no circumstances to open the coffin: the S.S. sent her a sum of money in recognition of her loss and their mistake. When she refused to accept it, Himmler rang up and told her to take the money and keep quiet. When she still refused, Hess called and eventually through his help, Frau Schmidt secured a pension: she should think of her husband's death, Hess told her, as the death of a martyr for a great cause.

Goebbels forbade German newspapers to carry obituary notices of those who had been executed or "had committed suicide." The ban only led to exaggerated rumours and to the intensification of the feeling of horror and fear. Not until 13 July did Hitler appear before the Reichstag and reveal a part of the story.

When Hitler came to describe the events leading up to 30 June he threw the whole blame on Roehm, who had forced him to act against his own wishes. Hitler gave great prominence to the charges of corruption, favouritism and homosexuality against Roehm's group, and went out of his way to represent them as betraying the ordinary, decent S.A. man. Hitler spoke of those who had become "revolutionaries who favoured revolution for its own sake and desired to see revolution established as a permanent condition." But, Hitler replied, "for us the Revolution is no permanent condition." Finally he repeated the promise, which to the Army leaders was the convenant in which they placed their faith: "In the State there is only one bearer of arms, and that is the Army; there is only one bearer of the political will, and that is the National Socialist Party."

The Officer Corps, intent only on preserving the privileged position of the Army, could see no further than the ends of their own noses. The menace of the S.A. was broken for good on the week-end of 30 June, but already a new and far more dangerous challenge to the autonomy of the Army was taking shape. As a reward for their service in the Roehm purge, Himmler's S.S. were now given their independence of the S.A., and placed directly under Hitler's orders with Himmler as *S.S. Reichsfuehrer*. At last Hitler had got what he had always wanted, an absolutely dependable and unquestioning instrument of political action. No group of men was to suffer so sharp a reversal as the Army officers, who, in the summer of 1934, ostentatiously held aloof from what happened in Germany and expressed an arrogant satisfaction at the Chancellor's quickness in seeing where the real power in Germany lay.

For anyone less blind than the generals, the way in which Hitler dealt with the threat of a second revolution must have brought consternation rather than satisfaction. Never had Hitler made so patent his total indifference to any respect for law or humanity, and his determination to preserve his power at any cost. Never had he illustrated so clearly the revolutionary character of his régime as in disowning the revolution.

When President von Hindenburg died on the morning of 2 August, there was neither hitch nor delay. Within an hour came the announcement that the office of President would henceforward be merged with that of the Chancellor, and that Hitler would become the Head of the State—as well as Supreme Commander-in-Chief of the Armed Forces of the Reich. Among the signatures at the foot of the law announcing these changes were those of von Papen, von Neurath, Graf Schwerin von Krosigk, General von Blomberg and Schacht: the representatives of Conservatism acquiesced in their own defeat.

The same day the officers and men of the German Army took the oath of allegiance to their new commander-in-chief. The form of the oath was significant. The Army was called on to swear allegiance not to the Constitution, or to the Fatherland, but to Hitler personally.

Between March, 1933, and August, 1934, the balance of power in Germany had shifted decisively in Hitler's favour. In that year and a half he had mastered the machine of State, suppressed the opposition, dispensed with his allies, asserted his authority over the Party and S.A., and secured for himself the prerogatives of the Head of the State and Commander-in-Chief of the Armed Forces. The Nazi revolution was complete: Hitler had become the dictator of Germany.

CHAPTER SIX

THE COUNTERFEIT PEACE

1933 — 1937

Hitler hated the routine work of government, and, once he had stabilized his power, each of the Party bosses, Goering, Goebbels, Himmler and Ley, created a private empire for himself, while the Gauleiters on a lower level enjoyed the control of their own local pashaliks. Hitler deliberately allowed this to happen; the rivalries which resulted only increased his power as supreme arbiter. Not until his own position, or special interests, were affected did he rouse himself to intervene actively.

Certain subjects, even in internal affairs, always interested Hitler—building plans, and anti-Semitic legislation, for instance—but he rapidly became absorbed in the two fields of foreign policy and preparation for war. Hitler was interested in power. The Party had been the instrument by which he acquired power in Germany; the State was now to be the instrument by which he meant to acquire power in Europe.

The aggressive—or, to use the favourite Nazi word, dynamic—foreign policy which Germany began to follow under Hitler gave expression to the long-smouldering rebellion of the German people against the defeat of 1918 and the humiliation of the Peace Settlement. Through the revived industrial activity stimulated by rearmament, it helped to overcome the economic crisis in which the Republic had foundered. The revolutionary impulse in Nazism was diverted into challenging the existing order outside Germany's frontiers and the creation of a European New Order, in which the big jobs and the privileges would go to the *Herrenvolk*. Above all, such a foreign policy was the logical projection of that unappeased will to power, both in Hitler himself and in the Nazi Party, which was now eager to extend its mastery further.

In the 1920s Hitler wrote in *Mein Kampf*: "What a use could be made of the Treaty of Versailles! . . . How each one of the points of that Treaty could be branded in the minds

135

and hearts of the German people until sixty million men and women find their souls aflame with a feeling of rage and shame; and a torrent of fire bursts as from a furnace, and a will of steel is forged from it, with the common cry: *'Wir wollen wieder Waffen!*—We will have arms again!"

In January, 1941, Hitler said, with considerable justification: "My programme was to abolish the Treaty of Versailles. It is nonsense for the rest of the world to pretend today that I did not reveal this programme until 1933, or 1935, or 1937. Instead of listening to the foolish chatter of *émigrés*, these gentlemen would have been wiser to read what I have written and rewritten thousands of times. No human being has declared or recorded what he wanted more often than I."

In practice, now that reparations had been ended, this could only mean Germany's right to rearm on terms of full equality with other nations, and the recovery of at least part of the territories lost in 1918—1919: the Saar, Alsace-Lorraine, the German colonies, above all Danzig and the lands incorporated in the new state of Poland.

But this was only a part of Hitler's programme in foreign policy, as Hitler had said quite plainly in *Mein Kampf*, his aim was to extend the frontiers of Germany to include those people of German race and speech who, even in 1914, had lived outside the Reich, the Germans of Austria and the Sudeten Germans of Czechoslovakia, who, before 1914, had formed part, not of the German Empire, but of the Hapsburg Monarchy.

Hitler was an Austrian. This is a fact of the greatest importance in understanding his foreign policy. For, in the 1860s, when Bismarck founded the German Empire, he deliberately excluded from it the Germans of the Hapsburg Monarchy. After the collapse of the Monarchy these Germans became citizens either of the Austrian Republic or of Czechoslovakia. It was amongst these Germans of the old Monarchy that there had sprung up before the war a violent Pan-German nationalism which sought to re-establish a union of all Germans in a single Greater Germany, and which was now violently opposed to the claims of the Czechs and the other former subject peoples of the Monarchy to nationhood and equality with the Germans. Born on the frontier between Germany and Austria, he felt—as he says on the opening pages of *Mein Kampf*—called upon to reunite the two German states which had been left divided by Bismarck's solution of the German problem. His hatred for the Czechs was the product of his early life in an empire where the Germans felt themselves on the defensive against the rising tide of Slav nationalism, most strongly represented in Hitler's experience by the Czech working men whom he met in Vienna. Here, too, is to be found one of the roots of the distinction Hitler made between the *Volk*, all those of German race and speech, and the State, which need not be co-extensive with the first, or might—as in the case of the old Hapsburg Monarchy and Czechoslovakia—include peoples of different races.

Even this does not exhaust the meaning of Hitler's remark about the inadequacy of Germany's 1914 frontiers. For in the Nazi Party programme, adopted as early as 1920, the culmination of Hitler's foreign policy is to be found in the demand for *Lebensraum*, living room for the future of the *Volk*, which formed the basis for his programme of expansion. Hitler advocated a continental policy of territorial expansion eastwards, seeking *Lebensraum* in the rich plains of Poland, the Ukraine and Russia. Such a policy would mean the resumption of that ancient struggle against the Slavs which had founded Austria, the old Ostmark, and had carried the Order of the Teutonic Knights along the southern shores of the Baltic into East Prussia and beyond. The continuity of Germany's eastern policy is impressive.

The logical consequence of such a policy was, of course, war with Russia. Hitler faced and accepted this as early as the 1920s and when the German armies invaded the Soviet Union in 1941 it was in execution of a policy the outlines of which are already to be found in *Mein Kampf*.

It was to the conquest of Eastern Europe and Russia that Hitler looked for the opportunity to build his New Order, the empire of the *Herrenvolk* based upon the slave-labour of the inferior races. Such plans involved the movement of populations, the deliberate depression of whole races to a lower standard of life and civilization, the denial of any chance of education or medical facilities, even, in the case of the Jews, their systematic extermination.

In these schemes for redrawing the map of the world and remodelling the distribution of power upon biological principles is found the authentic flavour of Nazi geopolitics. Hitler's over-inflamed imagination set no bounds to the expansion of Nazi power. In the early 1930s these appeared no more than the fantasies with which Hitler beguiled the early morning hours round the fire in the Berghof; by the early 1940s, however, the fantastic was on the verge of being translated into reality.

In the first year or two after Hitler had come to power, the prospects of accomplishing even the annexation of Austria,

still less of overrunning Russia, appeared remote. Germany
was politically isolated. Economically, she was only beginning to recover from the worst slump in her history. Her
army, limited by the Treaty to a hundred thousand men, was
easily outnumbered by that of France alone. A move in any
direction—in the west, against Austria, Czechoslovakia, or
Poland—seemed certain to run into the network of alliances
with which France sought to strengthen her security. So
impressed were the German diplomats and the generals with
the obstacles in Germany's way that indeed up to the Battle of
France in 1940, their advice was always on the side of
caution.

Hitler, on the other hand, became more and more convinced that he had a far keener appreciation of political—or
military—factors than the High Command or the Foreign
Office, and he dazzled them by the brilliant success of his
bold tactics. Hitler took office as Chancellor without any
previous experience of government. He had no knowledge of
any country outside Germany and Austria, and spoke no
foreign language. His sole experience of politics had been as
a Party leader and agitator. He knew nothing and cared less
for official views and traditions; he was suspicious of anyone
who might try to instruct him. In the short run, these were
assets. He refused to be impressed by the strength of the
opposition his schemes were likely to meet, or to be restricted
to the conventional methods of diplomacy. He displayed a
skill in propaganda and a mastery of deceit, a finesse in exploring the weaknesses of his opponents and a crudeness in
exploiting the strength of his own position which he had
learned in the struggle for power in Germany and which he
now applied to international relations with even more remarkable results.

No man was more of an opportunist, as the Nazi-Soviet
Pact shows. No man had more luck. But Hitler knew how to
turn events to his advantage. He knew what he wanted and
he held the initiative. His principal opponents, Great Britain
and France, knew only what they did not want—war—and
were always on the defensive. The fact that Hitler was perfectly ready to risk war, and prepared for it from the day he
came to power, gave him a still greater advantage while the
British and the French, eager to snatch at any hope of
avoiding a conflict, were only too ready to go on believing in
Hitler's pacific assurances.

The first and indispensable step was to rearm. Until he had
the backing of military power for his diplomacy, Hitler's
foreign policy was bound to be restricted. Until rearmament

reached a certain stage Germany was highly vulnerable to any preventive action which France or the other Powers might take, under the provisions of the Treaty. The first overriding objective of German foreign policy, therefore, was to secure the time and the freedom to rebuild Germany's military power.

Hitler's speeches from this period are masterpieces of carefully planned propaganda. Well aware that there were many abroad—especially in Great Britain—who had long felt uneasy about the shortcomings of the Peace Settlement, he hinged all arguments upon the unequal treatment of Germany after the war. This had three great advantages. It invoked sympathy for Germany as the defeated nation unfairly treated. It allowed Hitler to appear as the representative of reason and justice, protesting against the unreasonableness and injustice of Germany's former opponents. It enabled him to turn round and use with great effect against the supporters of the League of Nations all the slogans of Wilsonian idealism, from self-determination to a peace founded upon justice.

In October, 1933, when it became clear that the French—uneasily conscious of the inferiority of their manpower and industrial resources to those of Germany—were not prepared to disarm, Hitler pushed his argument a stage further. On 14 October he announced that Germany was driven, by the denial of equal rights, to withdraw from the Disarmament Conference and the League of Nations. Germany had tried to co-operate, but had suffered a bitter disillusionment and humiliation. In sorrow, rather than in anger, he had decided to take this step, which was demanded by the self-respect of the German people.

The withdrawal from the League was not without risks, in view of Germany's military inferiority, and a secret directive to the Armed Forces, in case the League should apply sanctions, was issued by General von Blomberg. It was the first of Hitler's gambles in foreign policy—and it succeeded. Events wholly justified his diagnosis of the state of mind of his opponents—their embarrassment in face of a case which they felt was not without justice; the divided public opinion of Great Britain and France; the eagerness to be reassured and to patch up a compromise, all those elements on which Hitler was to play with such skill time and again. With this in mind he issued a proclamation in which he declared force to be useless in removing international differences, affirmed the German people's hopes in disarmament and renewed his offer to conclude pacts of non-aggression at any time.

In an interview, published by *Le Matin* on 22 November, Hitler declared categorically that, once the question of the Saar had been settled, there were no further issues between Germany and France. He had renounced Alsace-Lorraine for good, and had told the German people so.

Hitler's cleverest stroke was to announce, on the same day as the withdrawal from the League, that he would submit his decision at once to a plebiscite. This was to invoke the sanctions of democracy against the democratic nations and resulted in a sweeping victory, with all the long-pent-up resentment of the German people against the loss of the war and the Treaty of Versailles expressed in the vote.

To Rauschning Hitler remarked that, now he had left the League, he would more than ever speak its language. "And my party comrades," he added, "will not fail to understand me when they hear me speak of universal peace, disarmament and mutual security pacts!" These were the tactics of legality applied to international relations with even greater success than in the fight for power in Germany.

Hitler had now manoeuvred himself into the strongest possible position in which to begin German rearmament. When the other Great Powers sought to renew negotiations, Hitler replied that disarmament was clearly out of the question. All that could be hoped for was a convention for the limitation of armaments, and Germany's terms for co-operation would be the recognition of her right to raise an army of three hundred thousand men. Rearmament had already begun, while Great Britain and France had placed themselves in the disadvantageous position, from which they were never to recover until the war, of asking the German dictator what concessions he would accept to reduce his price.

While negotiations continued, Hitler strengthened his hand in an unexpected direction. No feature of the Treaty of Versailles stirred more bitter feelings in Germany than the loss of territory to the new State of Poland and nowhere was the rise to power of the Nazis viewed with more alarm than in Warsaw.

It caused a diplomatic sensation, therefore, when, on 26 January, 1934, Hitler announced that the first country with which Nazi Germany had concluded a Non-Aggression Pact was Poland. It was an astute move for Hitler to make. Ultimately, there was no place for an independent Poland in Hitler's Europe; but Hitler could not move against Poland for years to come. Instead of accepting this situation with a bad grace, he turned it to his advantage, and made an ostentatious parade of his enforced virtue.

Hitler was thus able to substantiate his claim to peaceful intentions, and the pact with Poland was constantly used in Hitler's "peace" speeches from 1934 through 1936.

The importance of the Pact, however, was greater than its value as propaganda. Poland was one of the bastions of the French security system in Eastern Europe, but the Poles were becoming restive at the casual way in which they felt they were treated by France. The Polish Government was beginning to turn from France towards an independent neutrality, hoping to balance between her two great neighbours, Germany and Russia. The Nazi offer of a Ten-Year Pact fitted admirably into this new policy, and Hitler thereby first breached the French alliance system and first displayed his "one-by-one" tactics with which he was to achieve so much.

This was a good beginning, but there were reminders during 1934 of the dangers of the situation, notably in the case of Austria. The Austrian Nazis, who formed a part of the German Party under Hitler's leadership, lived and worked for the day when the *Anschluss* should take place. Local leaders kept up a violent propaganda campaign, backed by intimidation and acts of terrorism. Anyone in Austria had only to tune in to the Munich radio station to get confirmation of the financial support the Austrian Nazis were receiving from Germany. It appeared to be no more than a matter of months, possibly weeks, before the local Nazis would try to capture power by a rising.

German relations with Austria, however, were not simply a family affair, as Hitler tried to insist and Mussolini's suspicions were not removed by Hitler's assurances at their meeting at Venice in June. At last, on 25 July, while Madame Dolfuss and her family were actually staying with Mussolini, the Austrian Nazis broke into the Vienna Chancellery and shot Dolfuss, while others occupied the radio station and announced the appointment of Rintelen as Chancellor. Hitler was at Bayreuth and as he sat in his box listening to Wagner's *Rheingold*, his adjutants Schaub and Brückner kept coming in to whisper further news to him. "After the performance," Friedelind Wagner recalls, "the Fuehrer was most excited. . . . Although he could scarcely wipe the delight from his face, Hitler carefully ordered dinner in the restaurant as usual. 'I must go across for an hour and show myself,' he said, 'or people will think I had something to do with this'."

This was precisely what people did think, for the German Legation in Vienna had been heavily implicated in the plot, and rumours of an attempt had been rife in Munich and

Berlin twenty-four hours before the action began. Although Dolfuss died of his wounds, the *putsch* failed. Mussolini, furious at Hitler's bad faith, had ordered Italian divisions to the Austrian frontier, promising Italian support in the defence of Austria's independence.

The Nazis had over-reached themselves, and Hitler had promptly to repudiate all connection with the conspiracy. The initial announcement of the official German News Agency, couched in enthusiastic terms, was hurriedly suppressed; the murderers of Dolfuss were surrendered to the Austrian Government; the German Minister in Vienna was recalled in disgrace; and Hitler appointed Papen to go to Vienna as Minister-Extraordinary in order to repair the damage. The choice of Papen, a Catholic, a Conservative and Vice-Chancellor in Hitler's Cabinet, was intended to conciliate the Austrians; at the same time it was a convenient way of getting rid of the man who had made the Marburg speech and who had been lucky to escape with his life on the week-end of 30 June. These hasty measures tided over the crisis and preserved appearances. But it had been made plain enough to Hitler that the opposition to his schemes would have to be divided before it could be overcome.

For the rest of 1934 the unanimity of the other Powers in face of further German adventures was strengthened, rather than weakened, but the year ended not without some cause for congratulation on Hitler's part. On 9 October Louis Barthou, the energetic French Foreign Minister, who stood for a policy of firmness in face of Nazi demands, was assassinated at Marseilles. His successor at the Quai d'Orsay was Pierre Laval, a master of *combinazioni* and shady political deals. Despite appearances, Hitler held to his belief he had in 1927 when he told Otto Strasser: "There is no solidarity in Europe; there is only submission." This was the essential premise on which all his plans depended; the next year, 1935, was to show how just was his diagnosis.

From the summer of 1934 the principal object of the Western Powers' diplomacy was to persuade Germany to sign an Eastern Locarno pact of mutual assistance which would include Russia, Germany, Poland, Czechoslovakia and the other states of Eastern Europe and would involve the same obligation of automatic assistance in the case of an attack.

Hitler had no intention of entering into any such scheme: it was not aggression that he feared, but checks upon his freedom of action. German opposition, which had already been made clear in 1934, was powerfully assisted by that of Poland which continued its policy of balancing between

Moscow and Berlin, a policy that fatally overestimated Poland's strength, and fatally underestimated the danger from Germany.

Hitler courted the Poles assiduously, constantly urging on them the common interest Poland and Germany had in opposing Russia. Goering, who was used by Hitler in the role of a candid friend of the Poles, spoke plainly when he visited Warsaw at the end of January, 1935. In his talks with Polish generals and with Marshal Pilsudski, Goering "outlined far-reaching plans, almost suggesting . . . a joint attack on Russia. He gave it to be understood that the Ukraine would become a Polish sphere of influence and North-western Russia would be Germany's." In 1935 relations between the two governments became steadily closer, and after a visit of Foreign Minister Beck to Berlin in July the communiqué spoke of "a far-reaching agreement of views." The attention Hitler paid to Polish-German relations was to repay him handsomely.

Meanwhile, the British and French Governments renewed their attempts to reach a settlement with Germany, proposing that the existing Locarno Pact of mutual assistance, which applied to Western Europe, be strengthened by the conclusion of an agreement to cover unprovoked aggression from the air. At the same time it was to be supplemented by two similar pacts of mutual assistance, one dealing with Eastern Europe, the other with Central Europe.

Hitler faced a difficult decision. German rearmament had reached a stage where further concealment would prove a hindrance. It seemed clear that the Western Powers would waive their objections to German rearmament in return for Germany's accession to their proposals for strengthening and extending collective security. Yet Hitler had to avoid tying his hands, and also meet the need of some dramatic stroke of foreign policy to gratify the mood of nationalist expectation in Germany. On both these grounds a bold unilateral repudiation of the disarmament clauses of the Treaty of Versailles would suit him very much better than negotiations with the Western Powers, in which he would be bound to make concessions. Could he afford the risk?

Hitler's first reply welcomed the idea of extending the Locarno Pact to include air attack. The German Government invited the British to continue discussions on the other two proposed pacts, and a visit to Berlin by the British Foreign Minister, Sir John Simon, was arranged for 7 March. Before the visit could take place, however, on 4 March the British Government published its own plans for increased armaments, basing this on "the fact that Germany was . . . rearming openly on a large scale, despite the provisions of Part V of the Treaty of Versailles." Great indignation was at once expressed in Germany, and Hitler contracted a "chill" which made it necessary to postpone Sir John Simon's visit. On the 9th the German Government officially notified foreign governments that a German Air Force was already in existence. This seems to have been a kite with which to test the Western Powers' reaction. As Sir John Simon told the House of Commons that he and Mr. Eden were still proposing to go to Berlin and nothing else happened, it appeared safe to risk a more sensational announcement the next week-end. On 16 March, 1935, the German Government proclaimed its intention of building up a peacetime army of thirty-six divisions, with a strength of five hundred and fifty thousand men.

Four days before, the French Government had doubled the period of Army service and reduced the age of enlistment to make good the fall in conscripts due to the reduced birth-rate of 1914-1918. This served Hitler as a pretext for his own action. Germany, Hitler declared, was the one Power which had disarmed; now that the other Powers were actually beginning to increase their armaments, she had no option but to follow suit.

The announcement was received with enthusiasm in Germany, and on 17 March, Heroes Memorial Day, a brilliant military ceremony in the State Opera House celebrated the rebirth of the German Army. In this first open breach of the Treaty's provisions, Hitler had anticipated protests, what mattered was the action with which the Treaty Powers proposed to support their protests.

The result more than justified the risks. The British Government, after making a solemn protest, proceeded to ask whether the Fuehrer was still ready to receive Sir John Simon. The French appealed to the League, and an extraordinary session of the Council was at once summoned. But the French Note, too, spoke of the need to dispel the tension which had arisen. This was not the language of men who intended to enforce their protests. When Sir John Simon and Mr. Eden at last visited Berlin at the end of March they found Hitler charming, but perfectly sure of himself and firm in his refusal to consider any pact of mutual assistance which included the Soviet Union, or to discuss German rearmament. It was the Englishmen who had come to ask for cooperation and Hitler who was in the advantageous position of being able to say "no," without having anything to ask in return. The very presence of the British representatives in Berlin, after the announcement of 16 March, was a triumph for his diplomacy.

On 21 May Hitler appeared before the Reichstag to deliver a long and carefully prepared speech on foreign policy. It is a speech worth studying, for in it are to be found most of the tricks with which Hitler lulled the suspicions and raised the hopes of the gullible. His answer to the censure of the Powers was not defiance, but redoubled assurances of peace, an appeal to reason, justice and conscience. The new Germany, he protested, was misunderstood, and his own attitude misrepresented.

No man ever spoke with greater feeling of the horror and stupidity of war than Adolf Hitler.

> The blood shed on the European continent in the course of the last three hundred years bears no proportion to the national result of the events. In the end France has remained France, Germany Germany, Poland Poland and Italy Italy. . . . It has not substantially altered their fundamental characters. If these States had applied merely a fraction of their sacrifices to wiser purposes the success would certainly have been greater and more permanent. . . . If the nations attach so much importance to an increase in the number of the inhabitants of a country they can achieve it without tears in a simpler and more natural way. A sound social policy, by increasing the readiness of a nation to have children, can give its own people more children in a few years than the number of aliens that could be conquered and made subject to that nation by war.

Despite the failure of the other Powers to carry out their obligation to disarm, Germany was still prepared to co-operate in the search for security. But she had rooted objections to the proposal of multilateral pacts, for this was the way to spread, not to localize war. Moreover, in the east of Europe, Hitler declared, there was a special case, Bolshevik Russia, pledged to destroy European independence, a State with which a National Socialist Germany could never come to terms.

In place of the "unrealistic" multilateral treaties Hitler offered non-aggression pacts with Germany's neighbours . . . . Germany's improved relations with Poland, he did not fail to add, showed how great a contribution such pacts could make to the cause of peace: this was the practical way in which Germany set about removing international misunderstandings.

Hitler supported his offer with the most convincing display of good-will. The fact that Germany had repudiated the disarmament clauses of the Treaty of Versailles did not mean that she had anything but the strictest regard for the Treaty's other provisions—including the demilitarization of the Rhineland—or for her other obligations. She had no intention of annexing Austria and was perfectly ready to strengthen the Locarno Pact by an agreement on air attack. She was ready to agree to the abolition of heavy arms, to limit the use of the bomber and poison gas by international convention; indeed, to accept an over-all limitation of armaments provided it applied to all the Powers. Hitler laid particular stress on his willingness to limit German naval power to thirty-five per cent of the strength of the British Navy. He ended with a confession of his faith in peace. ". . . That Germany may make an imperishable contribution to this great work is our proud hope and our unshakable belief."

Hitler's mastery of the language of Geneva was unequalled. His grasp of the mood of public opinion in the Western democracies was startling. He understood intuitively their longing for peace, the idealism of the pacifists, the uneasy conscience of the liberals, the reluctance of the great mass of their peoples to look beyond their own private affairs. At this stage these were greater assets than the panzer divisions and bomber fleets he was still building, and Hitler used them with the same skill he had shown in playing on German grievances and illusions.

Although Hitler's attitude towards Britain was modified later by growing contempt for the weakness of her policy and the credulity of her governments, the idea of an alliance with her attracted him throughout his life. It was an alliance which could only, in Hitler's view, be made on condition that Britain accepted the prospect of a German hegemony on the Continent and left Germany a free hand in attaining it. Yet there was a section of British opinion sufficiently impressed by Hitler's arguments to be attracted to the idea of a settlement which would have left him virtually a free hand in Central and Eastern Europe, and Hitler was remarkably successful for a time in weakening the opposition of Great Britain to the realization of his aims. The policy of appeasement represented the acceptance by the British Government, at least in part, of Hitler's view of what British policy should be.

The speech of 21 May had been intended to influence opinion in Great Britain in Hitler's favour. The quickness of the British reaction was surprising. During his visit to Berlin in March Sir John Simon had been sufficiently impressed by a hint thrown out by the Fuehrer to suggest that German representatives should come to London to discuss the possibility of a naval agreement between the two countries.

Early in June Ribbentrop, whom Hitler now began to use for special missions, flew to London and scored a personal triumph over the German Foreign Office when he returned with the British signature of a naval pact. This bound the Germans not to build beyond thirty-five per cent of Britain's naval strength, but it tacitly recognized Germany's right to begin naval rearmament and specifically agreed that Germany could build up to one hundred per cent of the submarine strength of the British Commonwealth. The affront to Britain's partners, France and Italy, neither of whom had been consulted, was open and much resented. The unanimity of the Powers' condemnation of German rearmament was destroyed. The British Government, in its eagerness to secure a private advantage, had given a disastrous impression of bad faith. Like Poland, but without the excuse of Poland's difficult position, Great Britain had accepted Hitler's carefully calculated offer without a thought of its ultimate consequences.

In September the Fuehrer attended the Party's rally at Nuremberg. For the first time detachments of the new German Army took part in the parade and Hitler glorified the German military tradition: ". . . When we looked upon the Army our faith in the future of our people was always reinforced. This old glorious Army is not dead; it only slept, and now it has arisen again in you."

The Reichstag was summoned to Nuremberg for a special session, and Hitler presented for its unanimous approval the Nuremberg Laws directed against the Jews, the first depriving Germans of Jewish blood of their citizenship, the second forbidding marriages between Germans and Jews and the employment of German servants by Jews. These laws, Hitler declared, "repay the debt of gratitude to the movement under whose symbol (the Swastika, now adopted as the national emblem) Germany has recovered her freedom."

While Hitler was making use of his State power to gratify his hatred of the Jews, a quarrel began at Geneva which gave him opportunity to extend his power outside the German frontiers of 1914.

After the murder of Dolfuss, Mussolini had been outspoken in his dislike and contempt for the "barbarians" north of the Alps, and he had co-operated with the other Powers in their condemnation of Germany's unilateral decision to rearm. Mussolini, however, had long been contemplating a showy success for his régime in Abyssinia and it is almost certain that he hoped to profit by French and British preoccupation with German rearmament to carry out his adventure on the cheap.

Abyssinia had appealed to the League in March. In September the British Government, having just made a sensational gesture of appeasement to Germany by the Naval Treaty of June, astonished the world for the second time by taking the lead in demanding the imposition of sanctions against Italy. To the French, who judged Germany, not Italy, the greater danger to Europe, the British appeared to be standing on their heads and looking at events upside down. The Baldwin Government made the worst of both worlds. By insisting on the imposition of sanctions Great Britain made an enemy of Mussolini and destroyed all hope of a united front against German aggression. By her refusal to drive home the policy of sanctions, in face of Mussolini's bluster, she dealt the authority of the League as well as her own prestige a fatal blow, and destroyed all hope of finding in collective security an effective alternative to the united front of the Great Powers against German aggression. Thus the farce of sanctions dragged on to its inconclusive and discreditable end with the ultimate beneficiary of these blunders not Mussolini, but Hitler.

The advantages to be derived from the quarrel between Italy and the Western Powers did not escape Hitler and the further development of the dispute gave him greater cause for satisfaction. Not only was Italy driven into a position of isolation, in which Mussolini was bound to look more favourably on German offers of support, but the League of Nations never recovered. French confidence in England was further shaken, and the belief that Great Britain was a spent force in international politics received damning confirmation.

As Mussolini later acknowledged, it was in the autumn of 1935 that the idea of the Rome-Berlin Axis was born. No less important was the encouragement which the feebleness of the opposition to aggression gave Hitler to pursue his policy without regard to the risks. "There was now, as it turned out," wrote Sir Winston Churchill, "little hope of averting war or of postponing it by a trial of strength equivalent to war. Almost all that remained open to France and Britain was to await the moment of the challenge and do the best they could."

By March, 1936, Hitler judged the moment opportune for another *coup* in foreign policy. There had been ample warning of where his next move would be. In his speech of 21 May, 1935, he had put forward the view that the alliance concluded between France and Russia "brought an element of legal insecurity into the Locarno Pact," with the obligations of which, he argued, it was incompatible. After an interview with Hitler on 21 November the French Ambassador,

M. François-Poncet, reported to Paris that Hitler had made up his mind to use the pretext of the Franco-Soviet treaty to denounce Locarno and reoccupy the demilitarized zone of the Rhineland.

The treaty between France and Russia had still not been ratified. It had become a subject of bitter controversy in French politics, and Hitler was thus deliberately choosing as his pretext an issue which divided France; nor was he ignorant of the fact that in London, too, there was no enthusiasm for France's latest commitment.

On 11 February, 1936, the Franco-Soviet treaty was finally ratified and Hitler's reply, as François-Poncet had foreseen, was to march German troops into the demilitarized Rhineland. It was a proposal which thoroughly alarmed his generals. German rearmament was still far from complete and the first conscripts had only been taken into the Army a few months before. If the French and their allies marched, the Germans would be heavily outnumbered, and the reoccupation of the Rhineland represented not only a breach of the Treaty of Versailles but a *casus foederis* under the Locarno Pact. Hitler did not dispute these facts; he based his decision on the belief that the French would not march—and he was right.

On the morning of 7 March, as the German soldiers were marching into the Rhineland, greeted with flowers flung by wildly enthusiastic crowds, Neurath, German Foreign Minister, presented the British, French and Italian Ambassadors with a document which contained, in addition to Germany's grounds for denouncing the Locarno Pact, new and far-reaching peace proposals. As M. François-Poncet described it, "Hitler struck his adversary in the face, and as he did so declared: 'I bring you proposals for peace!' " In place of the discarded Locarno Treaty, Hitler offered a pact of nonaggression to France and Belgium, valid for twenty-five years and supplemented by the air pact to which Britain attached so much importance.

At noon Hitler addressed the Reichstag. His speech was another masterpiece of reasonableness.

. . . Why should it not be possible to put an end to this useless strife (between France and Germany) which has lasted for centuries and which has never been and never will be finally decided by either of the two nations concerned? Why not replace it by the rule of reason? The German people have no interest in seeing the French people suffer. And what advantage can come to France when Germany is in misery? . . . Why should it not be possible to lift the general problem of conflicting interests between the European states above the sphere of passion and unreason and consider it in the calm light of a higher vision?

It was France, Hitler declared, who had betrayed Europe by her alliance with the Asiatic power of Bolshevism, pledged to destroy all the values of European civilization—just as it was France who, by the same action, had invalidated the Locarno Pact. Once again, reluctantly but without flinching, he must bow to the inevitable and take the necessary steps to defend Germany's national interests. He ended with the sacred vow to work now more than ever to further the cause of mutual understanding between the nations of Europe, but the roar of enthusiasm with which the packed Reichstag welcomed the announcement of the reoccupation of the Rhineland belied the words of peace. It was the assertion of German power, not the offer of peace, that brought the Reichstag to its feet, stamping and shouting in their delight.

Hitler later admitted: "The forty-eight hours after the march into the Rhineland were the most nerve-racking in my life. If the French had then marched into the Rhineland we would have had to withdraw with our tails between our legs, for the military resources at our disposal would have been wholly inadequate for even a moderate resistance." Events, however, followed exactly the same pattern as the year before. There were anxious consultations between Paris and London; appeals for reason and calm, and talk of the new opportunities for peace offered by Hitler's proposals. The Locarno Powers conferred; the Council of the League conferred; the International Court at The Hague was ready to confer, and Germany's action was again solemnly condemned and the censure again rejected by Hitler. But no one marched—except the Germans.

Meanwhile Hitler dissolved the Reichstag and invited the German people to pass judgment on his policy. He came before them as the Peacemaker. " . . . Peoples must find a new relation to each other, some new form must be created. . . . They make a mistake who think that over the entrance to this new order there can stand the word 'Versailles.' That would be, not the foundation stone of the new order, but its gravestone."

If the election figures seemed to show a suspicious unanimity, there can be little doubt that a majority of the German people approved Hitler's action, or that it raised the Fuehrer to a new peak of popularity.

Meanwhile the Western Powers continued a futile exchange of notes with Berlin, and the other European governments began to accommodate themselves to the new balance of power.

No government was more uneasily conscious of the meaning of these events than the Austrian. The premise upon which Austrian independence was based, the unity and military superiority of Italy, France and Great Britain in face of Germany, was being destroyed. Sooner or later Mussolini's 1934 guarantee of Italian divisions on the Brenner frontier would be withdrawn.

In 1936 Papen, minister in Vienna, whose aim was to undermine Austrian independence from within and to bring about the Anschluss peacefully, gained his first success when on 13 May, Prince Starhemberg, the Austrian Vice-Chancellor and an outspoken opponent of the Austrian Nazis, was forced to resign.

The Austro-German Agreement of 11 July, 1936, was designed on the surface to ease and improve relations between the two countries, reaffirming Hitler's recognition of Austria's full sovereignty; promising non-intervention in each other's internal affairs; and covering her special relationship with Italy and Hungary established by the Rome Protocols of 1934. Most important of the secret clauses, the Austrian Government agreed to give representatives of the so-called National Opposition in Austria, "respectable" crypto-Nazis like Glaise-Horstenau and later Seyss-Inquart, a share in political responsibility.

Ostensibly, Austro-German relations were now placed on a level satisfactory to both sides. But, in fact, the Agreement, as it was exploited by the Germans, marked a big step forward in that policy of capturing Austria by peaceful methods to which Hitler resorted after the failure of the *putsch* in July, 1934. Also, the Agreement's signature materially improved Hitler's prospects of a *rapprochement* with Italy. Here again he had extraordinary luck when the League Powers tacitly admitted defeat and withdrew the sanctions they had tried to impose on Italy. Less than a fortnight later, on 17 July, civil war broke out in Spain and created a situation from which Hitler was able to draw even greater advantages than from Mussolini's Abyssinian adventure.

Hitler was at Bayreuth when a German business man from Morocco and the local Nazi leader there arrived with a personal letter from General Franco. After Hitler's return from the theatre he sent for Goering and his War Minister, Blomberg. That night he decided to give active help to Franco. In the course of the next three years German aid to Franco was never sufficient to win the war for him or even to equal the forces sent by Mussolini. But the advantages Germany secured in return were disproportionate—economic advantages (valuable sources of raw materials in Spanish mines); useful experience in training her airmen and testing equipment such as tanks in battle conditions; above all, strategic and political advantages.

France, for geographical reasons alone, was more deeply interested in what happened in Spain than any other of the Great Powers, yet the ideological character of the Spanish Civil War divided, instead of uniting, French opinion, and many Frenchmen were prepared to support Franco as a way of hitting at their own left-wing Blum Government. The Spanish Civil War exacerbated all those factors of disunity in France upon which Hitler had always hoped to play.

The common policy of Italy and Germany towards Spain created one of the main foundations on which the Rome-Berlin Axis was built, and the Spanish Civil War provided ample scope for such co-operation.

In September, 1936, Hitler judged circumstances favourable for creating a closer relationship between Germany and Italy in order to exploit a situation in which the two countries had begun to follow parallel courses. The July Agreement between Germany and Austria removed the biggest obstacle to an understanding between Rome and Berlin, and on 29 June the German Ambassador conveyed to Ciano, the Italian Foreign Minister, an offer from Hitler to consider the recognition of the new Italian Empire—a point on which the Duce was notoriously touchy—whenenver Mussolini wished. In September Hitler sent Hans Frank, his Minister of Justice, who spoke Italian fluently, on an exploratory mission to Rome.

Frank saw Mussolini in the Palazzo Venezia on 23 September. He brought a cordial invitation from the Fuehrer for both Mussolini and Ciano to visit Germany. After disclaiming any German interests or claims in the Mediterranean, declaring Germany now considered the Austrian question to have been settled, and after suggesting a common policy in presenting their colonial demands, Frank concluded by expressing Hitler's belief in the need for increasingly close collaboration between Germany and Italy. Throughout the interview Mussolini affected a certain disinterestedness, but a month later Ciano set out for Germany.

After a talk with Neurath, in Berlin, Ciano visited Hitler himself at Berchtesgaden on 24 October. Although Hitler monopolized the conversation he was obviously at pains to impress Ciano with his friendliness.

The gist of Hitler's remarks was the need for Italy and Germany to create a common front against Bolshevism and against the Western Powers. If England faced a strong German-Italian bloc, she might well seek to come to terms with it. If not, then Germany and Italy would have the power to defeat her.

> German and Italian rearmament [Hitler declared] is proceeding much more rapidly than rearmament can in Great Britain, where it is not only a case of producing ships, guns and aeroplanes, but also of undertaking psychological rearmament, which is much longer and more difficult. In three years Germany will be ready, in four years more than ready; if five years are given, better still. . . .

By the end of 1936 Hitler, by skilfully exploiting Mussolini's situation, had succeeded in establishing one of the two alliances on which he had counted in *Mein Kampf*. But the second alliance, that with Britain, still eluded him.

In August Hitler had determined on a new approach to London, and appointed Joachim von Ribbentrop as the German Ambassador to the Court of St. James. An ambitious man, Ribbentrop persuaded the new Chancellor that he could provide more reliable information about what was happening abroad than reached him through the official channels of the Foreign Office. With Party funds he set up a Ribbentrop Bureau on the Wilhelmstrasse.

Arrogant, vain, humourless and spiteful, Ribbentrop was one of the worst choices Hitler ever made for high office. But he shared many of Hitler's own social resentments (especially against the regular Foreign Service), he was prepared to prostrate himself before the Fuehrer's genius, and his appointment enabled Hitler to take the conduct of relations with Great Britain much more closely into his own hands.

What puzzled Hitler and Ribbentrop was the fact that although the British were only too prepared to put off awkward decisions, they were wary of committing themselves to co-operate with Germany. Hitler was reluctant to take open action which would alienate the British in the hope that he might still win them over, yet he was tempted at times to regard Britain as "finished" as a World Power. This alternation of moods never wholly disappeared from Hitler's ambivalent attitude towards Britain.

Hitler's best argument with the Conservative Government in Britain was one which he used more frequently after the outbreak of the Spanish Civil War: the common interest of the European States in face of Communism. The Spanish Civil War sharpened the sense of ideological conflict in Western Europe and many people in England as well as in France, were impressed by Hitler's anti-Communism; it served the same purpose as Russia's own peace campaign and similar moves after the Second World War. Again and again Hitler used the example of Spain as a land ravaged by Bolshevism, and pointed to the Popular Front Government in France as the equivalent of the Girondins who were replaced by the more extreme Jacobins. "Perhaps the time is coming more quickly than we think," he declared in November, 1936, "when the rest of Europe will no longer regard with resentment the founding of a National Socialist German Reich, but will rejoice that this dam was raised against the Bolshevik flood. . . ."

Anti-Communism could also be used to provide the basis for the power-bloc of which Hitler had spoken to Ciano. For months Ribbentrop had been working—quite independently of the German Foreign Office—to reach agreement with Japan. In November he succeeded, and flew to Berlin from London for the signature of the Anti-Comintern Pact. The ideological objectives of the pact—the defeat of the Communist "world-conspiracy"—gave it a universal character which a straightforward agreement aimed against Russia could not have had. It was expressly designed to secure the adherence of other States, and it was not long before Hitler began to collect new signatories. Besides the public provisions, there was also a secret Protocol which bound both parties to sign no political treaties with the U.S.S.R. In the event of an unprovoked attack or threat of attack by Russia on either Power, the Protocol added, each agreed to "take no measures which would tend to ease the situation of the U.S.S.R." This was still vague, but the statement made by Ribbentrop on the day the treaty was signed left little doubt that Germany hoped to make more of this new political grouping.

Hitler rounded off his first four years of office by a long speech to the Reichstag on 30 January, 1937, in which he formally withdrew Germany's signature from those clauses of the Treaty of Versailles which had denied her equality of rights and laid on her the responsibility for the war.

At Nuremberg in September, 1936, impatient with the difficulties raised by the economic experts, Hitler proclaimed a Four-Year Plan and put Goering in charge fully armed with the powers to secure results. German economy was henceforward subordinated to one purpose, preparation for war. It is this fact that explains why, although Germany made so remarkable an economic recovery . . . this was reflected, not in the standard of living which was deliberately stabilized at a low level, but in her growing military strength.

Moreover, the biggest single factor in the recovery of confidence and faith in Germany was the sense of this power, a renewed confidence and faith in "the German mission," expressed in an increasingly aggressive nationalism which had little use for the rights of other, less powerful nations. The psychology of Nazism, no less than Nazi economics, was one of preparation for war. Both depended for their continued success upon the maintenance of a national spirit and a national effort which in the end must find expression in aggressive action. War, the belief in violence and the right of the stronger, were the essence of Nazism. Recognition of the benefits which Hitler's rule brought to Germany in its first four years needs to be tempered therefore by the realization that for the Fuehrer—and for a considerable section of the German people—these were the by-products of his true purpose, the creation of an instrument of power with which to realize a policy of expansion that in the end admitted no limits.

Although throughout 1937 Hitler was still at pains to protest his love of peace, there was a new note of impatience in his voice. The demand for the return of Germany's colonies was raised with increasing frequency in 1937, and at the end of the year, speaking in Augsburg, Hitler declared: ". . .We shall voice our demand for living-room in colonies more and more loudly till the world cannot but recognize our claim."

There were two particular grounds for Hitler's confidence: the progress of German rearmament, and the consolidation of the Axis. Goering, now the economic dictator of Germany, had as little respect for economics as Hitler. His methods were crude, but not ineffective. At a meeting of ministers over which he had presided just before his appointment as Commissioner for the Four-Year Plan, Goering insisted that the shortages of raw materials must be overcome and that there could be no question of slowing down rearmament.

The wastefulness and danger of Hitler's and Goering's programme of autarky and of the search for *ersatz* raw materials were criticized by Dr. Schacht at the time, but his economic arguments fell on deaf ears. They were men in a hurry, indifferent to the cost or to the long-term economic consequences, provided they got the arms they wanted quickly. Goering continued to ride rough-shod over economic theories and economic facts alike. By the spring of 1939 Hitler had carried out an expansion of German military power unequalled in German history.

The consolidation of the Rome-Berlin Axis was marked by increased consultation between the two parties and frequent exchanges of visits culminating in Mussolini's State reception in Germany in September, and Italy's signature of the Anti-

Comintern Pact in November. The initiative still came from Berlin, and—as the captured diplomatic documents show—Hitler watched with some anxiety the attempts of the British and French to renew friendly relations with the Duce.

On 2 January, 1937, Ciano signed a "gentlemen's agreement" with England in which each country recognized the other's vital interests in the freedom of the Mediterranean, and agreed that there should be no alteration in the *status quo* in that region. Shortly afterwards Hitler sent Goering to Rome on an exploratory mission. It is evident that each side regarded with some suspicion the other's attempts to reach an understanding with England. Above all, Austria was still a danger-point in German-Italian relations. At his second conversation with the Duce, Goering confined himself to urging Mussolini to bring pressure to bear on Austria to observe the terms of the Austro-German Agreement, and although he made plain Germany's dislike of the Schuschnigg Government, he added the assurance that for Hitler's part there would be no surprises as far as Austria was concerned. According to Hassell, the German Ambassador, of special importance was Goering's clear statement "any German action on the Austrian question aiming at a change in the present situation would take place only in consultation with Rome. . . ."

These suspicions and difficulties were not easily removed. The Italians quickly took offence at any slighting reference, such as the Germans were only too prone to make, to their martial qualities, and Goering's talks with Mussolini showed that, over Austria, Hitler still needed to proceed with care.

None the less the pull of events was too strong for Mussolini. His anxiety to be on the winning side and to share in the plucking of the decadent democracies, pointed to the advantages of the partnership which Hitler persistently pressed on him. On 23 September the Duce set out for Germany in a new uniform specially designed for the occasion. For Mussolini it was the beginning of that surrender of independence which led his régime to disaster and himself to the gibbet in the Piazzale Loreto in Milan. . . .

Hitler received the Duce at Munich, where the Nazi Party put on a superbly organized show, including a ceremonial parade of S.S. troops. Mussolini had hardly recovered his breath when he was whisked away to a display of Germany's military power at the Army manoeuvres in Mecklenburg, and of her industrial resources in the Krupp factories at Essen. The visit reached its climax in Berlin, where the capital was put *en fête* to receive the impressionable Duce, and the two dictators stood side by side to address a crowd of eight hundred thousand on the *Maifeld*. Before the speeches were over a terrific thunderstorm scattered the audience in pandemonium, and in the confusion Mussolini was left to return to Berlin alone, soaked to the skin and in a state of collapse. But he returned bewitched by the display of power which had been carefully staged for him. There had been no time for diplomatic conversations but Hitler had achieved something more valuable than a dozen protocols: he had stamped on Mussolini's mind an indelible impression of German might from which the Duce was never able to set himself free.

On his part, Hitler's admiration for Mussolini was unfeigned. Mussolini, like himself—and like Stalin, whom Hitler also admired—was a man of the people; Hitler felt at ease with him as he never felt when with members of the traditional ruling classes. After the German visit Hitler presented the Axis to the world as a solid bloc of a hundred and fifteen million people.

Three weeks later Ribbentrop appeared in Rome to urge the Duce to put Italy's signature to the year-old Anti-Comintern Pact between Germany and Japan. Ribbentrop was disarmingly frank. He had failed in his mission to London, he told Mussolini, and had to recognize that the interests of Germany and Great Britain were irreconcilable. This was excellent hearing for the Duce, and, on 6 November, he made little difficulty about signing the Pact.

Ribbentrop's report on Mussolini's discussion of Austria can only have delighted Hitler. Now, in his November conversation, Mussolini told Ribbentrop that he was tired of mounting guard over Austrian independence, especially if the Austrians no longer wanted their independence.

> . . . France knows that if a crisis should arise in Austria, Italy would do nothing. This was said to Schuschnigg, too, on the occasion of the Venice conversation. We cannot impose independence on Austria. . . . It is necessary therefore to abide by the formula: nothing will be done without previous exchange of information.

Mussolini's embarrassment is obvious in every line of Ciano's minute, and was certainly not lost on Hitler. His exploitation of the quarrel between Italy and the Western Powers was beginning to yield dividends; in his cultivation of Mussolini's friendship Hitler had found the key to unlock the gate to Central Europe. Four months later the gate was swung back without effort, and German troops stood on the old Austro-Italian frontier of the Brenner Pass.

Hitler's interest in Italy did not lead him to neglect Poland, for the Rhineland reoccupation jolted Beck's complacency and under the immediate shock the Poles renewed their offer to the French to march.

Well aware of the stiffening in the Polish attitude, Hitler and Ribbentrop gave the most convincing assurances to the Polish Under-Secretary for Foreign Affairs in Berlin, August, 1936. In Danzig, Hitler declared, Germany would act entirely by way of an understanding with Poland, and with respect for all her rights. Ribbentrop, dismissing Danzig as a question of secondary importance, laid heavy emphasis on the common interests of Poland and Germany in face of the menace of Bolshevism, and shortly after Goering's return from Rome at the end of January Hitler sent him to Warsaw, where he used that bluff hypocrisy which was his diplomatic stock-in-trade, to disarm Polish suspicions.

"Germany (Goering told Marshal Smigly-Rydz) was completely reconciled to her present territorial status. Germany would not attack Poland. . . . 'We do not want the Corridor. I say that sincerely and categorically; we do not need the Corridor.' He could not give proof of this. . . ."

Indeed, Goering excelled himself on this occasion. He told the Poles that Germany needed a strong Poland; a weak Poland would be a standing invitation to Russian aggression, and for that reason Germany had no quarrel with the Franco-Polish alliance.

Hitler followed these reassurances by offering to negotiate a minorities treaty with Poland, which was signed in Berlin on 5 November—the date, as we shall see, is worth noting. So long as Poland refused to join forces against Germany, it was impossible to build up effective resistance to Hitler's eastern ambitions. If Italy's friendship was the key to Austria, Poland's was one of the keys to Czechoslovakia.

The German denunciation of the Locarno Pact had been followed by the reversion of Belgium to a professed policy of neutrality, which, in King Leopold's words, "should aim resolutely at placing us outside any dispute of our neighbours." The withdrawal of Belgium, was a further stage in the disintegration of the system of collective security. Yet London and Paris still did not give up their attempts to reach some form of general agreement with Hitler. A new impetus was given to these dragging negotiations by the replacement of Mr. Baldwin by Mr. Neville Chamberlain as Prime Minister at the end of May, 1937. Baldwin has been characterized by Sir Winston Churchill as possessing a genius for waiting upon events, knowing little of Europe and disliking what he knew.

"Neville Chamberlain, on the other hand, was alert, business-like, opinionated and self-confident in a very high degree. Unlike Baldwin, he conceived himself able to comprehend the whole field of Europe. . . . His all-pervading hope was to go down in history as the great Peacemaker; and for this he was prepared to strive continually in the teeth of facts, and face great risks for himself and his country."

The first fruits of Chamberlain's policy were the visit of Lord Halifax, then Lord President of the Council, to Germany in November, 1937. Hitler was willing to receive Lord Halifax at Berchtesgaden. Halifax's opening remark, however, that he brought no proposals, but had only come to sound out the ground, put the German leader in a bad temper. It was impossible, he declared, to make agreements with countries where political decisions were dictated by Party considerations. . . . The British could not get used to the fact that Germany was no longer weak and divided; any proposal he made was automatically suspected, and so on. He brought up the question of colonies, only to declare that the British were not prepared to discuss it reasonably; at the same time, he was careful to avoid defining Germany's colonial claims.

The German account of the interview gives the impression that Hitler threw doubt on the value of attempting to reach a comprehensive settlement, insisting that diplomatic exchanges would be preferable to the direct negotiations proposed by the British. Hitler could scarcely have expressed his indifference more plainly.

He was by now strong enough to risk taking action without worrying unduly about what Britain and France would do. Sure of himself and contemptuous of his opponents, Hitler was no longer concerned to keep up appearances.

Exactly a fortnight before he listened in irritation to Mr. Chamberlain's well-meant messages, on 5 November, Hitler disclosed something of his real intentions to a small group of men in a secret meeting at the Reich Chancellery. Only five others were present besides himself and Colonel Hossbach, the adjutant whose minutes are the source of our information. They were Field-Marshal von Blomberg, the German War Minister; Colonel-General von Fritsch, C.-in-C. of the Army; Admiral Raeder, C.-in-C. of the Navy; Goering, C.-in-C. of the Air Force, and Neurath, the Foreign Minister.

The Fuehrer was in an exalted mood, and from quarter past four in the afternoon to half past eight in the evening, Hitler talked as only he could talk. Silent and uneasy, the little group round the table listened without interrupting. Hitler put the problem in the simplest terms: how to secure and preserve the German racial community and enlarge it. Germany's future, Hitler declared, could only be safeguarded by acquiring additional *Lebensraum*. Such living space was to be sought, not overseas, but in Europe, and it could be found only at the risk of conflict. Germany had to reckon with two hate-inspired antagonists—not Russia despite all Hitler's talk of the Bolshevik menace, but Britain and France. Neither country was so strong as appeared. There were signs of disintegration in the British Empire—Ireland, India, the threat of Japanese power in the Far East and of Italian in the Mediterranean. France's situation was confronted with internal political difficulties. None the less, Britain, France, Russia and their satellites must be included as factors of power in Germany's political calculations.

Germany's problem, Hitler therefore concluded, could only be solved by means of force, and this was never without attendant risk. There remained to be answered the questions "when?" and "how?"

The peak of German power would be reached by the years 1943-1945. After that, equipment would become obsolete, and the rearmament of the other Powers would reduce the German lead. ". . . One thing only was certain, that we could not wait longer. . . . It was his unalterable resolve to solve Germany's problem of space at the latest by 1943-1945."

The first objective must be to overrun Austria and Czechoslovakia, and so secure Germany's eastern and southern flanks. He believed that Britain, and probably France too, had already written off the Czechs. In any case, France would be very unlikely to make an attack without British support, and the most that would be necessary would be to hold the western defence in strength. Once Austria and Czechoslovakia had been overrun, this would greatly increase Germany's economic resources and add twelve divisions to her army. . . .

In the case of France being crippled by internal division, that must be used at once for a blow against the Czechs, whenever it occurred. In case of a Mediterranean war, Hitler believed it coming nearer, and was resolved to take advantage of it, if need be as early as 1938. It was in Germany's interest to prolong the war in Spain. In such a war, the crucial point would be North Africa. Should such a conflict develop, Germany must take advantage of French and British preoccupations to attack the Czechs.

This, Hitler told his audience, was his political testament to the German nation in the event of his death. That events did not follow this course and that war came at a date, and as a result of a situation, he had failed to take into account, matters little, for Hitler was always prepared to profit by whatever might turn up. The importance of the conversation consists in the mood, the underlying attitude revealed. It provides documentary confirmation that despite the peace speeches and protestations of innocence, Hitler's original view as he had set is out in *Mein Kampf* ten years before had never changed: Germany's future lay in securing a continental *Lebensraum* by force. Secondly, it demonstrates that Hitler had already made up his mind that, whatever the occasion, the first stage in this solution must be the annexation of Austria and the overrunning of the whole of Czechoslovakia.

Finally, there is the date. Although Hitler fixed 1943-1945 as the latest period to take action, he added specifically that he was prepared to attack, in favourable circumstances, as early as 1938. The date at which he said this—November, 1937—points to the conclusion already suggested, that the end of 1937 marked a decisive stage in the development of Hitler's plans. The years of preparation and concealment were at an end: the Man of Peace gave way to the Man of Destiny.

CHAPTER SEVEN

THE DICTATOR

In the spring of 1938, on the eve of his greatest triumph, Adolf Hitler entered his fiftieth year. The falling lock of hair and the smudge of his moustache added nothing to a coarse and curiously undistinguished face, in which the eyes alone attracted attention. In appearance at least Hitler could claim to be a man of the people, a plebeian through and through, with none of the physical characteristics of the racial superiority he was always invoking. His face possessed an ability to express the most rapidly changing moods, at one moment smiling and charming, at another cold and imperious, cynical and sarcastic, or swollen and livid with rage.

Speech was the essential medium of his power, not only over his audiences but over his own temperament. Hitler talked incessantly, often using words less to communicate his thoughts than to release the hidden spring of his own and others' emotions, whipping himself and his audience into anger or exaltation by the sound of his voice. Talk had another function, too. "Words," he once said, "build bridges into unexplored regions." As he talked, conviction would grow until certainty came and the problem was solved.

Hitler always showed a distrust of argument and criticism. Unable to argue coolly himself, since his early days in Vienna his one resort had been to shout his opponent down. The questioning of his assumptions or of his facts rattled him and threw him out of his stride, for the introduction of intellectual processes of criticism and analysis marked the intrusion of hostile elements which disturbed the exercise of his power to manipulate emotion. Hence Hitler's hatred of the intellectuals: in the masses "instinct is supreme and from instinct comes faith. . . . While the healthy common folk instinctively close their ranks to form a community of the people, the intellectuals run this way and that, like hens in a poultry-yard. With them it is impossible to make history. . . ."

As an orator Hitler had obvious faults. His voice was harsh: he spoke at too great length; was often repetitive and verbose; lacked lucidity and frequently lost himself in cloudy phrases. But these, however, mattered little beside the extraordinary impression of force, the immediacy of passion, the intensity of hatred, fury and menace conveyed by the sound of the voice alone without regard to what he said.

One of the secrets of his mastery over a great audience was his instinctive sensitivity to the mood of a crowd, a flair for divining the hidden passions, resentments and longings in their minds.

One of his most bitter critics, Otto Strasser, wrote:

Hitler responds to the vibration of the human heart with the delicacy of a seismograph, or perhaps of a wireless receiving set, enabling him, with a certainty with which no conscious gift could endow him, to act as a loudspeaker proclaiming the most secret desires, the least admissible instincts, the sufferings and personal revolts of a whole nation. . . . I have been asked many times what is the secret of Hitler's extraordinary power as a speaker. I can only attribute it to his uncanny intuition, which infallibly diagnoses the ills from which his audience is suffering. If he tries to bolster up his argument with theories or quotations from books he has only imperfectly understood, he scarcely rises above a very poor mediocrity. . . . Adolf Hitler enters a hall. He sniffs the air. For a minute he gropes, feels his way, senses the atmosphere. Suddenly he bursts forth. His words go like an arrow to their target, he touches each private wound on the raw, liberating the mass unconscious, expressing its innermost aspirations, telling it what it most wants to hear."

As the French Ambassador, André François-Poncet, noted, there was in Hitler much of King Ludwig II of Bavaria. The fabulous dreams of a vast empire embracing all Europe and half Asia; the geopolitical fantasies of inter-continental wars and alliances; the plans for breeding an *élite,* biologically pre-selected, and founding a new Order to guard the Holy Grail of pure blood; the designs for reducing whole nations to slavery—all these are the fruits of a crude, disordered, but fertile imagination soaked in the German romanticism of the late nineteenth century, a caricature of Wagner, Nietzsche and Schopenhauer. After the outbreak of the war and the conquest of the greater part of Europe, all practical restraint upon Hitler's translation of his fantasies into brutal reality was removed. The S.S. extermination squads, the *Einsatzkommandos,* with their gas-vans and death camps; the planned elimination of the Jewish race; the treatment of the Poles and Russians, the Slav *Untermenschen*—these, too, were the fruits of Hitler's imagination.

All this combines to create a picture of which the best description is Hitler's own famous sentence: "I go the way that Providence dictates with the assurance of a sleepwalker." The former French Ambassador speaks of him as "a man possessed"; Hermann Rauschning writes: "Dostoevsky might well have invented him, with the morbid derangement and the pseudo-creativeness of his hysteria"; one of the Defence Counsel at the Nuremberg Trials, Dr. Dix, quoted a passage from Goethe's *Dichtung und Wahrheit* describing the Demoniac and applied this very aptly to Hitler. With Hitler, indeed, one is uncomfortably aware of never being far from the realm of the irrational.

But this is only half the truth about Hitler, for the baffling problem about this strange figure is to determine the degree to which he was swept along by a genuine belief in his own inspiration and the degree to which he deliberately exploited the irrational side of human nature, both in himself and others, with a shrewd calculation. For it is salutary to recall, before accepting the Hitler-Myth at anything like its face value, that it was Hitler who invented the myth, assiduously cultivating and manipulating it for his own ends. So long as he did this he was brilliantly successful; it was when he began to believe in his own magic, and accept the myth of himself as true, that his flair faltered.

It is this mixture of calculation and fanaticism, with the difficulty of telling where one ends and the other begins, which is the peculiar characteristic of Hitler's personality: to ignore or underestimate either element is to present a distorted picture.

The link between the different sides of Hitler's character wa his extraordinary capacity for self-dramatization. "This . . .ca pacity for self-delusion," Sir Nevile Henderson, the Britisl Ambassador, wrote, "was a regular part of his technique. I helped him both to work up his own passions and to make hi people believe anything that he might think good for them." Again and again one is struck by the way in which, having once decided rationally on a course of action, Hitler woul whip himself into a passion which enabled him to bear dow all opposition, and provided him with the motive power to enforce his will on others. This is the synthetic fury, which he could assume or discard at will. So long as good relations with Poland were necessary to his foreign policy he showed little interest in Poland's German minority. But when it suited hi purpose to make the "intolerable wrongs" of the Austrian Nazis, or the Germans in Czechoslovakia and Poland, a ground for action against these states, he worked himself into a frenzy of indignation, with the immediate—and calculated —result that London and Paris, in their anxiety for peace, exerted increased pressure on Prague or Warsaw to make further concessions to the German demands.

One of Hitler's most habitual devices was to accuse those who opposed or obstructed him of aggression and malice, and to pass rapidly from a tone of outraged innocence to the full thunders of moral indignation. In turn he denounced the Communists, the Jews, the Republican Government, or the Czechs, the Poles, and the Bolsheviks for their "intolerable" behaviour which forced him to take drastic action in selfdefense.

Hitler in a rage appeared to lose all control. His face became mottled and swollen with fury, he screamed at the top of his voice, spitting out a stream of abuse, waving his arms wildly and drumming on the table or the wall with his fists. As suddenly as he had begun he would stop, smooth down his hair, straighten his collar and resume a normal voice.

This skilful and deliberate exploitation of his own temperament extended to other moods than anger. When he wanted to persuade or win someone over he could display great charm. Until the last days of his life he retained an uncanny gift of personal magetism which defies analysis, but which many who met him have described. This was connected with the curious power of his eyes, which are persistently said to have had some sort of hypnotic quality. Similarly, when he wanted to frighten or shock, he showed himself a master of brutal and threatening language, as in the celebrated interviews with Schuschnigg and President Hacha.

Yet another role was the impression of concentrated willpower and intelligence, the leader in complete command of the situation and with a knowledge of the facts which dazzled the generals. To sustain this part he drew on his remarkable memory, which enabled him to reel off complicated orders of battle, technical specifications and long lists of names and dates without a moment's hesitation. Hitler cultivated this gift of memory assiduously. The fact that subsequently the details and figures which he cited were often found to contain inaccuracies did not matter: it was the immediate effect at which he aimed. The swiftness of the transition from one mood to another was startling: one moment his eyes would be filled with tears and pleading, the next blazing with fury, or glazed with the faraway look of the visionary.

Hitler, in fact, was a consummate actor, with the actor's and orator's facility for absorbing himself in a role and convincing himself of the truth of what he was saying at the time he said it. With the immense prestige of success behind him, and the resources of a powerful state at his command, there were few who could resist the impression of the piercing eyes, the Napoleonic pose and the "historic" personality.

Hitler had the gift of all great politicians for grasping the possibilities of a situation more swiftly than his opponents. He saw, as no other politician did, how to play on the grievances and resentments of the German people, as later he was to play on French and British fear of war and fear of Communism. His insistence upon preserving the forms of legality in the struggle for power showed a brilliant understanding of the way to disarm opposition, just as the way in which he undermined the independence of the German Army showed his grasp of the weaknesses of the German Officer Corps.

> No matter what you attempt [Hitler told Rauschning on one occasion], if an idea is not yet mature you will not be able to realize it. Then there is only one thing to do: have patience, wait, try again, wait again. In the subconscious, the work goes on. It matures, sometimes it dies. Unless I have the inner, incorruptible conviction: *this is the solution,* I do nothing. Not even if the whole Party tries to drive me into action.

Hitler knew how to wait. In 1939 he showed great patience while waiting for the situation to develop after direct negotiations with Poland had broken down and while the Western Powers were seeking to reach a settlement with Soviet Russia. Clear enough about his objectives, he contrived to keep his plans flexible.

Surprise was a favourite gambit of Hitler's, in politics, diplomacy and war: he gauged the psychological effect of sudden, unexpected hammer-blows in paralysing opposition. In war the psychological effect of the *blitzkrieg* was just as important in Hitler's eyes as the strategic: it gave the impression that the German military machine was more than life-size, that it possessed some virtue of invincibility against which ordinary men could not defend themselves.

To attend one of Hitler's big meetings was to go through an emotional experience, not to listen to an argument or a programme. Every device for heightening the emotional intensity, every trick of the theatre was used. The Nuremberg rallies held every year in September were masterpieces of theatrical art, with the most carefully devised effects. To see the films of the Nuremberg rallies even today is to be recaptured by the hypnotic effect of thousands of men marching in perfect order, the music of the massed bands, the forest of standards and flags, the vast perspectives of the stadium, the smoking torches, the dome of searchlights. The sense of power, of force and unity was irresistible, and all converged with a mounting crescendo of excitement on the supreme moment when the Fuehrer himself made his entry. Paradoxically, the man who was most affected by such spectacles was their originator, Hitler himself, and, as Rosenberg remarks in his memoirs, they played an indispensable part in the process of self-intoxication.

Hitler had grasped as no one before him what could be done with a combination of propaganda and terrorism. For the complement to the attractive power of the great spectacles was the compulsive power of the Gestapo, the S.S. and the concentration camp, heightened once again by skilful propaganda. Hitler was helped in this not only by his own perception of the sources of power in a modern urbanized mass-society, but also by possession of the technical means to manipulate them.

In making use of his formidable power Hitler had one supreme, and fortunately rare, advantage: he had neither scruples nor inhibitions. He was a man without roots, bound by no traditions, and felt respect neither for God nor man. Throughout his career Hitler showed himself prepared to seize any advantage that was to be gained by lying, cunning, treachery and unscrupulouness. He demanded the sacrifice of millions of German lives for the sacred cause of Germany, but in the last year of the war was ready to destroy Germany rather than surrender his power or admit defeat.

Wary and secretive, he entertained a universal distrust. He admitted no one to his counsels. He never let down his guard, or gave himself away. "He never," Schacht wrote, "let slip an unconsidered word. He never said what he did not intend to say and he never blurted out a secret. Everything was the result of cold calculation."

In Landsberg gaol, as long ago as 1924, Hitler had preserved his position in the Party by applying the principle of "divide and rule." After he became Chancellor there was always more than one office operating in any field. A dozen different agencies quarrelled over the direction of propaganda, of economic policy and the intelligence services. Before 1938 Hitler continually went behind the back of the Foreign Office to make use of Ribbentrop's special bureau or to get information through Party channels. The dualism of Party and State organizations was deliberate. In the end this reduced efficiency, but it strengthened Hitler's position by allowing him to play off one department against another. For the same reason Hitler insisted on dealing with ministers singly, so that they could not combine against him. "I have an old principle," he told Ludecke: "only to say what must be said to him who must know it, and only when he must know it." Only the Fuehrer kept all the threads in his hand and saw the whole design. If ever a man exercised absolute power it was Adolf Hitler.

He had a particular and inveterate distrust of experts. He refused to be impressed by the complexity of problems, insisting until it became monotonous that if only the will was there any problem could be solved. Schacht, to whose advice he refused to listen and whose admiration was reluctant, says of him: "Hitler often did find astonishingly simple solutions for problems which had seemed to others insoluble. He had a genius for invention. . . . His solutions were often brutal, but almost always effective."

In almost any situation, Hitler believed, force or the threat of force would settle matters—and in an astonishingly large number of cases he proved right.

In his Munich days Hitler always carried a heavy riding-whip, made of hippopotamus hide. The impression he wanted to convey—and every phrase and gesture in his speeches reflected the same purpose—was one of force, decision, will. Yet Hitler had nothing of the easy, assured toughness of *condottieri* like Goering and Roehm. His strength of personality, far from being natural to him, was the product of an exertion of will: from this sprang a harsh, jerky and over-emphatic manner which was very noticeable in his early days as a politician.

To say that Hitler was ambitious scarcely describes the intensity of the lust for power and the craving to dominate which consumed him. It was the will to power in its crudest and purest form, not identifying itself with the triumph of a principle as with Lenin or Robespierre—for the only principle of Nazism was power and domination for its own sake—nor finding satisfaction in the fruits of power, for, by comparison with other Nazi leaders like Goering, Hitler lived an ascetic life. For a long time Hitler succeeded in identifying his own power with the recovery of Germany's old position in the world, and there were many in the 1930s who spoke of him as a fanatical patriot. But as soon as the interests of Germany began to diverge from his own, from the beginning of 1943 onwards, his patriotism was seen at its true value—Germany, like everything else in the world, was only a vehicle for his own power, and he would sacrifice it with the same indifference as the lives of those he sent to the Eastern Front. By its nature this was an insatiable appetite, securing only a temporary gratification by the exercise of power, then restlessly demanding an ever further extension of it.

Resentment is so marked in Hitler's attitude as to suggest that from his Vienna and Munich days there sprang a compelling urge to revenge himself upon that comfortable bourgeois world which had slighted and ignored him. Hatred, touchiness, vanity are characteristics upon which those who spent any time in his company constantly remark. Hatred intoxicated Hitler. Many of his speeches are long diatribes of hate—against the Jews, against the Marxists, against the Czechs, the Poles and the French.

No less striking was his constant need of praise. His vanity was inappeasable, and the most fulsome flattery was received as no more than his due. The atmosphere of adulation in which he lived seems to have deadened the critical faculties of all who came into it. The most banal platitudes and the most grotesque errors of taste and judgment, if uttered by the Fuehrer, were accepted as the words of inspired genius. It is to the credit of Roehm and Gregor Strasser, who had known Hitler for a long time, that they were totally unimpressed by this Byzantine attitude towards the Fuehrer: no doubt, this was among the reasons why they were murdered.

A hundred years before Hitler became Chancellor, Hegel, in a famous course of lectures at the University of Berlin, had pointed to the role of "World-historical individuals" as the agents by which "the Will of the World Spirit," the plan of Providence, is carried out.

They may all be called Heroes, in as much as they have derived their purposes and their vocation, not from the calm regular course of things, sanctioned by the existing order; but from a concealed fount, from that inner Spirit, still hidden beneath the surface, which impinges on the outer world as on a shell and bursts it into pieces. (Such were Alexander,

Caesar, Napoleon.) They were practical, political men. But at
the same time they were thinking men, who had an insight
into the requirements of the time—what was ripe for development. . . .

To the objection that the activity of such individuals frequently outrages morality, and involves great sufferings for
others, Hegel replied:

> World History occupies a higher ground than that on which
> morality has properly its position, which is personal character
> and the conscience of individuals. . . . Moral claims which
> are irrelevant must not be brought into collision with world-
> historical deeds and their accomplishment. The litany of pri-
> vate virtues—modesty, humanity, philanthropy and forbearance
> —must not be raised against them. So mighty a form [he adds
> elsewhere] must trample down many an innocent flower—crush
> to pieces many an object in its path.

It may well be questioned whether Hitler ever read Hegel,
but like so many other passages in nineteenth-century German literature—in Nietzsche, in Schopenhauer, in Wagner—it
finds an echo in Hitler's belief about himself. Cynical though
he was, Hitler's cynicism stopped short of his own person: he
came to believe that he was a man with a mission, marked
out by Providence, and therefore exempt from the ordinary
canons of human conduct.

It was clear enough in the speech he made at his trial in
1924, and after he came out of prison those near him noticed
that he began to hold aloof, to set a barrier between himself
and his followers. After he came to power it became more
noticeable. Just before the occupation of Austria, in February,
1938, he declared in the Reichstag:

> Above all, a man who feels it is his duty at such an hour to
> assume the leadership of his people is not responsible to the
> laws of parliamentary usage or to a particular democratic
> conception, but solely to the mission placed upon him. And
> anyone who interferes with this mission is an enemy of the
> people.

It was in this sense of mission that Hitler, a man who believed neither in God nor in conscience ("a Jewish invention,
a blemish like circumcision"), found both justification and absolution. He was the Siegfried come to reawaken Germany to
greatness, for whom morality, suffering and "the litany of
private virtues" were irrelevant. So long as this sense of
mission was balanced by the cynical calculations of the pol-

itician, it represented a source of strength, but success was fatal. When half Europe lay at his feet and all need of restraint was removed, he became convinced of his own infallibility. But when he began to look to the image he had created to work miracles of its own accord—instead of exploiting it— his gifts deteriorated and his intuition deluded him. Ironically, failure sprang from the same capacity which brought him success, his ability to convince himself, yet it kept him going when the more sceptical Mussolini faltered. Hitler played out his "world-historical" role to the bitter end. The sin which Hitler committed was that which the ancient Greeks called *hybris*, the sin of overweening pride, of believing himself to be more than a man. If ever a man was destroyed by the image he had created it was Adolf Hitler.

After he became Chancellor Hitler had to submit to a certain degree of routine. He hated to submit to any discipline, even self-imposed. Administration bored him and he habitually left as much as he could to others, explaining the power of men like Hess and Martin Bormann, who relieved him of much of his paper-work.

When he had a big speech to prepare he would put off beginning work on it until the last moment. Once he could bring himself to begin dictating he worked himself into a passion, shouting so loudly that his voice echoed through the neighbouring rooms. The speech composed, he would in- vite his secretaries to lunch, praising and flattering them. Hitler wore spectacles in his office, but refused to be seen wearing them in public. To overcome this difficulty his speeches were typed on a special machine with characters twelve millimetres high.

Most North Germans regarded such *schlamperei*, slovenli- ness and lack of discipline as a typical Austrian trait. In Hitler's eyes it was part of his artist nature: he should have been a great painter or architect, he complained, and not a statesman at all. He passionately hated all forms of modern art, a term in which he included most painting since the Im- pressionists. He had a particular fondness for nineteenth- century painting of the more sentimental type, which he col- lected for a great museum to be built in Linz, the town he regarded as his home. He admired painstaking craftsmanship, and habitually kept a pile of paper on his desk for sketching in idle moments.

Architecture appealed strongly to him—especially Baroque —and he had grandiose plans for the rebuilding of Berlin, Munich and Nuremberg and the other big German cities. The qualities which attracted him were the monumental and the massive: the architecture of the Third Reich, like the Pyramids, was to reflect the power of its rulers.

Hitler also looked upon himself as highly musical. In fact, his liking for music did not extend very much further than Wagner, some of Beethoven and Bruckner, light opera like *Die Fledermaus* and such operettas as Lehar's *The Merry Widow* and *La Fille du Régiment*. For many years Hitler had a devoted admirer in Winnifried Wagner, and never missed a Wagner festival at Bayreuth. He was equally fond of the cinema, and at the height of the political struggle in 1932 he and Goebbels would slip into a picture-house to see *Mädchen in Uniform*, or Greta Garbo. When the Chancellery was rebuilt he had projectors and a screen installed on which he frequently watched films in the evening, including many of the foreign films he had forbidden in Germany.

Hitler rebuilt both the Chancellery and his house on the Obersalzberg after he came to power, the original *Haus Wachenfeld* becoming the famous Berghof. He had a passion for big rooms, thick carpets and tapestries. Rauschning, who was frequently in Hitler's company in 1933, speaks of "the familiar blend of *petit bourgeois* pleasures and revolutionary talk." He liked to be driven fast in a powerful car; he liked cream cakes and sweets (specially supplied by a Berlin firm); he liked flowers in his rooms, and dogs; he liked the company of pretty—but not clever—women.

It was in the evenings that Hitler's vitality rose. He hated to go to bed—for he found it hard to sleep—and after dinner he would gather his guests and his household, including the secretaries, and sit talking about every subject under the sun until two or three o'clock in the morning, often later. For long periods the conversation would lapse into a monologue, but to yawn or whisper was to incur immediate disfavour. Next morning Hitler would not rise until eleven.

There was little ceremony about life at the Berghof. Hitler had no fondness for formality or for big social occasions. Although he lived in considerable luxury, he was indifferent to the clothes he wore, ate very little, never touched meat, and neither smoked nor drank. The chief reason for this abstinence seems to have been anxiety about his health. He lived an unhealthy life, with little exercise or fresh air; he took part in no sport, never rode or swam, and he suffered a good deal from stomach disorders as well as from insomnia. He was depressed at the thought of dying early, before he had time to complete his schemes, and he hoped to add years to his life by careful dieting and avoiding alcohol, coffee, tea and tobacco. In the late-night sessions round the fireplace Hitler sipped peppermint-tea or some other herbal drink. He became a crank as well as a hypochondriac, and preached the virtues of vegetarianism to his guests at table with the same insistence as he showed in talking politics.

Hitler had been brought up as a Catholic and was impressed by the organization and power of the Church. For the Protestant clergy he felt only contempt: "They are insignificant little people, submissive as dogs, and they sweat with embarrassment when you talk to them. They have neither a religion they can take seriously nor a great position to defend like Rome." It was "the great position" of the Church that he respected, the fact that it had lasted for so many centuries; towards its teaching he showed the sharpest hostility. In Hitler's eyes Christianity was a religion fit only for slaves; its ethics he detested, and he mocked all talk of a life after death. From political considerations he restrained his anti-clericalism, seeing clearly the dangers of strengthening the Church by persecution. Once the war was over, he promised himself, he would root out and destroy the influence of the Christian Churches in Germany, but until then he was a good deal more cautious than some of his followers in attacking the Church publicly.

Earnest efforts to establish self-conscious pagan rites roused his scorn and ridicule. Nor has any evidence appeared to substantiate the belief that he resorted to astrology. The truth is that Hitler was a complete materialist, without understanding of either the spiritual side of human life or its emotional, affective side. Emotion to him was the raw material of power. The pursuit of power cast its harsh shadow like a blight over the whole of his life; hence the poverty of his private life and of his human relationships.

After his early days in Munich Hitler made few, if any, friends. In a nostalgic mood he would talk regretfully of the *Kampfzeit*, the Years of Struggle, and of the comradeship he had shared with the *Altkämpfer*, the Old Fighters. With almost no exceptions, Hitler's familiars belonged to the Nazi Old Guard: Goebbels, Ley, Hess, Martin Bormann; his two adjutants, Julius Schaub and Wilhelm Brückner; his chauffeur, Julius Schreck; Max Amann, the Party publisher; Franz Xavier Schwarz, the Party treasurer; Hoffmann, the court photographer. It was on the Old Guard alone that he believed he could rely, for they were dependent on him. More than that, he found such company, however rough, more congenial than that of the Schachts and Neuraths, the bankers and generals, high officials and diplomats, with their stiff manners and "educated" talk roused the suspicion that they sneered at him behind his back—as they did.

Hitler enjoyed and was at home in the company of women. At the beginning of his political career he owed much to the encouragement of women like Frau Hélène Bechstein, Frau Carola Hoffmann and Frau Winnifried Wagner. Many women were fascinated by his hypnotic powers; there are well-attested accounts of the hysteria which affected women at his big meetings, and Hitler himself attached much importance to the women's vote. If ladies were present at table he knew how to be attentive and charming—if he was in the mood to be so. Gossip connected his name with that of a number of women in whose company he had been frequently seen, and speculated eagerly on his relations with them, from Henny Hoffmann, the daughter of his photographer, and Leni Riefenstahl, the director of the films of the Nuremberg Rallies, to Unity Mitford, the sister-in-law of Sir Oswald Mosley, who attempted to commit suicide at Munich.

Much has been written, on the flimsiest evidence, about Hitler's sex life: he was impotent, he was affected by syphilis, he was incapable of normal intercourse, he suffered from Louis XIV's defect of phimosis or paraphimosis, he practised perversions, he was surrounded by an atmosphere of "furtive sexuality," and so on *ad nauseam*. Whatever may be the truth in these allegations, they only have a place in a study of Hitler's career if it can be shown that his relations with women directly affected his political judgment and decisions. It may well be true that a psychiatrist, provided with adequate knowledge of the facts, could show that the whole character of the man was altered by the nature of his sexual experience, but the evidence for a thorough psychological study of Hitler is lacking. In such a matter speculation and inspired guessing, especially by laymen, are misleading. What can be said with some certainty is that no woman ever played a part in Hitler's career comparable to that of a Madame de Maintenon, a Pompadour or even a Josephine. This is borne out by all that is known of his relations with the only two women in whom he showed more than a passing interest—his niece, Geli Raubal, and the woman he married on the day before he took his life, Eva Braun.

Geli and Friedl Raubal, the daughters of Hitler's widowed half-sister, Angela Raubal, accompanied their mother when she came to keep house for Hitler on the Obersalzberg in 1925. Geli was then seventeen, simple and attractive, with a pleasant voice which she wanted to have trained for singing. During the next six years she became Hitler's constant companion. This period in Munich Hitler later described as the happiest in his life; he idolized this girl, who was twenty years younger than himself, took her with him whenever he could

—in short, he fell in love with her. Whether Geli was ever in love with him is doubtful. She was flattered and impressed by her now famous uncle, she enjoyed going about with him, but she suffered from his hypersensitive jealousy. Hitler refused to let her have any life of her own; he refused to let her go to Vienna to have her voice trained; he was beside himself with fury when he discovered that she had allowed Emil Maurice, his chauffeur, to make love to her, and forbade her to have anything to do with any other man. Geli resented and was made unhappy by this domestic tyranny. So far there is little disagreement about the facts. It has also been said, however, that Hitler demanded that she should become his mistress, and that the peculiar nature of his demands repelled and disgusted her. The evidence for this so far consists of no more than dark hints and circumstantial gossip at secondhand.

On the morning of 18 September, 1931, Geli Raubal was found shot dead in Hitler's Munich flat. The coroner's verdict was one of suicide. Again there are dark hints and nothing that can be called evidence. If it was suicide, what was her motive? Was she driven to it by Hitler's importunity or by his despotic treatment of her? It has even been suggested that Hitler returned secretly after setting out for Hamburg and shot her at the height of a quarrel, in a passion of jealousy.

Whatever the degree of his responsibility for Geli's death —and suicide seems the most likely explanation—Hitler collapsed under the shock of his loss. For weeks he was inconsolable, refusing to see anyone and talking of suicide himself. For the rest of his life he never spoke of Geli without tears coming into his eyes; according to his own statement to a number of witnesses, she was the only woman he ever loved. Her room at the Berghof was kept exactly as she had left it, and remained untouched when the original *Haus Wachenfeld* was rebuilt. Her photograph hung in his room in Munich and Berlin, and flowers were always placed before it on the anniversary of her birth and death. Was it remorse, sentimentality, another pose or genuine passion? Who knows?

His relations with Eva Braun were on a different level. Over twenty years younger than Hitler, she came of a lower-middle-class Bavarian family, and was employed by Hoffmann in his photographer's shop. It was through Hoffmann that she met Hitler and some time after Geli's death became his mistress. The affair was managed with the utmost discretion on both sides. Hitler gave her a small villa in Munich and a car as well as a regular allowance. Not until Frau Raubal left the Berghof in 1936—after a quarrel over Eva— was she installed in Hitler's own house. Thereafter she took his sister's place as *Hausfrau*, and sat on Hitler's left hand when he presided at lunch. But when big receptions or dinners were given she had to stay upstairs in her room. Only after her sister married Fegelein, Himmler's personal representative with the Fuehrer in 1944, was she allowed to appear more freely in public; she could then be introduced as Frau Fegelein's sister, and the Fuehrer's reputation preserved untarnished.

If the original basis of the relationship was physical, it was confirmed by familiarity and became more domestic than erotic in character. In time Hitler became genuinely fond of Eva; her loyalty won his affection, and it was as a reward for her loyalty that, after more than twelve years as his mistress, Hitler finally gave way and married her. Before that he had always refused to discuss marriage on the grounds that it would be a hindrance to his career. In her company he was at ease and could cease to play a part. The nearest he came to being either human or happy in normal terms was during the hours he spent sprawling back in his chair beside her at tea-time, walking with her on the terrace at the Berghof or going for a picnic with a few friends.

Warm-hearted and impulsive, Eva made no pretensions to intellectual gifts or to any understanding of politics. She was an attractive, empty-headed blonde whose interests in life were sport—she was an excellent skier and swimmer—animals, the cinema, sex and clothes. Such ideas as she had were drawn from cheap novelettes and trashy films, the sole subject of which was "love." In return for her privileged position she had to submit to the same petty tyranny that Hitler had attempted to establish over Geli. She only dared to dance or smoke in secret, because the Fuehrer disapproved of both; she lived in constant anxiety lest a chance photograph or remark should rouse Hitler's anger at her being in the company of other men, yet herself suffered agonies of jealousy at Hitler's interest in the women he met. Sometimes he did not come to see her for weeks at a time. Fear that he would leave her for someone else, and her ambiguous status, left her with a feeling of insecurity. Twice she tried to commit suicide—or made a show of it—and this alarmed Hitler, if only because of possible scandal.

It has often been asserted that Eva Braun bore Hitler one or even two children, but no proof has been produced. Photographs of Hitler and Eva in the company of children are no evidence at all, for Hitler had a sentimental fondness for children—which went no further than giving them bars of chocolate—and was careful to be photographed with them as often as possible.

After the beginning of the war Hitler cut himself off from

all social life. Eva had no more rivals to fear, and the liaison had now lasted so long that Hitler accepted her as a matter of course. In the latter part of the war Hitler paid few visits to the Berghof and she was not allowed to move to the Fuehrer's headquarters. At no time was she in a position to influence the major calculations of policy or war. To the end she remained what she had always been, a kept woman, who never touched the essential Hitler.

Egotism is a malignant as well as an ugly vice, and it may well be doubted whether Hitler ever had the capacity to love anyone deeply. At the best of times he was never an easy man to live with: his moods were too incalculable, his distrust too easily aroused. He was quick to imagine and slow to forget a slight; there was a strong strain of vindictiveness in him which often found expression in a mean and petty spite. Generosity was a virtue he did not recognize: he pursed his enmities unremittingly.

Such sense of humour as he had was strongly tinged with *Schadenfreude*, a malicious pleasure in other people's misfortunes or stupidities. The treatment of the Jews only roused his amusement, and he would laugh delightedly at the description by Goebbels of the indignities the Jews had suffered at the hands of the Berlin S.A. Indifferent towards the sufferings of others, he lacked all feeling of sympathy, and was filled with contempt for the common run of humanity. Pity and mercy he regarded as humanitarian clap-trap and signs of weakness. The only virtue was to be hard, and ruthlessness was the distinctive mark of superiority. The more absorbed he became by the arrogant belief in his mission and infallibility the more complete became his loneliness, until in the last years of his life he was cut off from all human contact and lost in a world of inhuman fantasy where the only thing that was real or mattered was his own will.

Hitler was no fool. The calculation in his actions would never have been possible had he not possessed considerable intellectual powers. Reason, however, was the slave, not the master, of the passions, a faculty for discovering means, not for criticizing ends. He combined a technical virtuosity with the coarseness and ignorance of a moral illiterate.

The adjective "uneducated" can be applied to him in more than a formal sense. He refused to criticize, or allow others to criticize, his assumptions. He read and listened, not to learn, but to acquire information and find support for prejudices and opinions already fixed; his reading, like his thinking, was entirely pragmatic, never speculative.

Hitler delighted in amassing facts with which to impress his listeners, but cared little for the accuracy of his information, provided it suited his purpose. In the same way he used figures purely with an eye to effect. He claimed to have read widely in history, but his conversation and speeches show only a superficial knowledge of it, habitually distorted to fit his argument. Any of the quotations he used he might have got at second-hand. He liked to regard himself as a prophet and seems to have been genuinely unaware of the extent of his own unoriginality. He knew no foreign languages, and the imaginative and speculative world of European literature was closed to him.

The basis of Hitler's political beliefs was a crude Darwinism. "The whole work of Nature is a mighty struggle between strength and weakness—an eternal victory of the strong over the weak. . . . States which offend against this elementary law fall into decay." It followed from this that "through all the centuries force and power are the determining factors. . . . Only force rules. Force is the first law." Force was more than the decisive factor in any situation; it was force which alone created right. "Always before God and the world, the stronger has the right to carry through what he wills. . ."

The ability to seize and hold a decisive superiority in the struggle for existence Hitler expressed in the idea of race, the role of which is as central in Nazi mythology as that of class in Marxist. Hitler declared in *Mein Kampf*: "It was the Aryan who laid the groundwork and erected the walls of every great structure in human culture." But who were the Aryans?

Although Hitler frequently talked as if he regarded the whole German nation as of pure Aryan stock (whatever that may mean) his real view was rather different. It was only a part of any nation (even of the German nation) which could be regarded as Aryan. These constituted an *élite* within the nation (represented by the Nazi Party and especially by the S.S.) which stamped its ideas upon the development of the whole people, and by its leadership gave this racial agglomeration an Aryan character which in origin belonged only to a section. Thus Hitler's belief in race could be used to justify both the right of the German people to ride rough-shod over such inferior peoples as the uncouth Slavs and the degenerate French, and the right of the Nazis, representing an *élite*, sifted and tested by the struggle for power, to rule over the German people. As Hitler told Otto Strasser in May, 1930: "We want to make a selection from the new dominating caste which is not moved, as you are, by the ethic of pity, but is quite clear in its own mind that it has the right to dominate others because it represents a better race."

Just as he opposed the concept of "race" to the democratic belief in equality, so to the idea of personal liberty Hitler opposed the superior claims of the *Volk*.

National Socialism [Hitler declared] takes as the starting point of its views and its decisions neither the individual nor humanity. It puts consciously into the central point of its whole thinking the *Volk*. This *Volk* is for it a blood-conditioned entity in which it sees the God-willed building-stone of human society. The individual is transitory, the *Volk* is permanent. If the Liberal *Weltanschauung* in its deification of the single individual must lead to the destruction of the *Volk*, National Socialism, on the other hand, desires to safeguard the *Volk*, if necessary even at the expense of the individual. It is essential that the individual should slowly come to realize that his own ego is unimportant when compared with the existence of the whole people . . . above all he must realize that the freedom of the mind and will of a nation are to be valued more highly than the individual's freedom of mind and will.

Here was the justification for the campaign of the Nazis and other *Völkisch* groups against the Weimar Republic: justice, truth and the freedom to criticize must all be subordinated to the overriding claims of the *Volk* and its preservation.

The Strassers and the radical wing argued that if the same criterion were applied to the economic system it meant the socialist organization of the national economy in the interests of the *Volk*. Hitler's views about economics, however, were entirely opportunist. He was not at all interested in economics. He preached the true doctrine of the totalitarian State —which the rulers of Soviet Russia also practise, but find it embarrassing to admit—the supremacy of politics over economics. It is not economics but power that is decisive. As early as 1923, Hitler kept on saying: ". . . It is not an economic question which now faces the German people, it is a political question—how shall the nation's determination be recovered?" During the Inflation and the Depression this was clever propaganda. He was able to cut through the technicalities of the economists, declaring that all that was needed was the united will of the German people to end their troubles —given that, the rest would follow. It also corresponded to Hitler's own practice when he came to power: faced with economic problems, you gave orders that they were to be solved; if the orders were not carried out, you shot people. It was on this basis that Dr. Schacht and his successors had to find the answers.

As soon as Hitler began to think and talk about the organization of the State it is clear that he was thinking in terms of an army. He saw the State as an instrument of power in which the qualities to be valued were discipline, unity and sacrifice. It was from the Army that he took the *Fuehrerprinzip*, the leadership principle, upon which first the Nazi Party, and later the National Socialist State, were built.

In Hitler's eyes the weakness of democracy was that it bred irresponsibility by leaving decisions always to anonymous majorities, and so putting a premium on the avoidance of difficult and unpopular decisions. At the same time freedom of discussion and freedom of the Press sapped the unity of the nation. From this, he told the Hitler Youth, "we have to learn our lesson: one will must dominate us, we must form a single unity; one discipline must weld us together; one obedience, one subordination must fill us all, for above us stands the nation."

"Our Constitution," wrote Nazi Germany's leading lawyer, Dr. Hans Frank, "is the will of the Fuehrer." This was in fact literally true, since the Weimar Constitution was simply suspended by the Enabling Law, which placed all power in Hitler's hands. Hitler thus enjoyed a more complete measure of power than Napoleon or Stalin or Mussolini, since he had been careful not to allow the growth of any institution which might in an emergency be used as a check on him.

Yet Hitler was equally careful to insist that his power was rooted in the people; his was a plebiscitary and popular dictatorship, which distinguished the Third Reich from Imperial Germany. After each of his early *coups* in foreign policy Hitler duly submitted his action to the people for confirmation in a plebiscite. In the election campaign which followed the denunciation of the Locarno Pact and the reoccupation of the Rhineland, Hitler publicly declared:

> In Germany bayonets do not terrorize a people. Here a government is supported by the confidence of the entire people. I care for the people. . . . I have not been imposed by anyone upon this people. From the people I have grown up, in the people I have remained, to the People I return. My pride is that I know no statesman in the world who with greater right than I can say that he is the representative of his people.

Such statements may be taken for what they are worth, yet it is obvious that Hitler felt—and not without justification— that his power, despite the Gestapo and the concentration camps, was founded on popular support to a degree which few people cared, or still care, to admit.

Like all revolutionary movements, Nazism drew much of its strength from a new *carrière ouverte aux talents*, the formation of a new leadership drawn from other than the traditional classes. The Party's fourteen years of struggle served as a process of natural selection—"just as the magnet draws to itself the steel splinters, so did our movement gather together from all classes and callings and walks of life the forces in the German people which can form and also maintain States." In this way, even before coming to power, the Party created the cadres of leadership to take over the State. The difference between promise and practice will appear in the subsequent course of this history.

Once in power the Party remained the guarantor of the National Socialist character of the State. "Our Government is supported by two organizations: politically by the community of the *Volk* organized in the National Socialist movement, and in the military sphere by the Army." These, to use another phrase of Hitler's, were the two pillars of the State. The Party was a power held in reserve to act, if the State should fail to safeguard the interests of the *Volk*; it was the link between the Fuehrer and his *Volk*; finally it was the agent for the education of the people in the Nazi *Weltanschauung*. Education is an ambiguous word in this context; on another occasion Hitler spoke of "stamping the Nazi *Weltanschauung* on the German people." For its highest duty was intolerance: "it is only the harshest principles and an iron resolution which can unite the nation into a single body capable of resistance—and thereby able to be led successfully in politics." "The main plank in the National Socialist programme," Hitler declared in 1937, "is to abolish the liberalistic concept of the individual and the Marxist concept of humanity and to substitute for them the *Volk* community, rooted in the soil and bound together by the bond of its common blood."

While Hitler's attitude towards liberalism was one of contempt, towards Marxism he showed an implacable hostility. The difference is significant. Liberalism he no longer regarded as a serious threat; its values had lost their attraction in the age of mass-politics, especially in Germany, where liberalism had never had deep roots. Marxism, however, whether represented by revisionist Social Democracy or revolutionary Communism, was a rival *Weltanschauung* able to exert a powerful attractive force over the masses. Ignoring the profound differences between Communism and Social Democracy he saw in their common ideology the embodiment of all that he detested—mass democracy and a levelling egalitarianism as opposed to the authoritarian state and the aristocratic rule of an élite; equality and friendship among peoples as opposed to racial inequality and the domination of the strong; class solidarity versus national unity; internationalism versus nationalism.

Hitler regarded the Marxist conception of class war and of class solidarity cutting across frontiers as a particular threat to his own exaltation of national unity founded in the community of the *Volk*. The object of National Socialist policy was to create a truly classless society. "The slogan, 'The dictatorship of the bourgeoisie must make way for the dictatorship of the proletariat,' is simply a question of a change from the dictatorship of one class to that of another, while we wish for the dictatorship of the nation, that is, the dictatorship of the whole community. Only then shall we be able to restore to the millions of our people the conviction that the State does not represent the interests of a single group or class, and that the Government is there to manage the concerns of the entire community." This single-minded concept of the national interest was to be guaranteed by the absolutism of the State, as it had been in the time of Frederick the Great.

Just as Hitler ascribed to the "Aryan" all the qualities and achievements which he admired, so all that he hated is embodied in another mythological figure, that of the Jew. There can be little doubt that Hitler believed what he said about the Jews; from first to last his anti-Semitism is one of the most consistent themes in his career, the master idea which embraces the whole span of his thought. In whatever direction one follows Hitler's train of thought, sooner or later one encounters the satanic figure of the Jew. The Jew is made the universal scapegoat. Democracy is Jewish—the secret domination of the Jew. Bolshevism and Social Democracy; capitalism and the "interest-slavery" of the moneylender; parliamentarianism and the freedom of the Press; liberalism and internationalism; anti-militarism and the class war; modernism in art (*Kultur-Bolschewismus*), prostitution and miscegenation—all are instruments devised by the Jew to subdue the Aryan peoples to his rule. One of Hitler's favourite phrases, which he claimed—very unfairly—to have taken from Mommsen, was: "The Jew is the ferment of decomposition in peoples."

> . . . In the last resort it is the Aryan alone who can form States and set them on their path to future greatness. All this the Jew cannot do. And because he cannot do it, therefore all his revolutions must be international. They must spread as a pestilence spreads. Already he has destroyed Russia; now it is the turn of Germany, and with his envious instinct for destruction he seeks to disintegrate the national spirit of the Germans and to pollute their blood."

From this early speech of 1922, to the destruction of the Warsaw Ghetto and the death camps of Mauthausen and

Auschwitz, Hitler's purpose was plain and unwavering. He meant to carry out the extermination of the Jewish race in Europe, as the deliberate policy of the German State—and he very largely succeeded. The Prosecution at the Nuremberg Trials stated—and its figures have never been challenged—that of the nine million six hundred thousand Jews living in Europe at the outbreak of the war, sixty per cent are authoritatively estimated to have perished. History records few, if any, crimes of such magnitude and of so cold-blooded a purpose.

Stripped of their romantic trimmings, all Hitler's ideas can be reduced to a simple claim for power which recognizes only one relationship, that of domination, and only one argument, that of force. Every single one of Hitler's ideas—from the exaltation of the heroic leader, the racial myth, anti-Semitism, the community of the *Volk*, and the attack on the intellect, to the idea of a ruling *élite*, the subordination of the individual and the doctrine that might is right—is to be found in anti-rational and racist writers (not only in Germany but also in France and other European countries) during the century between the Romantic movement and the foundation of the Third Reich. By 1914 they had become the stale commonplaces of radical, anti-Semitic and pan-German journalism and café-talk in every city in Central Europe, including Vienna and Munich, where Hitler picked them up.

Hitler's originality lay not in his ideas, but in the terrifyingly literal way in which he set to work to translate fantasy into reality, and his unequalled grasp of the means by which to do this. To read Hitler's table talk at his headquarters in 1941-1942 is to feel continual astonishment at the lack of magnanimity and wisdom in his conversation, the main qualities of which were cunning and brutality, a cocksure ignorance and an ineradicable vulgarity. Yet this vulgarity of mind, like the badly fitting raincoat and the lock of hair plastered over his forehead, was perfectly compatible with brilliant political gifts. Accustomed to associate such gifts with the qualities of intellect which a Napoleon or a Bismarck possessed, or with the strength of character of a Cromwell or a Lincoln, we are astonished and offended by this combination. Yet to dismiss Hitler as an hysterical demagogue, is to make precisely the mistake that so many Germans made in the early 1930s.

It was not a mistake which those who worked closely with him made. However much they disagreed with this or that decision, they never underrated the ascendancy which he was able to establish over all who came into frequent contact with him. At Nuremberg, Admiral Doenitz, the Commander-in-Chief of the German Navy, admitted:

> I purposely went very seldom to his headquarters, for I had the feeling that I would thus best preserve my power of initiative, and also because, after several days at headquarters, I always had the feeling that I had to disengage myself from his power of suggestion. I am telling you this because in this connection I was doubtless more fortunate than his Staff, who were constantly exposed to his power and his personality.

Doenitz's experience can be matched a hundred times over. Generals who arrived at his headquarters determined to insist on the hopelessness of the situation not only failed to make any protest when they stood face to face with the Fuehrer, but returned shaken in their judgment and half convinced that he was right after all.

The events of these earlier years cannot be understood unless it is recognized that, however much in retrospect Hitler may seem to fall short of greatness, in the years 1938 to 1941, at the height of his success, he had succeeded in persuading a great part of the German nation that in him they had found a ruler of more than human qualities, a man of genius raised up by Providence to lead them into the Promised Land.

CHAPTER EIGHT

FROM VIENNA TO PRAGUE

1938—1939

The winter of 1937-1938 marks the turning-point in Hitler's policy from the restricted purpose of removing treaty limitations to the bolder course which brought the spectacular triumphs of the years 1938-1941. It was not so much a change in the direction or character of his foreign policy as the opening of a new phase in its development. The time was ripe, he judged, for the realization of aims he had long nurtured.

The prospects Hitler had unfolded at that meeting of 5 November, 1937, however, alarmed at least some of those who were present. The brief report of the discussion which followed Hitler's exposition shows clearly enough the opposition of the Army's leaders, Blomberg and Fritsch, to the risk of war with Great Britain and France, and their insistence on such material points as the incomplete state of Germany's western fortifications, France's military power and the strength of the Czech defences.

These doubts were not removed by Hitler's irritable assurances that he was convinced Britain would never fight and that he did not believe France would go to war on her own. On 9 November, Fritsch requested a further interview with Hitler and renewed his objections: Neurath, too, attempted to see Hitler and dissuade him from the course he proposed to follow. By this time, however, Hitler was so irritated that he left Berlin abruptly for Berchtesgaden and refused to receive the Foreign Minister until his return in the middle of January.

Reasoned criticism of any kind always roused Hitler's anger: he hated to have his intuition subjected to analysis. Those who were not prepared to follow blindly must go, and within less than three months of the meeting of 5 November, three of the men who had listened to him—Blomberg, Fritsch and Neurath—were removed from office, while those who remained were the two who had silenced whatever doubts they felt—Goering and Raeder.

Hitler's most persistent critic, Dr. Schacht, had already gone at the end of 1937. From May, 1935, Schacht had jeered at economic cranks in the Party who thought they could override economic laws, and protested at the Party's interference with business and industry. He was sceptical about the search for *ersatz* raw materials as a way of avoiding dependence on foreign sources, and pointed to the dangers of sacrificing foreign trade to the demand for armaments.

Schacht did not oppose German rearmament, but he warned Hitler and Goering that the demands they were making were greater than the German economy could stand. But Hitler needed Schacht, with his unrivalled grasp of finance, and foreign trade, to steer Germany through the first difficult years until she was strong enough to take what she wanted. Schacht, in short, was indispensable to Hitler, and this alone can explain why he was allowed a freedom of criticism unique in the Third Reich.

In April, 1936, Schacht had persuaded Hitler to appoint Goering as Commissioner for Raw Materials and Foreign Exchange, in the hope that this would put a stop to the extravagant waste of Germany's foreign exchange assets and her limited supplies of raw materials by Party agencies, such as the Ministry of Propaganda. Goering, however, having once entered the field of economic policy, began to take an interest in what was going on and to amass power. After Hitler made him Plenipotentiary for the Four-Year Plan in September, 1936, with the purpose of breaking down every obstacle to rearmament in the shortest possible time, his relations with Schacht, the Minister of Economics and President of the Reichsbank, became seriously strained. On 5 September, 1937, Schacht went on leave of absence from the Ministry of Economics, and after further protests his resignation was accepted on 8 December. To preserve appearances he remained Minister without Portfolio, and for the time being President of the Reichsbank as well, but from now on Goering was able to carry out Hitler's economic preparation for war without hindrance.

Schacht's successor as Minister of Economics was Walther Funk, but the post was now wholly subordinated to Goering as Plenipotentiary for the Four-Year Plan. Only after Goering had carried out a thorough reorganization of the Ministry was it finally transferred to Funk in February, 1938.

After replacing Schacht by Goering, Hitler turned to the two principal institutions which had so far escaped the process of *Gleichschaltung*—the Foreign Service and the Army. Both were strongholds of that upper-class conservatism which roused all Hitler's suspicion and dislike. Hitler rapidly came to feel contempt for the advice he received from the Foreign Office, whose political as well as social traditions he regarded as too respectable and too limited for the half-gangster tactics with which he meant to conduct his foreign policy. The social pretensions, squeamishness and lack of imagination of the Wilhelmstrasse irritated him. They still thought in terms of the old diplomacy, not of the revolutionary propaganda, fifth-column technique, corruption and incitement with which he proposed to conquer opposition. Now in the subservient Ribbentrop Hitler had found the man he wanted to replace Neurath, and by the beginning of 1938 he judged that this situation was too ripe for settlement.

But the critical relationship was that with the Army. So far the bargain of 1934 had worked well, but not without ominous signs of trouble. The generals, although delighted with the rearmament of Germany, were critical at the speed with which it had been rushed through. The flood of conscripts which began to pour into the depots was more than the four thousand officers of the small Regular Army could train satisfactorily. The figure of thirty-six divisions which Hitler announced in 1935 had been arbitrarily fixed without the agreement of the General Staff, who would have preferred a figure of twenty-one divisions. According to Manstein, then Chief of Staff of the important Military Area III (in Berlin), he and his commanding officer learned of Hitler's decision for the first time over the radio.

In 1936, again, Hitler had sprung his decision to reoccupy the Rhineland on the Army High Command with the least possible notice. On this occasion Blomberg and the Army C.-in-C., Fritsch, protested to Hitler at the risks he was running. Hitler did not forget their opposition, more especially as events justified his judgment, not theirs.

If Hitler found it difficult to get on with the stiff, buttoned-up hierarchy of the Army, the generals had their grievances as well. They knew little of what was discussed in the circle round the Fuehrer, and the one representative of the Army on friendly terms with Hitler—von Blomberg, the Minister of War—was regarded as so much under Hitler's influence that he was given the scornful nicknames of the "Rubber-Lion" (*Gummi-Löwe*), and "Hitler Youth Quex," after a highly enthusiastic Nazi film. The Army had lost the old independent position. There was a new master in Germany, and one with whose foreign and internal politics the generals were far from being in agreement. They disliked the Pact with Poland; they were inclined—following the Seeckt tradition—to be friendly with Russia and China, while they had little use for an alliance with Japan and nothing but scorn for Italy. The arrest of Pastor Niemoeller in July, 1937—roused considerable opposition in the Officer Corps. This was reinforced by dislike of the S.S. and S.A., whose ideas began to penetrate the Army as the inevitable result of conscription. The S.S. leader, Himmler, and his chief lieutenant, Heydrich —who had been expelled from the Naval Officer Corps for scandalous conduct in 1930—now entertained the ambition of humbling the proud Officer Corps, which treated the S.S. and its "officers" with icy contempt.

The key to the relationship between the Army and the Nazi régime was Hitler's own attitude. Closer acquaintance had reduced his original and exaggerated respect and after 1935-1936 he saw the generals as merely a group of men who, with few exceptions, lacked understanding of anything outside their own highly important but narrow field, whose pretensions were unsupported by political ability or, when put to the test, by solidarity in face of an appeal to their self-interest. Hitler indeed was one of the few Germans to emancipate himself from the legendary spell of German militarism. By the beginning of 1938, with his power securely established and with the foundations of German military rearmament solidly laid, he no longer felt the same need to buy the Army's support on its own terms. Thus when Blomberg and Fritsch attempted to apply a brake to his foreign policy, he disregarded both their judgment and the need of appeasing their doubts.

Hitler was still smarting with irritation at the opposition Fritsch had expressed in November, 1937, when an apparently unconnected series of events provided him with the chance to end once and for all the pretensions of the High Command to independent views. The trap was sprung by Himmler and Goering, and it is possible that Hitler was unaware of what was being planned by these two. But Hitler was nobody's dupe, and the use which he made of the opportunity thrust into his hands displayed his political gifts to sinister advantage.

The trouble began with Blomberg's eagerness to get married (for the second time) to a certain Fräulein Erna Grühn, who, Blomberg admitted, was a lady with a "past." Aware of the rigid views of the Officer Corps on the social suitability of the wife of a Field-Marshal and a Minister of War, Blomberg consulted Goering as a brother-officer. Goering not only encouraged him, but helped to ship an inconvenient rival off to South America. When the marriage took place— very quietly—on 12 January, Hitler and Goering were the two principal witnesses.

At this stage, however, complications arose. A police dossier disclosed that the wife of the Field-Marshal had a police record as a prostitute and had at one time been convicted of posing for indecent photographs. Blomberg had dishonoured the Officer Corps, and the generals saw no reason to spare a man whom they had long disliked for his attitude towards Hitler. Supported by Goering, the Commander-in-Chief, von Fritsch, requested an interview with Hitler and presented the Army's protest: Blomberg must go. Hitler, who appears to have felt that he too had been made to look a fool, eventually agreed. The question then arose who was to succeed Blomberg as Minister of War and Commander-in-Chief of the Armed Forces.

Fritsch was the obvious candidate, but Himmler regarded him as the man responsible for defeating his attempts to extend the power of the S.S. to the Army. For a long time he had been watching for an opportunity to get rid of Fritsch. Goering was ambitious to get Blomberg's place for himself. Indeed, the part played by Goering throughout the whole affair —his encouragement of Blomberg, and the fact that it was he who informed Hitler of the information which had come to light about Erna Grühn after the marriage—invites suspicion. Finally, Hitler too must have hesitated to appoint a man who had shown himself so lukewarm and unconvinced by the Fuehrer's genius at the secret conference on 5 November.

Whatever Hitler's doubts, Himmler and Goering settled the matter by again producing a police dossier, this time to show that General von Fritsch had been guilty of homosexual practices. They went further: when Hitler summoned Fritsch to the Chancellery on 26 January and faced him with the charges in the dossier, they arranged for him to be confronted with Hans Schmidt, a young man who made his living by spying on and blackmailing well-to-do homosexuals.

Schmidt identified Fritsch as one of those from whom he had extorted money. This flimsy evidence was later torn to shreds at the court of enquiry. The officer in question, it then emerged, was not Fritsch at all, but a retired cavalry officer of the name of Frisch. This was well known to the *Gestapo*, who later arrested Frisch in order to prevent the defence getting his evidence. Eventually Schmidt confessed in court that he had been threatened by the *Gestapo* if he did not agree to incriminate Fritsch, as Himmler ordered. Schmidt paid for this indiscretion with his life. But by then the trick had served its purpose. In face of Hitler's angry charges, General von Fritsch maintained an indignant silence, and when Hitler, either genuinely deceived or feigning conviction, sent him on indefinite leave, he refused to defend himself.

Fritsch's attitude frustrated the efforts of the little Army group who were later to form the secret opposition to Hitler and who now first came together in an attempt to use Fritsch's treatment as grounds for action against the régime. When Fritsch returned after his interview with Hitler, Beck, the Chief of the General Staff, urged him to carry out a *coup d'état* with the one force in Germany which still remained outside the Party's control—the Army. Fritsch declined.

Even so, for a few days it looked as if the affair might lead to a major crisis. A furious battle developed behind the scenes round the question whether there should be a court of enquiry into the charges against Fritsch and, if so, who should conduct it, the Army or the Party. Behind this loomed the far bigger question of who was to be given command of the Army, for now not only Blomberg's office of Minister of War and Commander-in-Chief of the Armed Forces, but also Fritsch's as Commander-in-Chief of the Army, had to be filled.

On 31 January Beck and Rundstedt, the senior general of the Army, had an interview in which Hitler raged against all generals. His one concession was a reluctant agreement to an enquiry into the Fritsch case. Hitler, however, had already seen how to turn the situation to his own advantage, without giving in to the demands of Goering and Himmler on the one hand, or of the Army on the other.

His solution was presented to the Cabinet, when it met for the last time during the Third Reich on 4 February. After announcing Blomberg's resignation, Hitler added that von Fritsch, too, had asked to be relieved of his duties because of ill-health. Hitler had been, since Hindenburg's death, the Supreme Commander of the Armed Forces, an office which went with that of Head of the State. Now he assumed in addition Blomberg's office of Commander-in-Chief of the Armed Forces and abolished the old post of War Minister, a position which could be used to represent the views of the Army against his own. The work of the War Ministry was henceforward to be done by a separate High Command of the Armed Forces (*Oberkommando der Wehrmacht*, the familiar O.K.W. of the War Communiqués), which in fact became Hitler's personal staff. To the head of the O.K.W. he appointed a man who was to prove quite incapable of withstanding him—General Wilhelm Keitel.

In General von Brauchitsch Hitler found a man acceptable to the Officer Corps in Fritsch's post of C.-in-C. Army and he eventually agreed that the case against Fritsch should be investigated by a military court. At the same time, however, he took the chance to retire sixteen of the senior generals and to transfer forty-four others. To console Goering, Hitler promoted him to Field-Marshal, which made him the senior German officer.

The purge extended further. Neurath was replaced at the Wilhelmstrasse by Ribbentrop. The ambassadors in the key posts of Vienna (Papen), Rome (Hassell) and Tokyo (Herbert von Dirksen) were replaced. Finally, the insignificant Walter Funk assumed office at the Ministry of Economics after it had been stripped of the powers.

Thus at one single blow Hitler succeeded in removing the few checks which remained upon his freedom of action by using a situation not of his making to establish a still firmer grip upon the control of the State. When put to the test the claim of the Army to stand apart in the totalitarian state had proved to be hollow. Nor had the solidarity of the Officer Corps prevented Hitler finding men who were eager enough to serve him. An Army court of enquiry to vindicate Fritsch finally met on 11 March, only to be adjourned because of the Austrian crisis. When it reassembled on the 17th, the régime, covered with the glory of the *Anschluss*, was unassailable. Once again Hitler showed his ability to make use of unexpected opportunities. Fritsch's reputation was vindicated, but he retired into private life as Colonel-in-Chief of his old regiment. With that the generals were content.

The Fritsch Affair marked the last stage in the revolution after power; the end of the Conservatives' hopes that they still preserved some slender guarantees against the recklessness of the Nazis. It was the prelude to the new era in foreign policy.

About nine o'clock on the evening of 4 February Franz von Papen, the Fuehrer's special representative in Vienna, was sitting in his study at the Legation when the telephone bell rang. It was the State Secretary, Lammers, speaking from the Reich Chancellery, with the brief announcement that Papen's mission in Vienna was at an end and he had been recalled.

Papen's surprise was considerable, for he had seen Hitler personally only the week before and nothing had then been said about his recall or transfer. The conclusion could only be that a sudden change in Hitler's policy was imminent, and that Vienna was one of the first places in which that change would be felt.

The fact that Papen's withdrawal had already been announced was sufficient indication to Chancellor Schuschnigg that he had little time left if he was going to persuade Hitler not to abandon the policy of which Papen had been the agent in favour of rougher methods of achieving the *Anschluss*. Schuschnigg tried to safeguard himself by asking for assurances that the Agreement of 1936 should remain the basis of Austro-German relations in the future, and that he should be told in advance precisely what Hitler wanted to discuss. Papen was perfectly ready to give all the assurances Schuschnigg demanded, and urged him again to take this last opportunity to reach a satisfactory agreement with the Fuehrer.

On the evening of 11 February Schuschnigg quietly left Vienna by train, accompanied by his Secretary of State for Foreign Affairs, Guido Schmidt, and the next morning was driven from Salzburg up the mountain roads to the Obersalzberg. It was a cold winter morning, but Papen met them at the frontier in the best of tempers, and only remarked casually that he hoped Schuschnigg would not mind the presence of one or two German generals who happened to be staying with Hitler. Hitler was waiting on the steps and at once conducted the Austrian Chancellor into his study for a private talk before lunch.

Scarcely had they sat down than Hitler, brushing aside Schuschnigg's polite remarks about the view from his window, launched into an angry tirade against the whole course of

Austrian policy. Schuschnigg's attempts to interrupt and defend himself were shouted down.

> The whole history of Austria [Hitler declared] is just one uninterrupted act of high treason. That was so in the past, and it is no better today. This historical paradox must now reach its long-overdue end. And I can tell you, here and now, Herr Schuschnigg, that I am absolutely determined to make an end of all this. The German Reich is one of the Great Powers, and nobody will raise his voice if it settles its border problems.

Hitler rapidly worked himself into a towering rage. He talked excitedly of his mission: "I have achieved everything that I set out to do, and have thus become perhaps the greatest German in history." Characteristically, he began to abuse Schuschnigg for ordering defence works to be constructed on the border. This was an open affront to Germany:

> Listen. You don't really think that you can move a single stone in Austria without my hearing about it the very next day, do you? You don't seriously believe that you can stop me, or even delay me for half an hour, do you? . . . After the Army, my S.A. and the Austrian Legion would move in, and nobody can stop their just revenge—not even I. Do you want to make another Spain of Austria? I would like to avoid all that, if possible.

Austria, Hitler sneered, was alone: neither France, nor Britain, nor Italy would lift a finger to save her. And now his patience was exhausted. Unless Schuschnigg was prepared to agree, at once, to all that he demanded, he would settle matters by force.

> Think it over, Herr Schuschnigg, think it over well. I can only wait until this afternoon. If I tell you that, you will do well to take my words literally. I don't believe in bluffing. All my past is proof of that.

For the moment, however, Hitler said nothing of what his demands were. After this two hour tirade, he suddenly broke off and led his guest in to lunch. Throughout the meal he was charm itself, but the presence of the generals at the table did not escape the Austrians' notice.

After lunch Hitler left Schuschnigg and Schmidt to a desultory conversation with the other guests, while he went off to talk to an Austrian Nazi leader, Mühlmann, and Keppler (Hitler's agent in Austria), whose visit had been timed to coincide with that of the Chancellor.

In the middle of the afternoon Schuschnigg was taken to

see Ribbentrop and Papen. They presented him with a draft of Hitler's demands. The Austrian Government was to recognize that National Socialism was perfectly compatible with loyalty to Austria, and even to Schuschnigg's Patriotic Front, so long as the Nazis conformed to the Austrian Constitution. Seyss-Inquart, a "respectable" crypto-Nazi, was to be Minister of the Interior, with control of the police and the right to see that Nazi activity was legally allowed to develop. An amnesty for all imprisoned Nazis was to be proclaimed within three days, and Nazi officials who had been dismissed were to be reinstated. To assure close relations between the German and Austrian Armies there was to be a systematic exchange of officers. Finally, the Austrian economic system was to be assimilated to that of Germany.

Schuschnigg's efforts to secure alterations in the draft, other than minor changes, were unavailing. When the Austrian Chancellor saw Hitler a little later he found him in the same intransigent mood: there was nothing to be discussed, not a word could be changed. When Schuschnigg explained that, although willing to sign, he could not, by the Austrian Constitution, guarantee ratification, or the observance of the time limit for the amnesty, Hitler flung open the door and, turning Schuschnigg out, shouted for General Keitel.

The reason for the presence of the generals now became clear. General Jodl records: "General Keitel tells us that the Fuehrer's order is to the effect that military pressure shamming military action should be kept up until the 15th." Another captured document gives the actual directive issued by Keitel—the recall of the German military attaché in Vienna, the assembly of rolling-stock, manoeuvres on the Austrian frontier and the spreading of rumours by German agents.

The effect of the summons to Keitel was well calculated. Schmidt remarked to the Chancellor that he would not be surprised if they were arrested in the next five minutes. Half an hour later, however, Hitler again sent for Schuschnigg. "I have decided to change my mind," he told him. "For the first time in my life. But I warn you—this is your very last chance. I have given you three more days before the Agreement goes into effect."

This was the limit of Hitler's concessions, and the Austrian Chancellor had little option but to sign. Schuschnigg's one anxiety now was to get away. The Austrians were silent as they drove down towards Salzburg, but Papen was still in the best of tempers. "Well, now," he remarked to Schuschnigg, "you have seen what the Fuehrer can be like at times. But the next time I am sure it will be different. You know, the Fuehrer can be absolutely charming."

Just twenty-four hours after they had arrived at Salzburg the Austrian Chancellor's train set out again for Vienna. Up at the Berghof the Fuehrer relaxed: it had been a highly successful day.

Hitler certainly expected the Berchtesgaden meeting to hasten events, and German reports from Vienna in the month following show the Austrian Nazis already boasting that within a matter of weeks, if not of days, they would be in the saddle and give Austria a taste of the whip.

At the end of the first week of March Schuschnigg resolved upon a desperate expedient which, he hoped, would destroy the strongest argument Hitler had so far used—that a majority of the Austrian people were in favour of an *Anschluss* with Germany. He determined to hold a plebiscite on Sunday, 13 March, in which the Austrian people should be invited to declare whether they were in favour of an Austria which was free and independent, German and Christian.

Hitler does not appear to have been informed of Schuschnigg's plebiscite until the afternoon of 9 March. That same evening while Schuschnigg was announcing it to a meeting of the Patriotic Front at Innsbruck, urgent summons were sent out from Berlin. Hitler was furious, but he had been taken by surprise. Goering and Keitel were at once called to the Chancellery, General von Reichenau was summoned back from a meeting of the Olympic Games Committee in Cairo, and Glaise-Horstenau, one of the crypto-Nazis in Schuschnigg's Cabinet, was rushed to Berlin. Ribbentrop was in London, and Neurath had to deputize for him at the Foreign Office.

Thursday, 10 March, was the day of decisions. Early in the morning Keppler, Hitler's special Austrian envoy and Globotcnik, an Austrian Nazi leader, reached Berlin by air with the latest news from Vienna. Between eleven and one o'clock Hitler discussed military plans; if the Army was to cross the frontier by Saturday—the plebiscite was fixed for Sunday—orders must go out that evening, and to this Hitler agreed. The question that most preoccupied him was Mussolini's reaction to the news that the German Army was about to march. Ciano had not disguised Italian annoyance at the fact that the Berchtesgaden meeting of 12 February had been sprung on Italy without any notice, and there were signs of an Anglo-Italian *rapprochement* which worried Hitler. At noon, therefore, Hitler sent off Prince Philip of Hesse to the Duce with a personal letter.

The letter began with an argument so unconvincing that the Germans later secured its omission when the text was published—the argument that Austria had been conspiring with the Czechs, in order to restore the Hapsburgs and "to throw the weight of a mass of at least twenty million men against Germany if necessary." Hitler then continued on more familiar ground, the oppression of the Germans in Austria by their own government. Both complaints, he said—Austria's designs against Germany and the maltreatment of the National-minded majority in Austria—he had presented forcefully to Schuschnigg at Berchtesgaden. Schuschnigg had then promised changes. With these assurances Hitler had been content, but Schuschnigg had broken his promise. Now, at last, the Austrian people were rising against their oppressors, and Austria was being brought to a state of anarchy. He could no longer remain passive in face of his responsibilities as Fuehrer of the German Reich and as a son of Austrian soil.

I am now determined to restore law and order in my homeland, and enable the people to decide their own fate according to their judgment in an unmistakable, clear and open manner. . . .

I now wish solemnly to assure Your Excellency, as the Duce of Fascist Italy:

(1) Consider this step only as one of national self-defence. . . . You, too, Excellency, could not act differently if the fate of Italians were at stake. . . .

(2) In a critical hour for Italy I proved to you the steadfastness of my sympathy. Do not doubt that in the future there will be no change in this respect.

(3) Whatever the consequences of the coming events may be, I have drawn a definite boundary between Germany and France and now draw one just as definite between Italy and us. It is the Brenner. This decision will never be questioned or changed.

While Philip of Hesse was flying south with this message, and orders for mobilization were beginning to go out, Vienna was quiet. Not until the evening did Globotcnik return from Berlin with the news that Hitler was in a fury and had rejected the plebiscite; Seyss-Inquart would get a letter by courier the next morning.

At two o'clock in the morning of Friday, 11 March, Directive No. 1 for Operation Otto was issued over Hitler's signature and by the time Hitler went to bed in the morning the Army trucks and tanks were already beginning to roll south, and the bombers to fly in to the Bavarian airfields. . . .

The same morning in Vienna, the telephone woke Schuschnigg from his sleep at half past five. The Chief of Police, Skubl, was on the line: the German border had been closed and all rail traffic between the two countries stopped. The

Chancellor dressed and drove through the still dark streets to early Mass at St. Stephen's Cathedral. At the deserted Chancellery Schuschnigg looked out the window and watched people in the streets hurrying to their jobs unconscious of what was already in train on the far side of the frontier.

There were other early risers in Vienna that morning. At dawn Papen left by air for Berlin, and not long afterwards the Austrian Minister of the Interior, Seyss-Inquart, was to be seen walking up and down at the airport waiting for the promised message from Hitler. It was brought by Glaise-Horstenau, and at half past nine the two Ministers called on the Chancellor to present Hitler's demands: the original plebiscite must be cancelled and replaced by another to be held in three weeks' time. The three men argued but not until after lunch did the Chancellor agree to the postponement of the plebiscite. But by now the German demands were being raised. At 2.45 p.m. Goering began a series of telephone calls from Berlin, the transcripts of which are among the most dramatic of the documents captured after the war.

Having secured the abandonment of the plebiscite, Goering now called for the resignation of Schuschnigg. When that was agreed to in the middle of the afternoon, he demanded the appointment of Seyss-Inquart. But here the Nazis encountered an unexpected obstacle in the Austrian President, Miklas, who stubbornly refused to make Seyss-Inquart Chancellor, and kept up his resistance until shortly before midnight. Keppler, who had arrived from Berlin and set up an improvised office in the Chancellery, went to see the President, accompanied by the German Military Attaché, General Muff. Keppler had brought the list of Seyss-Inquart's Ministers with him from Berlin; he threatened invasion if the President would not agree, but still Miklas held out.

At half past five an angry Goering, roaring down the wire from Berlin, demanded to speak to Seyss-Inquart:

> Look here, you go immediately together with Lieutenant-General Muff and tell the Federal President that, if the conditions which are known to you are not accepted immediately, the troops already stationed at the frontier will move in tonight along the whole line, and Austria will cease to exist. . . . Tell him there is no time now for any joke. . . . The invasion will be stopped and the troops held at the border only if we are informed by 7.30 that Miklas has entrusted you with the Federal Chancellorship. . . . Then call out the National Socialists all over the country. They should now be in the streets. So, remember, we must have a report by 7.30. If Miklas could not understand in four hours, we shall make him understand now in four minutes.

As the evening drew on, an excited mob filled the Inner City and surged round the Chancellery. On the stairs and in the corridors Schuschnigg noticed unfamiliar figures with swastika armbands, saluting each other with outstretched arms and pushing their way unceremoniously in and out of the offices. Shortly after half past seven Schuschnigg broadcast to the nation the news that Germany had delivered an ultimatum, and rebutted the lie that civil war had broken out in Austria. The President still refused to appoint Seyss-Inquart as Chancellor, and neither Keppler nor Muff could shake him.

Some time after eight o'clock Goering rang up again. If Schuschnigg had resigned, he told Muff, Seyss-Inquart should regard himself as still in office and entitled to carry out necessary measures in the name of the Government. If anyone objected or attempted to resist they would have to face a German court-martial by the invading troops. With Seyss-Inquart technically in office the façade of legality could be preserved. This was all that was needed. When Keppler telephoned to Berlin shortly before 9 p.m. to report that Seyss-Inquart was acting as instructed, Goering replied:

> Listen. You are the Government now. Listen carefully and take notes. The following telegram should be sent here to Berlin by Seyss-Inquart:
> "The provisional Austrian Government, which, after the dismissal of the Schuschnigg Government, considers it its task to establish peace and order in Austria, sends to the German Government the urgent request to support it in its task and to help it prevent bloodshed. For this purpose it asks the German Government to send German troops as soon as possible."

Goering added a few more instructions. Seyss-Inquart was to form a government from the names on the list sent from Berlin; Goering's own brother-in-law was to get the Ministry of Justice. The frontiers were to be watched, to prevent people from getting away. As to the telegram:

> Well, he does not even have to send the telegram—all he needs to do is to say: Agreed.

An hour later Keppler telephoned Goering: "Seyss-Inquart agrees."

Throughout the country the local Nazis were already seizing town halls and government offices. To their anger they had been largely excluded from the decisive events in the Chancellery, where the principal parts were played by Hitler's agent, Keppler, by General Muff, and by Seyss-Inquart, a

fellow-traveller long regarded with dislike by the true-blue
Nazis. None the less, by the threat of a seizure of power by
force, implicit in the noisy mob filling the street outside the
Chancellery, they contributed to the atmosphere of compulsion before which, just before midnight, the President had
to yield.

In the hope of securing at least the shadow of Austrian
independence, President Miklas nominated Seyss-Inquart as
Federal Chancellor of Austria. At two o'clock in the morning
General Muff rang up Berlin and, at Seyss-Inquart's request,
asked that the German troops should be halted at the frontier.
It was too late. An appeal to Hitler was turned down: the
occupation must go on.

The hour for crossing the frontier was fixed at daybreak on
Saturday, the 12th. Before then Hitler had received the mes-
sage he had been waiting for all day—news from Rome.
When Prince Philip rang up at 10.25 p.m. on the night of 11
March, it was Hitler, not Goering, who came to the telephone.

> *Hesse*: I have just come back from the Palazzo Venezia. The
> Duce accepted the whole thing in a very friendly manner. He
> sends you his regards. . . .
> *Hitler*: Then please tell Mussolini I will never forget him for
> this. . . . Listen, I shall make any agreement—I am no longer
> in fear of the terrible position which would have existed mili-
> tarily in case we had got into a conflict. You may tell him that
> I thank him ever so much; never, never shall I forget.
> *Hesse*: Yes, my Fuehrer.
> *Hitler*: I will never forget, whatever may happen. If he should
> ever need any help or be in any danger, he can be convinced
> that I shall stick to him, whatever may happen, even if the
> whole world were against him.
> *Hesse*: Yes, my Fuehrer.

With that load off his mind Hitler was content to leave
Goering to take over the direction of affairs in Berlin.

Shortly after lunch Hitler himself crossed the frontier, and
drove through decorated villages into the crowded, cheering
streets of Linz. Hitler was in an excited mood: he had come
home at last. The next day he went out to lay a wreath on his
parents' grave at Leonding. To the crowds he declared:

> . . . If Providence once called me forth from this town to be
> the leader of the Reich, it must, in so doing, have charged
> me with a mission, and that mission could be only to restore my
> dear homeland to the German Reich. I have believed in this
> mission, I have lived and fought for it, and I believe I have
> now fulfilled it.

So far no decision had been taken about the future of Austria, and it seems to have been under the influence of the enthusiastic reception he found in Linz that Hitler decided on the actual annexation. Next morning, the Sunday on which the ill-fated plebiscite was to have been held, one of Hitler's State Secretaries, Stuckart, flew to Vienna to place Hitler's plan before the new Austrian Government. The terms in which the suggestion was framed admitted of only one answer. A Cabinet meeting was hurriedly summoned, and when Seyss-Inquart reached Linz late on the night of the 13th he was able to present the Fuehrer with the text of a law already promulgated, the first article of which read: "Austria is a province of the German Reich." Hitler was deeply moved. Tears ran down his cheeks, and he turned to his companions with the remark: "Yes, a good political action saves blood." The same night the arrests began: in Vienna alone they were to total seventy-six thousand.

All day on the 13th crowds waited in Vienna for the Fuehrer to make his triumphant entry into the capital. It was not until the afternoon of Monday, the 14th, that he finally arrived. Among the reasons for the delay were Himmler's dissatisfaction with the security arrangements and, to Hitler's fury, the breakdown of a great part of the German mechanized and motorized troops on the road. When Hitler reached Vienna he was not in the best of tempers; he stayed only one night and then flew back to Munich. Yet the huge crowds filling the Heldenplatz and the Ring, the reception in the Hapsburgs' palace of the Hofburg, the element of personal triumph in his return to the city which had rejected him—all this must have given him deep satisfaction. Once he had cursed his generals and recovered his temper this sense of satisfaction, even of exaltation, is to be found in the speeches of the election campaign which followed. For Austria was to have its plebiscite after all, a plebiscite in which not only Austria but the whole of Greater Germany was to take part, this time under Nazi auspices.

When he presented his report to the Reichstag on 18 March Hitler announced the dissolution of the Reichstag and new elections for 10 April, appealing for another four years of power to consolidate the gains of the new *Gross-Deutschland*.

In the course of the electoral campaign Hitler travelled from end to end of Germany, with a closing demonstration at Vienna on the 9th. To the Burgomaster of Vienna he said: "Be assured that this city is in my eyes a pearl. I will bring it into that setting which is worthy of it and I will entrust it to the care of the whole German nation."

Under the Nazi system of voting there was no room for

surprises—99.08 per cent voted their approval of his actions; in Austria the figure was higher still: 99.75. "For me," Hitler told the Press, "this is the proudest hour of my life."

The union of Austria with Germany was the fulfilment of a German dream older than the Treaty of Versailles, which had specifically forbidden it, or even than the unification of Germany, from which Bismarck had deliberately excluded Austria. With the dissolution of the Hapsburg Monarchy at the end of the war many Austrians saw in such a union with Germany the only future for a State which, shorn of the non-German provinces of the old Empire, appeared to be left hanging in the air. If the rise of Nazism in Germany diminished Austrian enthusiasm for an *Anschluss*, yet the pull of sentiment, language and history, reinforced by the material advantages offered by becoming part of a big nation, was strong enough to awaken genuine welcome when the frontier barriers went down and the German troops marched in, garlanded with flowers. Austria had been living in a state of insecurity; no one could see where Schuschnigg's policy of independence was to lead, and there was a widespread sense of relief, even among those who were far from being Nazis, that the tension was at an end, and that what had appeared inevitable had happened at last, peacefully. Moreover, the Austrian Nazi Party had attracted a considerable following before 1938. Vienna, where the Jews had played a more brilliant part than in almost any other European city, was an old centre of anti-Semitism, and in provinces like Styria Nazism made a powerful appeal.

Disillusionment was not slow to come. The Austrian Legion returned from Germany with the two ideas of grabbing jobs and taking their revenge; some of the worst anti-Semitic excesses took place in Vienna, and many who had welcomed the *Anschluss* were shocked by the characteristic Nazi mixture of arrogance and ignorance, a régime of petty terrorism tempered by corruption. Even Austrian Nazis were soon to complain at the shameless way in which the new province was plundered. Vienna was relegated to the position of a provincial town and the historical traditions of Austria obliterated.

None the less, in 1938 Hitler had a plausible case to argue when he claimed that the *Anschluss* was only the application of the Wilsonian principle of self-determination, even if he was prepared to run the risk of war rather than allow a plebiscite to be held in Austria under any other auspices than his own. Those outside Austria who wanted to lull their anxieties to sleep again could shrug their shoulders and say it was inevitable—after all, the Austrians were Germans, and Hitler himself an Austrian. The Left found additional consolation in the thought that Schuschnigg, like Dolfuss before him, represented a Clerical-Fascist régime which had fired on the Vienna workers in February, 1934. The German Government strongly denied the story of an ultimatum, and played up the argument that Hitler's action alone had saved Austria from becoming another Spain in the heart of Europe. The bulwark against Bolshevism had been strengthened.

In Rome Mussolini made the best of a bad job and shouted down Italian doubts by loudly proclaiming the value and strength of the Axis. In Warsaw Goering had been the guest of Colonel Beck only a fortnight before: as they walked into dinner they passed an engraving of John Sobieski, the Polish king coming to the relief of the besieged city of Vienna in 1683. Beck drew Goering's attention to the title: "Don't worry," he remarked, "that incident will not recur." In London and Paris there was uneasiness, but reluctance to draw too harsh conclusions. The French reaffirmed their obligations to the Czechs, but Mr. Chamberlain, though indignant at Hitler's action in Austria, refused to consider giving a British guarantee to Czechoslovakia, or to France in support of her obligations under the Franco-Czech Alliance. He strongly deprecated the talk of force being used; it could only increase the feeling of insecurity. . . .

Yet those who, like Mr. Churchill, saw in the annexation of Austria a decisive change in the European balance of power and the unfolding of a calculated programme of aggression were to be proven right. To the south Germany now had a common frontier with Italy and Yugoslavia, no more than fifty miles from the Adriatic. To the north Hitler was in a position to press Czechoslovakia from three directions at once. Germany's strategic position, if Hitler was bent on a campaign of conquest, had been immeasurably improved. Nor was the contribution of Austria's iron, steel and magnesite to be disregarded.

The execution of the *Anschluss*, it is true, had been hastily improvised, but such a step had always been one of Hitler's first objectives in foreign policy, and the ease with which it had been accomplished was bound to tempt him to move on more rapidly to the next. Every step Hitler had taken in foreign policy since 1933 had borne an increased risk, and every time he had been successful in his gamble. To his astonishment and delight this time there had not even been a special session of the League of Nations to rebuke him. The door to further successful adventures appeared to be already half-open, needing only a vigorous kick to swing it right back.

His experience in the Austrian affair, therefore, confirmed

Hitler in the conclusions he had already reached at the end of 1937. German armaments were now increasing at a much more rapid rate. On 1 April, 1938, twenty-seven or twenty-eight divisions were ready; by the late autumn of 1938, this figure had grown to fifty-five divisions. Expenditure on rearmament was mounting by leaps and bounds.

This increase in German military strength did not yet amount to military supremacy in Europe, but taken with the fears, disunity and weakness of the opposition—those psychological factors to which he always attached the greatest importance—Hitler calculated that by the autumn of 1938 he would be in a position to press home his next demands with an even greater chance of success. Ten days after the result of the plebiscite on Austria had been announced, therefore, on 21 April, Hitler sent for General Keitel and set his Staff to work out new plans for aggression.

There was no doubt where Hitler would turn next. He had hated the Czechs since his Vienna days, when they had appeared to him as the very type of those Slav *Untermenschen* —"sub-humans"—who were challenging the supremacy of the Germans in the Hapsburg Monarchy. The Czechoslovak State was the symbol of Versailles—democratic in character, a strong supporter of the League of Nations, the ally of France and of Russia. The Czech Army, a first-class force, backed by the famous Skoda armaments works and provided with defences comparable with the Maginot Line in strength, had to be eliminated before he could move eastwards. For the Bohemian quadrilateral is of almost unequalled strategic value in the heart of Central Europe, within less than an hour's flying time from Berlin, and a base from which heavy blows could be dealt at important German industrial centres. As he had already insisted, the annexation of Czechoslovakia was the second necessary step in the development of his programme for securing Germany's future.

The Czechs had done their best to buttress their independence by alliances with France and Russia. On paper this meant that any attack on Czechoslovakia must inevitably lead to general war. Paradoxically, however, this was a fact in Hitler's favour: it meant that France and Great Britain, to avoid war, would go to great lengths to prevent the Czechs invoking the guarantees they had been given.

The value of these alliances had steadily depreciated. Russia could not come to the support of Czechoslovakia (except by air) unless she could secure passage through either Poland or Rumania. Both countries were bitterly anti-Russian and in any case the Russian alliance only came into operation if the French moved first to the Czechs' support. France, however, after retreating for the past three years in face of Hitler's demands had undermined the system of security it had built up in Central and Eastern Europe. No one was going to risk quarrelling with the new Reich, and there was already a rush to reinsure in Berlin. In 1938 the Czechs were, therefore, likely to be isolated unless the French should at last prepare to fight.

Nothing is more striking about Hitler's handling of foreign policy than his skill in diagnosing the state of public opinion in France, a country he had never visited and with whose language and thought he was totally unacquainted. While his generals continued to be impressed by the number of French divisions which could be mobilized, Hitler, with a shrewder eye for the psychological and social sources of military strength, was convinced that the French lacked the will to risk war, if they could possibly avoid it.

The people Hitler never understood, and whose actions continued to exasperate him to the end of his life, were the British. This is true even of 1938, when Chamberlain's policy, whatever its shortcomings, introduced an element of the incalculable which threw Hitler out of his stride and temporarily thwarted him. What puzzled and irritated Hitler was the illogical behaviour of the British, who could never be relied upon either to intervene or not to intervene, who refused to bind themselves in such a way as to organize effective opposition to his plans in Europe, yet continued to fuss and protest about what happened on the Continent. In the spring of 1938, however, Hitler believed that British intervention could be avoided as successfully in the case of Czechoslovakia as in that of Austria. The attitude of London in the first stages of the Czech crisis suggested that the British were even willing to act on Germany's behalf in exerting pressure on the Czechs.

The lever with which Hitler planned to undermine the Czech Republic was the existence inside the Czech frontiers of a German minority of some three and a quarter millions, former subjects of the old Hapsburg Empire. The grievances of these Sudeten Germans and their traditional hostility towards the Czechs had been a persistent source of trouble in Czech politics since the foundation of the Republic. The rise of the Nazis to power had been followed by sharpened demands from the Sudeten Germans for a greater measure of autonomy from Prague. From 1935 the German Foreign Office secretly subsidized the Nazi Sudeten German Party under the leadership of Konrad Henlein at the rate of fifteen thousand marks a month, and during 1938 Henlein succeeded in ousting the rival parties among the German minority from the field.

Aware of the dangers represented by this Trojan Horse within their walls, the Czech Government made a renewed effort towards the end of 1937 to reach a satisfactory settlement with the Sudeten German leaders. Ostensibly this remained the issue throughout the whole crisis—a square deal for the German minority in Czechoslovakia. By presenting the issue in this way Hitler succeeded in confusing public opinion in the rest of the world, and mobilizing sympathy for the wrongs of an oppressed minority, which would have been denied to a Great Power's aggressive demands on a smaller neighbour.

After the annexation of Austria, however, the rights or wrongs of the German minority ceased to be anything more than Hitler's excuse to push his foot in the door. For, on 28 March, 1938, Henlein, the Sudeten German leader, had a talk of three hours with Hitler, Ribbentrop and Hess in Berlin at which he was told that he must henceforth consider himself as the Fuehrer's representative and was instructed to make demands which would be unacceptable to the Czech Government. In this way Hitler planned to create a situation of permanent unrest in Czechoslovakia which could be progressively intensified until it reached a pitch where he could plausibly represent himself as forced, once again, to intervene, in order to prevent civil war.

The events in Austria had already led to big demonstrations in the Sudetenland, and the intimidation of Czechs living near the frontier. At Saaz, the day before Henlein saw Hitler, fifteen thousand Germans marched through the streets shouting the slogan: *Ein Volk, Ein Reich, Ein Fuehrer.* Rumours were current of troop movements on the German side of the frontier and an imminent invasion. But Hitler wanted no repetition of the improvisation of March, with German tanks and trucks stranded by the wayside. So Henlein was told to keep his supporters in hand, and Hitler laid it down that the attack must be prepared to the smallest detail.

The objective in Hitler's mind was, from the first, the destruction of the Czech State and the annexation of Bohemia-Moravia. This was only recognized in the west with the occupation of Prague a year later. On 24 April Henlein announced his Eight Points in a speech at Karlsbad, and these provided a programme with which to rally the Sudeten Germans, keep the Czech Government in play and bamboozle public opinion abroad.

Having put this in train, Hitler set out for Rome on 2 May on a State visit, the invitation for which had been given when Mussolini was in Germany the autumn before. Every Party boss and Nazi hanger-on tried to squeeze into the four special

trains which were needed to carry the German delegation and
its cumbrous equipment of special uniforms. Nothing appealed to the gutter-élite of Germany so much as a free trip,
entertainment and costly gifts waiting for them south of the
Alps.

Hitler was delighted with Italy. He was less pleased by the
fact that protocol required him, as head of the State, to stay
with the King. The formality of his reception at the Palace left
him with a permanent dislike of the Italian Royal House.

Since the two dictators had last met in September the Axis
had been subjected to considerable strain. The *Anschluss* was
not forgotten in Italy, where anxiety about the South Tyrol
had revived, while the Anglo-Italian Agreement of April had
been noted without enthusiasm in Berlin. When Ribbentrop
produced a draft German-Italian treaty of alliance, Mussolini
and Ciano were evasive. After such a display of friendship,
Ciano replied, a formal treaty was superfluous.

Hitler's references to the new Italy were in a generous vein,
and by the time he left he had succeeded in restoring cordiality between the two régimes. It seems probable that Hitler
informed Mussolini in general terms of his intention to deal
next with the Czechs. Mussolini, who disliked the Czechs,
made no objections, although by the end of the summer he
was to show considerable alarm as a result of Hitler's demands.

Back in Germany, Hitler found his preparations against
Czechoslovakia making even better progress than he had
hoped. At the end of April, 1938, the French Prime Minister
and Foreign Minister had conferred with Mr. Chamberlain
and Lord Halifax in London. The first fruits of the conference
were a joint *démarche* in Prague, urging the Czechs to make
the utmost concessions possible to the Sudeten Germans. Not
content with this, Lord Halifax then instructed the British
Ambassador in Berlin to tell Ribbentrop that Britain was
pressing the Czechs to reach a settlement with Henlein, and to
ask for German co-operation. Ribbentrop replied that the
British and French action was warmly welcomed by the
Fuehrer, who must have been delighted at the way in which
his two chief opponents were doing his work for him. A day
or two later the General Staff informed the Fuehrer's Adjutant that a dozen German divisions were on the Czech frontiers ready to march at twelve hours' notice.

At this juncture, however, Hitler's plans were thrown into
temporary confusion by an unexpected series of events which
transformed his attitude towards the Czechs.

On 20 May the Czech Government, alarmed by reports of
German troop concentrations near the frontier ordered a

partial mobilization. To Hitler's astonishment the British and French Governments promptly made the stiffest representations, warning Hitler and Ribbentrop of the grave danger of general war if the Germans made any aggressive move against the Czechs. At the same time the French, supported by the Russians, categorically reaffirmed their promise of immediate aid to Czechoslovakia. A council of war hastily summoned to the Berghof on Sunday, 22 May, and attended by Henlein, was faced with this impressive display of solidarity, which, in the unanimous opinion of Hitler's military advisers, left him with no option but to call a retreat. Hitler was furious—the more so because he had not in fact been preparing a move against the Czechs at so early a date. He had now, however, to calm the storm that had been aroused.

On 23 May the Czech Ambassador in Berlin was assured that Germany had no aggressive intentions; Henlein was packed off to resume negotiations with Prague, while indignant denials were made by the German Foreign Office of the reports of troop concentrations.

Unfortunately, the effect of the week-end of 21-22 May was largely lost upon the Western Powers; it was certainly not lost upon Hitler. London and Paris described the May crisis as a grave blunder and blamed President Benes for his "provocative" action, while Mr. Chamberlain determined never to run so grave a risk of war again. Hitler's reaction was different. For a week he remained at the Berghof in a black rage, which was not softened by the crowing of the foreign Press at the way in which he had been forced to climb down. Then, on 28 May, he suddenly appeared in Berlin and summoned another conference at the Reich Chancellery. Spread out on the table in the winter garden was a map, and on it Hitler sketched with angry gestures exactly how he meant to eliminate the State which had dared to inflict this humiliation on him.

The possibility of a general war was clearly reckoned with, but Hitler hoped by the swiftness of his action to forestall effective intervention. In any case, "the whole weight of all forces must be employed against Czechoslovakia." According to Hitler's later account, he demanded the immediate mobilization of ninety-six divisions to begin the operations, with X Day set for not later than 1 October, 1938. Hitler never forgave the humiliation of 21-22 May. He constantly referred to it in his later speeches, and from it sprang his venomous hatred of President Benes, and determination to obliterate the very name of Czechoslovakia.

Hitler's tactics for the next three months, June, July and

August of 1938, were devoted to preparing the ground for intervention. Everything was done to impress upon the British and French Governments the obstinacy and unreasonableness of the Czechs; the urgency of a situation in which Hitler might be forced to act himself, if nothing were done, and the folly of a war over the return of three million Germans to their Fatherland. In their anxiety to avoid war London and Paris pressed the Czechs to make more and more concessions to the Sudeten Germans. Hitler noted with satisfaction the strain to which the Czechs were being subjected by the intervention of the British and the French, by the feeling of being pushed and hurried by their friends, and by their sense of isolation.

To the east Hitler pressed the Rumanians not to make transit facilities available to the Russians and kept a watchful eye on Poland. The reports from Moltke, the German Ambassador in Warsaw, were highly satisfactory. Polish opinion was inflexible in its opposition to any idea of Soviet troops marching across its territory to come to the aid of the Czechs. The Polish Government—especially Colonel Beck—were unfriendly towards the Czechs, and preoccupied with the possibility of securing the valuable district of Teschen in Czech Silesia.

The Poles were not the only people whose appetite for territory might be encouraged at the expense of Czechoslovakia. At the end of the war Hungary had lost the whole of Slovakia to the new Czechoslovak State. Budapest's demand for the return at least of the districts inhabited by Magyars, better still of the whole province, had never wavered. To safeguard Slovakia against the claims of the Hungarian revisionists, Benes had concluded the Little Entente with Rumania and Yugoslavia, who were affected by similar Hungarian claims. The Hungarians were eager enough to take advantage of the Czechs' difficulties, but were worried lest in doing so they should provide a *casus foederis* for the Little Entente and commit themselves too completely to the German side. The tortuous efforts of the Hungarians to sit on the fence to the last moment met with little appreciation in Berlin. When the Hungarian Regent, Horthy, visited Germany towards the end of August, Hitler remarked contemptuously that he had nothing to ask of Hungary, but "that he who wanted to sit at table must at least help in the kitchen." The Hungarians' caution was a disappointment to Hitler; it was, none the less, a serious anxiety to the Czechs.

With Russia Hitler confined himself to putting obstacles in the way of her giving aid to the Czechs, and played heavily on British and French dislike of inviting Russian co-operation in order to keep any United Front from coming into existence.

So successful had been Hitler's anti-Bolshevik propaganda that the Franco-Russian and Russo-Czech Pacts were regarded by the British and French as liabilities rather than as assets. On the Russian side there was deep—and not unjustified—distrust of the Western Powers, and a determination not to go one step ahead of France and Britain in risking war with Germany. Hitler's remark to Otto Strasser—"There is no solidarity in Europe"—was the major premise of his diplomacy.

Meanwhile Henlein continued the negotiations with the Czech Government taking care always to find fresh objections to the successive Czech offers of a greater measure of Home Rule for the Sudeten Districts. Their other task was to keep feeling against the Czechs in the frontier districts at fever-pitch: by the end of the summer the tension between the Sudeten population and the Czech officials was reaching snapping-point.

On the German side of the frontier the military preparations for an attack in the autumn continued. Hitler, however, now began to encounter some resistance to his plans in the Army High Command. His readiness to risk a general war alarmed his staff officers, and not all were convinced by his declaration that intervention by France and Britain could be discounted. The opposition to Hitler was led by General Ludwig Beck, Chief of Staff of the Army, and in a series of memoranda he tried to persuade the Commander-in-Chief of the Army, General von Brauchitsch, to make a stand against Hitler.

Brauchitsch, although he agreed with Beck, tried to avoid taking action. In the first week of August, however, at Beck's insistence, a meeting of the leading commanders was held in Berlin under the chairmanship of Brauchitsch, with only two generals dissenting from Beck's views. This time Brauchitsch went so far as to submit Beck's memorandum to Hitler.

News of the conference and of Beck's memorandum had already reached Hitler. After a stormy argument with Brauchitsch, on 10 August Hitler summoned another conference, this time to the Berghof. The senior generals were excluded; Hitler appealed to the younger generation of the Army leaders, and for three hours he used all his skill to set before them the political and military assumptions on which his plans were based. Then, for the first—and last—time at a meeting of this sort, he invited discussion. The result was disconcerting. General von Wietersheim, Chief of Staff to the Army Group Commander at Wiesbaden, said bluntly that it was his own, and his superior's view that the western fortifications against France could be held for only three weeks. A furious scene followed, Hitler cursing the Army as good-for-nothing and shouting: "I assure you, General, the position will not only be held for three weeks, but for three years."

Brauchitsch declined to go further. When Beck thereupon resigned, and demanded that the Commander-in-Chief resign with him, Brauchitsch refused. In the meantime General Halder took over his duties as Chief of Staff. Hitler rejected any alteration in his policy, yet he was conscious that the opposition, although silenced, had not been convinced.

On 3 September, Hitler summoned Keitel, Chief of the O.K.W., and Brauchitsch, the Commander-in-Chief of the Army, to the Berghof to go over the final arrangements. Field units were to be moved up on 28 September and X-day fixed by noon on 27 September. The next day President Benes put an end to the Sudeten leaders' game by asking them to visit him in the Hradschin Palace and inviting them to set down on paper their full demands, with the promise to grant them immediately whatever they might be. Caught off their guard, the Sudeten Party found to their horror that the Czechs' fourth offer, virtually dictated by themselves, fulfilled the Eight Points Henlein demanded. In their embarrassment the Sudetan leaders usd the pretext of incidents at Moravska-Ostrava to break off the negotiations and send an ultimatum demanding the punishment of those responsible before they could be resumed. Immediately, Henlein left for Germany.

For some time past the foreign embassies in Berlin had been reporting that the opening of the final stage of the Czech crisis would coincide with the Nuremberg Party Rally. Hitler's closing speech at Nuremberg on 12 September, it was said, would perhaps decide the issue of peace or war.

Meanwhile a small group of conspirators, which included Dr. Schacht, Generals Witzleben (Commanding Officer of the Third Military District in Berlin), Oster (of the Army Counter-Intelligence), Beck, and Hoeppner (commanding an armed division in Thuringia), was discussing the possibility of seizing Hitler by force as soon as he gave the order to attack the Czechs, and putting him on trial before the People's Court. Much depended upon their ability to persuade Brauchitsch and Halder that a general war was inevitable, and soundings were made in London for proof that Britain and France would support the Czechs in the event of a German attack. Such evidence as they were able to get, however—including a letter from Mr. Churchill—failed to convince Brauchitsch or Halder, and the conspiracy hung fire. On 9 September Hitler held another military conference in Nuremberg, attended by Halder, Brauchitsch and Keitel. Hitler criticized the Army as too cautious, in failing to provide that concentration of forces which alone would secure the quick, decisive success he needed. His aim was to drive at once right into the heart of Czechoslovakia and leave the Czech Army in the rear. X-day was now fixed for 30 September, and was to be preceded by a rising in Sudetenland.

Appeals and warnings from London and Paris did not erase the indelible impression the British and French desire to avoid war had left on Hitler's mind. As if to confirm his view, *The Times*, on 7 September, published its famous leader suggesting the possibility of Czechoslovakia ceding the Sudetenland to Germany. When Hitler stood in the spotlights at the huge stadium on the final night of the Rally, all the world was waiting to hear what he would say—and they were not disappointed. Hitler made no attempt to disguise his anger at the humiliation of 21-22 May, which, he declared, had been deliberately planned by Benes, who spread the lie that Germany had mobilized.

You will understand, my comrades, that a Great Power cannot for a second time suffer such an infamous encroachment upon its rights. . . . I am a National Socialist, and as such I am accustomed on every attack to hit back immediately. I know, too, quite well that through forbearance one will never reconcile so irreconcilable an enemy as are the Czechs; they will only be provoked to further presumption. . . .

Herr Benes plays his tactical game: he makes speeches, he wishes to negotiate, after the manner of Geneva he wishes to clear up the question of procedure and to make little appeasement presents. But in the long run that is not good enough! . . .

I am in no way willing that here in the heart of Germany a second Palestine should be permitted to arise. The poor Arabs are defenceless and deserted. The Germans in Czechoslovakia are neither defenceless nor are they deserted, and people should take notice of that fact.

At every pause the deep baying of the huge crowd gathered under the stars, and the roar of *"Sieg Heil! Sieg Heil! Sieg Heil!"* supplied a sinister background. At last the one-time agitator of the Munich beerhalls had the world for audience. Yet, for all his tone of menace Hitler was careful not to pin himself down; he demanded only justice for the Sudeten Germans, and left in his own hands what constituted justice.

The speech was the signal for a rising in the Sudetenland, and in Eger and Karlsbad several people were shot. The Czechs proclaimed martial law, and by the 15th had the situation in hand. But the Sudeten leaders had used the proclamation of martial law to deliver an ultimatum demanding its immediate repeal and the withdrawal of the State police. When no reply was received within the time-limit, Henlein broke off all contact with Prague, and issued a proclamation

ending with the words: "We wish to live as free Germans. We
want peace and work again in our homeland. We want to return to the Reich." Thereupon, leading several thousand of his
followers, Henlein moved to Bavaria and organized a Sudetan
Freikorps for raids across the frontier. The withdrawal of
Henlein in fact led to a pacification of the Sudetenland, but
this did not stop the German headlines of the Czech "reign of
terror". All pretence that it was purely a matter between
Prague and the Sudeten Germans had now been dropped:
Henlein's Proclamation and flight brought Germany into the
centre of the picture.

So far events had followed the course Hitler had foreseen.
The unexpected element that now appeared, forcing him
eventually to postpone his triumph, was the initiative of
the British Prime Minister in offering to fly to Germany for a
personal discussion. Twenty-four hours after Hitler's speech
at Nuremberg the French Prime Minister, M. Daladier, appealed to Mr. Chamberlain to make the best bargain he
could with Hitler. Mr. Chamberlain on the same evening
(the 13th) sent a message proposing to fly to Germany (if
possible the next day), and try to find a basis for a peaceful
solution.

Hitler was taken by surprise, but delighted. His vanity was
gratified by the prospect of the Prime Minister of Great
Britain, a man twenty years older than himself, making his
first flight at the age of sixty-nine in order to come and plead
with him. Hitler did not even offer to meet him halfway, but
awaited him at the Berghof.

There, at four o'clock on 15 September, Chamberlain was
greeted by Hitler at the top of the steps and, after tea, went
with him to the study where Schuschnigg had been received.
They were accompanied only by Paul Schmidt, the interpreter. Sir Nevile Henderson had taken special pains to ex-
clude the touchy and malignant Ribbentrop with his particular
resentment against the British. Ribbentrop retorted by refusing Chamberlain Schmidt's record of the conference available afterwards.

Hitler began by a long, rambling account of all that he
had done for Germany in foreign policy, how he had
restored the equality of rights denied by Versailles, yet at the
same time had signed the Pact with Poland, followed by the
Naval Treaty with Britain, and had renounced Alsace-Lorraine. The question of the return of the Sudeten Germans,
however, was different, he declared, since this affected race,
which was the basis of his ideas. These Germans must come
into the German Reich. "He would face any war, even the

risk of a world war, for this. Here the limit had been reached
. . . he would not yield one single step."

Chamberlain, who had so far only listened and watched
Hitler, asked if this was all he wanted, or if he was aiming
at the dismemberment of Czechoslovakia. Hitler replied that
there were also Polish and Hungarian demands to be met—
what was left would not interest him. The Sudetenland was
the one remaining problem, but, he insisted again, he was
determined to solve it.

Chamberlain attempted to narrow the problem down to
practical considerations: if the Sudetenland was to be ceded
to Germany, how was this to be done, what about the areas
of mixed nationality, was there to be a transfer of populations
as well as a change of frontiers? Hitler could never submit to
such questioning. He became excited.

> All this seems to be academic; I want to get down to realities.
> Three hundred Sudetens have been killed, and things of that
> kind cannot go on; the thing has got to be settled at once. I
> am determined to settle it; I do not care whether there is a world
> war or not. I am determined to settle it and to settle it soon; I am
> prepared to risk a world war rather than allow this to drag on.

Outside the autumn day was dying, the wind howled and
the rain ran down the window-panes. Up in this house among
the mountains two men were discussing the issue of war or
peace, an issue that must affect millions of people they had
never seen or heard of. It was this thought which preoccupied
Chamberlain, and now he too began to grow angry.

"If the Fuehrer is determined to settle this matter by force,"
he retorted, "without waiting even for a discussion between
ourselves to take place, what did he let me come here for?
I have wasted my time."

Chamberlain's protest had its effect. Hitler hesitated, and
his mood changed. "Well, if the British Government were
prepared to accept the idea of secession in principle, and to
say so, there might be a chance then to have a talk." Chamberlain declined to commit himself until he had consulted
his Cabinet, but if Hitler would consider a peaceful separation
of the Sudeten Germans from Czechoslovakia, then he believed there was a way out, and would return for a second
meeting. Meanwhile he asked Hitler for an assurance that he
would not take action until he had received an answer. With
all the appearance of making a great concession, Hitler agreed,
knowing perfectly well that X-day was still a fortnight away.

Chamberlain next day flew back to London.

Hitler, as he later admitted to Chamberlain, never supposed
that the British Prime Minister would be able to secure the

Czechs' agreement to a voluntary surrender of the Sudetenland to Germany. He saw the interview only as a further
means of ensuring that Britain and France would not intervene. He had drawn the Prime Minister into advocating the
cession of the Sudetenland on the grounds of self-determination; and anticipated Prague's rejection so in Chamberlain's
eyes the responsibility of war would rest on the unreasonable
Czechs, and Britain would be less likely than ever to go to
Czechoslovakia's aid, or to encourage the French to do so.

During the week that followed, therefore, Hitler continued
his preparations to attack Czechoslovakia. On the 18th the
Army reported its plans for the deployment of five armies
against the Czechs. a total of thirty-six divisions, including
three armoured divisions.

Political preparations matched the military. On 20 September the Slovak People's Party, at Henlein's prompting, put
forward a claim to autonomy for the Slovaks. On the same
day Hitler sharply urged the Hungarian Prime Minister and
Foreign Minister demand from Czechoslovakia the return of
the districts claimed by Hungary. "In his opinion," he added,
"action by the Army would provide the only satisfactory solution. There was, however, a danger of the Czechs submitting
to every demand." On the 21st the Poles delivered a Note in
Prague, asking for a plebiscite in the Teschen district, a step
followed by the Hungarian Government the next day. By the
22nd the Sudeten Freikorps, armed and equipped in Germany,
had seized control of the Czech towns of Eger and Asch.

This same day Mr. Chamberlain again flew to Germany,
and was received by Hitler at Godesberg, on the Rhine. The
first meeting was held in Hitler's hotel in the late afternoon.
Mr. Chamberlain was in an excellent temper. As a result of
extreme pressure on the Czech Government he had returned
to Germany with the agreement of the British, French and
Czech Governments to the proposal he had discussed with
Hitler at Berchtesgaden. He was prepared to present a plan
for the transfer of the Sudeten districts to Germany, with a
commission to settle the details, and the transfer of populations where necessary. In addition, the existing alliances which
the Czechs had with Russia and France were to be dissolved,
while Britain would join in an international guarantee of
Czechoslovakia's independence and neutrality.

When Chamberlain had finished speaking, Hitler inquired
whether his proposals had been submitted to the Czech Government, and accepted by them. The Prime Minister replied:
"Yes." There was a brief pause. Then Hitler said, quite
quietly: "I'm exceedingly sorry, but after the events of the
last few days this solution is no longer any use."

Chamberlain was both angry and puzzled; he had, he declared, taken his political life in his hands to secure agreement to Hitler's demands—only for Hitler to turn them down. He could see no reason at all why Hitler should regard the situation as so changed in the past week that the Berchtesgaden solution was no longer applicable. Nor did Hitler give any reasons why he had changed his mind. He talked of the demands of the Poles and Hungarians, the unreliability and treachery of the Czechs; he argued himself into a fury over the wrongs and sufferings of the Sudeten Germans. The whole problem, he shouted, must be settled by 1 October. If war was to be avoided, the main areas to be ceded—marked by the Germans on a map—must at once be occupied by German forces. Afterwards a plebiscite could be held to settle the detailed line of the frontier.

Messages brought into the conference room reporting the death of more Sudetens that day enabled Hitler to work up his indignation to a new pitch. Yet, as they walked on the terrace at the end of the discussion, he said to Mr. Chamberlain with a complete change of manner: "Oh, Mr. Prime Minister, I am so sorry: I had looked forward to showing you this beautiful view of the Rhine . . . but now it is hidden by the mist."

Chamberlain took note of Hitler's new demands, but he refused to commit himself and withdrew to his hotel across the river.

The question which puzzled the Prime Minister, and which the historian must attempt to answer, was why Hitler had acted in this unexpected way. Hitler, it seems clear, had never taken seriously the possibility that Chamberlain could obtain Czech agreement to the cession of the Sudetenland which he had advanced at Berchtesgaden. The news, which he received the day before the Godesberg meeting, that the Czechs had been persuaded to accept, faced him with a new and awkward situation. Hitler's intention was to destroy Czechoslovakia, and the Sudeten demands were only a means to this end. Now he was offered the cession of the Sudetenland as a substitute for the overrunning of the whole of Czechoslovakia.

There were arguments in favour of accepting Chamberlain's offer, as Hitler saw perfectly well: the risk of a general war, if he persisted; the warnings of the General Staff that Germany was not yet prepared for such a conflict; a solid gain at no expense. But this was not enough to satisfy him. Since May he had been consumed with a lust for revenge on Benes, and with the desire to smash Czechoslovakia by force. The use of force had a natural attraction for him; he itched to spit in the face of the respectable, bourgeois world with its talk of respect for law, the rights of small nations and all the other League of Nations catchwords. The cession of the Sudetenland would give him a good part of what he wanted, since it would effectively cripple the Czechs' capacity to defend themselves. But it would rob him of the satisfaction of revenging himself for his humiliation in May, and would oblige him to proceed in two stages to the elimination of Czechoslovakia.

Hitler's new demand was for the Sudetenland's immediate occupation by the German Army before any plebiscite was held. If the Czechs agreed to this it would provide so striking a demonstration of his power, so severe a humiliation for the Czechs and for the prestige of the Western Powers, as to offer at least a temporary satisfaction to his resentment and ambition. If, on the other hand, the Czechs refused, then the way was still open to carry through his original programme.

The final agreement at Munich gave him substantially what he asked for at Godesberg. But there remained in his mind a feeling of irritation at having conceded even so much, and a continued conflict between the desire for a triumph on the cheap without risks, and the hope that the negotiations would still fail and he could launch his armies over the frontier. It was a conflict between temperament and calculation, which was not resolved indeed until six months later when he sat in the Hradschin Palace in Prague and wrote the words: "Czechoslovakia has ceased to exist."

Meanwhile, at Godesberg, an exchange of letters failed to persuade Hitler to give way, and Chamberlain confined himself to asking for a memorandum and maps of the German proposals, announcing his intention of returning to England.

Hitler invited Chamberlain to a further discussion at half past ten on the evening of the 23rd. By the time Chamberlain crossed the Rhine Hitler had recovered his temper, thanked the Prime Minister for all he had done and hoped that a peaceful solution was still possible. But a new time limit had now been added, requiring the Czechs to begin evacuation of the territory to be ceded by 26 September, and to complete it by the 28th. The exchanges between the two men had already become tart when Ribbentrop brought the news that the Czechs had ordered mobilization. That, Hitler declared, settled matters. But Chamberlain refused to give up. The argument continued, Hitler excitedly denouncing the Czechs, Chamberlain not concealing his indignation at Hitler's impatience and his anger at the way he had been treated. When Chamberlain described the document he had been given as an ultimatum, Hitler pointed to the word "Memorandum" at the top. The Prime Minister retorted that Hitler was already behaving like a conqueror: no, interjected Hitler, "like an owner with his property."

Yet, once again, Hitler seems to have been impressed by the way in which the Prime Minister stood up to him. Mr. Chamberlain only pledged himself to submit the Memorandum to the British and Czech Governments, and with this he returned to London.

Whatever Chamberlain's personal inclinations may have been, on Sunday, 25 September, the British Cabinet decided that it could not accept the terms Hitler had offered or urge them on the Czechs. On the 26th Mr. Chamberlain at last gave assurances of British support to France if she became involved in war with Germany as a result of her treaty obligations, and preparations for war were expedited in both Britain and France.

The British Prime Minister, however, resolved to make one last appeal to Hitler, in the hope of persuading him to moderate the tone of the speech he was due to make in the Berlin *Sportpalast* on the evening of the 26th. Sir Horace Wilson was at once sent off by plane with a personal letter to the Fuehrer reporting the Czech rejection of the Godesberg Proposals. But, he added, the issue could still be settled by peaceful means if Hitler would agree to direct negotiations with the Czech Government, with the British present as a third party.

In the interval Hitler had worked up his resentment, hatred and impatience to the pitch where they would provide him with the necessary stimulus for his speech. This was the mood in which Sir Horace Wilson and the British Ambassador found him when they arrived to present Chamberlain's letter three hours before the meeting in the *Sportpalast*. Hitler was so keyed up that he could scarcely bear to remain seated. When Schmidt, the interpreter, who was translating the letter, came to the words: "The Czech Government regard the proposal as wholly unacceptable," Hitler leapt up, and shouting: "There's no point at all in going on with negotiations," made for the door. Only with difficulty could Wilson persuade him to hear them out, and he continued to bark out interruptions. "The Germans were being treated like niggers; one would not dare treat even the Turks like that. 'On the 1st of October I shall have Czechoslovakia where I want her.' If France and England decided to strike, let them. He did not care a farthing." The utmost the British representatives were able to get out of him was agreement to conduct negotiations with the Czechs, on the basis of their acceptance of the Godesberg Memorandum. If he was to hold back his troops, Hitler demanded an affirmative reply within less than forty-eight hours, by 2 p.m. on Wednesday, 28 September.

Hitler's speech was a masterpiece of invective which even he never surpassed. He began with a survey of his own efforts to arrive at a settlement with the other Powers in the past five years. "And now before us stands the last problem that must be solved and will be solved. It is the last territorial claim which I have to make in Europe. . . . The origin of the Czech problem, he declared, was the refusal of the Peacemakers to apply their own principle of self-determination.

This Czech State began with a single lie, and the father of this lie was named Benes. . . . There is no such thing as a Czechoslovak nation, but only Czechs and Slovaks, and the Slovaks do not wish to have anything to do with the Czechs.

From this point Hitler's account became more and more grotesque in its inaccuracy. Having established a rule of terror over the subject peoples, the Slovaks, Germans, Magyars and Poles, Benes had set out systematically to destroy the German minority; they were to be shot if they refused to fire on their fellow Germans. The Germans were so persecuted that hundreds of thousands fled; thousands more were butchered by the Czechs. Meanwhile Benes put his country at the service of the Bolsheviks as a base from which to bomb Germany. . . .

Hitler briefly explained the Godesberg proposals, brushing aside the Czech objection that these constituted a new situation. The Czechs had already agreed to the transfer of the districts demanded; the only difference was the German occupation. In other words: "Herr Benes's promise must be kept. That is the 'new situation' for Herr Benes."

The Czechs, Hitler declared in his peroration, were working to overthrow the Chamberlain Government in Britain and Daladier in France; they placed their hopes on Soviet Russia. In this way they still thought to evade fulfilling their promises.

And then I can only say one thing. Now two men stand arrayed one against the other: there is Herr Benes, and here am I. We are two men of a different make-up. In the great struggle of the peoples, while Herr Benes was sneaking about through the world, I as a decent German soldier did my duty. and now today I stand over against this man as a soldier of my people . . . With regard to the problem of the Sudeten Germans, my patience is now at an end. I have made Herr Benes an offer which is nothing but the execution of what he himself has promised. The decision now lies in his hands: Peace or War. He will either accept this offer and now at last give the Germâns their freedom, or we will go and fetch this freedom for ourselves. The world must take note that in four and a half years of war, and through the long years of my political life, there is one thing which no one could ever cast in my teeth: I have never been a coward. Now I go before my people as its first soldier, and behind me—this the world should know—there marches a different people from that of 1918.

We are determined!

Now let Herr Benes make his choice.

Rarely has the issue of war or peace been so nakedly reduced to the personal resentment and vanity of one man.

The next day the process of self-intoxication with his own words was still at work. Sir Horace Wilson, calling that afternoon, asked where the conflict would end, if the Czechs rejected the German demands; Hitler retorted that the first end would be the total destruction of Czechoslovakia. When Wilson then added that the war could scarcely be confined to Czechoslovakia, and that Britain would feel obliged to support France if she went to the aid of the Czechs, Hitler twisted his words round:

> That means that if France chooses to attack Germany, England feels it her duty to attack Germany also. I can only take note of this communication. . . . If France and England strike, let them do so. It is a matter of complete indifference to me. I am prepared for every eventuality. It is Tuesday today, and by next Monday we shall all be at war.

As soon as Wilson had gone Hitler ordered the movement of the assault units, twenty-one reinforced regiments, totalling seven divisions, up to their action stations. They must be ready to go into action on 30 September. A concealed mobilization was put into operation, including that of five further divisions in Western Germany.

Yet Hitler had not slammed the door. Even at the height of his frenzy in the *Sportpalast* the night before he had still left open the alternative to war which he had put forward at Godesberg. While Ribbentrop and Himmler were in favour of war, others in Hitler's entourage pressed him to make a settlement, among them Goering. Events began to support their arguments. The news that Great Britain and France were making preparation for war, and Wilson's warning that Britain would support France impressed Hitler more than all Mr. Chamberlain's appeals.

At this moment the group of conspirators—Beck, Witzleben, Oster, Schacht, Gisevius—who planned to carry out a *coup d'état* and seize Hitler by force, were making renewed preparations, based on the use of the division commanded by General Brockdorff-Rantzau at Potsdam. This time they were convinced that they would carry Halder and even perhaps Brauchitsch, with them. Hitler's decision, of course, cannot have been influenced by a plot of which he remained ignorant, but the conspiracy reveals something of the dismay that was felt in the Army High Command at Hitler's willingness to run the risk of general war—and of this Hitler was perfectly well aware. Quite independently of the Witzleben-Schacht plot, a deputation of generals had called at the Chancellery on the 26th. Hitler refused to talk to them, and they came again on the 27th and left a memorandum giving grounds for the strong opposition in the Army to an attack on Czechoslovakia, drawing attention to deficiencies in armaments—especially in the western fortifications—deficiencies in morale, and the shortage of officers.

Meanwhile, during the afternoon of the 27th a mechanized division, in full field equipment, rumbled through Berlin and was greeted with almost complete silence by the crowds, who turned their backs and disappeared into subways rather than look on. For a long time, Hitler stood at the window to watch, and the total lack of enthusiasm is reported to have made a singularly deep impression on him. Later that evening, the Commander-in-Chief of the Navy, Raeder, arrived to reinforce the Army's arguments—an appeal that was given added weight by the sudden news that the British fleet was being mobilized.

Hitler, at any rate, was sufficiently interested in keeping open the line to London to send a letter delivered to Mr. Chamberlain at 10:30 p.m. on the 27th, in which he sought to defend his attitude and to answer the objections of the Czechs to accepting the Godesberg proposals. The letter contained no hint of modification, but the very fact that Hitler had bothered to write it at all, and the closing sentence —"I leave it to your judgment whether . . . you consider you should continue your effort . . . to bring the Government in Prague to reason at the very last hour"—spurred Mr. Chamberlain to make one final effort.

With the morning of 28 September—"Black Wednesday"—all hope of avoiding war seemed to have gone. A sense of gloom hung over Berlin, no less than over Prague and Paris and London. Only a few hours remained before Hitler's time-limit of two o'clock expired. Nowhere was the sense of tension greater than at the Reich Chancellery, where in the course of the next hour or two Hitler had to decide on peace or war.

Shortly after eleven o'clock Hitler was asked to receive the French Ambassador. François-Poncet brought an offer which went a good way to meet the Godesberg demands. The plan had not yet been accepted by the Czechs, but if it was agreed to by Hitler France would demand the Czech acceptance and would guarantee the smooth execution of the occupation.

The decisive move, however, appears to have been Britain's appeal to Mussolini, who had given general support to Hitler's claims against the Czechs but was now thoroughly alarmed at the prospect of a European war for which Italy was ill-prepared. He agreed to send Attolico, the Italian Ambassador in Berlin, to Hitler.

Breathless and hatless, Attolico arrived at the Chancellery while Hitler was still engaged with François-Poncet. The Fuehrer agreed to come out to speak to the Ambassador. Mussolini, Attolico began, sent assurances of full support whatever the Fuehrer decided, but he asked him to delay mobilization for twenty-four hours to examine the new proposals put forward by Paris and London. Mussolini's appeal made an impression on Hitler; after a slight hesitation he agreed. When he went back he was clearly preoccupied and said briefly that he would have a reply early in the afternoon.

The French Ambassador had not long been gone when Sir Nevile Henderson arrived, bringing Chamberlain's reply to Hitler's letter. In a last appeal the British Prime Minister put forward the suggestion of an international conference to discuss arrangements to give Hitler what he wanted. Hitler again declined a definite answer; he must consult first with Mussolini. Mussolini, meanwhile, was again on the telephone to Attolico, who was instructed to inform Hitler of the Duce's support for Chamberlain's proposal of a conference. Hitler was prepared to listen to advice from Rome that he would never have accepted from London or Paris; his brother dictator knew how to handle his excessive touchiness of temperament and pride, while, by sponsoring the conference himself, Mussolini enabled Hitler to agree to it without loss of face. At the same time, as Mussolini pointed out, the new proposals brought by François-Poncet, which would form the basis of any discussions, would allow Hitler to march his troops into the Sudetenland by 1 October, the date to which he had publicly committed himself.

Between one and two o'clock that afternoon Hitler agreed on condition that Mussolini should be present in person and the conference held at once, either in Munich or Frankfurt.

Mussolini accepted and chose Munich. The same afternoon invitations were sent to London and Paris—not, however, to either Prague or Moscow.

Hitler was eager to see Mussolini before the conference began, and early next day, 29 September, he boarded the Duce's train at Kufstein on the old German-Austrian frontier. According to Italian accounts, Hitler greeted Mussolini with an elaborate exposition of his plans for a lightning attack on Czechoslovakia, followed by a campaign against France. If these accounts are to be believed, it was Mussolini's influence which persuaded Hitler to give the conference a chance and not to assume that it would fail from the beginning.

The meeting of the two dictators with the British and French Prime Ministers began in the newly built *Fuehrerhaus* on the Königsplatz at 12:45 p.m. Hitler, pale, excited and handicapped by his inability to speak any other language but German, leaned a good deal on Mussolini. Hitler, however, left the meeting in little doubt of what was required of it. "He had already declared . . . that he would in any case march in on 1 October. He had received the answer that this action would have the character of an act of violence. Hence the task arose to absolve the action from such a character. Action, however, must be taken at once."

Mussolini produced a memorandum which eventually formed the basis of the Munich Agreement. This Memorandum had been drafted the day before by Neurath, Goering and Weizsäcker (the State Secretary in the Foreign Office) in order to forestall Ribbentrop; Goering had shown it to Hitler and then secretly gave it to Attolico for dispatch to Rome. Mussolini now brought it out as his own draft, before Ribbentrop could put forward an alternative, and so got the conference over its first hurdle. Attempts by Chamberlain and Daladier to secure representation for the Czechs produced no results: Hitler refused categorically to admit them to the conference. Either the problem was one between Germany and Czechoslovakia, which could be settled by force in a fortnight; or it was a problem for the Great Powers, in which case they must take the responsibility and impose their settlement on the Czechs.

The conference had been so hastily improvised that it lacked any organization. No minutes were taken; the delegations sat in easy chairs scattered round a large circle. The general discussion was constantly breaking down into individual arguments or conversations, and there were constant interruptions while members of one delegation or another went in and out to prepare alternative drafts. Finally, in the early hours of 30 September, agreement was reached, and the two Dictators left to the British and French the odious task of communicating to the Czechs the terms for the partition of their country.

On 1 October German troops marched into the Sudetenland, as Hitler had demanded. The promised plebiscite was never held and the frontiers when finally drawn followed strategic rather than ethnographical lines, leaving two hundred and fifty thousand Germans in Czechoslovakia, and including eight hundred thousand Czechs in the lands ceded to the Reich. Czechoslovakia lost her system of fortifications —which greatly impressed the German generals when they inspected them—together with eleven thousand square miles of territory. To this must be added crippling industrial losses and the disruption of the Czech railway system. President Benes was forced to go into exile and one of the first acts of the new régime was to denounce the alliance with Russia. On 10 October the Czechs ceded the Teschen district to Poland, and on 2 November Ribbentrop and Ciano dictated the new Czech-Hungarian frontier at a ceremony in the Belvedere Palace at Vienna from which the two other signatories of the Munich Agreement and the guarantors of Czechoslovakia were blatantly excluded.

Hitler's prestige rose to new heights in Germany, where relief that war had been avoided was combined with delight in the gains that had been won on the cheap.

Abroad the effect was equally startling, and Mr. Churchill described the results at Munich in a famous speech on 5 October, 1938:

> At Berchtesgaden . . . £1 was demanded at pistol's point. When it was given (at Godesberg), £2 was demanded at the pistol's point. Finally the Dictator consented to take £1 17s. 6d. and the rest in promises of good-will. . . . We are in the presence of a disaster of the first magnitude.

Austria and the Sudetenland within six months represented the triumph of Hitler's own methods of political warfare. His diagnosis of the weakness of the Western democracies which prevented the formation of a united front against him had been brilliantly vindicated. Five years after coming to power he had raised Germany from one of the lowest points of her history to the position of the leading Power in Europe—and this was not only without war, but with the agreement of Great Britain and France. The tactics of legality had paid as big dividends abroad as at home. Hitler can scarcely have failed to appreciate the fact that, twenty years after the end of the First World War, he had dictated terms to the victorious Powers of 1918 in the very city in the back streets of which he had begun his career as an unknown agitator.

Yet Hitler was more irritated than elated by his triumph. The morning after the Munich Agreement when Chamberlain called on him in his Munich flat, Paul Schmidt, the interpreter, describes Hitler as moody and preoccupied. The news that Chamberlain had been given an ovation as he drove through Munich—in contrast to Berlin's sullen reception of the mechanized division—further annoyed him. In Berlin he exclaimed angrily: "That fellow Chamberlain has spoiled my entry into Prague."

After Munich the view gained currency outside Germany that Hitler had been bluffing all the time, and that he laughed up his sleeve when Chamberlain took his threats at face value. This view is one of the assumptions which most strongly colour discussion of the Munich crisis even today. It does not, however, correspond with the impressions of those who saw Hitler at the time.

On the view taken here Hitler was genuinely undecided up to noon of 28 September, when he received the message from Mussolini, whether to risk war or not. The hesitation was not, as Chamberlain thought, between getting the Sudetenland by force or by negotiation, but between getting the Sudetenland and overrunning the whole of Czechoslovakia. Goering later told Wiezsäcker that "he knew from Hitler that two reasons had moved him to choose peaceful methods: first, doubts as to the warlike disposition of the German people; and second, the fear that Mussolini might definitely leave him in the lurch."

Even when he had agreed to the conference Hitler continued to have doubts. The indignation against the Czechs into which he had lashed himself, his pride and sensitivity to prestige, his ingrained dislike of negotiation, his preference for violence, his desire for a sensational success for the new German Army he had created, the recurrent thought of the original plan to secure the whole of Czechoslovakia—all these were factors liable to start up once more the conflict in his mind. This is borne out by his behaviour after the Agreement was signed.

The German High Command were only too relieved at avoiding war. But Hitler regarded his generals as defeatists. He was more impressed by the arguments of Ribbentrop and Himmler that Germany had failed to exploit the Western Powers' fear of war to the full. The fact that Britain and France had agreed to impose the Munich terms on Czechoslovakia suggested to Hitler that he had been baulked of the triumph he had really wanted: the German armoured divisions storming across Bohemia and a conqueror's entry into the Czech capital. This was still his objective.

The criticism which began to be heard of the Munich Agreement in Great Britain and France, and the fact that the British Government proposed to increase, not reduce, its rearmament programme, soon roused Hitler's anger. On 9 October, he retorted by announcing the strengthening of Germany's western fortifications, adding:

> It would be a good thing if people in Great Britain would gradually drop certain airs which they have inherited from the Versailles period. We cannot tolerate any longer the tutelage of governesses. Inquiries of British politicians concerning the fate of Germans within the frontiers of the Reich—or of others belonging to the Reich—are not in place. . . . We would like to give these gentlemen the advice that they should busy themselves with their own affairs and leave us in peace.

On reflection Hitler let matters stand for the time being, but his intention of going a stage further was never in doubt, and a new directive for the Armed Forces was issued on 21 October which listed, immediately after measures to defend Germany, preparations to liquidate the remainder of Czechoslovakia.

The well-meaning efforts of the appeasers during the next six months, far from mollifying, only irritated Hitler further. He objected to this attempt to put him on his best behaviour, to treat him as a governess treats a difficult child, appealing to sweet reason and his better instincts. He was more determined than ever not to be drawn into the kind of settlement which was the object of Chamberlain's policy. If England wanted a settlement with Germany it was quite simple, all she had to do was to give him a free hand in Europe and stop clucking like a fussy hen about what happened east of the Rhine, a sphere of influence which Germany now claimed as her own. Hitler was interested in appeasement only in so far as it was the equivalent of capitulation and the complete abandonment of British interest in continental affairs.

On the night of 9-10 November a carefully organized pogrom against the Jewish population throughout Germany was carried out as revenge for the murder of a Nazi diplomat by a young Jew in Paris. A reaction of horror and indignation followed in Great Britain and the United States. President Roosevelt recalled the American Ambassador in Berlin, and the British Press was unanimous in its condemnation. Hitler flew into a rage. Hatred of the Jews was perhaps the most sincere emotion of which he was capable. To his resentment

against Britain was added the fury that the British should
dare to express concern for the fate of the German Jews.
He now saw London as the centre of that Jewish world conspiracy with which he had long inflamed his imagination,
and Great Britain as the major obstacle in his path.

One of Hitler's diplomatic objectives during the winter of
1938-1939 seems to have been to detach France from Great
Britain. When the French Ambassador was about to leave
Berlin to take up a new appointment in Rome, Hitler invited
him to the Obersalzberg. He received him, not in the Berghof,
but in the pavilion he had built six thousand feet up in the
mountains. François-Poncet has described the approach up a
nine-mile-long road cut through the rock, and the ascent
in a lift with double doors of bronze. At the summit he
stepped out into an immense circular room surrounded by
pillars, with fantastic views of the mountain peaks. "In the
immediate vicinity of the house, which gives the impression
of being suspended in space, an almost overhanging wall of
bare rock rises up abruptly. The whole, bathed in the
twilight of an autumn evening, is grandiose, wild, almost
hallucinating."

Hitler launched into an angry tirade against Great Britain.
But he suggested a joint declaration guaranteeing the existing
Franco-German frontier, thus confirming Germany's abandonment of any claim to Alsace-Lorraine, together with an
agreement to hold consultations on all questions likely to
affect mutual relations.

The French Government proved amenable, and the proposed Declaration was signed on 6 December. Ribbentrop
visited Paris and had long talks with the French Foreign Minister, Georges Bonnet. Ribbentrop later claimed that Bonnet
agreed that Czechoslovakia was in the German sphere of interest and no longer an issue for discussion. This was
indignantly denied by Bonnet, but it is obvious that this was
the object which the Germans hoped to obtain.

France's alliances with Poland and the U.S.S.R., Ribbentrop claimed to have told Bonnet, were "an atavistic remnant
of the Versailles mentality." The price of German friendship,
in short, was a disavowal of France's old interest in Europe
east of the Rhine.

In the meantime Hitler turned toward Italy. At Munich
Ribbentrop had produced a draft for a defensive military
alliance between Germany, Italy and Japan, and at the end of
October he visited Rome to urge the Duce to sign the treaty.

The Fuehrer is convinced [Ribbentrop told the Italians] that
we must inevitably count on a war with the Western Democracies in the course of a few years. . . . The Czechoslovak

crisis has shown our power! We have the advantage of the initiative and are masters of the situation. We cannot be attacked. The military situation is excellent: as from the month of September (1939) we could face a war with the great democracies.

Mussolini was wary of committing himself to an outright military alliance, and he resented Ribbentrop's visit to Paris in December and the German-French Declaration at precisely the moment when Italy was raising her own claims to Tunisia, Corsica and Nice. Yet the very fact that Mussolini was beginning a new quarrel with France forced him back into his old position of dependence on Germany. As Hitler had astutely realized at the time of the Abyssinian War, if Mussolini continued to cherish his bombastic imperial ambitions he would always be forced to come begging to Berlin for support in the end, whether he liked it or not. Sure enough, after two months of hesitation, the Duce instructed Ciano to inform Ribbentrop that he was willing to accept the suggested treaty.

In his speech of 30 January Hitler was lavish in his praise of Fascist Italy and her great leader. It was to be some months yet before the Pact of Steel was actually signed, but Hitler had Mussolini where he wanted him, and he felt secure enough to make his next move—without, however, informing his partner in advance.

What would Hitler's next move be? No question more absorbed the attention of every diplomat and foreign correspondent in the winter of 1938-1939. Every rumour was caught at and diligently reported.

Immediately after Munich, Dr. Funk went on a tour of the Balkans. His visit underlined the state of economic dependence upon Germany in which Hungary, Rumania, Bulgaria and Yugoslavia now found themselves. Their political docility was secured by the organization of the German minorities; by subsidies to local parties on the Nazi model; by playing on internal divisions between different peoples and different classes in the same country; by encouraging the territorial claims of one country, like Hungary, and rousing the fears of another, like Rumania. After the capitulation of Munich these countries had to recognize that they were in the German sphere of influence and must shape their policy accordingly.

Precisely because of this dependence, however, it seemed unlikely that Hitler would attempt a *coup* in this direction. Rather the rumours persistently pointed to the occupation of the rest of Czechoslovakia, the annexation of Danzig, the return of Memel from Lithuania, or—the most interesting possibility of all—the use of the easternmost part of Czechoslovakia, Ruthenia, with its Ukrainian population, as a base from which to stir up discontent among the Ukrainians of the U.S.S.R. and of Poland.

After Munich Hitler did not hesitate to express his disappointment with the Hungarians for failing to press their claims on the Czechs more pertinaciously. He refused to agree to their annexation of Ruthenia, with a common Hungarian-Polish frontier. Instead an autonomous Ruthenia was set up within the new Czechoslovakia, in the same relationship towards its German patrons as the autonomous Slovakia. The little town of Chust, the capital of Ruthenia, soon became the centre of a Ukrainian national movement, eager to bring freedom to the oppressed Ukrainians of Poland and of the Soviet Union.

Poland and Russia took the threat sufficiently seriously to discover a common interest, despite their inveterate hostility and the pact of non-aggression between the two countries reaffirmed. This Polish-Soviet *rapprochement* may have played a part in persuading the Germans to postpone their plans for a Greater Ukraine. At any rate, by the end of January a different set of anxieties occupied the Foreign Ministries in London and Paris.

On 24 January Lord Halifax, the British Foreign Secretary, wrote an appreciation of the European situation, which was to be laid before President Roosevelt and which was subsequently sent to the French Government as well. Lord Halifax began by saying that he had received a large number of reports about Hitler's mood and intentions.

> According to these reports, Hitler is bitterly resentful at the Munich Agreement which baulked him of a localized war against Czechoslovakia and demonstrated the will to peace of the German masses in opposition to the warmongering of the Nazi Party. He feels personally humiliated by this demonstration. He regards Great Britain as primarily responsible for this humiliation, and his rage is therefore directed principally against this country which he holds to be the chief obstacle now to the fulfilment of his further ambitions.
>
> As early as November there were indications which gradually became more definite that Hitler was planning a further foreign adventure for the spring of 1939. . . . Since then reports indicate that Hitler, encouraged by Ribbentrop, Himmler and others, is considering an attack on the Western Powers as a preliminary to subsequent action in the east.

It is in the directives which he issued to the Armed Forces that we have the surest indication of the way in which Hitler's mind was moving. There are three such directives in the six months between Munich and Prague. In the first, issued on 21 October, the Army and the other Forces are ordered to be prepared at all times for three eventualities: the defence of Germany, the liquidation of Czechoslovakia, and the occupation of Memel. On 24 November Hitler added a fourth eventuality, the occupation of Danzig, and on 17 December he instructed the Army to make its preparations to occupy the rest of Czechoslovakia.

In point of time, the preliminary moves for securing Danzig overlap the preparations for the liquidation of Czechoslovakia, but it will be convenient to treat relations with Poland separately and to conclude this chapter, which began with the occupation of Vienna in March, 1938, with the occupation of Prague in March, 1939. . . .

After the cession to Poland and Hungary of a further five thousand square miles with a population of well over a million souls, Prague was obliged to grant far-reaching autonomy to the two eastern provinces of Slovakia and Ruthenia, each of which had its own Cabinet and Parliament and maintained only the most shadowy relation with the Central Government. Even this did not satisfy the Germans, and a long series of further demands was made upon the unfortunate Czechs.

The efforts of the Prague Government to comply with these demands entirely failed to assuage Hitler's hatred towards the Czech people. The German documents leave the clear impression that Hitler was only seeking a favourable opportunity to carry out the destruction of the Czechoslovak State of which he had been baulked at Munich.

There were considerable practical advantages to be derived from such a move. The German Army was anxious to replace the long, straggling German-Czech frontier with a short easily held line straight across Moravia from Silesia to Austria. The German Air Force was eager to acquire new air bases in Moravia and Bohemia. The seizure of Czech Army stocks and of the Skoda arms works, second only to Krupps, would represent a major reinforcement of German strength. The rearmament of Germany was beginning to impose a severe strain on the German economy and standard of living. To alleviate this strain, Czech reserves of gold and foreign currency, Czech investments abroad and the agricultural and manpower resources of the country could be put to good use. At the same time, another cheap success in foreign policy would distract attention from hardships at home and add to the prestige of the régime.

The role of fifth column, played by the Sudeten Germans

in 1938, was now assigned to the Slovaks, assisted by the German minority left within the frontiers of the new State. The demand of the Slovak extremists for complete independence was carefully cultivated by the Germans. As early as mid-October, 1938, Goering met with two of the Slovak leaders, Durcansky and Mach, and Karmasin, the leader of the German minority in Slovakia. After Durcansky had declared that the Slovak aim was complete independence, with very close ties with Germany, Goering assured him that the Slovak efforts would be suitably supported. On 12 February Hitler received Bela Tuka, the Slovak National Party leader, who, encouraged by the Fuehrer, declared that further association with the Czechs had become an impossibility for the Slovaks. "I entrust the fate of my people to your care."

The stage was therefore well set when, in March, the Prague Government played straight into Hitler's hands by taking drastic and unexpected action against the separatist intrigues in both the Slovak and Ruthene capitals. On 6 March the President of Czechoslovakia, Hacha, dismissed the Ruthenian Government from office, and, on the night of 9-10 March, the Slovak as well. For the moment Hitler was taken by surprise. It did not take him long, however, to grasp that here was the opportunity for which he had been waiting.

Some of the Slovak leaders showed a last-minute reluctance to play their assigned roles but they were prodded in the back by Karmasin and the well-organized German minority. Durcansky, one of the dismissed Ministers, was hurried across the border in the German Consul's car. Over the Vienna radio he denounced the new Slovak Government formed by Sidor, and called on the Slovak Hlinka Guard to rise. Arms were brought across the river from Austria and distributed to the Germans, who occupied the Government buildings in Bratislava. The British Consul reported that the Slovak enthusiasm was in fact very lukewarm, and continued so even after the declaration of Slovak independence. But Hitler was not interested in what the Slovaks thought; all he wanted was the declaration, and he took drastic measures to get it.

It had already been announced in Berlin on the morning of 11 March that Tiso, the deposed Slovak Premier, had appealed to Hitler. That night the two chief German representatives in Vienna, Buerckel and Seyss-Inquart, accompanied by five German generals, arrived in Bratislava and pushed their way into a meeting of the Slovak Government. Buerckel is reported to have told the new Premier, Sidor, that they must proclaim the independence of Slovakia at once, or Hitler would disinterest himself in the Slovaks' future.

For the moment Sidor gave an evasive answer, but early the next morning, Sunday the 12th, Tiso, the deposed Premier, held a further Cabinet meeting in the offices of the newspaper *Slovak*, to escape German interference. Tiso told the Cabinet that Buerckel had brought him an invitation from Hitler to go at once to Berlin. This he had accepted, for the consequences of refusal would be the occupation of Bratislava by German troops and of Eastern Slovakia by the Hungarians. Accordingly he proposed to leave by train for Vienna early on Monday and be back by Tuesday night. No sooner, however, did Tiso reach Vienna than he was bundled into a plane and flown to Berlin.

In the early evening of Monday, 13 March, Hitler received Tiso and Durcansky in the Reich Chancellery. Tiso, a short, stout Catholic priest, who once told Paul Schmidt: "When I get worked up, I eat half a pound of ham, and that soothes my nerves," had first to listen to a long, angry speech in which Hitler denounced the Czechs and expressed astonishment at his own forbearance.

The attitude of the Slovaks, Hitler continued, had also been disappointing. After Munich he had prevented Hungary from occupying Slovakia in the belief that the Slovaks wanted independence, and had thereby risked offending his Hungarian friends. The new Slovak Premier, Sidor, however, now declared that he would oppose the separation of Slovakia from Czechoslovakia.

> He had therefore [Hitler continued] permitted Minister Tiso to come here in order to clear up this question in a very short time: whether Slovakia wished to conduct her own affairs or not. . . . It was not a question of days, but of hours. . . . If Slovakia wished to make herself independent he would leave the destiny of Slovakia to the mercy of events. . . . .

To add point to Hitler's remarks, Ribbentrop conveniently produced a message reporting Hungarian troop movements on the Slovak frontiers.

After further conversations with Ribbentrop, Keppler and other Nazi officials, Tiso rang up Bratislava, to request the summoning of the Slovak Parliament for ten o'clock the next morning, and in the early hours returned to the Slovak capital. When the Deputies met, Tiso read out a proclamation of independence for Slovakia which he had received from Ribbentrop already drafted in Slovak. Whether they liked it or not, the Slovak Deputies had no option but to accept the independence thrust upon them, and by noon on Tuesday, 14 March, the break-up of Czechoslovakia had begun. In the House of Commons the next day Mr. Chamberlain gave the internal disruption of the Czechoslovak State by the action of the Slovaks, before the Germans marched in, as the reason why Great Britain could no longer be bound to guarantee the frontiers of Czechoslovakia. Once again Hitler had shown his understanding of the value of "legality."

Hitler was now ready to deal with the Czechs. By 13 March the news from Slovakia had been crowded out of the front pages of the German Press by violent stories of a Czech "reign of terror" directed against the German minority in Bohemia and Moravia. "German Blood Flows again at Brünn," "Humiliation of German Honour"—these were the familiar headlines. Not only the wording, the French Ambassador noted, but even the incidents reported were almost identical with those of August, 1938: the pregnant woman struck down and trampled on, the German students beaten up, and so on. There was little truth in any of these atrocity stories, but they served their purpose, not least in helping Hitler to whip up his own indignation.

On Monday the 13th the Czech Government made a last effort to avert German action by a direct appeal to Hitler, and the following day President Hacha and the Foreign Minister, Chvalkovsky, set out for the German capital by train. An hour before they left, the Hungarians presented an ultimatum demanding the withdrawal of all Czech troops from Ruthenia, and the President had not yet crossed the Czech frontier when news reached Prague that German troops had already occupied the important industrial centre of Moravska Ostrava.

In Berlin President Hacha was received with all the honours due to a Head of State, was lodged in the Adlon Hotel and, when he reached the Chancellery, found an S.S. Guard of Honour drawn up in the courtyard. The irony was barely concealed. Not until after 1 a.m. was the President admitted to Hitler's presence, and he was quite unable to discover in advance what would be discussed. He found the Fuehrer in his study, accompanied by Goering, General Keitel and four other men. Ill at ease, politically inexperienced, old, tired and without a card in his hand, Hacha tried to soften Hitler's mood by ingratiating himself. He said he had rarely met either Benes or Masaryk and had felt their régime to be alien to him—"so much so that after the sudden change he had asked himself whether it was really a good thing for Czechoslovakia to be an independent State." He had no complaint over what had happened in Slovakia, but he pleaded with the Fuehrer for the right of the Czechs to continue their own national life.

When Hacha had finished his abject plea Hitler began to speak.

. . . He had no longer confidence in the Czech Government. . . . This very morning at 6 a.m. the German Army would invade Czechoslovakia at all points and the German Air Force would occupy all Czech airports. There were two possibilities. The first was that the invasion of the German troops might develop into a battle. This resistance would then be broken by force of arms. The other was that the entry of the German troops should take place in a peaceable manner, and then it would be easy for the Fuehrer to give to the Czechs an individual existence on a generous scale, autonomy and a certain amount of national freedom. . . .

If it came to a fight, in two days the Czech Army would cease to exist. Some Germans would, of course, also be killed, and this would produce a feeling of hatred which would compel him to refuse any longer to grant autonomy. The world would not care a jot about this. He felt sorry for the Czech people when he read the foreign Press. It gave him the impression expressed by the German proverb: The Moor has done his duty; The Moor may go. . . .

This was the reason why he had asked Hacha to come here. That invitation was the last good deed he would be able to render to the Czech people. . . perhaps Hacha's visit might avert the worst. . . . The hours were passing. At six o'clock (it was then nearly 2 a.m.) the troops would march in. He felt almost ashamed to say that for every Czech battalion a German division would come. The military operation had been planned on the most generous scale. He would advise him to withdraw now with Chvalkovsky, in order to discuss what should be done.

When Hacha asked what could be done in so short a time, Hitler suggested he should telephone to Prague.

Hacha asks whether the purpose of the invasion is to disarm the Czech Army. This might, perhaps, be done in some other way. The Fuehrer says that his decision is irrevocable. Everyone knows what a decision by the Fuehrer means.

At this point Hacha and Chvalkovsky were taken into another room for talks with Goering and Ribbentrop. Goering threatened to destroy Prague by bombing and Hacha fainted. He was revived by an injection from Hitler's doctor, Morell, thoughtfully kept in attendance. Before they returned Hacha was put through to Prague by telephone, and the Czech Government ordered no resistance to the German advance.

In the meantime a communiqué was ready for Hacha's signature when the Fuehrer received him again in his study shortly before 4 a.m. It was a masterpiece of understatement. The Fuehrer had received President Hacha at the latter's request, and the President "confidently placed the fate of the Czech people in the hands of the Fuehrer." Not a word was said of threats or invasion.

Hitler could hardly contain himself. He burst into his secretaries' room and invited them to kiss him. "Children," he declared, "this is the greatest day of my life. I shall go down to history as the greatest German."

Two hours later German troops crossed the frontier. "Legality" had been preserved, and when the British and French Ambassadors called at the Wilhelmlstrasse to deliver their inevitable protests they were met with the argument that the Fuehrer had acted only at the request of the Czech President.

By the afternoon of 15 March Hitler was on his way to Prague, where he arrived the same evening, accompanied by Keitel, Ribbentrop and Himmler. His proclamation to the German people revived the stories of an "intolerable" reign of terror, which had forced him to intervene to prevent the "complete destruction of all order in a territory . . . which for over a thousand years belonged to the German Reich." That night he spent in the palace of the Kings of Bohemia with the swastika waving from its battlements. Hitler had paid off another of the historic grudges of the old Monarchy, the resentment of the Germans of the Empire in face of the Czech claim to equality, that impertinent claim he had first rejected in the working-class quarters of Vienna thirty years before.

The next day, in the Hradschin Castle overlooking Prague, Hitler reaffirmed the claim of the Germans to Bohemia and Moravia in which the upstart Czechs had dared to establish their own national state.

For a millennium [he wrote in the Proclamation of 16 March] the territories of Bohemia and Moravia belonged to the *Lebensraum* of the German people. Violence and stupidity tore them arbitrarily from their ancient historic setting and at last through their inclusion in the artificial construction of Czechoslovakia created a hot-bed of continual unrest. . . . The Czechoslovak State has proved its inability to live its own internal life, and in consequence has now fallen into dissolution.

As Secretary of State and Head of the Civil Administration, the Czechs were to receive the two former leaders of the Sudeten German Party, K. H. Frank and Konrad Henlein. Hitler's revenge was complete.

An exchange of telegrams between Tiso and Hitler on the 16th placed Slovakia, too, under German protection. German troops promptly moved in to guarantee Slovakia's newly won independence. Ruthenia, however, no longer of interest to the Germans, was abandoned to the Hungarians whose troops marched in, overrunning all opposition, and soon reached the Polish border, establishing the common frontier between Hungary and Poland which had been the aim of the two countries at the time of Munich.

Hitler was back in Vienna on the 18th. There the Treaty of Protection between Germany and Slovakia was drafted. Slovakia granted to Germany the right to maintain garrisons in her territory and promised to conduct its foreign policy in the closest agreement with her Protector. A secret protocol allowed Germany the fullest rights in the economic exploitation of the country.

As the year before in Austria, so now in Czechoslovakia, the speed of the operation staggered the world. Nowhere was the German action more resented than in Rome. Attolico, the Italian Ambassador in Berlin, had only been informed of the German intentions on 14 March, and the arrival of Philip of Hesse with his usual message of thanks for Italy's unshakeable support scarcely mollified Mussolini. "The Italians will laugh at me," he told Ciano; "every time Hitler occupies a country he sends me a message." The Duce was gloomy and worried at the prospect of German expansion down the Danube and in the Balkans, his own chosen sphere of interest, but anger was tempered by the calculation that Hitler was now too powerful to oppose and that it was best to be on the winning side. Expressing violent irritation with the Western Democracies, he declared: "We cannot change our policy now. After all, we are not political whores."

Mussolini was the prisoner of his own policy. Hitler's success roused his envy, yet the more he attempted to imitate the Fuehrer the more dependent he became upon him. A personal letter from Hitler on the twentieth anniversary of the Fascist movement helped to smoothe the Duce's ruffled feathers, and by 26 March he was making a speech full of aggressive loyalty to the Axis. The Duce's eyes began to wander towards Albania.

In London and Paris the effects of Hitler's *coup* were more far-reaching. Prague has rightly been taken as the turning point in British foreign policy, when the British Government, however belatedly, abandoned hope of appeasing Hitler, and set to work, however ineptly, to organize resistance to any

further aggressive move. It was this changed attitude of the
Western Powers which led logically to the outbreak of war
six months later, when Hitler attempted to repeat his usual
tactics in Danzig. Although he was extremely reluctant to
recognize it, the chances of further successes on the cheap
in foreign policy were steadily diminishing. A chapter was
closed. If he persisted in his plans, a new chapter would open
in which his triumphs would have to be achieved under new
conditions.

Yet it is easy to be misled by this. It was, after all, only
a change in the circumstances, not in the character, of Hitler's foreign policy which took place with the occupation of
Bohemia and Moravia. Much has been made of the fact that
by his seizure of lands inhabited by Czechs, not by Germans,
Hitler had now departed from the principle of self-determination to which he had hitherto appealed. But Hitler,
a master of opportunism, used whatever pretext came to
hand—equality of rights, the defence of Europe against
Bolshevism, the Wilsonian right of self-determination, Germany's need of *Lebensraum*. Prague destroyed a good many
illusions outside Germany, but it marked no essential change
in Hitler's policy. And Czechoslovakia was only the beginning,
as *Mein Kampf* was there to show.

Those who had been taken in by his arguments made the
same mistake as those who had imagined that Hitler would be
bound by the Nazi Party Programme: they had failed to recognize that Hitler had only one programme, power without
limit, and that the rest was window-dressing. This had been
his programme before Prague, as it remained his programme
afterwards. The only question was, Where next? Hitler,
however, knew very well what he wanted next, and had
already taken the first steps to get it: Europe was not to be
left wondering for long.

CHAPTER NINE

HITLER'S WAR

1939

After the annexation of Austria, Hans Dieckhoff, one of the
senior men in the German Foreign Office, remarked to Rib-

bentrop that Bismarck would have taken years to consolidate his position before making another move. "Then," Ribbentrop retorted, "you have no conception of the dynamics of National Socialism."

The obvious weakness of Hitler's policy, the fault which destroyed him as surely as it had destroyed Napoleon, was his inability to stop. By the end of 1938 Hitler had everything to gain by waiting for a year or two before taking another step, sitting back to profit from the divisions and hesitations of the other European Powers, instead of driving them, by the fears he aroused, into reluctant combination. Moreover, a temporary relaxation of the rearmament drive would have had considerable economic benefits for Germany. But success now strengthened his native arrogance and made him contemptuous of opposition and impetuous in the pursuit of his ambition.

About a month after the Munich Agreement at a meeting of the Reich Defence Council attended by all Reich Ministers and State Secretaries, as well as by the Commander-in-Chief and Chiefs of Staff, Goering spoke for three hours on the need to concentrate all the resources of the nation on raising the level of rearmament from a current index of 100 to one of 300. Everything was to be subordinated to this single task, regardless of the fact, which Goering frankly admitted, that the Germany economy was already showing strain.

Alarmed at the financial consequences, Schacht, as President of the Reichsbank, presented a memorandum, signed by the Directors, protesting against the Government's reckless expenditure. This was on 7 January, 1939. Hitler sent for Schacht and handed him his dismissal. "You don't fit into the National Socialist picture," he told him. Schacht was replaced by the docile Funk, and all but two of the Bank's directors were removed. A secret decree was promulgated placing it under direct orders of the Fuehrer, with the obligation to provide whatever credits the Government demanded.

There was no question about the purpose of this rearmament: it was to strengthen Hitler's hand in foreign policy. His successes in Austria and the destruction of the Czechoslovak State, as he had made clear in November, 1937, were only the preliminaries to the further development of his foreign policy.

If any country had good reason to fear Germany's intentions it was Poland. At the Peace Settlement of 1919, and afterwards when Germany was weak, the Poles had acquired territory, the loss of which was more resented by the Germans than perhaps any other part of the Versailles Settlement.

In order to provide Poland with access to the sea, Danzig was separated from Germany and made into a Free City, where the Poles enjoyed special privileges, while East Prussia was divided from the rest of the Reich by the Polish Corridor. There was justice on both sides. Much of the land regained by Poland had been first seized by Prussia at the time of the Partitions, and was inhabited by Poles. But the Poles had in turn taken more than they could legitimately claim. German public opinion was as solid in demanding that the eastern frontiers should be redrawn as Polish opinion was in refusing it. The rise of the Nazis to power in Germany had been followed by increasing Nazi influence in Danzig, and it appeared only a question of time before the city was reunited to the Reich.

Yet the first country with which Hitler had signed a Pact of Non-Aggression had been Poland, and for five years he treated Poland in the friendliest fashion, despite the unpopularity of such a policy in Germany. The obvious reason for Hitler's attitude was his need to placate the most suspicious of Germany's neighbours and France's principal ally in Eastern Europe, until he was strong enough to risk her hostility. In this he enjoyed a brilliant success. But there is also some evidence to show that, as Goering believed, Hitler was anxious to secure Polish support for his anti-Russian policy. With his Austrian outlook on European politics Hitler did not share the traditional North German dislike of the Poles, or the feeling of a common interest with Russia in suppressing an independent Polish State. The essential condition, in Hitler's view, was the willingness of the Poles to accept the restoration of Danzig to Germany, in return for which they would eventually find compensation against Russia.

The question was whether the Polish Government would accept the role of ally in Hitler's schemes of eastward expansion. This question was the more difficult for the Poles to answer since their policy aimed at independence of both her great neighbours, but the tragic result was to leave Poland isolated, and at the mercy of an agreement between Germany and Russia to partition her territory between them.

Hitler adopted the policy of such an agreement with Russia, however, only after the failure of his first plan, a German-Polish alliance against Russia. On 24 October, 1938, Ribbentrop invited the Polish Ambassador, Josef Lipski, to lunch at the Grand Hotel in Berchtesgaden. The time had come, Ribbentrop declared, for a general settlement of the issues outstanding between the two countries. He put forward proposals for Poland's return of the Free State of Danzig to the Reich, and the construction of a German road and railway across the Corridor to link East Prussia with the rest of Germany.

At this stage Ribbentrop was still quite friendly; he invited Colonel Beck, the Polish Foreign Minister, to Germany to discuss the situation. Besides providing Poland with a free port at Danzig, together with a Polish extraterritorial road and railway, Germany would be prepared to extend the German-Polish Pact and to guarantee her existing frontiers with Poland. The Polish account contains two further suggestions which the Germans took care to omit when they published their White Book.

> As a possible sphere for future co-operation between the two countries the German Foreign Minister specified joint action in colonial matters and the emigration of Jews from Poland, *and a joint policy towards Russia on the basis of the Anti-Comintern Pact.* . . .

There was nothing new in this suggestion of German-Polish co-operation against Russia; it had been made a score of times by Goering in the past five years. So far the invitation had been evaded by Beck, and Hitler had not been pressing. But for the first time the question of Danzig had been raised, and Beck could have little doubt that Ribbentrop's proposals were being made with a sense of immediacy which had been lacking from Goering's expansive gestures.

The success of Beck's policy of independence had so far rested on the fact that neither Germany nor the Soviet Union had wished to bring pressure to bear on the Poles. Hitler had limited his demands in the first place to Danzig and a road and railway across the Corridor, but not a single Pole believed that, once these had been conceded, Hitler would not demand the cession of the provinces of Posen and Polish Silesia. Nor did Beck consider Ribbentrop's vague offer of alliance against Russia seriously, since he saw quite correctly that it would reduce Poland to the status of a German satellite. On the other hand, although he did his best to renew such links as he had with Moscow, he was equally opposed to becoming too dependent upon Russia either. The most he could do was to try to persuade the Germans not to press their demands, at the same time making it clear that any attempt to annex Danzig by force would lead to war.

On 24 November, Hitler revised his secret Directive to the Armed Forces to provide for a further contingency: a lightning occupation of Danzig by German forces, for which plans were to be submitted by 10 January. Although he knew nothing of this, after his conversations at Berchtesgaden Beck told Ribbentrop that he was in a pessimistic mood. "Particularly in regard to the Danzig question, as it had been raised by the Chancellor, he saw no possibility whatever of agreement." But Hitler had first to complete the liquidation of Czechoslovakia. At Berchtesgaden he assured Beck that there would be no *faits accomplis* in Danzig, and in his speech of 30 January he made his customary friendly reference to Poland. After that there was silence for the next seven weeks.

The occupation of Bohemia-Moravia, and the German assumption of a protectorate over Slovakia at once transformed the situation. German garrisons in Slovakia on the southern flank of Poland (already German troops were on Poland's northern and western frontiers) were taken in Warsaw as explicitly against Polish security. The deliberate neglect of the Germans to inform them of what they were doing increased the Polish Government's alarm.

Nor was this the end of German surprises in store for Poland. Immediately after the occupation of Prague, Ribbentrop presented an ultimatum to Lithuania demanding the return of the Memelland, a strip of territory on the northern frontier of East Prussia which Germany had lost by the Treaty of Versailles. Yet Ribbentrop again refused to give any information in advance to the Polish Ambassador.

There was no question of Lithuanian resistance to Germany, and Hitler arrived in Memel to acclaim its return to the Reich. "You have returned," he told the Memellanders, "to a mighty new Germany . . . a Germany determined to be the mistress of her own destiny . . . even if that should not please the world without. . . ."

For the moment the focus of Western anxieties was Rumania, where Herr Wohlthat was engaged in negotiating a far-reaching economic agreement on behalf of the Reich, which was signed on 23 March. Since the Treaty established Germany's dominant position in the development of Rumania's agricultural and mineral resources, it appeared unlikely that Hitler would make a further move in that direction, and an uneasy peace descended on the Balkans.

For it was on Poland that Hitler's attention was now fixed. On 21 March Ribbentrop again asked the Polish Ambassador to call on him. Lipski complained of the German action in Slovakia, which had been undertaken without a word to the Poles. Ribbentrop replied that, if the matter of Danzig and the road and railway to East Prussia could be settled to Germany's satisfaction, the Slovak question could be settled. But the Fuehrer had been disagreeably surprised at the failure of the Poles to make any constructive reply to his proposals, and it was important that he should not come to the conclusion that Poland was rejecting his offer. For that reason Colonel Beck should come to Berlin as soon as possible and the Ambassador should report to Warsaw at once.

Hitler was now determined to press the Poles hard, but he was still thinking in terms of a peaceful settlement which would bind the Poles more closely to Germany. He would have been glad enough to recover Danzig without making enemies of the Poles. On the other hand, he was not prepared to wait indefinitely for the Poles, and, if he had to use force, then characteristically he would impose a really drastic settlement upon the Poles, the outline of which he had ready at the back of his mind. Everything depended upon the answer the Poles gave him in the next few days.

On Sunday, 26 March, Lipski, newly returned from Warsaw, informed Ribbentrop that the Polish Government was anxious to reach a settlement with Germany; but the return of Danzig and the extra-territorial road and railway, were unacceptable. Ribbentrop received Lipski coldly and began to threaten. The Poles had been taking mobilization measures. "It reminded him of certain risky steps taken by another State (obviously Czechoslovakia). He added that all aggression on our part (against Danzig) would be an aggression against the Reich."

The next day Ribbentrop told Lipski the Polish counter-proposals were wholly unsatisfactory, began blustering about Polish outrages against the German minority in Poland and warned him that the German Press could hardly be restrained much longer. On 28 March Beck sent for the German Ambassador in Warsaw and replied to Ribbentrop's statement on Polish aggression against Danzig with the announcement that the Polish Government would equally regard any attempt by the Germans, or by the Danzig State, to change the *status quo* in the Free City as an act of aggression against Poland.

"The German Ambassador: You want to negotiate at the point of the bayonet!

"Colonel Beck: That is your own method."

At this stage, however, the situation was complicated by the unexpected intervention of the British Government, which, to Hitler's anger, refused to mind its own business. Alarming reports were reaching London of German preparations for immediate action against Danzig and Poland. This time Mr. Chamberlain conveyed the determination of

Great Britain to risk war rather than acquiesce in further
German acts of aggression. The French Government asso-
ciated themselves with the British in these assurances.

Mr. Chamberlain's sudden decision to offer an unconditional guarantee to Poland, followed within a fortnight by
similar guarantees to Rumania and Greece, was criticized in
Great Britain at the time, and has continued to be criticized
since, as a maladroit method of meeting the threat of further
German aggression. But this criticism, however just, does not
alter the fact that, from Hitler's point of view, he was now
confronted with a new situation, principally as a result of
his own decision to overrun the remainder of Czechoslovakia
only six months after the Munich Agreement. However, if
his action strengthened Germany's military position, it also
served at last to awaken the British Government to the need
to call a halt to Hitler's demands if Europe was not to be
conquered piecemeal. In short, Hitler had now to face a
European coalition which would put an end to his tactics of
"one-by-one" and threaten him with a general war, if he
ventured on further adventures in foreign policy. During
the next five months, April to September, 1939, Hitler attempted to divide the forces against him, and to recover
that freedom of action he had enjoyed between March,
1938, and March, 1939.

Hitler was both surprised and angered by the British declaration. Admiral Canaris, who was with Hitler, soon after
the news came from London, reported that he flew into a
passion, hammered on the table-top and stormed up and
down the room. "I'll cook them a stew that they'll choke on,"
he shouted. When he spoke at Wilhelmshaven on 1 April,
the day after Chamberlain's announcement in the House,
he insisted excitedly that he was not to be turned from his
path. Germany could not submit to intimidation or
encirclement.

In the same mood Hitler issued a new directive to his
commanders on 3 April which listed as the three contingen-
cies for which they were to prepare, the defence of the frontiers, Operation White (war with Poland), and the seizure
of Danzig. Plans for the smashing of the Polish armed forces,
were to be ready by 1 September, 1939, the actual date of
the German invasion of Poland. Germany policy, the directive stated, continued to be based on the avoidance of
trouble with Poland. But "should Poland . . . adopt a
threatening attitude towards the Reich, we may be driven
to a final settlement, notwithstanding the existing Pact wih
Poland." For the moment, however, Hitler seems to have
been at a loss how to proceed. This time the British Prime

Minister showed no disposition to fly to Germany, and the Polish Foreign Minister, instead of coming to Berlin as Ribbentrop had demanded, visited London, where agreement was announced on a pact of mutual assistance between Great Britain and Poland.

Grégoire Gafencu, the Rumanian Foreign Minister, who paid a visit to the Chancellery on 19 April, the eve of Hitler's fiftieth birthday, found the mention of England brought him out of his chair, pacing up and down the room and shouting out his resentment. "Well, if England wants war, she can have it. It will not be an easy war, as they like to think. . . . And it will be a war of such destructiveness as no one has imagined. How can the English imagine what a modern war will be like when they are incapable of putting two fully-equipped divisions in the field?"

Some of the anger which Hitler felt at this check came out in his speech to the Reichstag at the end of the month. On 14 April, following the Italian invasion of Albania on the 7th, President Roosevelt had addressed a message to Mussolini and Hitler, asking if they were willing to give assurances against aggression to a list of thirty countries. It was announced that Hitler would reply to the President on 28 April.

Hitler began his speech with a lengthy and elaborate defence of his foreign policy, up to the present. This is so frequent a feature of his speeches on foreign policy as to suggest that this act of self-justification was psychologically necessary, in order to kindle the indignation and conviction with which he could defend the most blatant acts of aggression.

After describing his action in Czechoslovakia as a service to peace, Hitler passed to a consideration of German relations with Great Britain for which he had nothing but feelings of friendship, but friendship could only survive if it was based on mutual regard for each other's interests and achievements. This the British refused to recognize. The British now accepted war with Germany as inevitable, and had begun their old game of encircling Germany. With this the basis for the Anglo-German Naval Treaty of 1935 had been destroyed, and he therefore decided formally to denounce it.

With Poland, too, Hitler declared, he had been only too anxious to reach a settlement. He had never ceased to uphold the necessity for Poland to have access to the sea. But Germany also had legitimate demands, for access to East Prussia and for the return of the German city of Danzig to the Reich. To solve the problem Hitler had made an unprecedented offer to Poland, the terms of which he now re-

peated, with the careful omission of the German invitation to join against Russia. The Poles, however, had not only
rejected his offer, but had begun to lend themselves—like
the Czechs the year before—to the international campaign
of lies against Germany. Thus the German-Polish Agreement
of 1934 had no longer any validity, and Hitler had decided
to denounce this too. He was careful to add, however, that
the door to a fresh agreement between Germany and Poland
was still open, and that he would welcome such an agreement, provided it was upon equal terms.

Throughout this speech Hitler spoke in violent terms of
the "international warmongers" in the Democracies, whose
one objective was to misrepresent German aims and to stir
up trouble. He boasted of the part German and Italian forces
had played in Franco's victory, and exalted the strength of the
Axis, congratulating Mussolini on the occupation of Albania
and the establishment of order in a territory which naturally
belonged to Italy's *Lebensraum*.

Hitler had by now worked himself into the state of mind
to answer President Roosevelt. Now his speech was marked by
a display of sarcasm which produced roars of applause from
the Reichstag, and from the delighted Goering, who presided. It is not difficult to pull holes in Hitler's argument when
it is set down in cold print, or to point to the cheapness of
his retorts, but to see and hear it brought to life on the film
is to be struck once again by Hitler's mastery of irony and
every other trick of the orator. As he delivered it, it was a
masterpiece of political propaganda, directed with equal
skill at his German audience and at public opinion in the
U.S.A.

The American President had read him a lesson on the
wickedness and futility of war: who should know better,
Hitler retorted, than the German people, who had suffered
from an unjust peace treaty for twenty years? Mr. Roosevelt
believed that all problems could be solved round the conference table: yet the first nation to express distrust of the
League of Nations was the U.S.A., which refused to join it
from the beginning. "The freedom of North America was
not achieved at the conference table, any more than the
conflict between the North and South."

President Roosevelt pleaded for disarmament: the German
people, trusting in the promises of another American President,
had laid down their arms once before . . . only to see the
other States repudiate their promises: the German people
had had enough of unilateral disarmament.

Mr. Roosevelt was much concerned about German intentions in Europe. If Germany enquired about American policy

in Central and South America she would be referred to the Monroe Doctrine and told to mind her own business. None the less, Hitler had approached each of the States mentioned by the President and has asked them if they felt threatened by Germany. . . . The reply in all cases had been negative. Not all the States mentioned by the President, however, had been able to reply. In Syria and Palestine the views of the inhabitants could not be ascertained owing to the occupation by French and British—not German—troops. The German Government was still willing to give assurances against aggression to any of the States referred to by the President, provided only that they asked for such assurances themselves.

Mr. Roosevelt! I fully understand that the vastness of your nation and the immense wealth of your country allow you to feel responsible for the history of the whole world and for the history of all nations. I, sir, am placed in a much smaller and more modest sphere.

I once took over a State, which was faced by complete ruin, thanks to its trust in the promises of the rest of the world and to the bad régime of democratic governments. . . .

Since then, Mr. Roosevelt . . . as this world took no interest in the pitiful fate of my own people, I have regarded myself as called upon by Providence to serve my own people alone. . . . I have lived day and night for the single task of awakening the powers of my people, in view of our desertion by the rest of the world. . . .

I have conquered chaos in Germany, re-established order, enormously increased production. . . . I have succeeded in finding useful work once more for the whole of seven million unemployed. . . . Not only have I united the German people politically, but I have also rearmed them. I have also endeavoured to destroy sheet by sheet the treaty which in its 448 articles contains the vilest oppression which peoples and human beings have ever been expected to put up with.

I have brought back to the Reich provinces stolen from us in 1919, I have led back to their native country millions of Germans who were torn away from us and were in misery, I have re-established the historic unity of German living-space—and, Mr. Roosevelt, I have endeavoured to attain all this without spilling blood and without bringing to my people, and consequently to others, the misery of war.

I, who twenty-one years ago was an unknown worker and soldier of my people, have attained this, Mr. Roosevelt, by my own energy. . . . You, Mr. Roosevelt, have a much easier task in comparison. You became President of the United States in 1933 when I became Chancellor of the Reich. From the very outset you stepped to the head of one of the largest and wealthiest States in the world. . . .

Your concerns and suggestions, therefore, cover a much

larger area than mine, because my world, Mr. Roosevelt, in which Providence has placed me and for which I am therefore obliged to work, is unfortunately much smaller—although for me it is more precious than anything else, for it is limited to my people.

I believe, however, that this is the way in which I can be of the most service to that for which we are all concerned, the justice, well-being, progress and peace of the whole human community.

This speech of 28 April, 1939, is one of the most effective defences Hitler ever made of his use of the power he had secured in 1933. Yet Hitler's real skill lay in his evasion of the simple question which President Roosevelt had posed: was Nazi Germany entertaining further schemes of aggression?

To this question Hitler, for obvious reasons, confused the issue by repeating his own highly selected and exaggerated account of the history of Germany since 1918, by pointing to the inconsistencies and shortcomings of his critics, and by playing upon that historical pariah-complex of self-pity and self-justification which the German people had developed after 1918. Even to question his intentions was made to appear as part of a denial of equal rights to the German people.

The speech marked the close, rather than the opening, of a period of activity on Hitler's part. Hitler was content to sit back and wait. Even in regard to Poland the door had been left open to further negotiations, if the Poles should change their minds.

Throughout the summer of 1939, from the end of April to August, Hitler was little to be seen in public. His silence was as much the product of uncertainty as of calculation. Yet he could have devised no better tactics for the occasion. Once the tension was relaxed, there was a good chance that London and Paris might be tempted to reduce rather than extend the obligations they had assumed. In Paris, in particular, the currents of appeasement and defeatism still ran strongly beneath the surface. Nor were the guarantees which had been given to Poland and to Rumania of value, unless they could be supported by the construction of a coherent system of collective security. The policy of appeasement hitherto followed by the two Powers made it difficult to create such a system in a short time.

The key to their success lay in Moscow. Only with the backing of Russia could collective security in Eastern Europe be made into something more than a phrase. Not only however, did the Russian Government look upon British and French policy with intense distrust, but the Poles, the Rumanians and the peoples of the Baltic States were strongly adverse to accepting help from a country they regarded with as much suspicion as Germany. Given time and a relaxation of pressure, here was a situation from which Hitler should not find it hard to extract profit.

Throughout the summer the remilitarization of Danzig, the training of the local S.S. and S.A. with arms smuggled across the frontier, and a series of incidents designed to provoke the Poles, continued with little remission. In the middle of June Goebbels appeared in the city and made two violent speeches, reaffirming the German claim to its return.

While pressure was kept up on Poland, German propaganda through the radio and the Press hammered home the argument that Danzig was not worth a war, and that war was only likely because of the obstinacy of the Poles. In their turn the Poles were warned not to trust their new friends, the British, who would soon tire of their energetic attitude, and sell them down the river, as they had sold the Czechs at Munich.

The centre of diplomatic activity during the summer was Moscow, where the British and French were attempting to reach an agreement with the Russians. From time to time, however, Weizsäcker, the State Secretary at the Wilhelmstrasse, saw the British and French Ambassadors in Berlin in order to sound them out. His arguments always followed the same course: the rashness of Britain and France in handing over the decision of peace or war to an irresponsible people like the Poles.

Meanwhile relations with the other States in the German sphere of influence were strengthened, in order to keep Poland isolated. The visit of the Hungarian Prime Minister and Foreign Minister to Berlin, at the end of April, was followed by the State visit of Prince Paul, the Regent of Yugoslavia, at the beginning of June. A month later the Bulgarian Prime Minister was fêted in the German capital. The Pact of Non-Aggression signed with Lithuania after the cession of Memelland was matched by similar pacts with Latvia and Estonia.

Hitler's principal concern, however, was the alliance with Italy. The invasion of Albania in April, which Mussolini and Ciano regarded as the assertion of Italian independence, only bound them more closely to the Axis. Hitler was delighted and the Germans now began to press for the signature of the military alliance which Mussolini had so far evaded. Ciano was uneasy about German-Polish relations; therefore he invited Ribbentrop to come to Italy, in the hope of learning what was in Hitler's mind, and set off for their meeting at Milan (on 6 May) with the Duce's memorandum which stressed Italy's need of peace for at least three more years.

Ribbentrop did not disguise Hitler's determination to recover Danzig and secure his motor-road to East Prussia, but he was sympathetic to Mussolini's insistence on the need to defer war. After dinner Ciano telephoned to Mussolini and reported that the conversations were going well. Thereupon the Duce, apparently swayed by a gust of anti-British irritation ordered Ciano to publish the news that an Italo-German alliance had been agreed upon. Ribbentrop would have preferred to wait until he could bring in Japan as well, but when he telephoned to Hitler he found the Fuehrer eager to seize the chance offered by Mussolini's sudden change of mind. The announcement of the alliance, Hitler was convinced, would further weaken the British and French resolution to stand by Poland. The Italians accepted the German draft and on 21 May Ciano arrived in Berlin for the formal signature of the Pact of Steel.

The Chancellery was crowded with brilliant uniforms, resplendent with decorations. Ciano had invested Ribbentrop with the Collar of the Annunziata the evening before, thereby making him the cousin of the King of Italy, and seriously offending Goering, who noisily declared that he should have received the decoration as the real architect of the Alliance. Hitler, in the best of tempers, presided while the two Foreign Ministers affixed their signatures. He had every reason to be pleased.

The preamble of the Treaty announced that "the German and Italian nations are determined to act side by side and with united forces for the securing of their living-space and the maintenance of peace."

> *Article III:* If, contrary to the wishes and hopes of the contracting parties, it should happen that one of them is involved in hostilities with another Power or Powers, the other contracting party will come immediately to its side as ally and support it with all its military forces on land, sea and in the air. . . .
>
> *Article V:* The contracting parties undertake now that in the event of a war conducted in common they will conclude an armistice and peace only in full agreement with each other.

When due allowance is made for the conventional ambiguity of diplomatic language, this may well be considered one of the most plain-spoken and openly offensive alliances concluded in modern times.

Mussolini's chief anxiety, however, continued to be the possibility of war. On 30 May, the day before General Cavallero left Rome to serve on the military commission set up under the new Pact, the Duce gave him a secret memorandum for Hitler which re-emphasized Italy's need of a preparatory period of peace extending as far as the end of 1942. Hitler's reply was a vague suggestion that he should meet the Duce for a discussion some time in the near future. Beyond that he made no comment, and his silence seems to have been accepted by the Italians as assent.

Had Mussolini known what Hitler told his senior Army, Navy and Air Force officers on 23 May, the day after the Pact of Steel had been signed, his anxiety would have been vastly increased.

Hitler began from the same premises as in November, 1937: the problem of *Lebensraum*, and the need to solve it by expansion eastwards. Once again he ruled out a colonial solution as an alternative. This time, however, he came almost at once to the military problem. The shift from political to military considerations between November, 1937, and May, 1939, is striking.

War, Hitler told his officers, was inevitable.

Danzig is not the object of our activities. It is a question of expanding our living-space in the east, of securing our food-supplies and of settling the Baltic problem. . . . There is no question of sparing Poland and we are left with the decision: To attack Poland at the first suitable opportunity.

We cannot expect a repetition of the Czech affair. There will be war. Our task is to isolate Poland. The success of this isolation will be decisive. . . . There must be no simultaneous conflict with the Western Powers.

If it is not certain that a German-Polish conflict will not lead to war in the west, the fight must be primarily against England and France.

Basic principle: Conflict with Poland—beginning with an attack on Poland—will only be successful if the Western Powers keep out. If this is impossible, then it will be better to attack in the west and incidentally to settle Poland at the same time.

Hitler then went on to discuss the character of a war with the British, whom he described as the driving force against Germany, and of whose strength he spoke with appreciation. It would, he declared, be a life-and-death struggle and probably of long duration. "The idea that we can get off cheaply is dangerous; there is no such possibility. We must burn our boats. It is no longer a question of right or wrong, but of life or death for eighty million human beings."

Much that Hitler said about the conduct of a war with

Britain is of interest in the light of events a year later. He saw the Ruhr as Germany's vital point, and so made the occupation of Holland and Belgium, to protect the Ruhr, a first objective. Britain's weakness was her need of sea-borne supplies. The Army's task, therefore, must be to overrun the Low Countries and France in order to provide bases from which the Navy and Air Force could blockade Britain and cut off her supplies. Analysing the lessons of the First World War, Hitler argued that a wheeling movement by the German Army towards the Channel ports at the outbreak of war—instead of towards Paris—might well have been decisive. This was in fact to be his own strategy in 1940.

Granted Hitler's purpose of pursuing an expansionist policy, it was a sober and shrewd calculation of the risks. Its weakness was Hitler's failure to push his predictions far enough into the future, and to reckon with the importance of the U.S.A., or the strength of the Soviet Union. But, in the short run, Hitler was quite right in thinking that he could ignore both America and Russia, while his estimate of France's weakness and his grasp of how to attack Britain are noteworthy.

As it happens, we have a precise account of what German rearmament had achieved so far, given by General Thomas, Head of the War Economy and Armaments Office, the day after Hitler's conference. From the Peace Treaty army of 7 infantry and 3 cavalry divisions, which Hitler had found on taking office, the German Army had been expanded to a peacetime strength of 30 infantry divisions (including 4 fully motorized and 3 mountain divisions), 5 newly equipped Panzer divisions, 4 light divisions and 22 machine-gun battalions.

Behind these forces there stood a steadily increasing number of reserves and the most powerful armaments industry in the world. Nor had the Army been built up at the expense of the other branches of the armed forces. Since 1933 the German Navy had put into service two battleships of 26,000 tons; two armoured cruisers of 10,000 tons; 17 destroyers and 47 U-boats. It had launched, and was engaged on completing, two more battleships of 35,000 tons (actually much larger, for one of them was the *Bismarck*); 4 heavy cruisers of 10,000 tons; an aircraft carrier; 5 destroyers and 7 U-boats. The German Air Force, which had been entirely built up since 1933, now had a strength of 260,000 men, with 21 squadrons consisting of 240 echelons. Its anti-aircraft forces, equipped with four standard types of A.A. guns, numbered close on three hundred batteries.

If, numerically, the number of divisions Germany could put in the field was still smaller than that of the French or

Russian Armies, in quality, leadership and equipment it was almost certainly an instrument without equal—and this time Hitler was determined to put it to use. On 14 June, the Commander-in-Chief of the Third Army Group, General Blaskowitz, issued orders from his H.Q. at Dresden to have all preparations for the attack on Poland complete by 20 August. On 22 June, the O.K.W. presented a detailed timetable for the attack, for which reserves were to be called up on the pretext of autumn manoeuvres. On the 24th, the Army was ordered to prepare plans for capturing the bridges over the Lower Vistula intact. A month later, on 27 July, the order was drafted for the occupation of Danzig, only the date being left blank for the Fuehrer to write in.

Yet Hitler was in no hurry to move. He was still preoccupied with the problem of localizing the war. Three months had passed since his speech of 28 April; the resolution of the Poles, and the determination of the British and French to stand by their guarantees, had been subjected to strains, but had not been weakened. Only in one direction could Hitler see an opening, in Moscow. Talks between British, French and Russian representatives began in Moscow on 15 June. It was no secret, however, that agreement was still very far off, and that neither side had lost its suspicions of the other.

Hitler followed the course of these negotiations with interest. Without the support of Russia, the one Great Power near enough to give active help to Poland, the Anglo-French guarantees must lose much of their value. True, France and Britain could still attack Germany from the west; but this would not prevent the German Army overrunning Poland, and presenting the Western Powers with a *fait accompli* which would make their continuation of the war futile. Or could a Russo-German agreement undercut the Western Powers and guarantee Russia's neutrality in the event of a war between Germany and Poland? In that case, Britain and France would be forced to recognize the impossibility of trying to aid Poland.

These possibilities were already being canvassed in the group around Hitler as early as March and April. Hitler was slow to make up his mind. The basis for a deal was obvious. In the long run war between Germany and Russia was inevitable, so long as Hitler persisted in looking for Germany's living-space in the east. But, in the short run, there was no conflict of interests. The last thing Hitler wanted was to become involved with Russia while occupied with Poland. Stalin, on his side, had few illusions about Hitler's ultimate objectives, but was eager to postpone the clash with Germany as

long as possible. Stalin had an inveterate distrust of the
Western Powers, doubted their determination to resist Hit-
ler and suspected them of trying purposely to embroil the
Soviet Union with Germany.

In such a frame of mind, Stalin was likely to look on a
separate deal with Germany as very much to Russia's advantage. It would enable him to buy time at the expense of
Poland, and possibly secure important territorial and strategic
advantages in Eastern Europe as part of his price. These
could be used to strengthen the Soviet Union against the
day when Hitler should feel free to carry out his designs
against Russia.

The obstacles in the way were twofold: the extreme distrust each side entertained towards the other, and the public
commitments each had undertaken against the other. Hitler
had made anti-Bolshevism a principal item of his propaganda
stock-in-trade for twenty years, both in Germany and
abroad; he had built up his foreign relations around the
Anti-Comintern Pact. However cynical his intentions towards
Russia once the Pact had served its purpose, Hitler was
bound to hesitate in face of such a repudiation of his own past.

But most people would be far more impressed by his
astuteness in getting the Russians to sign than troubled
about his inconsistency. In the German Army, always preoccupied with the danger of a war on two fronts, there had
always been a school of thought which favoured active collaboration with Russia. In the German Foreign Office, too, a
policy of friendship with Russia had not lacked advocates
after 1918, and had found expression in the Treaty of Rapallo
in 1922, when the two countries had formed a common
front against the victor powers. To those who were struggling
with the economic problems of the Four-Year Plan, the
ability to draw upon Russian resources in raw materials
would be a godsend. Finally—and this weighed most of all
with Hitler—this was the surest way to isolate Poland and
to deter the Western Powers from interfering.

These discussions were given added point by the news
on 3 May that Litvinov, the man most closely identified
with the policy of collective security and co-operation
with the Western Powers, had been dismissed from the office
of Soviet Foreign Minister and replaced by Molotov. Litvinov's dismissal raised great hopes in the circle round the
Fuehrer. Trade negotiations between the two countries had
been unaccountably delayed, but now the Germans proposed
to start them in earnest, and the first difficult contacts were
made in May.

At last, on the evening of 26 July, Schnurre, in charge of

the talks on the German side, took Astakhov, the Soviet *Chargé,* and Babarin, the head of the Russian Trade Mission, out to dinner. Schnurre's instructions were to raise once more the possibility of political, as well as economic, negotiations. "What could England offer Russia?" he asked his two guests. "At best, participation in a European war and the hostility of Germany, but not a single desirable end for Russia. What could we offer, on the other hand? Neutrality in a possible European conflict, and . . . a German-Russian understanding on mutual interests which would work out to the advantage of both countries."

Ribbentrop followed up Schnurre's conversation by instructing the German Ambassador to see Molotov and propose political talks along the lines Schnurre had indicated.

> In *any* development of the Polish question [Ribbentrop wrote], either in a peaceful manner or in any other way, we would be prepared to safeguard all Soviet interests . . . . If the talks proceed positively . . . the idea could be advanced that we will adjust our stand with regard to the Baltic . . . to respect the vital Soviet interests . . . .

Hitler was now convinced that, if his approach to Moscow were successful, he had hit upon the way of prising open the door barred by the British guarantee to Poland, and enforcing his will on the Poles without the risk of a general war.

In his dispatch of 3 August, the French Chargé d' Affaires in Berlin reported: "In the course of the last week a very definite change in the political atmosphere has been observed in Berlin. . . . The period of . . . hesitation . . . has been succeeded by a new phase."

The most obvious sign of this change was the renewal of the Press campaign, which was now enlarged to include German claims not merely to Danzig, but to the whole of the Corridor, and even Posen and Upper Silesia, claims supported by a steady stream of reports describing Polish oppression of the German minority in these provinces.

At the same time the interference of the Germans in Danzig with the Polish customs and frontier guards in the Free Territory, and Polish economic reprisals, led to the most serious crisis so far in the dispute over the city. On 7 August, Forster, the Gauleiter of Danzig, was summoned to the Obersalzberg, and on his return told Carl Burckhardt, the League High Commissioner, that Hitler had reached the extreme limits of his patience. On the 11th, when Burckhardt himself visited Hitler, the Fuehrer threatened that "if the slightest thing was attempted by the Poles he would fall upon them like lightning with all the powerful arms at his disposal, of which the Poles had not the slightest idea. M. Burckhardt said that that would lead to a general conflict. Herr Hitler replied that if he had to make war he would rather do it today than tomorrow, and that he would fight without mercy up to the extreme limit."

Hitler was still waiting with growing impatience for news of the Russian reception of his proposal before he punished Poland for her insolent refusal of his earlier offer. Schulenberg, the German Ambassador, saw Molotov on 3 August and reported hopefully that Molotov had shown considerable interest in the offer to provide for Soviet interests in Poland and the Baltic States. British and French Military Missions to extend the scope of their talks were en route to Moscow, where they arrived on 11 August. It was clear that a decision by the Soviet Government, promised by Molotov at the interview on the 3rd, could not be much longer delayed.

In Rome, meanwhile, Ciano decided that the time had come for him to learn what the Germans were planning. Towards the end of July Italian suggestions for an international conference, in which Mussolini saw himself repeating his Munich success, were rejected by Ribbentrop. Ciano began to feel a little uneasy: silence and evasiveness of the German leaders were the usual signs that they meant to spring a surprise on their allies. But this time a surprise might mean war. At Ciano's urgent request Ribbentrop agreed to meet him at Salzburg on 11 August. "Before letting me go," Ciano recorded in his Diary, "Mussolini recommends that I should frankly inform the Germans that we must avoid a conflict with Poland, since it will be impossible to localize it, and a general war would be disastrous for everybody. . . . "

When they met at Salzburg the two Foreign Ministers spent altogether ten hours in each other's company. Ciano pleaded with all the eloquence at his command for a peaceful settlement of the dispute with Poland; he found himself up against a brick wall. Ribbentrop proclaimed a German-Polish conflict inevitable but refused, however, to tell Ciano what Germany proposed to do—"all decisions were still locked in the Fuehrer's impenetrable bosom." So convinced was he that the Western Powers would not intervene that he wagered Ciano a collection of old armour against an Italian painting that he would be proven right. Four years later, sitting in gaol at Verona, waiting to be shot by the Germans, Ciano reflected with some bitterness that Ribbentrop had neglected to pay his debt.

Ciano described the atmosphere of his talks with Ribbentrop as icy. Hitler, whom he was taken to see the following day at the Berghof, was more cordial, but equally implacable. He received Ciano with his staff-maps spread out on the table before him and demonstrated the strength of Germany's military position: "After the conquest of Poland (which could be expected in a short time) Germany would be in a position to assemble for a general conflict a hundred divisions on the West Wall." As for Poland, she was too weak to withstand the German attack, and Hitler repeated Ribbentrop's suggestion that Italy should take advantage of the occasion to dismember Yugoslavia.

In reply Ciano set out with a wealth of detail Italy's weakness and lack of preparations for war, complaining that, despite the alliance so recently signed, the Germans had never informed their allies of the gravity of the situation or of their own intentions. But Hitler, he noted, listened with a far-away look. "The Fuehrer was determined to use the opportunity of the next political provocation . . . to attack Poland within forty-eight hours and to solve the problem in that way."

Ciano did his best to argue with Hitler but without effect. Convinced that the Western Powers would not intervene, Hitler was prepared to dispense with Italian aid, and said so. While they were still talking a telegram arrived from Moscow announcing Russian agreement to the dispatch of a German delegation to negotiate. This incident bears all the marks of having been staged for Ciano's special benefit: it confirmed the impression that everything had been decided already, and that Hitler only continued to listen to the views of his Italian allies out of politeness.

The next day, 13 August, when the conversation was renewed, Ciano made no further effort to alter Hitler's mind. Hitler added that Britain and France were not in any case prepared to allow the Axis the further period of preparation which Mussolini desired. "The Western Democracies were dominated by the desire to rule the world, and would not regard Germany and Italy as their class. This psychological element of contempt was perhaps the worst thing about the whole business. It could only be settled by a life-and-death struggle."

Hitler added the usual assurances regarding the Mediterranean, and declared himself fortunate to have been born "at a time in which, apart from himself, there was one other statesman who would stand out as great and unique in history; that he could be this man's friend was for him a matter of great personal satisfaction."

Ciano wrote: "I return to Rome, completely disgusted with

the Germans, with their leader, and with their way of doing things. They have betrayed us and lied to us. Now they are dragging us into an adventure which . . . may compromise the régime and the country as a whole."

There is no need to look far for an explanation of Hitler's indifference towards the ally he had welcomed with such effusiveness three months before. It was the prospect of an agreement with Russia which now dazzled the Fuehrer and Ribbentrop. There was always a strong element of personal feeling in all Hitler's policies; to sign a treaty with a government he had hitherto treated with unremitting hostility, at the very moment when the British and French Missions were still negotiating in the Russian capital—this was the sort of revenge which appealed to his vanity.

Yet the agreement was far from being so certain as Ribbentrop had suggested to Ciano. Hitler, with his eyes on the deadline he had fixed for the attack on Poland, began to press for the negotiations to start at once.

Molotov still found reasons for delay. Did the Germans wish to conclude a pact of non-aggression? If so, what were to be its provisions, and so on. Ribbentrop at once replied, accepting all Molotov's suggestions and reiterating the need for haste. Molotov, quick to take advantage of the Germans' eagerness, fell back on the need to prepare for the conference in the most thorough way. If the agreement could be signed at once, for example, the German Foreign Minister might come to Moscow say, on 26 or 27 August: in the meantime Molotov handed the German Ambassador a draft of the proposed Pact which his Government could study. The Germans immediately signed the economic agreement, but they were not prepared to wait another week. On Sunday the 20th, Hitler telegraphed Stalin, asking him to receive Ribbentrop on the 22nd, or at the latest 23 August.

Throughout the rest of Sunday and all day Monday Hitler waited on tenterhooks for Stalin's reply. Would the Russians still go through with the deal? Would they agree to his need of a quick decision? Worst of all, would they, at the last moment, reach agreement with the British and French? Unable to sleep, Hitler rang up Goering in the middle of the night to express his anxiety at Stalin's delay.

At last, Monday morning, Schulenburg telegraphed Stalin's reply:

To the Chancellor of the German Reich, A. Hitler:
I thank you for your letter. I hope that the German-Soviet Non-Aggression Pact will mark a decided turn for the better in the political relations between our two countries . . . .
The Soviet Government has authorised me to inform you

that it agrees to Herr von Ribbentrop's arriving in Moscow
on 23 August.

J. Stalin.

Hitler had already accepted Molotov's draft of the Pact,
but the Russian proposal contained a postscript of far
greater importance than the text to be published. Put in crude
terms, the Soviet Government did not propose to sign until it
learned what its share of the spoils was going to be, and how
Eastern Europe was to be parcelled into spheres of influence.
It was to complete this process of horse-trading that Ribbentrop was now to fly to Moscow. But to Hitler the one
thing that mattered was the Pact. For the Pact, whatever its
precise wording, would mean the neutrality of Russia, the
end of the Western Powers' hopes of building a system of
collective security in Eastern Europe, and the isolation of
Poland. To get Stalin's signature he was prepared to promise
anything, and without a moment's hesitation he signed the
scrap of paper conferring plenipotentiary powers on Ribbentrop, who, early on the 22nd, was on his way by plane to
Moscow.

Later that day one after another of the senior commanders of the Armed Services drove up the mountain road to the
Berghof for a conference specially summoned by the Fuehrer. Hitler stood behind a large desk, while the officers sat in
a half-circle before him. No discussion was permitted; they
were there to listen. No official record was kept, but sur-
reptitious notes were taken by more than one officer, and
these supply a substantial version of what Hitler said.

Hitler set out the factors which made the present situation
unusually favorable for Germany to act against Poland.

First of all two personal factors: my own personality and
that of Mussolini. Essentially it depends on me, on my existence, because of my political ability. Probably no one will
ever again have the confidence of the German people as I
have. There will probably never again be a man with more
authority than I have. My life is, therefore, a factor of
great value. But I can be eliminated at any time by a criminal or an idiot.

The second personal factor is the Duce. His life is also
a decisive factor. If something happens to him, Italy's loyalty
. . . will no longer be certain. . . .

For us it is easy to make decisions. We have nothing to
lose; we can only gain. Our economic situation is such that
we cannot hold out for more than a few years. Goering can
confirm this. We have no other choice; we must act. Our
opponents risk much and can gain only a little. England's
stake in a war is unimaginably great.

The West has only two possibilities in a fight against us: (1)

Blockade: it will not be effective because of our autarky and because we have sources of aid in the East. (2) Attack in the west from the Maginot Line: I consider this impossible.

The enemy had another hope, that Russia would become our enemy after the conquest of Poland. The enemy did not count on my great power of determination. Our enemies are little worms: I saw them in Munich. I was convinced that Stalin would never accept the English offer. . . . Litvinov's dismissal was decisive. . . . The day after tomorrow Ribbentrop will conclude the treaty. Now Poland is in the position in which I wanted her.

We need not be afraid of a blockade. The East will supply us with grain, cattle, coal, lead and zinc. It is a big aim which demands great efforts. I am only afraid that at the last minute some *Schweinhund* will produce a plan of mediation. The political aim goes farther. A beginning has been made with the destruction of England's hegemony. The way is open for the soldier, now that I have made the political preparations.

Then Hitler returned to the need for iron resolution.

. . . In 1918 the nation fell because the mental prerequisites were not sufficient.

The destruction of Poland stands in the foreground. . . . I shall give a good propaganda reason for starting the war, whether plausible or not. The victor will not be asked, later on, whether he told the truth or not. In starting and making war it is not right, but victory, that matters.

Have no pity. Brutal attitude. Eighty million people must get what is their right. Their existence must be secured. Might is right. Greatest severity.

With this exhortation Hitler dismissed his generals. The creation of Greater Germany had been an achievement politically, he told them, but militarily it was questionable, since it had been achieved by bluff. It was now necessary to test the Army, although he had little doubt that it would come up to requirements. As for the opening of the war, the probable time would be at dawn on Saturday, 26 August.

Hitler stayed on at the Berghof, waiting for news from Moscow, for the rest of the 22nd and for the whole of Wednesday, the 23rd. It was here that Henderson, the British Ambassador, found him on Wednesday afternoon after flying from Berlin. On the previous day the British Cabinet had met to discuss the announcement that Germany and Russia were about to conclude a Pact of Non-Aggression. Contrary to Hitler's expectation, they announced: "The Cabinet had no hesitation in deciding such an event would in no way affect their obligation to Poland, which they have repeatedly stated and which they are determined to fulfil." To leave no doubt that they meant what they said, the British Government began to call up reservists and ordered their Ambassador in Berlin to deliver to Hitler personally a letter from the Prime Minister.

It was a letter couched in the most unambigious terms:

> It has been alleged [Mr. Chamberlain wrote] that if H.M. Government had made their position more clear in 1914 the great catastrophe would have been avoided. Whether or not there is any force in this allegation, H.M. Government are resolved that on this occasion there shall be no such tragic misunderstanding.
>
> If the case should arise, they are resolved, and prepared, to employ without delay all the forces at their command, and it is impossible to foresee the end of hostilities once engaged.

Mr. Chamberlain expressed the view that there was no issue between Germany and Poland which could not be settled by negotiation, and suggested ways in which such negotiations might be begun.

The effect of this letter was to rouse Hitler to a fury. No sooner had he received Henderson than he launched into a violent tirade against the British: it was the British guarantee to Poland, he declared, which had prevented the whole affair being settled long ago. He gave the wildest account of Polish excesses against the German minority in Poland, refused even to consider the suggestion of negotiations, and bitterly reproached the British for the way in which they had rejected his offers of friendship.

To all appearance Hitler was a man whom anger had driven beyond the reach of rational argument, yet Weizsäcker, who was present, records: "Hardly had the door shut behind the Ambassador than Hitler slapped himself on the thigh, laughed and said: 'Chamberlain won't survive that conversation; his Cabinet will fall this evening'."

At a second interview, later in the afternoon, Henderson found the Chancellor in a calmer frame of mind, but as unprepared as before to make a single concession. "I spoke of the tragedy of war," Henderson reported, "and of his immense responsibility, but his answer was that it would be all England's fault. . . . He was, he said, fifty years old: he preferred war now to when he would be fifty-five or sixty." Hitler took note of the British intention to fulfil their guarantee to Poland, but this, he added, could make no difference to his determination: "Germany, if attacked by England, will be found prepared and determined."

Meanwhile, Saturday, 26 August, at four-forty in the morning, was confirmed as the date of the invasion.

The news from Moscow was good. Ribbentrop reached the Russian capital at noon on the 23rd. He drove almost immediately to the Kremlin for his talks with Stalin and Molotov.

The evening appears to have been passed in the most cordial atmosphere. Toasts were drunk while copies of the Agreement were being prepared for signature.

The first document was a straightforward pact of non-aggression, but to this public treaty was appended a protocol of the utmost secrecy, which only became known after the war. By this Germany and Russia agreed to divide the whole of Eastern Europe into spheres of influence, the limits of which were outlined in three clauses. In the first, Finland, Estonia and Latvia were recognized to lie in the Soviet sphere, Lithuania and Vilna in the German. In the second, a partition of Poland was foreshadowed along the line of the Rivers Narew, Vistula and San. In the third article Russia stated her interest in the Rumanian province of Bessarabia. Ribbentrop, with an eye to German economic interests in that part of the world, was content to declare Germany's "complete political disinterestedness in these areas."

In the early hours of the 24th both documents were signed, and by one o'clock in the afternoon Ribbentrop was on his way back to Berlin filled with enthusiasm for Germany's new friends. Stalin was less easily carried away. As the German delegation left the Kremlin he took Ribbentrop by the arm and repeated: "The Soviet Government takes the new Pact very seriously. I can guarantee on my word of honour that the Soviet Union will not betray its partner." The doubts were barely concealed.

Perhaps the most striking aspect of Ribbentrop's discussions in Moscow was the careful way in which both sides avoided mention of the State, on the partition of which they had virtually signed agreement. Yet if ever the death warrant of a nation was signed in cold blood it was at Moscow, and Ribbentrop returned to Berlin in the firm belief that he brought with him an agreement which gave Hitler a free hand to deal the Poles a blow from which they would not recover for fifty years. To get this Ribbentrop had been prepared to risk straining Germany's relations with the Italians and the Japanese, to make nonsense of the Anti-Comintern Pact of which he had himself been the architect, and to grant sweeping concessions to the Russians in Eastern Europe. Immediately, these appeared a small price to pay for one of the most dramatic diplomatic *coups* in history, which at a blow wrote off the Franco-Soviet Alliance of 1935, the long-drawn-out negotiations of the British and French in

Moscow, and—as Ribbentrop was quite convinced—the British and French guarantees of support to Poland.

Hitler was in Berlin to greet his Foreign Minister as "a second Bismarck"—a remark that indicates the unique place in German history which he now claimed for himself. Hitler, while impressed by the advantages of securing Russia's neutrality, was still profoundly disappointed by the news from London. Instead of the fall of the Chamberlain Government, which he had confidently anticipated, there came reports of Chamberlain's and Halifax's speeches in Parliament, re-affirming Britain's determination to stand by her obligations. He had first looked to the passage of time and skilful propaganda to cause the British and French to lose interest in Poland. When these hopes proved unfounded, he had looked to the Pact with Russia to produce a reversal of policy in London and Paris. Now this too appeared to have failed.

On one issue Hitler's mind was made up: either the Poles capitulated unconditionally under threat of force, or he would attack. Hitler wanted war—but only a localized war. To secure that he was now prepared to make one last bid to separate the British and French from the Poles.

This last approach to London and Paris was made by two separate means. The first—the initiative for which came from Goering, not Hitler—was the dispatch of an unofficial envoy to sound out the British by the back door. On the morning of the 25th Hr. Birger Dahlerus, a Swedish friend of Goering's, left by plane for London and saw Lord Halifax later that afternoon. Unaware of Hitler's determination to enforce his will on the Poles, Herr Dahlerus acted in all good faith. What he took to London, however, was simply an assurance of Hitler's willingness to come to an agreement with England.

At the same time Hitler proposed to make a more direct approach through the British and French Ambassadors. His first task on the morning of the 25th was to dispatch a long and somewhat embarrassed letter to Mussolini, with a tardy explanation of the negotiations in Moscow and assurances that the Pact with Russia could only strengthen the Axis. The end of the letter suggested that war was imminent. Then Hitler summoned the British Ambassador to the Chancellery.

In a wholly different mood from that in which he had greeted Henderson forty-eight hours before, Hitler began by recalling Henderson's hope, expressed at the end of their last conversation, that an understanding between Britain and Germany might still be possible. "After turning things over in his mind once more he desired to make a move as regards

England which should be as decisive as the step taken in regard to Russia, the result of which had been the recent Pact." Hitler spoke with regret of the general war to which it seemed the British attitude must now lead.

After naming certain conditions Hitler then made this offer: a German guarantee of the existence of the British Empire, with the assurance of German assistance, irrespective of where such assistance might be required. With this he coupled his willingness to accept a reasonable limitation of armaments, and to regard Germany's western frontiers as final.

Hitler added a few more characteristic touches—"that he was by nature an artist not a politician, and that once the Polish question was settled he would end his life as an artist and not as a warmonger . . . that once the Polish question was settled he himself would settle down," and so on. But these did not alter the essentials of his offer, which, reduced to simple terms, was a bribe in return for looking the other way while he strangled Poland. In Hitler's mind, no doubt, an exact parallel to the bribe which he had persuaded Stalin to accept two days before. The one condition was a free hand over Poland. Finally, Henderson agreed to transmit the offer to London, Hitler urging him to spare no time and offering to put a German plane at his disposal, so that he could fly to London and add personal representations to Hitler's message.

No sooner had Henderson left than Hitler confirmed the order for the German Army to march into Poland the following morning at dawn. There could be no clearer proof that Hitler intended the offer he had sent by Henderson solely as a means of averting British intervention.

Hitler, however, had still two more visitors to receive that afternoon. The first was Attolico from whom he was expecting a reply to the letter he had sent Mussolini. When he learned that no reply had yet reached Berlin he sent Ribbentrop to telephone Ciano.

At half past five the French Ambassador, Coulondre, arrived. Hitler once again insisted that there was no issue between France and Germany which could justify shedding the blood of "two equally courageous peoples." "I say again, it is painful to me to think we might come to that. . . . But the decision does not rest with me. Please tell this to M. Daladier."

A message was brought in to Hitler announcing the signature of the Pact of Mutual Assistance between Britain and Poland. This would explain Hitler's anxiety, which Coulondre as well as Schmidt noticed, to cut the interview short. The final signature of the Agreement had been held up for months by one delay or another: the fact that it should be signed on this very day, after Hitler had made his final offer to Great Britain, and on the eve of war, was the clearest possible answer the British Government could give to his attempts to detach them from the Polish side.

A second piece of news of still greater importance now came from Rome. Hitler's message with its hint of imminent action against Poland, had found Mussolini still in a state of painful hesitation. On his return from Berchtesgaden, Ciano had urged on the Duce the need to recover his independence of Germany, while there was still time. "The Duce's reactions," he noted in his Diary, "are varied. At first he agrees with me. Then he says that honour compels him to march with Germany. Finally, he states that he wants his share of the booty in Croatia and Dalmatia."

On the 18th Ciano records: "A conversation with the Duce: his usual shifting feelings. He still thinks . . . that Germany might do business cheaply, from which business he does not want to be excluded. Then, too, he fears Hitler's rage. He believes that a denunciation of the Pact of Steel might induce Hitler to abandon the Polish question in order to square accounts with Italy. This makes him nervous and disturbed."

After expressing his satisfaction at the agreement with Russia, Mussolini wrote:

> As for the *practical* position of Italy . . . If Germany attacks Poland, and the conflict remains localized, Italy will afford Germany every form of political and economic assistance which is requested. If Germany attacks, and Poland's allies open a counter-attack against Germany, I wish to warn you now that it would be better if I did not take the *initiative* in military operations in view of the *present* situation of Italian war preparations. . . . Our intervention can, however, take place at once if Germany delivers to us immediately the military supplies and the raw materials to resist the attack which the French and English would direct against us.

After the way he had treated the Italians and his refusal to take them into his confidence Hitler had little reason to be surprised at Mussolini's reply, but, coming immediately after the news from London, its effect was to plunge him once more into uncertainty. As Schmidt showed Attolico out of the Chancellery he passed Keitel hurrying in to see Hitler, and when he met him on his way back he heard the general excitedly instructing his adjutant with the words: "The order to advance must be delayed again."

By 28 August, possibly earlier, Hitler had restored the decision to invade Poland, with 4.45 a.m. on Friday, 1

September, as zero-hour. He used the interval for fresh efforts to secure the neutrality of the Western Powers. To give himself more time for this was almost certainly one of the reasons which led him to postpone the attack.

How long was Hitler prepared to wait and how far was he prepared to go in making concessions—at least on paper—in order to accomplish this? The answer appears to have been a matter of fierce dispute between the Nazi leaders, on which no clear decision was taken right up to the end of the negotiations. Here is the first source of uncertainty in interpreting the documents, since at no time is it possible to be certain how seriously Hitler took his own offers.

Goering had another purpose in mind—and this is a second cause of confusion. Unlike Hitler, Goering was not at all eager for war, even for a local war. He preferred a dictated settlement in which Britain and France should take the responsibility of forcing the Poles to accept demands imposed by Germany under the threat of force.

A third factor complicating the history of this last stage of the crisis was the rivalry between Goering and Ribbentrop. As in September, 1938, the Foreign Minister was avid for war, even at the risk of nominal British and French intervention on Poland's side. He regarded Goering's approach to London through Dahlerus as an encroachment on his own prerogatives and did his best to see that it should fail.

Hitler's own attitude defies analysis. He was engaged in probing the strength of the opposition he had encountered, searching for a weak point, trying to gauge how far he could go, exploring every possibility that turned up, but refusing to commit himself. At every crisis in his career he had found it difficult to make up his mind, hesitating, waiting for some sudden impulse to carry him forward. In the hectic, over-wrought atmosphere of the Reich Chancellery in the last days of August half the decisions made were bound to be incoherent and contradictory. Hitler's conversations with Henderson and Dahlerus show him constantly talking in the wildest fashion. The German Press stories of atrocities committed on the Germans in Poland—particularly, it was noted, reports of castration—roused Hitler to a pitch of barely controlled excitement. Shouting and waving his arms, he poured out a stream of words in which recrimination, self-justification, deliberate misrepresentation and grotesque exaggeration were all jumbled together. It may well be a mistake, in such circumstances, to try to make too much sense of all that was said and done in these days.

The negotiations conducted between the postponement of the attack on 25 August and the invasion of Poland on the morning of 1 September fall into three groups: those with Rome, those with Paris, and those with London. Of these, the last, which involved a double approach, officially through the British Embassy and unofficially through Herr Dahlerus, are by far the most important. It is noteworthy that no serious attempt was made by the Germans to renew the talks wih the Poles which had remained in abeyance since the spring.

Hitler's immediate reply to Mussolini had been to ask him what he needed to complete his preparations, in order to see whether Germany could supply the deficiencies. The Italian answer was such as to rule out any hope of this. Hitler thereupon contented himself with three requests to Mussolini: support for Germany in the Italian Press and radio; the immobilization of as large English and French forces as possible; and, as a great favour, Italian manpower for industrial and agricultural work.

The Duce, Ciano reports, was beside himself at the poor figure he was obliged to cut. In the hope of saving face at the last moment, on the evening of 31 August, Mussolini himself offered to mediate. Hitler thanked Mussolini for his trouble but told Attolico that he was "not in the mood to be slapped in the face time and again by Poland, and does not want to bring the Duce into an uncomfortable position through acceptance of his mediation. . . . To the question of Attolico whether herewith everything is at an end, the Fuehrer answered yes." There was no open breach between the Axis partners, but Hitler refused to alter his plans in order to save Mussolini's reputation.

Apart from a letter to Daladier, in which he repeated with considerable skill the argument that Danzig and Poland did not represent a sufficient issue to justify war between France and Germany, Hitler paid little attention to France in the final stages of the crisis. He judged, correctly, that it was on London that everything depended, and the French Government, with M. Bonnet still at the Ministry of Foreign Affairs, were glad enough, as at Munich, to leave the chief responsibility to the British, a tacit confession of Hitler's success in weakening French unity.

Despite his remark to Goering that he must try to eliminate British intervention, Hitler took no fresh initiative in this direction, apparently waiting to see what would be the reaction in London to his offer of the 25th and the visits of Henderson and Dahlerus to London.

On the evening of the 26th Dahlerus returned, bringing with him a letter which he had persuaded Lord Halifax to write to Goering expressing Britain's desire for peace and wish to come to an understanding with Germany. The letter appears to have been written in the most non-committal terms. None the less, when Dahlerus read it to Goering, the Field-Marshal declared it to be of enormous importance and drove with Dahlerus to see Hitler. When they reached the Chancellery at midnight the building was in darkness and Hitler in bed, but Goering insisted on waking him up. Dahlerus, kept waiting in an ante-room, had time to notice the exquisite carpets—always a weakness of Hitler's—and the masses of orchids. Then he was shown in.

Entirely ignoring the letter, Hitler began with a twenty-minute lecture justifying German policy and criticizing the British. After that he spent half an hour eagerly questioning Dahlerus about the years he had passed in England. Only then did he return to the current crisis.

> Hitler . . . suddenly got up, and, becoming very excited and nervous, walked up and down saying, as though to himself, that Germany was irresistible. . . . Suddenly he stopped in the middle of the room and stood there staring. His voice was blurred, and his behaviour that of a completely abnormal person. He spoke in staccato phrases: "If there should be war, then I shall build U-boats, build U-boats, U-boats, U-boats, U-boats." His voice became more indistinct and finally one could not follow him at all. Then he pulled himself together, raised his voice as though addressing a large audience and shrieked: "I shall build aeroplanes, build aeroplanes, aeroplanes, aeroplanes, and I shall annihilate my enemies." He seemed more like a phantom from a story-book than a real person. I stared at him in amazement and turned to see how Goering was reacting, but he did not turn a hair.

Dahlerus agreed to return to London with a new offer from Hitler to the British Government. It comprised six points:

(1) Germany wanted a pact or alliance with Britain.
(2) England was to help Germany to obtain Danzig and the Corridor, but Poland was to have a free harbour in Danzig, to retail Gdynia and a corridor to it.
(3) Germany would guarantee the Polish frontiers.
(4) Germany was to have her colonies, or their equivalent, returned to her.
(5) Guarantees were to be given for the German minority in Poland.
(6) Germany was to pledge herself to defend the British Empire.

Dahlerus was not allowed to write these points down. When Dahlerus asked what Hitler claimed in the Corridor, Goering tore a page out of an atlas and drew in the lines with a red

pencil. Such was the way in which affairs of State were conducted under the Third Reich.

Dahlerus reached London again just after midday on
Sunday the 27th, and was at once taken, by a roundabout
route, to No. 10 Downing Street. The British Government
had now two different sets of proposals before them, the
first the offer Hitler had made to Henderson on the 25th, to
which no reply had yet been sent, and the second, that now
brought by Dahlerus. The circumstances in which the proposals had been thrown together, however, and Dahlerus's
account of Hitler's state of mind, made the British Government extremely sceptical as to their value. Finally it was
agreed that Dahlerus should return to Berlin at once with
a reply to the second offer, and report on its reception by
Hitler, before the official reply to the first offer was drafted
and sent over by Henderson.

So, once again, Dahlerus flew back to Berlin, and soon
after eleven o'clock on the Sunday night delivered the British
Government's message to Goering. In principle the British
were willing to come to an agreement with Germany, but
they stood by their guarantee to Poland; they recommended
direct negotiations between Germany and Poland to settle
questions of frontiers and minorities, stipulating that the
results would have to be guaranteed by all the European
Powers, not simply by Germany; they rejected the return of
colonies at this time, under threat of war, though not indefinitely; and they emphatically declined the offer to defend
the British Empire. Goering at once went off to Hitler, this
time alone. To Dahlerus's surprise, and also to Goering's,
Hitler accepted the British terms. Dahlerus got the British
Chargé d' Affaires out of bed at 2 a.m. and sent an account of
his reception off to London. Everything now depended upon
the message Henderson would bring.

Sir Nevile Henderson flew back to Berlin the same evening,
Monday the 28th, and was received in state, with a guard of
honour and a roll of drums, when he presented himself at the
Chancellery at half past ten o'clock. Despite further outbursts on Hitler's part against the Poles, the interview was
conducted in a reasonable manner. The official reply which
Henderson brought with him confirmed the report which
Dahlerus had given, but it made perfectly clear that "everything turns upon the nature of the settlement with Poland
and the method by which it is reached." The British politely
declined Hitler's bribe: "They could not, for any advantage
offered to Great Britain, acquiesce in a settlement which put
in jeopardy the independence of a State to whom they have
given their guarantee." "In the view of H. M. Government, it

follows that the next step should be the initiation of direct discussions between the German and Polish Governments." The British Government had already secured the agreement of the Polish Government to such discussions: they now asked the German Government if they too were prepared to negotiate.

Hitler promised to reply on the following day, Tuesday, 29 August, after he had talked with Ribbentrop and Goering.

Had Hitler wanted to avoid war the British reply offered him a clear opportunity. But what he wanted, as he had aimed for from the first, was a free hand to deal with the Poles in a localized war. Hitler had now to decide how far he was prepared to go in humouring the British by a show of willingness to negotiate with the Poles.

Ribbentrop urged Hitler to take the risk of Britain intervening and to attack. Even if Britain and France declared war, in order to save face, once Poland was overrun they would accept the *fait accompli* and condone Hitler's action. Goering, more impressed than Ribbentrop by the advantages of an agreement with Great Britain, was prepared to go further, although not even Goering thought in terms of anything other than Poland accepting the German demands. As he told Dahlerus, he regarded the Polish question as a bagatelle when weighed against possible understanding between Germany and England.

Characteristically, Hitler tried to get the best of both courses. In his reply he made a great show of the lengths to which he was ready to go to please England, but imposed such conditions for the talks with the Poles that it was virtually certain nothing would come of his concessions. The German Note, handed to Henderson at 7.15 p.m. on 29 August began with a lengthy indictment of the Poles, their refusal of the German demands, their provocation and threats offered to Germany, and their persecution of the German minority—a state of affairs intolerable to a Great Power. All this was skilfully used to heighten the effect of the concession Hitler was ready to make in order to win Britain over.

. . . The German Government are . . . prepared to accept the English proposal and to enter into direct discussions . . . solely as a result of the impression made upon them by the written statement received from the British Government that they too desire a pact of friendship. . . .

The German Government, accordingly, in these circumstances agrees to accept the British Government's offer of their good offices in securing the dispatch to Berlin of a Polish emissary with full powers. They count on the arrival of this Emissary on Wednesday, 30 August.

The catch was in the last two lines: the Polish emissary was to leave at once and reach Berlin the following day—and he was to come provided with full powers. If the Poles accepted, it meant capitulation. To send a plenipotentiary to Berlin, with full powers to commit the Polish Government, was to invite a repetition of what had happened to the Austrian Chancellor, Schuschnigg, and to President Hacha. But if the Poles refused, Hitler hoped, the British and French might come to regard them in the same light as Benes and the Czechs the year before, as the sole obstacles to a peaceful settlement, which Germany was only too eager to sign. After all, was Danzig worth a war?

It was a clever trick, but this time the British Government did not fall into the trap. Although they continued to work for negotiations between Germany and Poland and to urge this course in Warsaw, they declined to put pressure on the Poles to comply with Hitler's demand for a plenipotentiary within twenty-four hours, a condition which they described as wholly unreasonable. A last attempt by Goering to influence the British by sending Dahlerus to London on the 30th failed to alter the situation.

During the course of Wednesday, the 30th, a precise statement of the German claims against Poland was for the first time drawn up under sixteen heads. It included the return of Danzig; a plebiscite, under international control, on the Corridor; extra-territorial communications between Germany and East Prussia, and between Poland and Gdynia; an exchange of populations, and the guarantee of minority rights. This might have been of some importance, for Hitler had taken care hitherto to avoid committing himself, and there were wide variations between the different verisons of the German demands. But it was a statement drawn up with an eye to propaganda, not to diplomacy. Hitler himself later said in Schmidt's presence: "I needed an alibi, especially with the German people, to show them that I had done everything to maintain peace. That explains my generous offer about the settlement of Danzig and the Corridor."

Ribbentrop saw Henderson at midnight on the night of 30-31 August. In an interview, during which both men lost their tempers and shouted at each other, Ribbentrop read through the Sixteen Points but refused to give the British Ambassador the text on the grounds that the time-limit for the appearance of a Polish plenipotentiary was up, and that the proposals were therefore out of date. Ribbentrop could scarcely have demonstrated more blatantly his desire to see the negotiations come to nothing.

Through Dahlerus, Goering was prevailed on to provide

the text of the Sixteen Points surreptitiously, and this Henderson passed on to Lipski, the Polish Ambassador. Later on the 31st the Polish Government, pressed by the British, instructed Lipski to seek an interview with Ribbentrop, and after some difficulty he was received by the German Foreign Minister at half past six in the evening. But since Lipski had not come with plenipotentiary powers to accept the German proposals, the Foreign Minister brusquely ended the interview.

There was not much longer to wait. The High Command of the Army was pressing Hitler for a decision one way or the other. Half an hour after noon, on Thursday, 31 August, Hitler signed "Directive No. 1 for the Conduct of the War."

Every preparation was complete, even down to the necessary "incidents." Since 10 August one of Heydrich's S.S. men, Naujocks, had been waiting at Gleiwitz, near the Polish frontier, in order to stage a faked Polish attack on the German radio station there. At Oppeln he got in touch with the head of the Gestapo, Mueller. "Mueller," Naujocks explained in an affidavit taken after the war, "had twelve or thirteen condemned criminals who were to be dressed in Polish uniforms and left dead on the ground. For this purpose they were to be given fatal injections by a doctor employed by Heydrich. Then they were also to be given gunshot wounds. After the incident, members of the Press and other persons were to be taken to the scene." At 8 p.m. on 31 August Naujocks picked up one of these men, already unconscious, near the Gleiwitz radio station, seized the station as he had been ordered, broadcast a short proclamation and fired a few pistol shots, leaving the body behind. Naujocks' story is confirmed by General Lahousen, of the German Counter-Intelligence, whose job it was to provide the Polish uniforms. The "attack" on Gleiwitz was one of the Polish infringements of German territory cited as justification for their attack.

While these "incidents" were being staged on the frontier, the Berlin radio broadcast the Sixteen Points of the German demands as proof of the moderation and patience of the Fuehrer in face of intolerable provocation. The Poles were represented as stubbornly refusing to undertake negotiations, and the Sixteen Points had been "to all intents and purposes rejected." The use of the Points as an alibi now became clear: even William Shirer, a seasoned foreign correspondent, admits that he was at first taken aback by their reasonableness.

Away to the east of Berlin, tanks, guns, lorries and division after division of troops were moving up the roads towards the Polish frontier all through the night. It was a beautiful, clear night. At dawn on 1 September, the precise date fixed in the Fuehrer's directive at the beginning of April, the guns opened fire. Hitler had got his war. Not for five and a half years, until he was dead, were they to be silenced.

On 1 September, 1939, there were no scenes of enthusiasm, no cheering crowds in Berlin like those in Munich in which Hitler had heard the news of the declaration of war twenty-five years before. When he drove to address the Reichstag at the Kroll Opera House at 10 a.m. the streets were emptier than usual.

Hitler's speech to the Reichstag was on a characteristic note of truculent self-defence. Not only was the whole blame for failure to reach a peaceful settlement thrown on the Poles, but they were actually accused of launching an offensive against Germany, which compelled the Germans to counter-attack. It was not one of Hitler's best speeches. He made a great deal of the Pact with Russia, but was uncertain in his attitude towards the Western Powers, disclaiming any quarrel with France or Britain and insisting on his desire for a final settlement with both. He was also clearly embarrassed by the need to refer to Italy. Towards the end he announced that, if anything should happen to himself, Goering would be his successor, and after him, Hess.

The nomination of Goering was as much a purely personal decision on Hitler's part as the decision to attack Poland. No Cabinet had now met for two years past, and anything that could be called a German Government had ceased to exist. By assuming the right to name his own successor Hitler demonstrated the arbitrary character of his rule.

Shortly after Hitler's return from the session of the Reichstag, Goering took Dahlerus to see him in the Chancellery. Goering was still interested in the possibility of a settlement with Great Britain, and still hopeful of averting British intervention. They found Hitler alone in a small room. Dahlerus writes," . . He was obviously determined to snatch at every argument, however far-fetched, that would serve to absolve him personally for the decisions he had made."

He grew more and more excited, and began to wave his arms as he shouted in my face: "If England wants to fight for a year, I shall fight for a year; if England wants to fight for two years, I shall fight two years. . . ." He paused and then yelled, his voice rising to a shrill scream and his arms milling wildly: "If England wants to fight for three years, I shall fight for three years. . . ." The movements of his body now began to follow those of his arms, and when he finally bellowed: *"Und wenn es erforderlich ist, will ich zehn Jahre kampfen,"* he brandished his fist and bent down so that it nearly touched the floor. The situation was highly embarrassing, so embarrassing in fact that Goering reacted perceptibly to the spectacle Hitler was making of himself by turning on his heel so that he had his back to both of us.

Despite his remark that he was prepared to meet the British halfway, Hitler refused to make any concessions to avoid British and French intervention. Hitler had still some hopes that the British and French would in the end do nothing: these hopes were encouraged by their delay in declaring war. Not until more than forty-eight hours after the attack on Poland had begun did Poland's allies enter the war. When it became certain that the British and French meant to honour their obligations to Poland, Hitler's diasppointment was alleviated by the belief that their aid would remain purely nominal.

The British ultimatum was delivered by Sir Nevile Henderson at nine o'clock on the morning of Sunday, 3 September. Ribbentrop sent Paul Schmidt, the interpreter, to act in his place, and it was Schmidt who brought the message across to the Chancellery immediately afterwards. Pushing through the crowd of Nazi leaders who filled the anteroom, he entered the Fuehrer's study.

Hitler was sitting at his desk and Ribbentrop stood by the window. Both looked up expectantly as I came in. I stopped at some distance from Hitler's desk, and then slowly translated the British Government's ultimatum. When I finished, there was complete silence.

Hitler sat immobile, gazing before him. He was not at a loss, as was afterwards stated, nor did he rage as others allege. He sat completely silent and unmoving.

After an interval, which seemed an age, he turned to Ribbentrop, who had remained standing by the window. "What now?" asked Hitler with a savage look, as though implying that his Foreign Minister had misled him about England's probable reaction.

Ribbentrop's only answer was to explain that they could now expect a French ultimatum.

Outside, in the ante-room, Schmidt's news was also received in silence. Goering contented himself with the remark: "If we lose this war, then God help us!" Goebbels stood apart, lost in his own thoughts.

Hitler's embarrassment was soon relieved by the remarkable progress of the German armies in Poland. This seems to have been almost the only campaign of the Second World War in which the German generals did not have to submit to Hitler's direct interference. Hitler's interest in what was happening, however, was so great that he at once left Berlin for the Eastern Front. He established his headquarters in his special train near Gogolin. Every morning he drove up to the front line. On 18 September, he moved to the luxurious Casino Hotel at Zoppot, on the Baltic, and from there made his triumphal entry into Danzig the following day.

Despite the utmost bravery the Polish forces were overwhelmed by the speed and impetus of the German armoured and motorized divisions, supported by an air force which had swept all opposition out of the skies in the first two or three days. By the end of the second week the Polish Army had virtually ceased to exist as an organized force. Warsaw and Modlin alone held out, much to Hitler's anger.

At Danzig Hitler was certainly in no mood to hold out any olive-branches. After the inevitable justification of his actions, Hitler turned angrily upon the British warmongers, who, he declared, had manoeuvred the Poles into provoking and attacking Germany. Poland would never rise again in the form of the Versailles Treaty: that was guaranteed, not only by Germany, but by Russia as well. Poland, however, was only the pretext; the real British motive was hatred of Germany. Hitler thereupon burst into a series of threats. "Today you have the Germany of Frederick the Great before you. . . . This Germany does not capitulate. We know too well what would be in store for us: a second Versailles, only worse."

The authentic Hitler touch appears in his references to the Poles. Poland, like Czechoslovakia, was dismissed as an artificial creation, and his contempt for the Poles as a people of inferior culture and inferior rights was both emphatic and ominous.

The speed of the German advance in Poland took the Soviet Government by surprise. They had hastily to prepare for an immediate occupation of the territory allotted to them by the August Agreement. This was begun on 17 September and completed within a few days. The German and Russian armies met at Brest-Litovsk. The Russian advance brought Soviet troops to the frontiers of Hungary, news which raised the utmost alarm throughout the Balkans and in Rome. Hitler and Ribbentrop did not share this feeling and relations between the two Governments continued to be cordial. The Russians, however, showed anxiety about the future of Poland and urged the Germans to open discussions with them at once. After an unsuccessful attempt to persuade Stalin or Molotov to come to Berlin, Ribbentrop left for Moscow on 27 September.

It was Stalin who now took the initiative and, in the three meetings held in the Kremlin on 27 and 28 September, largely succeeded in altering the August Agreement to his own satisfaction. So skilfully did Stalin play his hand that the final result of the German campaign in Poland was to strengthen the Russian, even more than the German, position in Eastern Europe, and to hand over to the Soviet Union half Poland and the three Baltic States. The Germans had even to withdraw their troops from the oil region of Borislav-Drohobycz, which they were eager to acquire, but which Stalin insisted on retaining in the Soviet half of Poland. The only concession offered in return was a Russian promise to export to Germany a quantity of oil equal to the annual production of the area.

Why did Hitler attach so much importance to maintaining good relations with Russia? The main reason was the advantage in shelving the problems of Eastern Europe, at least for a time, and leaving himself free to concentrate all his forces on dealing with the West.

In a joint communiqué published in Moscow on 28 September Ribbentrop and Molotov expressed the view that, "after the definite settlement of the problems arising from the collapse of the Polish State . . . it would serve the true interest of all peoples to put an end to the state of war existing between Germany on the one side, and England and France on the other." The same argument was given great prominence in the German Press and radio, and there is every indication that the German people—and the Army leaders, too—would have warmly welcomed peace after the successes in the east.

The talk of a peace offensive, widespread in Berlin after Hitler's return from Poland, found a fervent echo in Rome. The elimination of Catholic Poland, a country for which Italians felt a traditional friendship; the advance of Russia to the threshold of the Balkans; Hitler's neglect of Italy for his newfound Russian friends, the feeling of being left out and no longer informed of what was afoot, greatly increased the mixed emotions of chagrin, envy and resentment with which the Duce had watched Hitler's success in the past month. Mussolini was eager for peace, if only to save his own face. He was also anxious to discover Hitler's intentions, and an invitation to Ciano to visit Berlin immediately after Ribbentrop's return from Moscow was at once accepted.

Ciano's record of his conversation on 1 October leaves no doubt that, while still nominally committed to a peace offer, Hitler was already thinking in terms of the deliberate extension of the war to the west. The effect of his victories in Poland had been to sharpen his taste for more. The inactivity of the Western Powers during the campaign presented itself only as an invitation to rid himself of their interference for good. The hesitations which had beset him during the previous months were now, as Ciano recognized, replaced by a serene self-confidence. The Pact with Russia now guaranteed his freedom of action in the west, without the need to worry about his rear. The fact that Hitler no more trusted the Russians than they trusted him was an additional argument for speedily settling with France and Britain.

Thus the much-advertised peace offer of 6 October, to which so much importance had been attached in advance, was largely discounted by Hitler before it was made. Hitler's main purpose in making the speech seems to have been to convince the German people that, if the war continued, it was through no fault of his. The longing for peace impressed everyone who was in Berlin in the autumn of 1939. It was, almost certainly, with this undercurrent of disaffection in view that the German Press had been ordered to build up Hitler's peace offer in advance, and that Hitler now presented himself in his most plausible mood.

Hitler had flown to Warsaw the day before to review the victorious German troops. Full of pride at what he had seen, he opened his speech to the Reichstag with an exultant description of the triumph of German arms, followed by a venomous attack upon the Polish nation and its leaders, ending with a grossly distorted account of a deliberate campaign of atrocities which was represented as rising to new heights of infamy after the British guarantee. Only when he had vented these twin emotions of arrogance and hatred did Hitler turn to review the present situation.

He began by underlining the importance of Germany's new relationship with Russia—the turning-point in German foreign policy. Germany and Russia had clearly defined their respective spheres of interest, in order to prevent any friction arising between them. Where the League of Nations had totally failed to provide the much promised revision of the Peace Treaties, Germany and Russia had carried out a resettlement which had removed part at least of the material for a European conflict.

Hitler pointed to the new settlement with Poland as the culminating achievement in his policy of ridding Germany of the fetters fastened on her by the Treaty of Versailles. This last revision of the Treaty, too, could have been brought about in the same peaceful way as in the other cases, but for the malignant opposition of the warmongers abroad. Hitler then proceeded to recite all the efforts he had made to improve relations and live in peace with Germany's neighbours.

> My chief endeavour has been to rid our relations with France of all trace of ill-will and render them tolerable for both nations. . . . Germany has no further claims against France, and no such claim shall ever be put forward. . . . . I have always expressed my desire to bury forever our ancient enmity and bring together these two nations, both of which have such glorious pasts. . . . I have devoted no less effort to the achievement of an Anglo-German . . . friendship. . . .
>
> Why should this war in the west be fought? For the restoration of Poland? The Poland of the Versailles Treaty will never rise again. This is guaranteed by two of the largest States in the world.

Hitler made it quite clear that the reorganization of Central Europe was a subject on which he would not permit "any attempt to criticize, judge or reject my actions from the rostrum of international presumption." But the future security and peace of Europe was a matter which must be settled by international conference and agreement. One day such a conference would have to meet and these problems would have to be tackled.

> If, however, these problems must be solved sooner or later, then it would be more sensible to tackle the solution before millions of men are first uselessly sent to their death. . . . Continuation of the present state of affairs in the west is unthinkable. Each day will soon demand increasing sacrifices. . . . One day there will again be a frontier between Germany and France, but instead of flourishing towns there will be ruins and endless graveyards. . . .
>
> If, however, the opinions of Messrs. Churchill and his followers should prevail, this statement will have been my last. Then we shall fight, and there will never be another November, 1918, in German history.

Every paper in Germany at once broke into headlines: "Hitler's Peace Offer. No war aims against France and Britain. Reduction of armaments. Proposal of a conference." As propaganda it was a well-turned trick; as a serious offer of peace it was worthless. When Daladier replied on 10 October and Chamberlain on the 12th, they left no doubt that they were not prepared to consider peace on terms which, as Chamberlain put it, began with the absolution of the aggressor. On the 13th an official German statement announced that Chamberlain had rejected the hand of peace and deliberately chosen war. Once again Hitler had established his alibi.

necessary was to stand on the defensive might well produce a compromise settlement, and seemed to the generals
an irresponsible gamble. They did not share Hitler's confidence in the superiority of the German Army over the
French; and were sceptical of the claims which Hitler made
for their advantage in armour and in the air. If no quick
victory was obtained, Germany would find herself involved
in a second world war, for which, they felt, her resources
were inadequate. In the background the same group of men
who had urged Brauchitsch and Halder to remove Hitler by
force in 1938 was again active—among them General Beck,
the former Chief of Staff; Goerdeler; Hassell, the former
Ambassador in Rome; General Oster, of the Counter-Intelligence (the *Abwehr*), and General Thomas, Head of the War
Economy and Armaments Office.

A lull followed, during which the generals began to hope
that they had dissuaded Hitler from going on with his plans.
But at the end of October Hitler announced that the attack
would begin on 12 November, and Brauchitsch, as Commander-in-Chief of the Army, was faced with the choice between giving orders for an offensive which he believed was
bound to end disastrously for Germany, and organizing a
putsch against the man who was the Commander-in-Chief of
the German Armed Forces and the Head of the State.

The one institution in Germany which possessed the
authority and the forces to carry out a *coup d'état* was the
Army. As a result the history of the active German Opposition is a history of successive attempts to persuade one or
other of the military leaders to use armed force against
the Nazi régime. It may well be argued that to expect the
commander-in-chief of any army to stage a mutiny in time
of war is to ask more than is reasonable.

For a few days at the beginning of November the conspirators were hopeful. Their argument that, if Hitler were
removed, it would be possible to reach a settlement with
the Western Powers and save Germany from the disaster
of another 1918, appeared to be making an impression on
the Army High Command. Discussions were held with the
Army Chief of Staff, General Halder, and his deputy, General
Stuelpnagel, on 2 and 3 November, and General Oster was
assured that preparations for a military *putsch* had been
made, if Hitler should insist on giving the final order for the
attack. A meeting between General Brauchitsch and Hitler
was fixed for Sunday, 5 November, after which the Army
leaders promised a final decision.

The interview between Hitler and Brauchitsch in the
Reich Chancellery did not last long. Hitler listened quietly

enough as Brauchitsch set out his anxieties over the proposed attack, but when the Commander-in-Chief remarked that the spirit of the German infantry in Poland had fallen far short of that of the First World War Hitler flew into a rage, shouting abuse at Brauchitsch and forbidding him to continue with his report. Under this direct attack the Commander-in-Chief, who seems to have been not far from a nervous breakdown, crumpled. Furious at the defeatism of the High Command, Hitler peremptorily ordered the preparations to continue and the attack to begin at dawn on the day fixed, 12 November.

After the dressing-down he received from Hitler, Brauchitsch (and Halder) hastily disavowed all interest in the conspiracy. Chance offered them a way out. On 7 November the attack had to be postponed, owing to an unfavourable weather forecast, and the High Command was able to make use of the same excuse to secure further postponements throughout the winter.

Hitler, however, did not abandon his plans. On 20 November Directive No. 8 ordered the state of alert to be maintained, so that immediate advantage could be taken of an improvement in the weather, while on 23 November Hitler summoned the principal commanding officers of the Army, Navy and Air Force to the Reich Chancellery for another conference.

The arguments which Hitler used were the same as those he had put forward on 10 October, but he spoke more freely and the arguments were driven home with greater force.

He laid great stress on the fact that, for the first time since the foundation of the German Empire by Bismarck, Germany had no need to fear a war on two fronts. The Pact with Russia brought no security for the future, but for the present the situation was favourable to Germany.

Everything is determined by the fact that the moment is favourable now: in six months it may not be so any more. As the last factor I must in all modesty name my own person: irreplaceable. Neither a military nor a civil person could replace me. Assassination attempts may be repeated. I am convinced of my powers of intellect and decision. . . . Time is working for our adversaries. Now there is a relationship of forces which can never be more propitious, but can only deteriorate for us. . . .

My decision is unchangeable. I shall attack France and England at the most favourable and quickest moment. Breach of the neutrality of Belgium and Holland is meaningless. No one will question that when we have won.

Hitler, carried away by his theme, was disarmingly candid:

. . . The question is not the fate of National Socialist Germany, but who is to dominate Europe. . . . No one has ever achieved what I have achieved. My life is of no importance in all this. I have led the German people to a great height, even if the world does hate us now. I am setting this work on a gamble. I have to choose between victory and destruction. I choose victory. Greatest historical choice, to be compared with the decision of Frederick the Great before the First Silesian War. Prussia owes its rise to the heroism of one man. Even the closest advisers were disposed to capitulate. Everything depended on Frederick the Great. . . .

The spirit of the great men of our history must hearten us all. . . . I shall shrink from nothing and shall destroy everyone who is opposed to me. . . . In the last years I have experienced many examples of intuition. Even in the present development I see the prophecy. If we come through this struggle victoriously—and we shall—our time will enter into the history of our people. I shall stand or fall in this struggle. I shall never survive the defeat of my people. No capitulation to the forces outside; no revolution from within.

Although Hitler had designed the whole occasion in order to stamp the impression of an inspired leadership upon his commanders, it is difficult to believe that he was still only acting a part; the megalomania of the later years is already evident. He failed to convince the senior generals—Brauchitsch unsuccessfully offered his resignation after the meeting—but it was certain that the vacillating doubts of the High Command could not halt Hitler in this mood. All that the generals could do—assisted, it appears, by Goering, who also was loth to risk his Air Force—was to make use of the continued bad weather to delay the start of the offensive until well into 1940.

Meanwhile the impression which Hitler had formed of the lack of enthusiasm for war among his senior commanders, strengthened the distrust with which he was coming to regard the professional soldiers. The clash between Hitler and his generals in the winter of 1939-1940, bore fruit in his refusal ever again to let himself be influenced by their advice, even in military matters. When the attack in the west was followed, not by the disaster they had foretold, but by the most startling victories of the war, Hitler was encouraged to believe that his judgment was as superior to theirs in strategy, and even tactics, as he had always known it to be in politics—with disastrous results for both Hitler and the Army.

Throughout the autumn and winter of 1939-1940 Hitler's mind was filled with the prospects of the offensive which

he meant to launch in the west. Despite the successive postponements, he still thought of the attack as no more than
a few days distant, and not until the New Year did he reluctantly agree to defer it to the spring or early summer.
His mood was bellicose: in December Weizsäcker heard him
say that a campaign in the west "would cost me a million
men, but it would cost the enemy that too—and the enemy
cannot stand it." In the meantime awkward problems were
raised by German relations with Italy and with Russia.

The brief honeymoon of the Pact of Steel was long since
over. The alliance was popular in neither country, and
Hitler admitted at the meeting with his commanders on 23
November that Italy's reliability depended solely upon Mussolini's continuation in power. The Duce's own attitude was
far from stable. On 20 November Ciano noted in his
Diary: "For Mussolini, the idea of Hitler's waging war, and
worse still, winning it, is altogether unbearable." A month
later, on 26 December, Mussolini was hoping for a German defeat, and told Ciano to let the Dutch and Belgian
Governments know surreptitiously that their countries were
threatened with an imminent German invasion.

At other times Mussolini swung round and talked of intervening on Germany's side. But the ill-concealed contempt
which many Germans felt for their "non-belligerent" ally
kept Mussolini's resentment alive, while German policy
on a number of important issues was strongly criticized in
Rome. The first part of January Mussolini sent Hitler a letter
which represents the high-water mark of the Duce's independence towards his brother-dictator.

The main burden of Mussolini's letter was the unfortunate
consequences of Hitler's Pact with Russia—discontent in Spain
and Italy; the sacrifice of Finland in a war for which Italian
volunteers had come forward in thousands, and the failure
to preserve an independent Polish State. Opposed to an
extension of the war in the west, Mussolini urged Hitler to
seek Germany's *Lebensraum* in the east, in Russia.

No one knows better than I [he wrote], that politics has to
admit the demands of expediency. This is true even of revolutionary politics. . . . None the less, the fact is that in Poland
and the Baltic it is Russia which has been the great beneficiary
of the war—without firing a shot. I, who was born a revolutionary and have never changed, I say to you that you cannot
sacrifice the permanent principles of your revolution to the
tactical needs of a passing phase of policy. I am sure that you
cannot abandon the anti-Bolshevik and anti-Semitic banner
you have brandished for twenty years . . . and I have a duty

to perform in adding that one step further in your relations with Moscow would have catastrophic results in Italy.

Mussolini's letter was not only evidence of the troubled state of the relations between the two allies; its arguments touched on a side of his own policy—the Nazi-Soviet Pact —about which Hitler was never altogether at ease.

After the partition, while part of the western half of Poland was annexed to the Reich, the rest was formed into the Government-General, under Hans Frank, once the Party's defence-lawyer in the lean years before they came to power. The Government-General was a testing ground for those principles of racial superiority on which Himmler had built up the S.S. In Poland the S.S. tried out their methods of racial extermination (directed in the first place against the Jews, in the second against the Poles themselves), and created the first model of the Nazi New Order based upon the complete subjugation of inferior races, like the Slavs, to the Aryan master-race represented by the S.S.

The test of German-Russian relations in the winter of 1939-1940 was not Poland, but Finland. Hitler had accepted the absorption of the three Baltic States into the Russian sphere of influence and the painful sequel of the evacuation of the long-established German population from those countries. Now he had to sit by silently while the Russians used force to coerce the Finns, a people who had close ties with Germany and whose brave resistance to the Russians inevitably aroused admiration. The role of a neutral was humiliating for the man who had continually summoned all Europe to join him in throwing back the Bolshevik horde. Germany, however, expressed complete disinterest in the fate of Finland, and the Foreign Office instructed all German Missions abroad to avoid any gesture of sympathy with the Finns or criticism of the Russians.

Hitler can scarcely have been blind to the fact that the measures taken by Russia to strengthen her position in the Baltic were obviously aimed at defending herself against an attack by Germany. Yet he still judged the price of co-operation with the Soviet Union to be worth paying. The advantages were threefold: economic, political and strategic.

So important were the Russian supplies of raw materials for Germany that, on 30 March, Hitler ordered the delivery of German equipment to the U.S.S.R. to be given priority over deliveries to Germany's own Armed Forces. The amounts promised by Russia in the Agreement of February, 1940, ranged as high as a million tons of grain for cattle, nine hundred thousand tons of oil, half a million tons of phosphates and half a million tons of iron ore. In addition, the Soviet Union agreed to act as a purchaser on Germany's behalf of metals and raw materials from other countries.

In the autumn of 1939 Russian propaganda and the Communist parties abroad gave support to the German thesis that the responsibility for continuing the war rested upon the Western Powers—the so-called Peace Offensive. Also, the two Governments co-operated in bringing pressure on Turkey to prevent the Turks from abandoning their neutrality.

But the supreme advantage, which Hitler rated above everything else, was strategic: the possibility of making his attack in the west without worrying about the defence of Germany's eastern frontiers. After the war Goering estimated the Pact with Russia to have been worth fifty divisions to Hitler, the forces he would otherwise have had to keep in the east. The Pact was as indispensable a condition of Hitler's attack in the west as of the attack on Poland.

Like Stalin, Hitler was taking advantage of a situation which neither side expected to last long. For the moment the balance of advantage appeared to be in Stalin's favour, but Hitler was undismayed. If he could use Russian neutrality to inflict a defeat upon the Western Powers, he would more than redress the balance. All Russia's gains would be forgotten if he could overrun the Low Countries and France, drive the British Army into the sea and dictate terms in the west. In October, 1939, when talking to Keitel about the future of Poland, Hitler had made one exception to the general policy of neglect to be followed in the Government-General:

The territory is important to us [he told Keitel] from a military point of view as an advanced jumping-off point and can be used for the strategic concentration of troops. To that end the railroads, roads and lines of communication are to be kept in order.

Hitler had shelved his eastern ambitions for the present but he had not forgotten them.

On 10 January, 1940, Hitler ordered the attack in the west to begin on the 17th, that day week, at fifteen minutes before sunrise. The very day of Hitler's decision—10 January—a German major with the 2nd Air Fleet made a forced landing in Belgium while flying from Münster to Bonn. He had with him the complete operational plan for the opening of Hitler's offensive, and although he burnt part of it, enough fell into

Belgian hands to alarm the Germans. To the barely disguised relief of the High Command, until the winter was over, and new plans could be prepared, Hitler at last agreed that there was no further point in postponing the start of the operation from day to day.

Hitler was partly reconciled to this decision by the interest he began to feel in a new project, the initiative for which came from the Naval High Command. The Commander-in-Chief of the German Navy, Admiral Raeder, believed that by 1944 there would have been a "good chance of settling the British question conclusively"; but in 1939 the German Navy had neither sufficient surface ships nor U-boats to make a serious challenge to British naval supremacy.

Searching for a means of increasing the Navy's power of attack against Britain's sea-routes, Raeder hit on the idea of securing bases in Norway, and on 10 October he made the suggestion to Hitler in one of the Fuehrer's conferences on naval affairs. Hitler at that time was entirely absorbed in the plans for invading the Low Countries and France, and the Norwegian project was not mentioned again until the middle of December.

By December with the Russian attack on Finland, allied aid for the Finns was under discussion in London and Paris, and the possibility of British and French troops being sent to Finland through Norway, even of an allied occupation of Norway, was taken seriously by the Germans. For the most vulnerable link in Germany's war economy was her dependence on supplies of iron-ore from Sweden. By occupying Norway the Western Powers could not only interfere with this vital traffic, but could carry the war into the Baltic and block the movement of German ships into the North Sea and the Atlantic. Raeder was able to support his argument that, if Norway fell into British hands, this might decide the outcome of the war.

At the same time Raeder suggested a means for securing Norway which at once attracted Hitler. Through Rosenberg, head of the Party's Foreign Policy Bureau, and who had always been interested in the peoples of Scandinavia, the Admiral had been put in touch with Quisling and Hagelin, the leaders of the small Norwegian Nazi Party known as the Party of National Unity. Quisling, a former General Staff officer and Norwegian Minister of War from 1931 to 1933, encouraged the belief that, with German support, he would be able to carry out a *coup d'état*. In this way the German forces needed could be reduced to proportions which would not disturb the main concentration on the western frontier or endanger the plans already made to attack France.

Hitler was sufficiently impressed to see Quisling three times between 14 and 18 December, and to give orders for German support to be made available to him. Hitler preferred the *coup d'état* because of its obvious economy, but, in case of its failure, he agreed to plans for an occupation of Norway by force. The final postponement of the offensive in the west, in the middle of January, freed his hands, and was followed on 27 January by the establishment of an inter-services staff to work out the details. The occupation of Denmark was to be carried out at the same time as the operation against Norway.

On 17 February the British destroyer *Cossack* intercepted the German prison-ship *Altmark* in Norwegian waters and rescued a number of British prisoners. This incident roused Hitler's anger and he demanded the immediate appointment of a commander for the expedition and agreed at once to see the man proposed by Keitel, General Nikolaus von Falkenhorst, who had served in Finland in 1918.

On 20 February, Hitler saw him for a few minutes before his daily military conference and gave him instructions to take over the preparations for the occupation of Norway. Falkenhorst, a little bewildered by his new commission, was then dismissed and told to return at five o'clock the same afternoon with his plans ready to lay before the Fuehrer. He bought a Baedeker and retired to his hotel bedroom. By five o'clock he had a rough plan sketched out, sufficient to satisfy Hitler, and before he returned to Coblenz his new command had been confirmed.

In the week that followed the interview with Falkenhorst, Hitler was taking a greatly increased interest in the Norwegian expedition. The force was to be kept as small as possible, and Falkenhorst was given only five divisions. Quisling's part had dwindled into insignificance, and the Germans were preparing to carry out a military occupation, relying on surprise to supplement the small forces Hitler was willing to spare.

The risks involved in such an operation were great. As Raeder pointed out to Hitler it was contrary to all the principles of naval warfare to attempt such an undertaking without command of the sea. Reports of British and French preparations for the occupation of Norwegian ports as part of the plan to come to Finland's aid kept the German High Command in a state of constant alarm.

Their anxiety was relieved when the Finns were driven to ask the Russians for an armistice. This was signed on 15 March, and the danger of an Anglo-French landing receded. But, having gone so far, Hitler refused to turn back. *Exercise Weser* (Norway) was to come before *Case Yellow* (the attack in the west), and on the afternoon of 2 April, Raeder, Goering and Falkenhorst reported that the preparations were complete, and Hitler confirmed the order for operations to begin on 9 April.

The plan to attack Norway and Denmark was one of the best-kept secrets of the war. The German troop concentrations in the west could not be hidden, but activity along the Baltic coast passed unnoticed, and Hitler gave nothing away. He signed the preliminary directive for *Exercise Weser* on 1 March, and received Sumner Welles, the U.S. Under-Secretary of State, on the 2nd. The purpose of Welles's visit was to sound out the possibilities for the re-establishment of peace before the conflict began in earnest, and in particular to strengthen the reluctance of the Italians to be drawn into the war. Sumner Welles's reception in Berlin was cool.

The American envoy's visit to Berlin, as he soon recognized, was a waste of time, so Welles returned to Rome after visits to Paris and London. The possibility that in Rome he would find a more sympathetic audience than in Berlin caused Hitler some anxiety. The Duce's letter of January had been left unanswered for two months: now, quite unexpectedly, the German Ambassador informed Ciano on 8 March that Ribbentrop would arrive in Rome in two days' time, before Welles returned, bringing with him Hitler's long-delayed reply.

The letter was couched in the most cordial terms, and Ribbentrop used every opportunity to stress the identity of Italian and German interests. Although inclined to argue on relations with Russia—Mussolini accepted the German argument without dispute.

Ribbentrop failed to pin Mussolini down to a specific date when the Duce mentioned that "at the given moment" Italy would enter the war, but he made good use of Italian resentment at the effect of the British blockade. In particular the sudden ability of the Germans to find up to twelve million tons of coal a year, and the trucks to move it, left a considerable impression on the Italians. To clinch matters, Ribbentrop invited Mussolini to meet Hitler on the Brenner at any time after 19 March.

Even Ciano admitted that Ribbentrop had succeeded in reinforcing the Axis by his visit. Sumner Welles, who saw Mussolini again on 16 March, was impressed by the change in the Duce. " . . . He seemed to have thrown off some great weight. Since that time I have often wondered whether . . . during Ribbentrop's visit (Mussolini) had not decided to force Italy into the war."

As soon as he returned to Berlin, Ribbentrop telephoned to Rome to ask for the Brenner meeting to be brought forward to the 18th. Mussolini cursed—"These Germans are unbearable; they don't give one time to breathe or to think matters over"— but he agreed. Ciano wrote gloomily: "It cannot be denied that the Duce is fascinated by Hitler, a fascination which involves something deeply rooted in his make-up. The Fuehrer will get more out of the Duce than Ribbentrop was able to."

Mussolini could not overcome the sense of inferiority he felt in face of Hitler. As Ciano saw, the sole successes which Mussolini valued were military successes. Hitler had dared to risk war, and he had not. Hitler had only to play on this feeling of humiliation to stimulate the Duce's longing to assert himself and revive his flagging belligerency. When they met on the Brenner, Hitler overwhelmed Mussolini with a flood of talk, describing the Polish campaign and the preparations for the attack in the west. Mussolini used the few minutes left him to re-affirm his intention of coming into the war.

Back in Rome the Duce might grumble at the way in which Hitler talked all the time, but face to face with him he was unable to conceal an anxious deference. Hitler handled him with skill. The impression of German strength which he created and the confidence with which he spoke stirred Mussolini's old fear of being left out at the division of the spoils. As the two dictators parted on the station platform, Hitler could congratulate himself on the ease with which he had re-asserted his ascendancy: three months later Italy entered the war.

Hitler said not a word to Mussolini of his intention of attacking Norway. From the beginning of April, however, all his attention was directed to the Baltic and the north.

Meanwhile, exactly one day after Hitler confirmed 9 April as the date for *Excercise Weser*, the British Cabinet at last authorized the Royal Navy to mine Norwegian waters, an operation fixed for 8 April. In case of German counter-action, British and French forces were embarked to occupy the very same Norwegian ports selected by the German Navy as its own objectives. Thus, between 7 and 9 April, two naval forces were converging on Norway, and the scraps of news which reached Berlin of British preparations heightened the tension in Hitler's headquarters. Raeder was staking virtually the whole German fleet on the Norwegian gamble, and if it had the ill-luck to encounter the British fleet in any force, disaster could follow within a few hours.

The tactics of surprise proved brilliantly successful. Oslo, Bergen, Trondheim, Stavanger and Narvik were captured at a blow. Quisling's *coup* was a miserable failure; the Norwegian King and Government escaped, and six weeks' hard fighting lay ahead before the allied troops, now hurriedly landed, were driven out. None the less, the British had been taken by surprise and "completely outwitted" (the phrase is Mr. Churchill's) on their own native element of the sea. The British Navy inflicted considerable losses on the German forces, but not much greater than Raeder had anticipated, and they were a small price to pay for safeguarding the iron-ore supplies, securing the Baltic, and breaking out into the Atlantic, with bases along the whole of the Norwegian coast at the disposal of the German Navy and Air Force.

In the Norwegian expedition, Falkenhorst was directly responsible to Hitler, and Hitler's own command organization (the O.K.W., the Supreme Command of the Armed Forces) replaced the Army High Command (O.K.H.) for the planning and direction of operations. This led to considerable friction and departmental jealousy. More important still was the way in which it foreshadowed future developments. For Norway marks the beginning of that continuous personal intervention in the daily conduct of operations which was more and more to absorb Hitler's attention and drive his generals to distraction.

Hitler's temperament was singularly ill-fitted for the position of a commander-in-chief. He easily became excited, talked far too much and was apt to blame others for his own mistakes, or for adverse circumstances out of their control.

At the end of April Hitler felt sufficient confidence in the outcome of the Norwegian operations to fix a provisional date for the opening of the western campaign in the first week of May. A slight delay due to bad weather caused a change from 8 May to 10 May, a decision which threw Hitler into a state of agitation. But this proved to be the final postponement, and at dawn on 10 May, 1940, the battle in the west was joined at last.

Little though Hitler may have realized it then, he owed his success in the Battle of France more than anything else to the long delay in opening the attack which had so much irked him at the time.

The original plan for the attack had assigned the chief role to the most northerly of the three German Army Groups in the west, Army Group B under von Bock. This was to carry out a wide sweeping movement through the Low Countries, supported by Army Group A (Rundstedt), which held the centre of the German line opposite the Ardeenes, and Army Group C (Leeb), which held the left wing facing the Maginot Line. For this purpose virtually the whole of the German panzer forces were assigned to Bock on the right wing. But this was a repetition of the German advance in 1914 and so unlikely to take the Western Allies by surprise, and it meant sending the tank forces into country broken by innumerable canals and small rivers. Here they would come into head-on collision with the pick of the British and French armies advancing into Belgium, and even if forced back they would only be driving the Allies nearer to their fortified positions.

An alternative plan had already been worked out by Rundstedt's Chief of Staff, General von Manstein who argued that the decisive thrust should be made not on the German right wing, where the Western Allies would almost certainly expect it, but in the centre through the Ardennes, aiming at Sedan and the Channel coast. Such a move would take the French completely by surprise, for they (like many of the German generals) had written off the Ardennes as unsuitable for tank operations, and this part of the French Front was weakest. Finally, if the German plan proved successful, it would destroy the hinge upon which the British and French advance into Belguim depended, severing their lines of communication, cutting them off from France and forcing them into a trap with their backs to the Belgian coast.

Manstein's plan was frowned on by the Army High Command, but, thanks to delays, his scheme was brought to Hitler's attention. Manstein's proposals had precisely those qualities of surprise and risk to which Hitler attached so much importance, and in the course of February he ordered the whole plan of attack to be re-cast along Manstein's lines, transferring the all-important panzer forces to the centre under von Rundstedt.

This change proved decisive, although professional jealousy got Manstein transferred to play a minor part in the offensive. But by March Manstein's plan had become Hitler's own—he seems to have believed that he had thought of it himself—and by May the new orders were ready to be put into operation.

The German Army which invaded the Low Countries and France on the morning of 10 May consisted of eighty-nine divisions, with a further forty-seven held in reserve. It included the formidable weapon of ten panzer divisions, with three thousand armoured vehicles, a thousand of which at least were heavy tanks. The first sensational success was the overrunning of the Dutch and Belgian defence systems. The key to this was the use of small forces of highly trained parachute and glider troops which captured the vital bridges before they could be destroyed, together with the famous fortress of Eben Emael on the Albert Canal. Hitler had personally conceived the capture of Eben Emael by landing on the roof less than a hundred parachute engineers equipped with a powerful new explosive, built up by German propaganda as one of Germany's secret weapons.

But still unsuspected by the Allies was the thrust through the Ardennes by Rundstedt's Army Group, from Aachen to the Moselle, disposing forty-four divisions, including three panzer corps under General von Kleist. The armoured column was over a hundred miles long, stretching back fifty miles the other side of the Rhine.

The German armour quickly traversed the Ardennes, passed the French frontier on 12 May and were over the Meuse on the 13th. The High Command indeed became alarmed at the ease with which Kleist was advancing.

Hitler shared this anxiety. He was preoccupied with the possibility of a French counter-attack from the south, and personally intervened to halt the advance of General Guderian's leading panzer divisions, which had reached the Oise on the night of the 16th. A note in Halder's diary on 17 May reads:

> Fuehrer is terribly nervous. Frightened by his own success, he is afraid to take any chance and so would rather pull the reins on us.

The next day Halder wrote:

> Every hour is precious, Fuehrer's H.Q. sees it quite differently. Fuehrer . . . rages and screams that we are on the way to ruin the whole campaign. He won't have any part in continuing the operation in a westward direction.

On the evening of the 18th Hitler allowed the tanks to resume their advance. Backed by an irresistible superiority in the air, the German armoured thrust broke right through the French front and threw the allied plans into confusion, trapping the British Expeditionary Force and the First French Army between Bock's Army Group on the north and Rundstedt's on the south.

The German plan of encirclement was only defeated by the brilliant improvisation of the Dunkirk evacuation. Between 27 May and 4 June a total of three hundred and thirty-eight thousand British and allied troops were got away by sea from the beaches and harbour of Dunkirk. Yet the possibility of such an evacuation might well have been denied to the British if Guderian's tanks had not been ordered to halt a few miles south of Dunkirk on 24 May, before the British Army had fought its way back to the coast.

The responsibility for this order the German generals themselves place on Hitler. At an angry interview on the afternoon of 24 May with the Commander-in-Chief of the Army and the Chief of Staff, Hitler insisted on holding back the tanks, against their advice and that of the field commanders. Hitler was determined not to be diverted from his principal aim, the defeat of the French Army, and he eagerly seized upon Goering's boastful promise that he could finish off the British from the air. At all costs he wanted to conserve his armoured force for the next phase which would decide the battle for Paris and France.

These were far from being short-sighted arguments, but for once Hitler's intuition betrayed him. Forty-eight hours later, Hitler allowed them to resume their advance. But by then the British had had time to strengthen their defences and were able to hold off the Germans long enough to complete their evacuation. The first of Hitler's military mistakes was to have momentous consequences for the future of the war.

At the time, however, the failure at Dunkirk appeared slight beside the continuing news of German successes. So Mussolini, as well as Hitler, judged. Fear of the consequences of going to war gave place to fear of arriving too late. Gauging the mood of his brother dictator with skill, Hitler wrote a series of letters to Mussolini in which he poured scorn on the feebleness of the British and French. Mussolini's replies were each more enthusiastic than the last, culminating in the announcement, delivered by the Italian Ambassador on 31 May, that Italy would declare war on 10 June, and hostilities began on the 11th.

Hitler was delighted at Mussolini's decision, and great efforts were made by Goebbels to convince the German people of the importance of Italian intervention. The German people, however, showed no more enthusiasm for the alliance than the Italians. Mussolini's timing, indeed, was so bad that his declaration of war in June, 1940, made their new allies appear even more contemptible in German eyes than the Italian failure to fight in September, 1939.

Meanwhile, on 5 June, the German Army drove south across the Somme. The French has lost nearly a third of their Army in Belgium, and only two out of the fourteen British divisions now remained in France. In eleven days the battle was over. On 14 June Paris was occupied by the Germans and the panzer divisions were racing for the Rhone Valley, the Mediterranean and the Spanish frontier. On the evening of 16 June M. Reynaud resigned, and the same night Marshal Pétain formed a new French Government, whose sole aim was to negotiate an armistice. Less than six weeks after the opening of the campaign Hitler was on his way to Munich to discuss with Mussolini the terms to be imposed on France.

Before the war Hitler had scored a series of political triumphs, culminating in the Nazi-Soviet Pact, which could challenge comparison with the diplomacy of Bismarck. Now within a little more than two months' time, he had led the German Army to a series of military triumphs which eclipsed the fame of Moltke and Ludendorff and challenged comparison with the victories of Frederick the Great and even Napoleon. Hitler, the outsider who had never been to a university or a staff college, had beaten the Foreign Office and the General Staff at their own game.

It is customary to decry this achievement, to point, for instance, to the luck Hitler had in encountering such weakness and incompetence on the other side, to his good fortune in finding a Manstein to construct his plan of campaign for him and men like Guderian to put it into operation. But if there were weakness and incompetence on the other side, it was Hitler who divined it. He was the one man who consistently refused to be impressed by the military reputation of France, the one man who insisted that a quick victory in the west was possible, and who forced the Army against his generals' advice to undertake a campaign which was to prove the most remarkable in its history. If Manstein designed the plan of campaign it was Hitler who took it up. If Guderian was the man who showed what the German panzer divisions could do when used with imagination it was Hitler who provided the new German Army with ten such divisions at a time when there was still strong opposition inside the Army itself to such ideas. If Hitler, therefore, is justly to be made responsible for the later disasters of the German Army, he is entitled to the major share of the credit for the victories of 1940: the German generals cannot have it both ways.

But what use did Hitler intend to make of his victory? The conflict with Britain and France arose not from any demands he had to make on the Western Powers themselves, but from their refusal to agree to a free hand for Germany in Central and Eastern Europe. This had been the issue between Britain and Germany throughout 1938 and 1939, and it remained the issue now, in 1940.

Hitler, however, far from abandoning his hopes of a settlement with Great Britain as a result of the war, looked upon the victories he had won in Poland and the west as clearing the ground for such an agreement. The British had now, he felt, lost any reason for continuing to adhere to their former policy. Their last ally on the Continent had gone, their Army had been driven into the sea, they must now surely accept the impossibility of preventing a German hegemony in Europe and, like sensible people, come to terms—the more so as

Hitler had no desire, at this stage, to interfere with their independence or their Empire. For his part, he was perfectly ready to conclude an alliance with Great Britain and to recognize the continued existence of the British Empire, which (he told Rundstedt), must be looked on, together with the Catholic Church, as one of the corner-stones of Western civilization. England would have to return the German colonies and recognize Germany's dominant position in Europe, but that was all.

In this frame of mind, daily expecting to receive an approach from London, Hitler turned to the question of the armistice with France. A final settlement with France could be allowed to wait until the end of the war, but the character of the armistice terms offered to France now might have considerable influence on the British. In particular, a French decision to continue the fight from North Africa or the departure of the French Fleet to join the Royal Navy would strengthen the British determination to go on fighting themselves. On the other hand, French acceptance of the German armistice terms might well make the British think twice.

Mussolini was in a very different mood. He was eager to become the heir of the French Empire in North Africa and to secure the mastery of the Mediterranean. As guarantees, the Duce wanted to occupy the whole of French territory and to enforce the surrender of the French Fleet. But, as he confessed with some bitterness to Ciano, Hitler had won the war and Hitler would have the last word.

At Munich the German reception of the Italians was cordial, but Ribbentrop made it quite plain that Hitler would not agree to make demands of the French which might drive them to continue the war from North Africa or England. For this reason, no less than for the effect on British opinion, Mussolini's annexationist ambitions would have to be deferred. Hitler proposed to occupy only three-fifths of France, to allow a French Government in Unoccupied France, to promise not to make use of the French Fleet during the war and to leave the French colonies untouched.

These were heavy blows for Mussolini, but he was in no position to argue. Hitler agreed not to conclude an armistice with France until she had come to terms with Italy as well, but he declined Mussolini's suggestion of joint German-Italian negotiations with the French. He had no intention of sharing his triumph.

For the signing of the armistice Hitler had appointed the exact place in the Forest of Compiègne, north-east of Paris, where Foch had dictated the terms of capitulation to the German delegation on 11 November, 1918. The old restaurant car in which the negotiations had taken place was brought from its Paris museum and set up on the identical spot it had occupied in 1918.

It was a hot June afternoon, with the sun casting shadows through the elms and the pines, when Hitler—in uniform, with the Iron Cross on his chest—stepped out of his car and strode into the clearing. He was accompanied by an impressive retinue, Goering, with his Field-Marshal's baton, Keitel, Brauchitsch, Raeder, Ribbentrop and Hess. Silently he led the little procession up to the block of granite on which the French inscription read: "Here on 11 November, 1918, succumbed the criminal pride of the German Reich . . . vanquished by the free peoples which it tried to enslave." Fifty yards away, in the shelter of the trees, Bill Shirer, the C.B.S. Correspondent, was watching intently through fieldglasses. As Hitler turned Shirer caught his expression, a mixture of scorn, anger, hate and triumph:

> He steps off the monument and contrives to make even this gesture a masterpiece of contempt. . . . He glances slowly round the clearing. . . . Suddenly, as though his face were not giving quite complete expression to his feelings, he throws his whole body into harmony with his mood. He swiftly snaps his hands on his hips, arches his shoulders, plants his feet wide apart. It is a magnificent gesture of defiance, of burning contempt for this place and all that it has stood for in the twenty-two years since it witnessed the humbling of the German Empire.

Shortly afterwards the French delegates arrived. Hitler received them in silence. He stayed to listen to the reading of the preamble, then rose, gave a stiff salute with his outstretched arm, and, accompanied by his retinue, left the railway car. As he strode back down the avenue of trees to the waiting cars the German band played the German national anthem, *Deutschland über alles,* and the Nazi Horst Wessel Song. The one-time agitator, who told the Munich crowds in 1920 that he would never rest until he had torn up the Treaty of Versailles, had reached the peak of his career. He had kept his promise: the humiliation of 1918 was avenged.

With France Hitler had every reason to be satisfied. The French Government had been relieved by the comparative moderation of the German demands, and the armistice was signed without further difficulty. But the news which Hitler had been waiting for since the middle of June, a sign from London that the British were willing to consider peace negotiations, still failed to come. Tentative soundings through the neutral capitals produced no result. On 18 June Mr.

Churchill, speaking in the House of Commons, declared the Government's determination to fight on, whatever the odds, and on 3 July the British Government underlined its resolve by ordering the British Navy to open fire on the French warships at Oran. Ciano found Hitler unwilling to commit himself to any course, but prepared to admit the possibility that the war would have to continue.

Hitler waited another twelve days and then at last summoned the Reichstag for 19 July, more than a month after the collapse of France. His speech has often been described as a peace offer, although in fact it marks the end of Hitler's hopes of a settlement with Britain. After waiting in vain for a move on the part of the British Government Hitler decided to make a direct appeal himself, as a last gesture. "It almost causes me pain," he told the Reichstag, "to think that I should have been selected by Fate to deal the final blow to the structure which these men have already set tottering. . . .

"In this hour, I feel it to be my duty before my own conscience to appeal once more to reason and common sense in Great Britain as much as elsewhere. I consider myself in a position to make this appeal since I am not the vanquished begging favours, but the victor speaking in the name of reason. I can see no reason why this war must go on."

The occasion was a splendid one, marked by the promotion of Goering to the special rank of Reichsmarshal and of twelve generals to be field-marshals. Hitler himself conveyed an unusual sincerity in what he said. Outwardly it was a scene of triumph, yet Ciano reported that there was ill-concealed disappointment among the Germans he met at the unfavourable British reaction to Hitler's offer.

Hitler had already issued the directive for the invasion of Britain three days before his speech. This was the obvious answer: if Britain would not come to terms she must be forced to submit. So, throughout the rest of the summer of 1940 and well into the autumn, the preparations for a direct assault on the British Isles continued, and all the world waited for the news that Hitler had launched his invasion armada across the Channel.

How then did it come about that, five months after his speech to the Reichstag, Hitler signed the order for the invasion, not of Britain, but of the Soviet Union? Why did he change his mind, why did he make the mistake of attacking Russia before he had finished with Britain, thereby deliberately incurring the dangers of a war on two fronts? To find an answer to these questions it is necessary to examine more closely Hitler's attitude to the war during the latter half of 1940.

Admiral Raeder had set his staff to work on the problems involved in an attack across the English Channel as early as November, 1939. Hitler himself, however, showed no interest in such an operation until after the conclusion of the campaign in France. His plans for that campaign contained no provision for a subsequent attack on Britain; Raeder's attempts to raise the matter at conferences with the Fuehrer on 21 May and 20 June proved unsuccessful, and until the end of June Hitler's view of the future was based on the British coming to terms.

It was not until 2 July that Keitel issued instructions to the three Services to prepare plans, and not until 16 July that Hitler signed his own directive fixing the middle of August as the date by which preparations must be completed. Even then the opening sentences revealed Hitler's reluctance: "As England, in spite of the hopelessness of her military position, has so far shown herself unwilling to come to any compromise, I have decided to begin to prepare for, and if necessary to carry out, an invasion of England."

Five days later, after the failure of his Reichstag speech to elicit a change of heart in London, Hitler again spoke to Raeder in gloomy terms of the difficulties of the operation:

> The invasion of Britain is an exceptionally daring undertaking, because even if the way is short this is not just a river crossing, but the crossing of a sea which is dominated by the enemy. This is not a case of a single-crossing operation as in Norway; operational surprise cannot be expected; a defensively prepared and utterly determined enemy faces us and dominates the sea area which we must use. For the Army forty divisions will be required; the most difficult part will be the continued reinforcement of military stores. We cannot count on supplies of any kind being available to us in England. The prerequisites are complete mastery of the air, the operational use of powerful artillery in Dover Strait, and protection by minefields. . . . If it is not certain that preparations can be completed by the beginning of September, other plans must be considered.

The discussions which continued throughout the summer confirmed rather than reduced the difficulties Hitler had foreseen. An acrimonious debate was conducted between the Army and the Navy on the number of divisions which could be put across the Channel and the width of the front on which landings were to be made. Raeder would have preferred to concentrate Germany's naval and air forces on starving Britain into surrender. He had the greatest difficulty in providing sufficient transport for the thirteen divisions (instead of forty) to which the Army was eventually limited. Although the movement of shipping to the embarkation ports began on 1 September and operational schedules were issued on the 3rd, no final order could be given until the Luftwaffe had achieved superiority in the air, and this —despite Goering's boast—was still denied them. On 14 September Hitler took the view that it would be inadvisable to call off *Operation Sea-Lion* partly in view of the loss of prestige involved, but postponements continued, and finally the operation, after being shelved for a year, was quietly cancelled in January, 1942.

Most striking is the fact that Hitler himself, who so often forced through a project in the face of difficulties and against the advice of his professional advisers this time failed to provide the necessary impetus to convince those most concerned that he was wholehearted in his order for the operation.

One explanation of Hitler's lack of conviction is that he regarded the preparations as an elaborate bluff, which he was obliged to drop when the British refused to be frightened into capitulation. This seems to have been the view of Rundstedt, who was appointed to command the invading force.

Again, Hitler, it can be argued, came reluctantly to accept the need of continuing the war in the west. He then made up his mind to invade Britain, but rapidly lost faith in it, largely on account of a growing preoccupation with Russia.

To appreciate the force of this argument it is necessary to recall that Hitler's ultimate aim had always been the old dream of finding Germany's future in the east. The Pact with Russia, which he had never regarded as more than a temporary expedient, had been made for limited purposes, to secure first the isolation of Poland, and later freedom of action against the west. The campaign in the west, however, did not represent any final aim. On the contrary, it was in its turn a necessary preliminary to turning back to the east. In his speech to the generals on 23 November, 1939, he had repeated this condition, first laid down in *Mein Kampf*: "We can oppose Russia only when we are free in the west."

The lightning campaign in the west had been designed to secure this. With France out of the war, and Britain obliged to make a compromise peace, Hitler would then be able to resume his eastern ambitions without anxiety about Germany's western frontiers. By July it was clear to Hitler that he had realized only a part of his plan. It was at this point, some time in the summer of 1940, that Hitler made his fatal decision and determined to launch his attack on Russia, *whether or not he had first brought Britain to terms.*

The stages by which Hitler came to this resolution are unknown to us, but what is clear is that, once Hitler began seriously to consider a major campaign in the east, he had very good reasons for hesitating to take the risky gamble of an invasion of the British Isles. This was reinforced by his resentment at the advantage which the Russians were taking of his preoccupaion with the west. In June, 1940, while the Battle of France was still in progress, the Soviet Government annexed the Baltic States without informing the Germans in advance, and followed this by heavy pressure on Rumania to make a futher cession of territory. Always sensitive to any change in the east, Hitler's suspicions of the Russians mounted in proportion to the treachery of his own intentions.

At a discussion in Berlin on the last day of July Halder records Hitler as saying:

". . . Britain's hope lies in Russia and the U.S.A. If Russia drops out of the picture, America too, is lost for Britain, because the elimination of Russia would greatly increase Japan's power in the Far East. . . . Decision: Russia's destruction must therefore be made a part of this struggle. . . . The sooner Russia is crushed the better. The attack will achieve its purpose only if the Russian State can be shattered to its roots with one blow. . . . If we start in May, 1941, we will have five months in which to finish the job."

In fact, the preliminary planning for *Barbarossa* (code name for the invasion of Russia) started at the beginning of August, little more than a fortnight after Hitler signed the first directive for the invasion of Britain. On 29 July General Jodl visited the O.K.W.'s planning section, and told its head, General Warlimont, that Hitler had made up his mind to prepare for war against Russia.

Warlimont's Staff at once set to work, and on 9 August got out the first directive (*Aufbau Ost*) to start work in the deployment areas in the east for the reception of the large masses of troops which would be needed.

At roughly the same time Hitler also gave orders to the Army General Staff under Halder, quite independently of Warlimont's team, to prepare a plan of campaign for operations against the Soviet Union. A skeleton operational plan for the offensive was completed by the beginning of November. The plan was presented to Hitler by General Halder on 5 December, and Hitler then gave it his approval, stressing that the primary aim was to prevent the Russian armies withdrawing into the depths of the country and to destroy them in the first encounter. The number of divisions to be committed was fixed at 130-140 for the entire operation.

The movement of troops to the east began in the summer of 1940. In November the Economic Section of the O.K.W. set to work on the economic preparations for the attack. On 14 August the Section's head, General Thomas, was informed that the Fuehrer desired punctual deliveries to the Russians to continue only until the spring of 1941. A special department for Russia was established and among its tasks was a survey of the whole of Russian industry (especially the arms industry) and of the sources of raw material supplies (especially of petroleum).

These dates, pieced together from a dozen different sources, show that more than four months before he signed the first formal directive for the invasion of Russia, detailed preparations were steadily going forward on Hitler's instructions.

Why then, it may be asked, did Hitler continue with the preparations for the invasion of Britain until October?

Even when he had made up his mind finally in favour of *Barbarossa*, there was every reason why he should not advertise his decision. It suited him very well to keep attention focused on the Channel coast as long as possible. This is borne out by the extreme secrecy in which the plans for *Barbarossa* were drawn up. The Commander-in-Chief of the Navy, Admiral Raeder, in a memorandum written in January, 1944, admitted that he had no idea in September, 1940, of what was in Hitler's mind, although he later came to believe that at that time "the Fuehrer was already firmly resolved on a surprise attack against Russia. . . ." Goering himself was also kept in the dark until November.

A further reason was the hope that Britain might yet be bombed into submission. In the late summer of 1940 the German Air Force concentrated all its forces against Britain, and throughout the winter of 1940-1941 maintained the blitz on London and the other big cities. Hitler, now that he had postponed the attack on Russia to the spring of 1941, was willing to see whether the heavy German air-raids, added to the threat of invasion, might not shake the British resolution to continue the war. And it was for this reason that the air attacks on Britain, begun as the preliminary to invasion, were continued well after intention of such an operation had been abandoned.

There was a third possibility, an alternative to the invasion of either Britain or Russia, which Admiral Raeder persistently urged Hitler to consider—the Mediterranean, and the adjacent territories of North Africa and the Middle East. Here, Raeder argued, was the most vulnerable point in Britain's imperial position, the weak link against which Germany ought to concentrate all her strength.

As he developed his case in two discussions with Hitler, on 6 and 26 September, Raeder brought forward additional arguments, the economic importance of this area for supplying the raw materials Germany so badly needed, and the dangers of a British, or even American, landing in French West Africa by way of the Spanish and Portuguese islands in the Atlantic. Raeder proposed that Gibraltar and the Canary Islands should be secured, and the protection of North-west Africa strengthened in co-operation with Vichy France. At the same time, the Germans, in co-operation with Italy, should launch a major offensive against Suez, and from there advance northwards through Palestine and Syria to Turkey.

There was much to be said for his proposals. They kept Britain in the centre of the picture as the chief enemy, a natural conclusion for the German Naval Staff; they made full use of Germany's alliances with Italy and Spain, and the projected operations were much more within the compass of German strength than the conquest of Russia.

At the time Hitler showed interest in his suggestions, and undertook to discuss them with Mussolini and possibly with Franco. Nor were these promises left unfulfilled. In the last four months of 1940 Hitler devoted considerable time and energy to plans for operations in the Western Mediterranean. None the less, Hitler's interest in the Mediterranean, it subsequently became clear, was governed by very different assumptions from those of the German Naval Staff.

Hitler's aims in the Mediterranean and African theatres were twofold. The first was to add to Britain's difficulties by closing the Mediterranean to her shipping and so bring additional pressure on her to come to terms. However, the last thing Hitler wanted to do was to launch out on a major offensive in the south when the concentration of troops in the east was already beginning.

Hitler's second purpose was defensive, to safeguard Northwest Africa and the Atlantic Islands—the Cape Verde group, the Azores, the Canaries and Madeira—against possible allied landings, and use of the Atlantic Islands as a stepping-stone to West Africa, and Africa as the back door to Europe. In August French Equatorial Africa had declared for General de Gaulle, and it was a common-sense precaution on Hitler's part to secure that area.

From beginning to end, however, Hitler looked to Franco's Spain to undertake the main responsibility in the western Mediterranean, and, less hopefully, to Vichy France for the

defence of North-west Africa, just as he insisted that the burden of operations in the eastern Mediterranean must fall on
Italy. There is no evidence at all that he ever seriously considered Raeder's proposals as an alternative to his own plan for
attacking Russia. What he did was to single out, against
Raeder's advice, those parts—notably the attack on Gibraltar
and its corollary, the occupation of the Atlantic Islands—
which fitted in with his own very different view of the future
of the war. At the same time, he did all he could to secure the
entry of Spain, and if possible France as well, into the war to
keep Britain fully occupied while he turned to the east.

Even these limited objectives proved to be beyond Hitler's
power to achieve, largely because of the superior skill of the
Spanish dictator in avoiding the trap, into which Mussolini
had fallen, of identifying his régime too closely with a German
alliance.

General Franco had first expressed his willingness to enter
the war in June, 1940, at a time when it seemed likely that
the war was about to end and the division of the spoils about
to begin. As the summer wore on, however, and the capitulation or invasion of Britain failed to take place, Franco's enthusiasm cooled and he began to lay stress on the conditions
which were a prerequisite of Spanish intervention. These included North African territorial claims as well as demands for
large-scale economic assistance in grain and petroleum, and
the provision of military equipment. In September, 1940,
Franco sent his future Foreign Minister, Serrano Suñer, to
Berlin, partly in order to allay the growing German irritation
with Spain and partly in order to spy out the land.

Ribbentrop pressed Suñer hard for a definite date by
which Spain would enter the war; while describing the Spanish
demands for aid as excessive, and was evasive on the question
of Morocco and Spain's other territorial claims. In his turn,
Suñer avoided any definite commitments and continued to
insist that Spain's demands must be met before she could risk
intervention.

Suñer took a violent dislike to Ribbentrop, to his prepos-
terous vanity and to his overbearing methods to get his own
way. Hitler made a different impression. After he had passed
through the portico of the massive new Reich Chancellery,
with its row of Doric columns, and crossed the vast marble
gallery which stretched into the distance, he was ushered into
the Fuehrer's presence. Hitler had assumed the role of the
"world-historical" genius for the occasion, exhibiting the calm
confidence of the master of Europe and leaning over the maps
to demonstrate with assured gestures the ease with which he
could take Gibraltar. He greeted Suñer with the famous mag-

netic stare, and walked across the room with carefully controlled, cat-like steps. His glance took in whole continents, and he spoke of organizing Europe and Africa as a single bloc for which he would proclaim a new Monroe Doctrine of nonintervention. Unlike Ribbentrop, he took care neither to utter any complaints nor to exert pressure on his visitor.

For the rest of Suñer's visit everything possible was done to impress him with the power and efficiency of the Third Reich. At the end, exhausted and oppressed, the Spanish Minister escaped with relief to the more congenial atmosphere of Italy.

From the point of view of the war nothing had been decided.

A week later, on 4 October, Hitler and Mussolini met on the Brenner when Hitler gave a double reason for refusing to cede French Morocco to Spain. The first was his plan for a large German empire in Central Africa, for which part of the Moroccan coast would be needed as an intermediate base. The second was his fear that such a step would lead the French colonies in North and West Africa to join de Gaulle. Hitler developed the corollary of his second theme, collaboration with France, at some length, much to the irritation of Mussolini, who feared that Vichy might be ingratiating itself with Hitler, and so depriving him of his anticipated reward, the major share of the French colonial empire. The idea of drawing France more fully into the Axis camp, however, continued to intrigue Hitler, despite the Duce's protests, and towards the end of October he resolved to clear up his difficulties by a personal visit to Franco on the Spanish frontier and a meeting with the leaders of Vichy France on the way.

Much to Hitler's surprise, the meeting with Franco proved to be one of the few occasions since he had become the Dictator of Germany on which Hitler found himself worsted in a personal encounter. The memory of his failure never ceased to vex him. For Hitler went out of his way to flatter the Spanish leader and he offered Spain immediate aid in the capture of Gibraltar. Admittedly, Hitler was unwilling to agree to the cession of French Morocco, if only because he wanted to keep Vichy in play. Nevertheless he was confident that with vague promises for the future and with the impression which his dynamic personality was bound to leave on Franco he would succeed in persuading the Spaniards to enter the war soon and play the part for which he had cast them.

The two dictators met at the Spanish frontier town of Hendaye on 23 October. Hitler began with an impressive account of the strength of Germany's position and the hopelessness of England's. He then proposed the immediate conclu-

sion of a treaty, by which Spain would come into the war in
January, 1941. Gibraltar would be taken on 10 January by
the same special troops which had captured the Belgian fortress of Eben Emael, and would at once become Spanish.

To Hitler's mounting irritation, however, Franco appeared
unimpressed and began to insist on Spain's need of economic
and military assistance, and to ask awkward questions about
Germany's ability to give either in the quantities required. He
even ventured to suggest that, if England were conquered, the
British Government and Fleet would continue the war from
Canada with American support. Barely able to control himself, Hitler at one point stood up and said there was no point in
continuing the talks, only to sit down and renew his efforts to
win Franco over.

The departure of the trains was delayed for two hours, and
Ribbentrop stayed on until the morning to work out a draft
treaty which would satisfy the Spaniards. But neither Hitler
nor Ribbentrop could get Franco to commit himself to anything beyond vague generalities. The Fuehrer for once had to
admit defeat, after a conversation lasting nine hours, "rather
than go through which again," he told Mussolini, "he would
prefer to have three or four teeth taken out."

By contrast, Hitler's interview with Pétain at Montoire on
the following day appeared to go well. The aged Marshal was
one of the few men who ever impressed Hitler, perhaps because, like Lloyd George, he had played a prominent part in
the defeat of Germany in 1918. Hitler made no attempt to
disguise the difficulty of France's position. "Once this struggle
is ended," he told the Marshal, "it is evident that either
France or England will have to bear the territorial and material costs of the conflict." When however, Pétain, expressed
himself ready to accept the principle of collaboration, it was
agreed that the Axis Powers and France had an identical interest in seeing Britain defeated as soon as possible and that
France should support the measures they might take to this
end. In return, Hitler agreed that France should be left with
an empire equivalent to the one she still possessed.

The meeting with Mussolini took place almost immediately
after Hitler had seen Franco and Pétain. Its occasion was an
item of news which took Hitler by surprise and was to prove
the turning-point in his plans for the Mediterranean and Africa.

On 28 October the Italians attacked Greece, not merely
without Hitler's agreement, but in flat contradiction of his
wishes. This affected the whole future of the war, but here we
are concerned only with its effects on Hitler's interest in the
southern theatre.

These did not at first appear to be great. True the Italian setbacks in Greece faced Hitler with the prospect of having to come to Mussolini's aid in the Balkans. This, and the improvement in Britain's position as a result of her occupation of Crete and a number of the Aegean Islands certainly put an end to any idea of German offensive operation in the eastern Mediterranean. Even German aid for the Italian drive on Suez, was only to be given, if at all, after the Italians had reached Mersa Matruh. But the conference of 4 November and the directive of 12 November in which these decisions were embodied, confirmed the plans for action in the western Mediterranean.

Orders were given for *Operation Felix*, the projected occupation of Gibraltar and the Atlantic Islands, to be carried out with German troops supporting the Spaniards in the assault on Gibraltar. Hitler, it soon appeared, was still relying on Spain's intervention, and a memorandum prepared by the Naval Staff on 14 November showed how little Hitler's plans, even at their boldest, corresponded with the Navy's view of what ought to be undertaken in the Mediterranean. Criticizing *Operation Felix* as insufficient, the Naval Staff argued that Germany must fight for the African area as "the foremost strategic objective" and, at the same time as she closed the western Mediterranean, herself launch an offensive against Suez, occupy Greece and march through Turkey.

There was never any prospect that Hitler would adopt such a plan. Although, later, German troops occupied Greece and Crete, and led the Italians in the drive for Suez, Hitler regarded all these operations as either defensive in character or as entirely secondary to the main theatre of war in the east.

During November Hitler pressed Franco hard, and on 7 December Admiral Canaris presented the Spanish Dictator with a proposal from Hitler to send German troops across the frontier on 10 January against the British. This time Franco gave Hitler a blunt refusal. He had little confidence in the plans nor was Spain in an economic condition to enter the war yet. The sudden opening of the first British Desert Offensive and the victory of Sidi Barrani confirmed all Franco's doubts, and the Italian Army was soon in full retreat across the desert. Forced to recognize his failure with Franco, on 11 December Hitler issued the brief notice:*"Operation Felix* will not be carried out as the political conditions no longer obtain."

For a moment Hitler even feared that the British successes might lead to the break-away of the French colonial empire under General Weygand, and on 10 December he ordered preparations to be made for an emergency operation, *Attila*, which would secure, if necessary, the occupation of the whole of France and the capture of the French Fleet and Air Force. On 13 December Laval, the advocate of collaboration, was dismissed from the Vichy Government and placed under arrest. The Germans soon secured his release, but not his return to office, and Marshal Pétain stubbornly refused to go to Paris to receive the ashes of the Duke of Reichstadt, Napoleon's son, which Hitler had ordered to be sent from Vienna as a symbolic gesture to the French. The Montoire promises of collaboration were evidently worthless. Although the troops were held in readiness to the spring of 1941, Hitler had to abandon hope of winning the French over to active co-operation against the British.

In the New Year Hitler made one final effort to persuade Franco to come into the war, writing personally to the Caudillo on 6 February and invoking Mussolini's intervention as well. Mussolini met Franco at Bordighera on 12 February, 1941, but, far from changing the Spanish point of view, only echoed Franco's complaints of Hitler's illusions about France. Hitler's own letter to Franco was strongly worded.

> . . . Spain will never get other friends than those given her in the Germany and Italy of today. . . . Caudillo, I believe that we three men, the Duce, you and I, are bound together by the most rigorous compulsion of history, and that thus we in this historical analysis ought to obey as the supreme commandment the realization that, in such difficult times, not so much an apparently wise caution as a bold heart can save nations.

Three weeks later Hitler received Franco's reply. The Caudillo was profuse in his protestations of loyalty, but he maintained that attitude of polite evasion which, throughout the negotiations, had baffled Hitler's clumsy efforts to pin him down.

The Spanish dictator, indeed, was to appear high on the list of those who disappointed the Fuehrer by their failure to fulfil the historic role for which he had cast them. It was a stigma which that wily politician knew how to bear with fortitude and eventually to turn to profit.

CHAPTER ELEVEN

"THE WORLD WILL HOLD ITS BREATH"

1940—1941

In the summer of 1940 the Russians, alarmed by the extent of the German victories in the west, had hurriedly taken advantage of Hitler's preoccupation to occupy the whole of their sphere of influence under the 1939 Agreement. By August Estonia, Latvia and Lithuania were incorporated in the Soviet Union. The Russian ultimatum to Rumania at the end of June, demanded the cession of the two provinces of Bessarabia and the Northern Bukovina. Hitler could only advise the Rumanians to comply, but henceforward he was determined to prevent any further Russian move towards the west.

His immediate object was to avoid the development of a situation in the Balkans which would provide the Soviet Government with an excuse for intervention. The danger came from Rumania's neighbours, whose territorial ambitions had been aroused by the Russian acquisition of Bessarabia. The Bulgarian claim to the South Dobrudja was soon settled, but the Hungarian demand for Transylvania was more than Rumanian national pride would accept, and relations between the two States rapidly deteriorated to a point where war was a possibility.

Hitler could not afford to see Russian troops occupying the Rumanian oilfields in the event of the Rumanian State disintegrating. Behind the scenes, therefore, he sought to bring the Hungarians and the Rumanians into a more reasonable frame of mind, and Ribbentrop summoned both parties to Vienna at the end of August to accept a settlement dictated by the two Axis Powers.

Ribbentrop only obtained the Hungarians' consent by shouting at them in a threatening manner, while the Rumanian Foreign Minister, Manoilescu, fell across the table in a faint when he saw Ribbentrop's line of partition. But Hitler was indifferent to Hungarian or Rumanian feelings. What mattered was to secure the oilfields: so he offered Rumania a guarantee of her new frontiers and secretly ordered a force of twelve divisions to be prepared for open intervention.

The crisis, in fact, ended very much to Hitler's advantage. A few days after the Vienna Award, King Carol abdicated in favour of his son, and General Antonescu, an admirer of the

Fuehrer, became Rumanian Prime Minister. Before the end of September Antonescu set up a dictatorship, adhered to the Axis Pact (23 September) and "requested" the dispatch of German troops to help guarantee the defence of Rumania against Russia. A secret order from the Fuehrer's H.Q. on 20 September directed:

> The Army and Air Force will send Military Missions to Rumania. To the world their tasks will be to guide friendly Rumania in organizing and instructing her forces.
>
> The real tasks—which must not become apparent either to the Rumanians or to our own troops—will be:
> (a) To protect the oil district against seizure by third Powers or destruction.
> (b) To enable the Rumanian forces to fulfil certain tasks according to a systematic plan worked out with special regard to German interests.
> (c) To prepare for deployment, from Rumanian bases, of German and Rumanian forces in case a war with Soviet Russia is forced on us.

The reorgnization of the Rumanian Army on German lines began in the autumn of 1940, and the German Military Mission was followed by German troops, including A.A. regiments to protect the oilfields, and the 13th Panzer Division. Hitler had soon established a hold over Rumania as a satellite State which was not to be shaken until the end of the war.

These German moves were far from welcome in Moscow. On 1 September Molotov summoned the German Ambassador and described the Vienna Award as a breach of the Nazi-Soviet Pact, which provided for previous consultation. Molotov took equal exception to the German guarantee to Rumania, as directed against the U.S.S.R.

Must more serious was the resentment with which news of the German protectorate over Rumania was received in Rome.

Mussolini had for long entertained ambitions to extend Italian influence in the Balkans and along the Danube, ambitions to which he had always recognized the growth of German power must be a threat, and all Hitler's fair words since the *Anschluss* had failed to eradicate the suspicion with which he watched any German move in the direction of the Danube or the Adriatic. Hitler was well aware of Mussolini's ambitions in the Balkans and was also alive to the possibility of Mussolini taking action there to forestall him. At the interview he had with Ciano on 7 July, 1940, Hitler was at pains to impress on the Italian Minister the need to delay any such action in the case of Yugoslavia, a country long marked down by the Duce as an object of his imperial designs. This warning was renewed in the succeeding weeks and extended to Greece, the other possible objective of an Italian move. In both cases the same reason was given, the danger of Balkan complications at this time—although Hitler added that he accepted as a matter of course Mussolini's right to settle his claims on Yugoslavia and Greece as soon as the situaion became more settled.

These German hints were not much to the Duce's liking but in a letter of 27 August Mussolini assured Hitler that the measures he had taken on the Greek and Yugoslav frontiers were purely defensive: all the Italian resources would be devoted to the attack on Egypt. Hitler took care to associate the Italians with him in the settlement imposed on Hungary and Rumania, and when Ribbentrop visited Rome in the middle of September he repeated that ". . . Yugoslavia and Greece are two zones of Italian interest in which Italy can adopt whatever policy she sees fit with Germany's full support." Mussolini did not conceal his intention of attacking Greece after Britain had been driven out of the eastern Mediterranean.

Mussolini readily fell in with Ribbentrop's proposal of a new Tripartite Pact to be signed by Germany, Italy and Japan. Ribbentrop had first put forward this suggestion as long ago as October, 1938, and he repeated in September, 1940, the same arguments he had used then, the effect such an alliance would have in strengthening isolationist opinion in America in its opposition to Roosevelt's policy.

At the end of September Ciano travelled to Berlin for the signature of the Pact. Every effort was made to impress its importance on the minds of a people who were becoming more sceptical as the war entered on its second year. A week later another meeting between the Fuehrer and the Duce on the Brenner Pass appeared to confirm the solidarity of the Axis partnership.

"Rarely," Ciano wrote in his journal, "have I seen the Duce in such good humour. . . . Hitler put at least some of his cards on the table and talked to us about his plans for the future. . . . Hitler was energetic and again extremely anti-Bolshevist. 'Bolshevism,' he said, 'is the doctrine of people who are lowest in the scale of civilization'." What Hitler did not mention, however, was the steps he was already taking to secure German control over Rumania.

When the movement of German troops became known during the next week, Mussolini's anger at Hitler's duplicity showed how fragile were the bonds of confidence between the two régimes. Once again the Italian dictator felt that Hitler had stolen a march on him and the indignant Duce burst out to Ciano:

Hitler always faces me with a *fait accompli*. This time I am going to pay him back in his own coin. He will find out from the newspapers that I have occupied Greece. In this way the equilibrium will be re-established. . . . I shall send in my resignation as an Italian if anyone objects to our fighting the Greeks.

Little more than a fortnight after the Axis partnership had been ostentatiously strengthened by the Tripartite Pact, Mussolini issued orders to prepare for an attack on Greece in the same childish mood of pique which had led to the occupation of Albania as a tit-for-tat after Hitler's march into Prague. This time the consequences were more serious. The role which Hitler had assigned the Italian forces in his strategic plan was the invasion of Egypt, and on 13 September the Italian Army under Graziani had crossed the Egyptian frontier and begun a slow advance eastwards. Even against the scanty British forces opposing them this soon proved to be a task demanding all the resources Mussolini could command, and Marshal Badoglio, the Chief of the Italian General Staff, was firmly set against any extension of Italy's commitments. Mussolini's sorely bruised vanity demanded a bold *coup* to restore Fascist prestige, and early on 28 October Italian troops began the invasion of Greece from Albania.

A long letter written on 19 October did not reach Berlin until the 24th and was only communicated to Hitler personally late that night after his interview with Pétain at Montoire. At precisely the moment when he had succeeded in pacifying the Balkans by the virtual occupation of Rumania, the Italians were about to set the whole peninsula in turmoil again by their ill-timed attack. Bulgaria and Yugoslavia, both with claims on Greece, were bound to be aroused; Russia would be provided with a further pretext for intervention, while the British would almost certainly land in Greece and acquire bases on the European shores of the Mediterranean. On top of his unsatisfactory interview with Franco on the 23rd the news from Rome strained Hitler's temper to the limit. Yet the manner in which Mussolini had acted was a clear enough indication of the resentment he felt at high-handed behaviour by the Germans, and Hitler, quick to see the danger of alienating his one reliable ally, resolved to go to Italy in the hope that a personal appeal to the Duce before the attack began might persuade him to change his mind.

A meeting was hurriedly arranged at Florence, and the Fuehrer's special train, in which he had journeyed to the Spanish frontier, was rerouted. Two hours before he reached Florence Hitler was informed that Italian troops had begun the assault that morning, and Mussolini, smirking with self-satisfaction, could not wait to leave the station platform before announcing his first successes.

It is an interesting sidelight on Hitler's character that, in such provocative circumstances, he controlled himself without difficulty and throughout the talks which followed in the Pitti Palace showed no trace of his real feelings. On the contrary, he began by offering the Duce Germany's full support in the new campaign and placed German parachute troops at his disposal if they should be required for the occupation of Crete. He followed this with a long report to his Italian partner on his negotiations with Spain and Vichy France—clever tactics in view of Mussolini's suspicion of France—and ended with a belated but reassuring account of his relations with Rumania.

Hitler had preserved appearances, but his actions on returning to Germany show that he had no illusions about the problems with which the Italians' blunder confronted him. New orders, discussed during the first ten days of November, were issued in the directive of 12 November.

Although the dispatch of German forces to the support of the Italian drive on Suez was to be considered only after the Italians had reached Mersa Matruh, provision was made for the rapid transfer of a German armoured division to North Africa if necessary. Meanwhile the German forces in Rumania were to be reinforced, and an Army Group of ten divisions assembled to march into Greek Thrace if the need should arise. Hitler still hoped to be able to carry *Operation Felix* out against Gibraltar, but it is evident that he anticipated trouble in the Balkans, either from British air attacks on Rumania or from an Italian failure in Greece, and was already making preparations to meet it in advance.

Hitler, moreover, had to look still further ahead. The plans for an attack on Russia, on which the Army General Staff had been engaged since August, were now taking shape. During the intervening period, Hitler was most anxious to prevent the Balkans becoming a main theatre of war, partly to avoid delays in his own preparations, and partly to deny the Russians any opportunity for intervening before he was ready to attack them. While his immediate anxiety, therefore, was the possibility of a British landing in Greece and an Italian collapse, he was bound to view any action he might be obliged to take in the context of his larger design.

Russian suspicions had already been aroused, not only by the guarantee given to Rumania, but also by an agreement reached between the German and Finnish Governments for the movement of German troops through Finland to the outlying garrisons in northern Norway. When the German Chargé d'Affaires in Moscow called on Molotov on 26 September he was pressed by the Soviet Foreign Minister to provide a copy of the agreement recently concluded between Germany and Finland, "including its secret portions." The German Foreign Office at once complied with the Russian request, but Molotov was not satisfied, asking for more information about the agreement and about the dispatch of a German Military Mission to Rumania. Anxious to allay Russian fears, Ribbentrop suggested that Molotov should visit Berlin. After a week's consideration Stalin agreed that Molotov should come to Berlin in the first half of November. The extension of the war to the Balkans in the meantime, and the possibility of German intervention in Greece—which would necessitate the passage of German troops through Bulgaria—added to the importance of the Soviet Foreign Minister's visit.

Molotov arrived in the German capital on 12 November, and was received by Hitler the same day. The Fuehrer at once placed the discussion on the most lofty plane: ". . . an attempt had to be made to fix the development of nations . . . so that friction could be avoided and the elements of conflict precluded so far as was humanly possible. This was particularly in order when two nations such as the German and Russian nations had at their helm men who possessed sufficient authority to commit their countries to a development in a definite direction. . . ."

The occasion for such a settlement was the approaching and final defeat of Great Britain.

> After the conquest of England, the British Empire would be apportioned as a gigantic world-wide estate in bankruptcy of forty million square kilometres. In this bankrupt estate there would be for Russia access to the ice-free and really open ocean. Thus far, a minority of forty-five million Englishmen had ruled the six hundred million inhabitants of the British Empire. He was about to crush this minority. . . . Under these circumstances there arose world-wide perspectives. . . . All the countries which could possibly be interested in the bankrupt estate would have to stop all controversies among themselves and concern themselves exclusively with the partition of the British Empire.

To this main theme of the division of the British Empire Hitler added the exclusion of the U.S.A., which was seeking to establish itself as Britain's heir. A new Monroe Doctrine must be erected to keep her out.

These were the "world perspectives" with which Hitler sought to dazzle his Russian guest. It was left to Ribbentrop to discuss the details, a task which he carried out with singular lack of tact, trying to rush Molotov into accepting a draft treaty before his visitor had had any chance to examine what he was being asked to agree to. The result, as anybody but Ribbentrop might have foreseen, was to increase the resistance of the Russian Foreign Minister, who was the last person to let himself be carried away by this barnstorming diplomacy.

Ribbentrop's proposals were contained in a draft agreement and two draft protocols which he offered to Molotov on the second day of his visit. The agreement was to be concluded between Germany, Italy and Japan on the one side, and the U.S.S.R. on the other; its purpose was to associate the Soviet Union with the Tripartite Pact. The core of the treaty was Article II, an undertaking to respect each other's natural spheres of influence (including "the present extent of the possessions of the U.S.S.R."), and Article III, a further undertaking to join no combination directed against any of the Four Powers.

The significance of the proposed treaty was made clear by the two accompanying protocols, both of which were to remain secret. The first defined the Four Powers' spheres of influence.

> Germany declares that, apart from territorial revisions in Europe . . . her territorial aspirations centre in the territories of Central Africa.
>
> Italy declares that, apart from territorial revisions in Europe, her territorial aspirations centre in . . . northern and north-eastern Africa.
>
> Japan declares that her territorial aspirations centre in the area of eastern Asia to the south of the Island Empire of Japan.
>
> The Soviet Union declares that its territorial aspirations centre south of the national territory of the U.S.S.R. in the direction of the Indian Ocean.
>
> The Four Powers declare that, reserving the settlement of specific questions, they will mutually respect these territorial aspirations. . . .

If he could persuade Molotov and Stalin to accept such a settlement, Ribbentrop believed that he would be able to divert Russia from her historic expansion towards Europe, the Balkans and the Mediterranean—areas in which she was bound to clash with Germany and Italy—southwards to the Persian Gulf and the Indian Ocean, where Russia would at once become embroiled with the British. It was a bold but transparent proposal which cut right across both the traditions and the interests of Russia. Ribbentrop hoped, however, to make it more attractive by the second protocol, which promised German and Italian co-operation in winning over

Turkey to collaboration with the new bloc of Powers. In addition, the German Foreign Minister spoke in vague but tempting terms of German help in securing for Russia a Non-Agression Pact with Japan, as a result of which Japan might be persuaded to recognize the Soviet spheres of influence in Outer Mongolia and Sinkiang and to do a deal over the island of Sakhalin, with its valuable coal and oil resources.

Such were the German proposals, characteristic of Hitler alike in their boldness and their vagueness. Molotov, a cold and stubborn negotiator, precise to the point of pedantry, in characteristic fashion, met Hitler's attempts to bewitch him by turning to ask a series of pointed questions about German-Russian co-operation in the present.

Foreseeing that the Russians were likely to raise such issues as Finland and the Balkans, Hitler tried to forestall them. "Thus, for instance," he told Molotov, "Germany has no political interests whatsoever in the Balkans and is active there at present exclusively under the compulsion of securing for herself certain raw materials."

The Russian Foreign Minister, stolidly refusing to be diverted, pursued his enquiries in a systematic manner, beginning with Finland.

Hitler accepted the fact that Finland was a part of the Russian sphere of influence as defined at Moscow, but he insisted that for the duration of the war Germany had economic interests in Finland's nickel and lumber which she expected to be considered. At the same time he pointed out that Germany had lived up to her side of the Agreement, while Russia had occupied the Northern Bukovina and part of Lithuania, neither of which had been mentioned in the Agreement at all. Germany accepted these revisions because they were in Russia's interests; she expected Russia to show the same consideration for her temporary interests in Finland and Rumania. This was an argument which Molotov was not prepared to admit, and a sharp exchange followed. Hitler, nettled by Molotov's persistence, seized an opportunity to bring the discussion back to the more attractive theme of the partition of the British Empire.

Once again Molotov sat impassively while the Fuehrer used all his skill to distract his attention. But as soon as Hitler finished, Molotov resumed where he had left off: the next question was the Balkans and the German guarantee to Rumania, "aimed against the interests of Soviet Russia, if one might express oneself so bluntly." With mounting impatience Hitler went over the familiar ground again: Germany had no permanent interests in the Balkans, the guarantee was not directed against Russia, and so on.

If Germany would not revoke her guarantee to Rumania, Molotov then asked, what would she say to a Russian guarantee to Bulgaria? Hitler was at once on his guard. ". . . He did not know of any such request by Bulgaria." When Molotov pressed him, Hitler refused to commit himself, although he conceded that Germany, as a Danubian Power, was only directly interested in the passage into the Black Sea, adding ominously that "if she were looking for sources of friction with Russia she would not need the Straits."

With this, Hitler's part in the talks ended, leaving him in a state of violent irritation. Franco had only angered him by evasion, Molotov had answered back and argued with him, a liberty which Hitler never forgave and which had already cost others their lives. That night he was not present at the banquet which Molotov gave to his hosts in the Russian Embassy, but Ribbentrop, who had his final conversation with Molotov in the air-raid shelter during a British air raid, brought back further reports which only added to Hitler's determination to settle with the Russians in his own way as soon as possible.

At this last meeting Molotov made it unmistakably clear that Russia would not disinterest herself in Europe. Not only Turkey and Bulgaria,

> but the fate of Rumania and Hungary was also of interest to the Soviet Union and could not be immaterial to her under any circumstances. It would further interest the Soviet Government to learn what the Axis contemplated with regard to Yugoslavia and Greece, and likewise what Germany intended with regard to Poland. . . . The Soviet Government was also interested in the question of Swedish neutrality . . . and the question of the passages out of the Baltic Sea. . . .

Ribbentrop, complaining that he had been "queried too closely" by his Russian colleague, made one last effort to pull the conversation back to the agenda which he had proposed. But to Ribbentrop's repeated assurances that Britain was finished Molotov replied: "If that is so, why are we in this shelter and whose are these bombs which fall?"

In fact, Stalin's reaction to Ribbentrop's proposals was not so negative as Molotov suggested. On 25 November, less than a fortnight after Molotov's visit to Berlin, the Soviet Government sent an official reply accepting Ribbentrop's suggested Four-Power Pact, on condition that the Germans agreed to a number of additional demands. These included the immediate withdrawal of German troops from Finland; a mutual assistance pact between Russia and Bulgaria, including the grant of a base for Russian land and naval forces within range of the

Straits; a further Russian base to be granted by Turkey and Japan's renunciation of mineral concessions in northern Sakhalin. Provided these claims were accepted, Russia was prepared to sign the Pact, rewriting the definition of her own sphere of expansion.

No reply was ever sent to the Soviet counter-proposals, despite German assurances that the Russian Note was being studied. Once the diplomatic manoeuvre to divert Russia away from Europe had failed, Hitler had no further interest in continuing negotiations.

The precise purpose of the proposals put forward during Molotov's visit remains uncertain. They may well have been no more than an elaborate camouflage with which Hitler hoped to deceive the Russians while he completed his preparations for attacking them. It is difficult to believe that they can ever have represented Hitler's serious suggestion for the future of German-Russian relations. Immediately after his final talk with Molotov Hitler saw Goering and told him of his intention to attack Russia in the spring. Goering, who supported Raeder's view that Germany's first object should be to clear the British out of the Mediterranean, attempted to dissuade Hitler, but his arguments made no impression.

Hitler was now able to reinforce his determination to invade Russia by the argument, of which he soon convinced himself, that Russia was preparing to attack Germany. Russian objections to German intervention in Finland and the Balkans were twisted into evidence of a Russian intention to cut off German iron-ore supplies from Sweden and oil supplies from Rumania. From this it was only a step to postulating the existence of an agreement between Russia and Great Britain. Thus Germany was once more threatened with encirclement, and Hitler was able to adopt the indignant attitude of the innocent man driven to defend himself. This pretext he used to justify his action to the German people in the proclamation published on the morning of the attack in June, 1941; this was the defence repeated again and again by Hitler's lieutenants at the Nuremberg Trials. The captured German documents tell of the systematic preparation of a deliberate act of aggression on a people whose Government to the last day was only anxious to restore the co-operation established by the Pact of August, 1939.

In a letter to Mussolini on 20 November, 1940, Hitler told the Duce frankly that the consequences of the Italian action in Greece were grave. The reluctance of Bulgaria, Yugoslavia, Turkey and Vichy France to commit themselves had been fortified; Russian alarm about the Balkans and the Straits had been increased, while Britain had been given the opportunity to secure bases in Greece from which to bomb Rumania and southern Italy.

The measures with which Hitler proposed to meet these difficulties were comprehensive. In addition to political campaigns in Spain, Turkey and the Balkans, Hitler added increased air attacks on the British Navy and its bases in the eastern Mediterranean, in which the German Air Force would assist the Italians. The German squadrons must, however, be sent back by 1 May at the latest, and land operations against Egypt would have to be abandoned for the time being. A German attack to clear the British out of Thrace could be mounted by March, 1941, but not before.

Mussolini's comment on reading Hitler's letter was brief: "He has really smacked my fingers." However, he accepted Hitler's proposals.

Ciano, who had seen Hitler at the Berghof a few days before, reported that Hitler was genuinely worried about the situation created by Mussolini's blunder, but became more cheerful when Ciano agreed to negotiations to win over Yugoslavia, the other object of Mussolini's ambitions.

Meanwhile Hitler was engaged in securing the political prerequisites for his intervention in Greece. A succession of Balkan rulers was imperiously summoned to Germany, and on 5 December Hitler wrote again to Mussolini. Yugoslavia and Bulgaria were proving difficult—the latter under Russian pressure—but he had hopes of bringing them over, and Mussolini was much relieved at the more confident tone of the letter.

Unfortunately for Mussolini, the degree of Fascist incompetence had not yet been fully revealed. On 7 December the Italian Ambassador, newly returned from Rome, saw Ribbentrop and begged for immediate help to relieve the situation in Albania where the Italians were in danger of a complete rout. When Hitler received the Ambassador the next day and asked for an early meeting with the Duce, Mussolini refused to face him. To add to the Duce's troubles, the Battle of Sidi Barrani, which began on 9 December, led to the collapse of the Italian threat to Egypt and the headlong retreat of Graziani's forces back across Libya.

In this crisis Hitler refused to be diverted from his main objectives. Between 10 December and 19 December he issued a series of orders which were designed not only to prop up his failing Italian ally, but to carry out his long-range plans.

On 10 December Hitler ordered formations of the German Air Force to be moved to the south of Italy, from where they were to attack Alexandria, the Suez Canal and the Straits between Sicily and Africa.

On 13 December Directive No. 20 for the invasion of Greece (*Operation Marita*) was issued. A German task force was to be formed in Rumania ready to thrust across Bulgaria as soon as favourable weather came, and to occupy the Thracian coast of Greece. The first objective was to deny the British air bases in Thrace, from which they could bomb Rumania and Italy, but if necessary the operation was to be extended to the occupation of the whole of the Greek mainland.

On 18 December Hitler signed Directive No. 21 for *Barbarossa*:

> The German Armed Forces must be prepared to crush Soviet Russia in a quick campaign even before the end of the war against England. For this purpose the Army will have to employ all available units with the reservation that the occupied territories must be safeguarded against surprise attack. . . .
>
> Preparations requiring more time to start are to be begun now—if this has not yet been done—and are to be completed by 15 May, 1941. . . . The ultimate objective of the operation is to establish a defence line against Asiatic Russia from a line running approximately from the Volga River to Archangel.

Hitler made it perfectly clear that from the beginning the active co-operation of Finland, Hungary and Rumania was counted on, and this same month of December both the Chief of the Finnish General Staff and the Hungarian Minister of War visited Germany.

Finally, on 19 December, Hitler saw the Italian Ambassador and promised increased economic aid for Italy, on condition that German experts should go to Italy and advise on its use. In return more Italian workmen were to be sent to Germany. This was one more step in the reduction of Italy to the status of a German satellite.

With these measures put in train Hitler was confident that he could master the crisis and still be ready for the attack on Russia by 15 May. He said nothing of such a possibility to Mussolini, but his letter to the Duce on the last day of 1940 was cordial in tone and did his best to encourage Mussolini and to assure him of his own unshaken confidence in the future.

Early in the New Year the chiefs of the three Services were summoned to the Berghof, where a war council lasting two days was held, on 8-9 January, 1941. Hitler reviewed what could be done for Italy, and his general mood was still one of confidence.

The Fuehrer [the Minutes record], is firmly convinced that

the situation in Europe can no longer develop unfavourably for Germany even if we should lose the whole of North Africa. . . . The British can hope to win the war only by beating us on the Continent. The Fuehrer is convinced that this is impossible.

Ten days later Mussolini visited the Berghof. He was most reluctant to make the journey and went on board the train in a bad temper. Smarting under the humiliations of Libya and Greece, he looked forward without relish to the Germans' patronizing condolences. To the Duce's and Ciano's surprise Hitler behaved with tact and impressed both of them with his cordiality during their two days as guests at the Berghof.

Mussolini found Hitler in a very anti-Russian mood, and Ribbentrop called a sharp halt to ill-timed Italian attempts to improve their relations with Moscow. On the second day of the visit, Monday, 20 January, Hitler made a speech of two hours on his coming intervention in Greece, his exposition ranging over the whole of Europe, Africa and the Middle East. Demonstrating his points with expressive gestures on the map, he impressed upon his audience the picture of a master of strategy who had foreseen every possibility and who was in complete command of the situation. He did not reveal his intention of attacking Russia, but he did not conceal his intense distrust of his nominal ally.

Mussolini returned—so Ciano reported—in the mood of elation which a meeting with Hitler frequently produced in him. Alfieri, the Italian Ambassador in Berlin, who had accompanied the party, was less sure. Mussolini, he believed, was profoundly resentful at the position of dependence in which he now found himself placed.

Hitler's concealment of his plans for *Barbarossa*, during his talks with Mussolini, has already been remarked. It could, of course, be argued that Italy was in no position in 1941 to give any help at all in the operations about to begin in Eastern Europe. But this argument could certainly not be applied to the second of Hitler's partners in the Tripartite Pact, Japan, whose relations with the U.S.S.R. had balanced precariously on the edge of war since the Japanese invasion of Manchuria in 1931. Yet Hitler made no effort to bring Japan into the projected war against Russia; on the contrary, he did everything he could to divert her away from Russia's Far Eastern territories towards the south.

Hitler wanted Japan to enter the war at the earliest possible moment, but it was against England, not against Russia, that he sought her co-operation. The war in Europe, Hitler and Ribbentrop assured Foreign Minister Matsuoka, when he visited Berlin at the end of March, 1941, was virtually over; it was only a question of time before Britain was forced to admit that she had been defeated. An attack by Japan upon Singapore would not only have a decisive effect in convincing Britain that there was no further point in continuing the war, it would also provide the key to the realization of Japanese ambitions in Eastern Asia. "There could never in human imagination," Hitler told Matsuoka, "be a better condition for a joint effort of the Tripartite Pact countries than the one which had now been produced. . . . Such a moment would never return. It was unique in history. . . ."

Hitler admitted that there were risks, but he dismissed them as slight. England was in no position to defend her possessions in Asia. America was not yet ready, and an attack on Singapore would strengthen the tendency towards non-intervention in the United States. If, none the less, America should attack, Japan could rely on German support. As for Russia, Hitler allowed Ribbentrop to give an explicit assurance that Germany would at once attack Russia if she moved against Japan.

In all their conversations Hitler and Ribbentrop persistently urged on Matsuoka the importance of an attack on Singapore at the earliest possible date. Ribbentrop asked the Japanese Foreign Minister for maps of the British base, "so that the Fuehrer, who must certainly be considered the greatest expert of modern times on military matters, could advise Japan as to the best method for the attack on Singapore." Japan, in short, was to play in the Far East the role for which Hitler had cast Franco's Spain and Mussolini's Italy: the capture of Singapore was the Far Eastern version of the capture of Gibraltar and the drive on Suez.

Had Hitler succeeded in persuading his allies to fall in with his plans, Britain's strength would have been stretched to the limit. After the defeat of France Hitler conducted a considerable number of diplomatic negotiations: it is a striking fact that, in every case where he was unable to use the threat of force these negotiations failed. Spain, Italy, Vichy France and now Japan, all chose different paths from those the Fuehrer had mapped out for them. It is not difficult to see why. Hitler's overbearing manner and his total inability to co-operate with anyone on equal terms; Ribbentrop's belief that the most effective method of diplomacy was to nag and, if possible, to threaten, produced in most of their visitors only a feeling of relief when the interview came to an end. It was too patent on every occasion why the Germans wanted what they were asking for, too obvious who was to benefit from it. Ciano wrote ". . . if Spain falls away the fault rests in great part with the Germans and their uncouth manners."

To clumsiness the Germans added falseness. If Mussolini's invasion of Greece was a blunder for which the Nazis had eventually to pay a high price, Hitler had only himself to blame for the way in which he had misled his partner and then stolen an advantage over him in Rumania. Hitler's golden rule in politics remained: Trust nobody.

It is not surprising, therefore, that Hitler should have concealed his purpose to attack Russia from the Japanese Foreign Minister. It is one more piece of evidence pointing to Hitler's confidence in his ability to conquer Russia, as he had conquered France, in a single campaign and without the need of help from outside which, when victory had been won, might prove an embarrassment. Meanwhile, Matsuoka was sufficiently deceived to ignore Ribbentrop's hints, with the result that when Germany attacked Russia three months later his failure to warn the Japanese Government led to his fall. Thereby Hitler lost his best ally in the Tokyo Cabinet, and the Japanese quickly made up their minds to follow their own plans and keep the Germans in ignorance.

With the spring of 1941 Hitler looked forward eagerly to the moment when he could once more give the order to advance, this time to sweep the British out of the Balkans as a preliminary to the greatest of all his schemes, the attack on Russia.

Between Germany and Greece lay four countries—Hungary, Rumania, Yugoslavia and Bulgaria—whose compliance had to be secured before Hitler could reach the Greek frontier. Hungary and Rumania had already accepted the status of German satellites, and throughout the winter months German troop trains steadily moved across Hungary to Rumania, where a task force of nearly seven hundred thousand men was built up. In Bulgaria a sharp tussle for influence took place between the Germans and the Russians. The Germans won, and on the night of 28 February German forces from Rumania crossed the Danube and began to occupy key positions throughout the country. The following day Bulgaria joined the Tripartite Pact.

Yugoslavia proved more difficult. Recognizing this, Hitler did not ask for the passage of German troops, but he put strong pressure on the Yugoslav Government to follow the example of Hungary, Rumania and Bulgaria in acceding to the Tripartite Pact. In the middle of February the Yugoslav Prime Minister and Foreign Minister went to Berchtesgaden, and on 4-5 March the Prince Regent Paul also paid a secret visit to the Fuehrer. Hitler's bribe was the offer of Salonika, and it was taken. On 25 March, Tsetkovitch, the Yugoslav

Foreign Minister, signed the Pact in Vienna. Given favourable weather, Hitler told Ciano in Vienna, the decision in Greece could be brought about in a few days. The sharp eyes of Winston Churchill did not miss the fact, reported by British agents, that, immediately on Yugoslavia's agreement, three of the five German armoured divisions which had moved southwards through Rumania were switched north to Cracow in Poland.

Hitler's satisfaction was premature. On the night of 26-27 March a group of Yugoslav officers, rebelling against adherence to the Axis carried out a *coup d'état* in Belgrade in the name of the young King Peter II.

The insolence of a nation which ventured to cross him roused Hitler's fury. To his imperious temper this was intolerable, and must be paid for by the most terrible punishment he could inflict.

A hurried council of war summoned to the Chancellery learned of the Fuehrer's decision while the Japanese Foreign Minister, Matsuoka, was kept waiting in another room. Determined to destroy those who had dared to cross him, he took the decision, then and there, to postpone the attack on Russia up to four weeks, so completely was he prepared to sacrifice everything to the satisfaction of his desire for revenge.

"The Fuehrer is determined," the official record of the meeting runs, "to make all preparations to destroy Yugoslavia militarily and as a national unit, without waiting for any possible declarations of loyalty from the new government."

Never was the man's essential character more clearly illuminated. The brutal tone of the orders reflects this mood. Not content with taking steps to ward off any threat to his plans from Yugoslavia, he was bent upon the entire destruction of the State and its partition. The blow, he insisted, must be carried out with "merciless harshness."

The military preparations for this new and unexpected campaign had to be improvised, but Hitler issued his directive that very day, and again included the sentence: "Yugoslavia, despite her protestations of loyalty, must be considered as an enemy and crushed as swiftly as possible." General Jodl, at four o'clock on the morning of 28 March was able to give the liaison officer with the Italian General Staff a memorandum on the joint measures to be taken. Hitler had already requested Mussolini to cover the Yugoslav-Albanian frontier. Mussolini's agreement was received in the early hours of the 28th. At the same time imperious messages had been sent to Hungary and Bulgaria, and General von Paulus hastily dispatched to Budapest to co-ordinate the measures to be taken by the satellite forces against the isolated Yugoslavs. Hitler's political preparations contained provision not only for stirring up the hatred and greed of Yugoslavia's neighbours, but also for its internal disruption by appealing to the Croats, whose grievances against the Belgrade Government had long been fostered by Nazi agents.

By 5 April, ten days after he had received the news of the *coup d'état*, Hitler had completed his preparations, and at dawn on the 6th, while German forces pushed across the frontiers, squadrons of German bombers took off for Belgrade to carry out *Operation Punishment* lasting three whole days and designed to destroy the Yugoslav capital. Flying at rooftop height, the German pilots systematically bombed the city without fear of intervention, killing more than seventeen thousand people.

Simultaneously, other German divisions operating from Bulgaria began the invasion of Greece. Both operations, mounted with overwhelming force, were rapidly carried to success. On 17 April the Yugoslav Army was driven to capitulate; six days later the Greeks, after their six months' heroic resistance to the Italians, were forced to follow suit. On 22 April the British troops, who had landed in Greece less than two months before, began their evacuation. On the 27th the German tanks rolled into Athens, and on 4 May Hitler presented his report to a cheering Reichstag. The Balkan war, which Mussolini had begun in an attempt to assert his independence, had ended in a German triumph which completely eclipsed the Italian partner of the Axis, and which was by implication a public humiliation of the Duce.

In his speech to the Reichstag Hitler did his best to disguise this unpalatable fact:

> I must state categorically that this action was not directed against Greece. The Duce did not even request me to place one single German division at his disposal for this purpose. . . . The concentration of German forces was therefore not made for the purpose of assisting the Italians against Greece. It was a precautionary measure against the British attempt to entrench themselves in the Balkans.

The real relationship between Berlin and Rome, however, was revealed by the partition of Yugoslavia. The new frontiers were drawn by the Fuehrer in a directive issued on 12 April. Not until 21 April, when he was summoned to Vienna, did Ciano learn that Italy's share was on a level with those of the other satellites, and the Duce had perforce to accept Hitler's unilateral decisions.

Italian dependence upon Germany was further emphasized by the course of events in North Africa. There the continuing

Italian failure to check the British advance led to the British conquest of Cyrenaica. At a conference on 3 February Hitler discounted the danger in losing North Africa, but he was worried about the effect on Italy.

> Britain [he remarked] can hold a pistol to Italy's head and force her either to make peace and retain everything, or after the loss of North Africa to be bombarded. . . . We must make every effort to prevent this. Italy must be given support. We are already doing this in *Marita*. We must however, attempt to render effective assistance in North Africa.

The steps which Hitler ordered to make good this decision proved as successful in Africa as they had in Greece—from Hitler's point of view almost embarrassingly successful. He reluctantly agreed to the transfer of an armoured division from the Balkans and secured Mussolini's consent to the creation of a unified command of all mechanized and motorized forces in the desert under General Rommel, and Rommel took not only the British, but the German High Command, by surprise. Ordered to submit plans for consideration by 20 April, he actually began his attack on 31 March, and by 12 April had recaptured Bardia within a few miles of the Egyptian frontier.

Indeed, by the early summer of 1941, the situation in the eastern Mediterranean had been changed out of recognition. The British had been thrown out of Greece and pushed back to the Egyptian frontier. In Iraq the pro-German Prime Minister, Rashid Ali, led a revolt against the British garrison, and at the beginning of May appealed to Hitler for help for which Syria provided a convenient base. Finally, between 20 May and 27 May, German parachute troops captured the island of Crete.

With the small British forces available stretched to the limit to hold Egypt, Palestine and Iraq, it appeared to the German Naval Staff and to Rommel that it needed only a sharp push to destroy the whole edifice of Britain's Middle Eastern defence system. Accordingly, on 30 May, Raeder revived his demand for a "decisive Egypt-Suez offensive for the autumn of 1941 which [he argued] would be more deadly to the British Empire than the capture of London." The anxiety revealed in Mr. Churchill's and General Wavell's dispatches at this time lends retrospective support to the German Naval Command's arguments. Even a quarter of the forces then being concentrated for the attack on Russia could, if diverted to the Mediterranean theatre in time, have dealt a fatal blow to British control of the Middle East.

But Hitler, his mind wholly set upon the invasion of Russia, declined to look at the Mediterranean as anything more than a sideshow to be left to the Italians with a stiffening of

German troops. In vain both Raeder and Rommel tried to interest him in the possibilities in the south. He preferred to dictate rather than take advantage of events. It was to prove one of the supreme blunders of his strategy.

Hitler's mind had been made up at the beginning of the year. On 15 February he announced that any large-scale operations in the Mediterranean must wait until the autumn of 1941, when the defeat of Russia would have been accomplished. Then Malta could be taken and the British expelled from the Mediterranean—but not before. This decision was inflexible. Goering admitted that at the time of its capture Crete was the end of the operations in the Balkans, not a stepping-stone to Suez and the Middle East. On 25 May Hitler gave orders to support Rashid Ali's revolt in Iraq, but help was to be limited to a military mission, some assistance from the German Air Force and the supply of arms.

The utmost Raeder could do was to extract from Hitler promises of a major effort in the Mediterranean and Middle East after Russia had been defeated. Hitler was lavish in such promises, including an attack on Egypt from Libya, an advance into Asia Minor from Bulgaria, and the invasion of Persia. But the condition was the same in each case—not until Russia had been defeated.

All this time the building up of the German forces in the east had steadily continued. On 3 February General Halder presented the Army's detailed estimate of the situation to the Fuehrer. The huge forces to be engaged and the vast distances to be covered excited his imagination. Hitler brushed aside arguments based on Russia's reserves of manpower with the assurance that the Bolshevik régime was so hated that initial defeats would lead to its collapse or overthrow. References to Russia's armament strength he met by reeling off from memory the figures for Russian arms production since the 1920s, adding that nobody with any spirit would allow himself to be impressed by such obsolete equipment. He insisted that everything depended upon the encirclement of the main Russian forces as near to the frontier as possible. The participation of Finland, Rumania and Hungary in the attack was assured, but Hitler added that—with the exception of Rumania—agreements could be made only at the eleventh hour, in order to keep the secret well guarded. After examining the operational plans for each Army Group, Hitler expressed himself as satisfied. "It must be remembered," he declared, "that the main aim is to gain possession of the Baltic States and Leningrad. . . . When *Barbarossa* begins, the world will holds its breath and make no comment."

A month later, early in March, Hitler held another military conference, of all the senior commanders to take part in the attack. Hitler presented the invasion as a step forced on him by Russia's imperialistic designs in the Baltic and the Balkans. A Russian attack on Germany was a certainty, he assured them, and must be forestalled. A secret agreement had even been arrived at between Russia and England, and this was the reason for the British refusal to accept German peace offers.

Hitler laid particular stress upon the ideological character of the war with Russia. It could not be conducted in a chivalrous manner, he told the generals, but must be waged in merciless fashion. In particular the Russian Commissars were to be liquidated as the bearers of an ideology hostile to National Socialism. If Halder is to be believed, Hitler added that breaches of international law by German soldiers were to be excused since Russia had not participated in the Hague Convention and had no rights under it. Halder's account is certainly in keeping with Hitler's later orders, and according to Brauchitsch a number of the generals protested to him after the conference that such a way of waging war was intolerable. The most Brauchitsch felt able to do was surreptitiously to issue an order instructing officers to preserve strict discipline and to punish excesses.

The generals were even more disturbed at the proposals for the administration of the territories occupied in the east. These, as they were set out in a special directive issued on 13 March, provided that "in the area of operations, the *Reichsfuehrer S.S.*" (Himmler) is entrusted, on behalf of the Fuehrer, with special tasks for the preparation of the political administration. Within the reach of these tasks, the *Reichsfuehrer S.S.* shall act independently and under his own responsibility."

Although the authority of the Army Commander-in-Chief was formally safeguarded, this could only mean that Himmler and the S.S. were to be given a free hand to stamp out all traces of the Soviet system. The directive also provided for handing over the areas occupied as soon as possible to the political administration of special commissioners appointed by Hitler himself, and for the immediate economic exploitation of the territory seized under the direction of Goering. Even the most unpolitical of German generals can have had little doubt that Hitler was making sure that no scruples or conservatism on the part of the Army Commanders should obstruct the treatment of the occupied territories on thoroughgoing National Socialist lines.

On 20 April Hitler appointed Alfred Rosenberg, the half-forgotten figure who had played a great part in forming his views on German expansion in the east, as Commissioner for the East European Region. It was an unhappy choice. Himmler, in his capacity as *Reichsfuehrer* of the S.S. *corps d'élite* already claimed the responsibility for laying the racial foundations of the New Order in the east, and this claim had been recognized in the directive of 13 March which has already been quoted. Goering was equally outraged by Rosenberg's appointment: in his capacity as Plenipotentiary for the Four-Year Plan he claimed the right to organize the economic exploitation of the territories in the east so as to guarantee Germany's present and future needs in food and raw materials. This claim, too, was confirmed by Hitler, in a secret decree of 20 May, despite Rosenberg's protests. There was thus from the beginning a conflict of authority in the east between the Army, Himmler, Goering and the nominal Commissioner, Rosenberg, which only became worse as time went on.

The ruthlessness of the German treatment of the occupied territories in the east was part of a methodical system of exploitation and resettlement planned in advance and entered upon with a full appreciation of its consequences. This can be well illustrated from a directive of Goering's Economic Staff East, dated 23 May, 1941, and dealing with the future of Russian agriculture. The overriding need was defined as the use of the food-producing areas of the east to supplement Germany's and Europe's supplies both during and after the war. The Directive goes on to discuss the consequences for Russia's industrial population:

> . . . Many tens of millions of people in the industrial areas will become redundant and will either die or have to emigrate to Siberia. Any attempt to save the population there from death by starvation by importing surpluses from the Black Soil Zone would be at the expense of supplies to Europe. It would reduce Germany's staying-power in the war, and would undermine Germany's and Europe's power to resist the blockade. This must be clearly and absolutely understood.

A memorandum summarizing a discussion of plans for *Barbarossa* on 2 May begins in similar fashion: "The war can only be continued if all the armed forces are fed by Russia in the third year of the war. There is no doubt that as a result many millions of people will be starved to death if we take out of the country the things we need."

This, it should be pointed out, is not Hitler talking late at night up on the Obersalzberg; this is the translation of those grim fantasies into the sober directives and office memoranda of a highly organized administration, methodically planning economic operations which must result in the starvation of millions. Not far away, in the offices of Himmler's S.S., equally methodical calculations were being made of how this process could be accelerated by the use of gas chambers (including mobile vans) for the elimination of the racially impure.

On 30 April with the Balkan operations all but completed, Hitler fixed 22 June as the new date for the opening of the attack in the east. By May an ominous lull settled over the battle fronts.

The few remaining weeks were an anxious time for Hitler. Conscious of his own duplicity, Hitler watched carefully for any sign of a Russian move to forestall it.

In order to camouflage his intentions Hitler ordered goods delivered to Russia till the last moment. The Russians continued to make a prompt dispatch of raw materials and food to Germany up to the day of the attack. Indeed, the Soviet Government, while building up its defences in the west, did everything it could to conciliate and appease the Germans. When Matsuoka, on his return to Tokyo, passed through Moscow in April, Stalin made an unexpected appearance at the station to see him off and publicly asked for the German Ambassador. When Schulenburg presented himself, Stalin put his arm round his shoulders and declared: "We must remain friends and you must now do everything to that end." The German Ambassador had no doubt that this unusual display on Stalin's part had been specially contrived to impress those present with Russo-German friendship. At almost the same time the Russian Government suddenly accepted the German proposals for settling frontier questions arising out of the Soviet annexation of Lithuania.

Early in May Stalin took over the Chairmanship of the Council of People's Commissars, a step university regarded as indicating the prospect of a crisis with which only Stalin himself could deal. Immediately afterwards, however, on 8 May, Tass denied reports of troops concentrations in the west; on 9 May the U.S.S.R. withdrew its recognition from the legations of the exiled Governments of Belgium, Norway and Yugoslavia, and on 11 May established relations with the pro-Nazi Government in Iraq. All through this period the Soviet Press was kept under the strictest restraint and as late as 14 June Tass put out a statement categorically denying difficulties between Germany and Russia.

There is, in fact, not a scrap of evidence to show that, in the summer of 1941, the Soviet Government had any intention of attacking Germany. But Hitler was interested only in reports that could be used to support the pretext for his decision, a decision reached long before without regard to Russia's attitude or the threat which he now alleged of Russian preparations to strike westwards.

In May Antonescu paid his third visit to Hitler, this time at Munich, and agreed that Rumania should take part in the attack. At the end of the month the Finnish Chief of Staff spent a week in Germany to discuss detailed arrangements for co-operation between the two armies. Still Hitler said nothing to Mussolini. When they met at the Brenner on 2 June the most that Ribbentrop admitted was that Russo-German relations were not so good as they had been. Stalin, he told Ciano, was unlikely to commit the folly of attacking Germany, but if he did the Russian forces would be smashed to pieces. Hitler and Ribbentrop were more concerned to reassure Mussolini about Admiral Darlan's visit to Berchtesgaden in May and his attempt to interest Hitler again in the possibilities of Franco-German collaboration in North Africa and the Middle East.

A fortnight later Ribbentrop was more forthcoming, or more indiscreet when he met Ciano at Venice. As they went out to dinner in their gondola Ciano asked his colleague about the rumours of an impending German attack on Russia.

"Dear Ciano," was Ribbentrop's expansive reply, "I cannot tell you anything as yet because every decision is locked in the impenetrable bosom of the Fuehrer. However, one thing is certain: if we attack, the Russia of Stalin will be erased from the map within eight weeks."

From Venice Ribbentrop sent a telegram to Budapest warning the Hungarians to be ready. On 18 June a Non-Aggression Pact between Germany and Turkey was announced. Satisfied with the preparations, in the following week Hitler left for his new headquarters, *Wolfsschanze* ("Wolf's Liar"), in East Prussia.

There, on 21 June, the eve of the attack, he dictated a letter to Mussolini with the first official news of his intentions.

Duce!
I am writing this letter to you at a moment when months of anxious deliberation and continuous, nerve-racking waiting are ending in the hardest decision of my life. I believe—after seeing the latest Russian situation map and after appraisal of numerous other reports—that I cannot take the responsibility for waiting longer, and above all, I believe that there is no other way of obviating the danger. . . .

As so often before, Hitler proceeded to justify himself at length. Britain had lost the war, but held out in the hope of aid from Russia. On their side, the Russians, reverting to their old expansionist policy, maintained a massive concentraton of forces in the east. Until he had safeguarded his rear, Hitler declared, he dared not take the risk of attacking England.

> . . . Even if I should be obliged at the end of the year to leave sixty or seventy divisions in Russia, that is only a fraction of the forces I am now continually using on the Eastern Front.

Once again Mussolini was roused in the middle of the night with the usual urgent message from the Fuehrer. "I do not disturb even my servants at night," he grumbled to Ciano; "but the Germans make me jump out of bed at any hour without the least consideration." While the Duce was still reading Hitler's letter the attack was already beginning. From the Arctic Circle to the Black Sea more than a hundred and fifty German, Finnish and Rumanian divisions were pressing forward across the Russian frontiers. The German forces, divided into three Army Groups commanded by Leeb, Bock and Rundstedt, included nineteen armoured divisions and twelve motorized, supported by over two thousand seven hundred aircraft.

In the 1920s Hitler, whose following numbered only a few thousands, had written at the end of *Mein Kampf*:

> And so we National Socialists. . . . when we speak of new territory in Europe today we must think principally of Russia and her border vassal states. . . . This colossal Empire in the east is ripe for dissolution, and the end of the Jewish domination in Russia will also be the end of Russia as a state.

Hitler concluded his letter to Mussolini with these words: "Since I struggled through to this decision, I again feel spiritually free. The partnership with the Soviet Union, in spite of the complete sincerity of my efforts to bring about a final conciliation . . . seemed to me to be a break with my whole origin, my concepts and my former obligations. I am happy now to be delivered from this torment."

It was to prove an irrevocable decision.

CHAPTER TWELVE

THE UNACHIEVED EMPIRE

1941—1943

At most Hitler's arguments for his attack on Russia reinforced a decision already reached on other grounds. Hitler invaded Russia for the simple but sufficient reason that he had always meant to establish the foundations of his thousand-year Reich by the annexation of the territory lying between the Vistula and the Urals.

The novelty lay in Hitler's decision to drop the provision he had hitherto regarded as indispensable, a settlement with Britain first. He had failed to secure this by diplomacy, he had now failed to secure it by war, but nevertheless Hitler convinced himself that Britain was already as good as defeated. Why then waste time forcing the British to admit that Germany should have a free hand on the Continent, when this was already an established fact to which the British could make no practical objection?

Most important of all was the belief that the Soviet armies could be defeated in a single campaign. Hitler knew that he was taking a risk in invading Russia, but he was convinced that the war in the east would be over in two months, or three at the most. He not only said this, but acted on it, refusing to make any preparations for a winter campaign. "We have only to kick in the door," Hitler told Jodl, "and the whole rotten structure will come crashing down." Hitler was not blind to the numerical superiority of the Russians, but he was certain that the political weakness of the Soviet régime, together with the technical superiority of the Germans, would give him a quick victory.

The invasion of Russia represented the realization of those imperial dreams which he had sketched of the closing section of *Mein Kampf*. At the same time he would be able to guarantee German victory and the creation of that European New Order which was to be the permanent memorial to his genius. This was the prize—and it was to be had, so he convinced himself, at the cost of no more than a single campaign which would be over before the winter came.

The opening of the campaign seemed to justify Hitler's optimism but, although the German troops rapidly gained ground, they did not succeed in destroying the Russian armies.

At this point a divergence appeared between Hitler's and the Army High Command's views of the objectives. Hitler laid the greatest stress on clearing the Baltic States and capturing Leningrad; once the initial battles were over, the Centre Army Group was to support this northerly drive through the Baltic States and not to press on to Moscow. At the same time the Southern Army Group was to drive south-east to secure the agricultural and industrial resources of the Ukraine.

Brauchitsch and Halder believed that the best chance of destroying the Russian forces was to press on to Moscow. They were in favour of concentrating, not dispersing, the German effort. This view, supported by Bock, commanding the Centre Army Group, and by his two panzer commanders, Guderian and Hoth, was rejected by Hitler, who ordered part of Bock's mobile forces to swing north to assist the Northern Army Group's drive on Leningrad, and the rest to wheel south and help the Southern Army Group in its advance into the Ukraine.

Brauchitsch temporized and the Centre Army Group remained halted east of Smolensk.

By September Hitler agreed that the Centre Army Group should prepare to launch a major offensive against Moscow, but he insisted that the battle of encirclement in the Ukraine must be put first and that Bock's Army Group must make the fullest possible contribution to this before resuming its advance eastwards.

Reluctantly the General Staff were forced to assent, but General Halder has since argued that Hitler threw away the chance of inflicting a decisive defeat on the Russians for the sake of a prestige victory and the capture of the industrial region of the Ukraine.

For not only had this dispute seriously worsened the relations between Hitler and his generals, it also led to the waste of valuable time. The southern encirclement proved a great success and over six hundred thousand Russians were taken prisoner east of Kiev, but it was late in September before the battle was ended. The onset of the autumn rains, which turned the Russian countryside, with its poor roads, into a quagmire, promised ill for the attack on Moscow, which the Army High Command had wanted to launch in August and beyond autumn there loomed the threat of the Russian winter. Hitler, however, elated by his success in the south, now pushed the attack on Moscow which he had held back for so long.

On 2 October the advance of the Centre Army Group was resumed, after a halt of two months. On the 3rd Hitler spoke in Berlin, boasting that "behind our troops there already lies a territory twice the size of the German Reich when I came to power in 1933. Today I declare, without reservation, that the enemy in the east has been struck down and will never rise again." Between Vyazma and Bryansk, another six hundred thousand Russians were trapped and taken prisoner. A week later the German spearheads reached Mozhaisk, only eighty miles from the Russian capital.

Yet even now Hitler could not make up his mind to concentrate on one objective. In the north the pressure on Leningrad was maintained and Hitler spoke of his intention of razing the city to the ground. In the south Rundstedt was ordered to clear the Black Sea coast (including the Crimea) and strike beyond Rostov, eastwards to the Volga and southeastwards to the Caucasus. "We laughed aloud when we received these orders," Rundstedt later declared, "for winter had already come and we were almost seven hundred kilometres from these cities."

Thus, with forces numerically inferior to the Russians, Hitler had fallen into the same trap against which he had warned his generals before the invasion began, that of allowing the Russians to retreat and draw the Germans farther and farther into the illimitable depths of their hinterland. When the dreaded winter broke over them, the German armies, despite their victories and advances, had still not captured Leningrad and Moscow, or destroyed the Russian capacity to continue the war.

All through the summer and autumn of 1941 Hitler was entirely occupied with the Eastern Front. Not content with fixing the strategic objectives of his armies, he began to interfere in the detailed conduct of operations. "What had been comparatively infrequent in previous campaigns," General Halder writes, "now became a daily occurrence."

Churchill and Roosevelt met off Newfoundland, and issued on 12 August the Joint Declaration of War Aims known as the Atlantic Charter. The later meeting of Hitler and Mussolini was a counter-demonstration.

Mussolini reached East Prussia by train on 25 August and was at once taken by Hitler to his headquarters, *Wolfsschanze* in the heart of a thick forest. The dim light of the forest produced a feeling of gloom in everyone who went there.

Two conversations took place between Fuehrer and Duce on the 25th. The first meeting was taken up with an exposition of the military situation in the east, during which Mussolini was reduced to the role of admiring listener. Hitler, he noted, spoke with great confidence but admitted that faulty intelligence work had misled him as to the size and excellence of the Russian forces as well as the determinaion with which they fought. In their second talk, the same evening, the two dictators ranged over the rest of the world. Hitler spoke bitterly of Franco and was evasive on the subject of the French, as always, the object of jealous complaints by Mussolini.

Hitler showed some embarrassment at the Duce's pressing offer of more Italian troops for the Eastern Front, but "concluded by expressing the most lively desire to come to Italy —when the war is over—in order to pass some time in Florence, a city dear to him above all others for the harmony of its art and its natural beauty."

Hitler and Mussolini flew to Rundstedt's H.Q. in the Ukraine. There Mussolini inspected an Italian division and lunched with the Fuehrer in the open air, surrounded by a crowd of soldiers. At the end of the meal Hitler walked about among the crowd talking informally, while Mussolini, to his annoyance, was left with Rundstedt. Mussolini had his revenge, however, on the return flight, when he insisted on piloting the plane in which he and Hitler were flying. Hitler's own pilot, Bauer, remained at the controls all the time, but Hitler never took his eyes off Mussolini and sat rigid in his seat until Mussolini left Bauer to his job. The Fuehrer's congratulations were mingled with undisguised relief. Mussolini was childishly delighted and insisted on his performance being recorded in the communiqué.

A feature of the communiqué was the "European New Order," which the Dictators pledged themselves to establish by removing the causes of war, eradicating the threat of Bolshevism, putting an end to "plutocratic exploitation" and establishing close and peaceful collaboration among the peoples of Europe. This was an expansion of Hitler's earlier idea of a "Monroe doctrine for Europe" directed against the Anglo-Saxon powers and a counter-blast to the Anglo-American Charter.

In Munich for the traditional celebration of the 8 November anniversary, Hitler developed an argument which was to provide a companion theme to the European New Order in Nazi propaganda, the New Germany in the New Europe.

What distinguishes the present from what went before [he said] is simply this: then the people were not behind the Kaiser. . . . Then the leaders had no roots in the people, for when all is said and done it was a class state. Today the National Socialist community of the people takes its place at the front, and you will notice how the Armed Forces from month to month become more National Socialist, how they increasingly bear the stamp of the New Germany, how all privileges, classes, prejudices and so on are more and more removed; how, from month to month, the German national community gains ground.

At the end of November Hitler and Ribbentrop staged a demonstration of the European solidarity which, they claimed, had come into existence under Germany's benevolent leadership. Representatives of nine European countries, together with those of Japan and Manchukuo, were summoned to Berlin to renew the original Anti-Comintern Pact.

What the New Order would mean in practice can best be judged from Goering's comment on the fear that the Greeks might soon be suffering from famine: "We cannot worry unduly about the hunger of the Greeks," he said. "It is a misfortune which will strike many other peoples besides them. In the camps for Russian prisoners they have begun to eat each other. This year between twenty and thirty million persons will die of hunger in Russia. Perhaps it is well that it should be so, for certain nations must be decimated."

Throughout this same month of November the German armies had been fighting their way nearer to Moscow under steadily worsening weather conditions. Bitter cold (against which they had no winter clothing), the few hours of daylight and the long nights handicapped the attacking forces, fighting in an unfamiliar land far from home. More and more doubts were felt by commanders as to the wisdom of continuing the attack, but Hitler was insistent: the Russian resistance, he declared, was on the verge of collapse.

Warnings and appeals were of no avail. Hitler categorically refused to admit that he had been wrong. Whatever the cost in men's lives, his armies must make good his boasts, and he drove them on relentlessly. On 2 December Kluge's Fourth Army made a last desperate effort to break through the Russian defences in the forests west of Moscow. A few troops from the 258th Infantry Division actually reached the outskirts of the capital but had to be pulled back.

At that moment, on 6 December, to the complete surprise of Hitler and the German High Command, the Russians launched a major counter-offensive along the whole Central Front with one hundred fresh divisions, and swept away the German threat to Moscow. The German troops, already driven to the limit of endurance, wavered; for a few days there was great confusion and the threat of a Russian breakthrough. Hitler was faced with the most serious military crisis of the war so far. Even if he surmounted it, one thing was already clear: the great gamble had failed, and 1941 would end without the long-heralded victory in the east.

On 7 December, the day after the Russians opened their offensive to relieve Moscow, the Japanese took the American Fleet by surprise in Pearl Harbour. Four days before, the

Japanese Ambassadors in Berlin and Rome had informed the
German and Italian Foreign Ministers that the negotiations
between Japan and the U.S.A. had reached a deadlock, that
war might be imminent, and that Japan requested the support
of her allies in the event of a conflict breaking out, but the
news of the attack on Pearl Harbour came as a surprise to
Hitler.

Nevertheless, he rapidly decided to follow the Japanese
example by declaring war on the United States himself. When
Ribbentrop pointed out that the Tripartite Pact only bound
Germany to assist Japan in the event of an attack on her,
and that to declare war on the U.S.A. would be to add to the
number of Germany's opponents. Hitler dismissed these as
unimportant cnnsiderations. He seems never to have weighed
the advantages of deferring war with America as long as
possible.

Hitherto Hitler had shown considerable patience in face
of the growing aid given by the U.S.A. to the British. But he
was coming to the conclusion that a virtual state of war already existed with the U.S.A. and that there was no point in
delaying the open clash which he regarded as inevitable. The
violence of Hitler's attack on President Roosevelt in his
speech of 11 December suggests the force of the resentment
accumulated under the restraint he had so far practised.

Two other factors affected Hitler's decision. The first was
his disastrous underestimate of American strength. The mixture of races in its population, as well as the lack of authoritarian discipline in its life, predisposed him to regard it as
another decadent bourgeois democracy, incapable of any
sustained military effort. The ease with which the Japanese
struck their blow at Pearl Harbour confirmed these prejudices. Hitler certainly never supposed that he would have to
reckon with a major American intervention, nor did he fore-
see the possibility of an invasion on the scale of that which
the British and the Americans mounted two and a half years
later.

The second factor is more difficult to assess. The prospect
of a war embracing the whole world excited Hitler's imagination. Elated by the feeling that his decisions would affect
the lives of millions of human beings, he declared in the speech
of 11 December, in which he announced Germany's declaration of war on America: "I can only be grateful to Providence that it entrusted me with the leadership in this historic
struggle. . . . A historical revision on a unique scale has
been imposed on us by the Creator."

Most of Hitler's speech was devoted to abuse of the America
of President Roosevelt, whom he depicted as the creature of

the Jews. He compared the success of National Socialism in rescuing Germany from the Depression to what he described as the catastrophic failure of the American New Deal: it was the desire to cover up this failure which led Roosevelt to divert American attention by a provocative foreign policy. The old demagogic tricks were employed to underline this comparison between Nazi Germany, a "have-not" nation, and the wealthy United States:

> I understand only too well that a world-wide distance separates Roosevelt's ideas and mine. Roosevelt comes from a rich family and belongs to the class whose path is smoothed in the democracies. I was only the child of a small poor family and had to fight my way by work and industry. I shared the fate of millions, and Franklin Roosevelt only the fate of the so-called upper ten thousand.

At the end of his speech Hitler announced that a new agreement had been concluded between Germany, Italy and Japan, binding them not to conclude a separate armistice or peace with the U.S.A. or with England, without mutual consent.

It was with Russia, however, far more than with the United States or Great Britain, that Hitler was still concerned in the winter of 1941-1942. The Russian counter-offensive, launched on 6 December, faced him with a crisis, which, if mishandled, might well have turned to disaster.

Hitler rose to the occasion. By a remarkable display of determination he succeeded in holding the German lines firm. It was his greatest achievement as a war-leader.

Hitler's method of dealing with the crisis was simple. In face of the professional advice of his generals and in total disregard of the cost to the troops, he ordered the German armies to stand and fight where they were, categorically refusing all requests to withdraw. This order was enforced in the most ruthless fashion.

The toll taken by the Russians, and even more by the terrible winter, was high. Thousands of German soldiers died of the cold, for Hitler had obstinately refused to consider the possibility of a winter campaign or to provide adequate clothing. In certain places Hitler had reluctantly to accept the withdrawal of decimated German divisions. But when the spring came the German Army still stood deep in the interior of Russia. More than this, by drawing on his own country and his allies, Hitler brought up the forces to sufficient strength to enable him to propose a resumption of the offensive in 1942. Some two hundred to two hundred and twenty German divisions—reduced in size from between twelve and fifteen thou-

sand men to between eight and ten thousand men—together
with another sixty-five divisions of more doubtful value from
Finland, Rumania, Hungary and Italy, were available to
carry out his plans.

The winter crisis marks a decisive stage in the development
of Hitler's relations with the Army which was to have considerable consequences for the future.

After the invasion of Russia there was no longer a High
Command or General Staff in Germany comparable with that
over which Hindenburg and Ludendorff had presided in the
First World War. Hitler ordered the C.-in-C. of the Army
and his Staff (O.K.H.) to confine themselves to the conduct of
the war in the east (excluding Finland). The other fronts
were to be left to his own Supreme Command of the Armed
Forces (O.K.W.). But the O.K.W. was in turn excluded from
the Eastern Front. The responsibility for the conduct of operations was thus divided, and the strategic picture of the war
as a whole remained the concern of Hitler alone.

Hitler was far from being a fool in military matters. He
had read widely in military literature and he took an eager
and well-informed interest in such technical matters as the
design of weapons. His gifts as a politician gave him mastery
of the psychological side of war, quick to see the value of
surprise, bold in the risks he was prepared to take and receptive of unorthodox ideas such as Raeder's proposal for the
occupation of Norway, and Manstein's for the thrust through
the Ardennes. Nor was Hitler far from the truth when he
argued that if he had listened to the High Command he would
never have dared to take the risks which brought the German
Army its sensational triumphs of 1940-1941.

His faults as a military leader were equally obvious. His
experience in the First World War, to which he attached un-
due importance, had been extremely limited. He allowed himself to become intoxicated with figures, with the crude numbers of men or of armaments production.

A combination of Hitler's often brilliant intuition with the
orthodox and methodical planning of the General Staff could
have been highly effective. But this was ruled out by Hitler's
distrust of the generals.

Well aware of the Army's unrivalled prestige as the embodiment of the national tradition, he was quick to suspect
its leaders of a lack of enthusiasm. The German generals,
Hitler complained, had no faith in the National Socialist
idea. His class-resentment was never far below the surface;
he knew perfectly well that the Officer Corps despised him as
an upstart, as "the Bohemian corporal," and he responded
with a barely concealed contempt for the "gentlemen" who

wrote "von" before their names and had never served as privates in the trenches.

To political distrust and social resentment was added Hitler's inveterate suspicion of the expert. It required great tact to get him to accept a view which differed from his own, and this was a quality which few of the German generals possessed. Thus, far from welcoming the very different talents of his military advisers as complementary to his own, he despised them as men hidebound by tradition.

The moment Hitler was faced with a situation like that on the Eastern Front in the winter of 1941-1942 he made it only too clear that he had no faith at all in the High Command's ability to deal with it. Brauchitsch, feeling that he was placed in an impossible position, offered his resignation on 7 December. Ten days later Hitler accepted his offer, and announced that he would himself take over the command-in-chief of the German Army in the field.

This step was the logical conclusion to the policy of concentrating all power in his own hands which Hitler had steadily pursued since 1933.

To General Halder, Hitler remarked:

> This little affair of operational command is something that anybody can do. The Commander-in-Chief's job is to train the Army in the National Socialist idea, and I know of no general who could do that as I want it done. For that reason I've decided to take over command of the Army myself.

So, seven years after his death, Roehm's object was realized, and the Army *Gleichgeschaltet*—by the man who had had Roehm murdered.

After visiting Hitler's headquarters three months later, Goebbels wrote in his diary:

> The Fuehrer spoke of Brauchitsch only in terms of contempt . . . By his constant interference and consistent disobedience he completely spoiled the entire plan for the eastern campaign as it was designed with crystal clarity by the Fuehrer. The Fuehrer had a plan that was bound to lead to victory. Had Brauchitsch done what was asked of him and what he really should have done, our position in the east today would be entirely different.

Even when he had been most calculating in his exploitation of the image of the inspired Fuehrer, Hitler had never lacked belief in the truth of the picture he was projecting. But as success followed upon success the element of calculation was completely overshadowed by the conviction that he was what he had so long claimed to be, a man marked out by

Providence and endowed with more than ordinary gifts. The image he had himself created took possession of him.

His success in checking the Russian counter-offensive exalted his sense of mission and his confidence in his military genius. After the winter of 1942 he was less prepared than ever to listen to advice—or even information—which ran contrary to his own wishes. This was the reverse side of the strength which he derived from his belief in himself—and it was the weakness which was to destroy him, for in the end it destroyed all power of self-criticism and cut him off from all contact with reality.

This can already be seen in 1941. For, if Hitler saved the German Army in the winter of that year, it was principally as the result of his miscalculation that it had ever been placed in such a position.

Yet his fatal facility for convincing himself of the truth of whatever he wanted to believe soon created the unshakeable conviction that the failure of 1941 had been due to the shortcomings of the Army High Command, and that, now he had taken over the direction of operations himself, 1942 would infallibly produce the knock-out blow which had eluded him the previous year. Thus, as belief in Nazi victory claims weakened in Germany under the ineluctable pressure of events, it only grew stronger in Hitler's own mind, in defiance of events, until he became the last victim of his own propaganda.

This same sense of confidence was equally marked in Hitler's private conversation during these months. An anthology of his table-talk has been published since the war, based upon the notes taken at the time by two men who were present at the Fuehrer's headquarters from July, 1941, to the end of July, 1942.

The form is the same in every case, a monologue listened to in respectful silence by those who had attended the meal. The greater part of the four hundred printed pages is devoted to politics and war, but there are shorter sections which record Hitler's opinions on moral questions, human relations, religion, education and the arts. His views on the relative merits of Bruno Walter and Furtwängler as orchestral conductors are duly recorded alongside those on the correct training of dogs, the pernicious habit of smoking and the advantages of a vegetarian diet.

The lasting impression is of the vulgarity of his mind, as commonplace as it was brutal, as unabashed as it was ignorant. A single example will be sufficient to illustrate this quality. One evening Hitler was discussing the need to warn the rising generation against what he called the "racial danger." On these grounds alone, he went on, he would permit the continuation of the Oberammergau Passion Play. "Nowhere has the Jewish danger in the case of the Roman Empire been so vividly depicted as in the representation of Pontius Pilate in the Oberammergau performance. His superiority as a Roman, both racially and intellectually, is so apparent that he stands like a rock amid the Near Eastern scum and swarm." In his recognition of the value of this drama for the enlightenment of the coming generation, Hitler added, he was a hundred per cent Christian.

The Hitler of the *Tischgespräche* indeeds reveals nothing new; it is the same harsh and uncouth figure already familiar from the pages of *Mein Kampf* or the earliest of his speeches. Success had altered little of the essential Hitler, and as for the set-back of the winter, it left his belief in his own cocksure genius strengthened rather than impaired.

This was the mood in which Hitler began to draw up his plans for the new campaigning season of 1942. When Goebbels saw him at his headquarters in March, he reported:

> The Fuehrer again has a perfectly clear plan of campaign for the coming spring and summer. He does not want to overextend the war. His aims are the Caucasus, Leningrad and Moscow. . . . Possibly this may mean a hundred years' war in the east, but that need not worry us.

When Halder told him that the Army Intelligence Service had information that six or seven hundred tanks a month were coming out of the Russian factories, Hitler thumped the table and said it was impossible.

> The Russians were "dead." This winter offensive had consumed the last of their strength, and it was only a question of giving a push to what was already tottering. Nietzsche and Clausewitz were quoted in support of his "heroic" decision.

The Home Front, no less than the Army, needed its faith in the Fuehrer's leadership restored, and in the first four months of 1942 Hitler found time to make three big speeches.

In his third speech on 26 April Hitler, with the winter now behind him, gave the fullest expression to his renewed faith in Germany's eventual triumph. He deliberately exaggerated the seriousness of the situation on the Eastern Front in order to throw into more effective contrast his own decision to assume personal responsibility and the news that the crisis had been mastered. Then, picking up the allusion to Napoleon's Retreat from Moscow, so often invoked during the winter, he added: "We have mastered a destiny which broke another man a hundred and thirty years ago."

Hitler's picture of the conditions under which the Army had fought in the east was a prelude to a demand for still greater powers, the counterpart on the Home Front to his decision to take over the Eastern Front operations. The law, duly passed by the Reichstag without discussion, proclaimed:

> The Fuehrer must have all the rights demanded by him to achieve victory. Therefore—without being bound by existing legal regulations—in his capacity as Leader of the Nation the Fuehrer must be in a position to force, with all the means at his disposal, every German, if necessary, whether he be common soldier or officer, low or high official or judge, leading or subordinate official of the Party, worker or employer, to fulfil his duties. In case of violation of these duties the Fuehrer is entitled, regardless of rights, to mete out punishment and remove the offender from his post, rank and position without introducing prescribed procedures.

Hitler's request for a confirmation of the arbitrary power which he already possessed is at first sight puzzling. The explanation of this decree is found in Goebbels' Diaries, in which the Minister of Propaganda continually complains of the shortcomings of State and Party administration, to meet the demands of "total" war. In March Goebbels pressed Hitler to adopt much more drastic measures to control war-profiteering and the black market, to increase production, reduce the swollen staffs of overgrown ministries, and provide additional manpower.

Goebbels and Hitler laid the blame for these shortcomings on the conservatism of the German civil service and judiciary. But they were only paying the penalty for treating the administration of the State as "spoils" for the Nazi Party once it had come to power. The Nazis remained what they had always been, gangsters, spivs and bullies—only now in control of the resources of a great State. It is astonishing that they had not ruined Germany long before the end of the war. The fact that they did not was due to the stolid virtues and organizing ability of the permanent officals of the civil service, of local government and industry, who, however much abused, continued, like the German Officer Corps, to serve their new masters with an unquestioning docility.

Hitler was the last man to remedy this situation. Without administrative gifts, disliking systematic work and indifferent to corruption, Hitler was at the same time far too jealous of his authority to make any effective delegation of his powers.

In the 1930s Hitler spoke of the Party as "a chosen Order of Leadership" whose task was "to supply from its membership an unbroken succession of personalities fitted to undertake the supreme leadership of the State." On closer inspection the new *élite* was far from impressive. Even amongst the Reich leaders of the Party there were few men of ability, integrity or even education. One of the exceptions was Goebbels. Goering, too, undoubtedly displayed ability in 1933-1934, but by 1942 this had long been overlaid by the habits of indolence and the corruption of power. Men like Ley, Ribbentrop, Funk, Darré and Rosenberg were wholly unfitted to hold positions of responsibility.

In February, 1942, however, Hitler had the luck to make one of the few good appointments he ever made. Albert Speer, whom he chose as Minister for Armaments and Munitions in place of Dr. Todt (killed in an air accident), was a young architect who had been set to complete the new Reich Chancellery. Disinterested as well as able, he soon showed himself to be an organizer of remarkable powers and became virtual dictator of the whole of German war production. Faced with great difficulties in procuring manpower from the obstruction of the Gauleiters, Speer shrewdly suggested that one of them should be made responsible for increasing Germany's labour force. This led in March, 1942, to the appointment as Plenipotentiary-General for Manpower of Fritz Sauckel, a former sailor and a Party Member since 1921, who was Gauleiter of Thuringia. These measures produced a sensational rise in German war-production in 1942 and 1943 without which Hitler could never have continued the war at all.

In the 1942 campaign a bigger part was to be played by the armies of the satellite States. Hitler had not seen the Duce since August, 1941, and, now he thought it desirable to revive Mussolini's flagging faith in an Axis victory. Accordingly the Duce and Ciano set out for the north at the end of April, 1942, and spent two days with Hitler at Salzburg.

> Hitler talks, talks, talks, talks. Mussolini suffers—he, who is in the habit of talking himself, and who instead has to remain silent. On the second day, after lunch, when everything had been said, Hitler talked uninterruptedly for an hour and forty minutes.

On the way back Mussolini complained that he could not see why Hitler had asked them to make the journey. Resentment at his own reduced role was beginning to be tinged with the uneasy fear that he, as well as the Germans, would have to pay for the mistakes of an over-confident Hitler.

Before the attack on Russia Hitler had evaded Raeder's proposals for intensifying the war in the Mediterranean, with the promise to take up these plans after Russia was defeated.

Although Hitler was forced to send stronger forces to the Mediterranean theatre, throughout 1941 and the winter of 1941-1942, the sole purpose behind these moves was defensive, to prevent an Italian collapse in North Africa. At the end of the winter, however, Raeder returned to the attack and succeeded in rousing Hitler's interest in the Mediterranean, largely because of the grandiose way in which the plan (known as the "Great Plan") was dressed up as a drive through the Middle East to join the Japanese in a vast encirclement of Britain's Asian Empire. Hitler agreed to a twofold operation for the summer of 1942—*Operation Hercules* for the capture of Malta (the key to the security of Rommel's supply route), and *Operation Aida*, the renewal of the desert offensive against Egypt, Suez and beyond to Persia. These two operations were to serve as the prelude to the "Great Plan."

The operations began well with Rommel's capture of Tobruk and the invasion of Egypt. By 30 June, 1942, a month after the offensive had opened, the *Afrika Korps* reached the El Alamein line, only sixty-five miles from Alexandria. But Hitler showed a curious reluctance to undertake the second part of the plan, the assault on Malta. He had already postponed *Operation Hercules* until Rommel could capture Tobruk: now he postponed it again, arguing that Malta's capture was no longer necessary with Rommel on the verge of occupying Egypt.

As the summer passed, the British had time to build up their forces in Egypt and to strengthen Malta; the losses on the Italy-North African run began to mount again. By the autumn the *Afrika Korps* was still at El Alamein and Malta still unsubdued.

At the beginning of September Hitler saw Rommel (who was on sick leave) and reassured him: "I mean to give Africa all the support needed. Never fear, we are going to get Alexandria all right." While agreeing to the "Great Plan," Hitler never once displayed that energy and singleness of purpose in forcing it through which had held the Eastern Front firm in the winter. Hitler never grasped North Africa's importance in the total picture of the war, as Churchill had done even when Britain's power was reduced to its lowest ebb.

For all his talk of a war between continents Hitler showed little understanding of sea-power, which bound together the alliance which opposed him.

For years Admiral Raeder had tried to persuade Hitler that the one certain way of defeating Great Britain was by attacking her trade routes and blockading her ports. Even after the directive for *Barbarossa* had been issued, Raeder argued:

"What is being done for U-boat and naval-air construction is much too little. . . . Britain's ability to maintain her supply lines is the decisive factor for the outcome of the war."

This was in December, 1940. Hitler's reply was to promise Raeder—as in the case of the Mediterranean—that once Russia had been defeated he should have all he asked for. Meanwhile the Navy had to be content with what it could scratch together in face of the competition of the Army and the Air Force. Raeder was not allowed to establish a naval air force, nor was he able to secure the effective co-operation of the Luftwaffe in attacks on British shipping, harbours and shipyards. Goering, on bad terms with the Navy, was a law unto himself, and Hitler simply let the quarrel between the two Services drag on.

Up to February, 1941, Raeder found it impossible to keep more than some six U-boats at sea at a time. By the end of 1941 this had been increased to sixty. With these limited forces the U-boats achieved remarkable successes in 1942, sinking six and a quarter million gross tons, nearly three times the figure for 1941. These results were so striking that Hitler began to talk of the U-boats as the factor which would decide the outcome of the war. In May, 1942, Doenitz, the Flag Officer U-boats, was summoned to attend the Fuehrer conferences for the first time. When Raeder demanded that no workman engaged on U-boat construction or repair should be drafted for military service, Hitler at once agreed, and more than three hundred U-boats were in fact completed during 1942.

But Hitler's interest in the possibilities of the U-boats came too late. Although the shipping losses between the beginning of 1942 and the spring of 1943 taxed the Allies to the limit, they now had at their disposal resources which Hitler, deeply committed in Russia, could not hope to equal. In the end the Battle of the Atlantic, which might—as Raeder had so often argued—have proved decisive, was destined to prove one of Hitler's greatest failures. It was a failure which sprang from his defective grasp of the war as a whole and which was confirmed by the decision to invade Russia, a campaign into which a disproportionate amount of Germany's resources in men and machines was drawn at the expense of every other front.

On the third front, the western seaboard of Europe and Northern Africa, Hitler was not blind to the threat of an Anglo-American landing, but the problem of how to defend so vast a coastline was one to which he never found a satisfactory answer. Moreover from the autumn of 1941, he displayed a growing conviction that Britain and the U.S.A.—possibly in co-operation with Russia—were planning a large-scale assault on Norway.

There was little enough evidence to support such a view, but so impressed was Hitler by his intuition that he insisted on concentrating virtually the whole of the German surface fleet in Norwegian waters. Not until 1943 was Hitler prepared tacitly—never openly—to admit that he had been wrong. By then the allied armada had safely landed an army in Northwest Africa, unmolested by the German naval forces a thousand miles away to the north, where they remained vainly keeping guard against an attack which never came.

A much more ominous threat from the west began to develop in 1942. The German Air Force, already roughly handled in the Battle of Britain, never recovered from the demands made on it in Russia. It could not prevent the first thousand-bomber raid, on Cologne, the night of 30-31 May, 1942, which was a portent for the future. The war was beginning to come home to Germany.

Hitler had chosen the south as the main theatre for his operations on the East Front in 1942, and powerful German forces drove fast down the corridor between the Don and Donetz rivers. While one wing pushed east towards the Volga at Stalingrad, the other drove past Rostov and, covering another four hundred and fifty miles, reached the Caucasus and the more westerly oilfields round Maikop in the first half of August.

Hitler moved his H.Q. to Winniza, in the Ukraine, during July, and from here he followed the progress of his armies with mounting excitement. Now, he declared, his faith and determination in the winter had been justified: Russia was on the verge of defeat.

Hitler, however, made exactly the same mistake he had made the year before. Overestimating the German strength, he did not limit himself to his original objective, to capture Stalingrad, but tried to break into the Caucasus with its valuable oilfields. By September the Battle for Stalingrad was beginning to assume proportions which made Halder doubt whether its capture was worth the effort or the risks. For the city's name and it historical association with Stalin during the Civil War made the Russians as eager to defend it as Hitler was to take it. As the Germans fought their way forward they exposed their long-drawn-out northern flank to grave danger from a Russian counter-attack across the Don.

Halder's attempts to point out the dangers of the situation

led Hitler again to accuse the General Staff of cowardice, and ridicule the Intelligence reports of Russian preparation for a counter-attack.

> When a statement was read to him [Halder recalls] which showed that Stalin would still be able to muster another one to one and a quarter million men in the region north of Stalingrad (besides half a million more in the Caucasus), and which proved that the Russian output of first-line tanks amounted to twelve hundred a month, Hitler flew at the man who was reading with clenched fists and foam in the corners of his mouth, and forbade him to read such idiotic twaddle.

When Halder recommended the breaking off of the attack at the end of September, Hitler dismissed him and replaced him as Chief of the Army General Staff by General Zeitzler.

Meanwhile, the thrust into the Caucasus had been halted short of the main oilfields. Hitler, beside himself with impatience, sent Jodl to investigate. When Jodl, on his return, ventured to defend the C.-in-C. in the Caucasus, Field-Marshal List, Hitler flew into fury. What particularly angered him was Jodl's citation of his own earlier directives to prove that List had only been obeying orders.

From that day on Hitler refused to eat with his staff officers at the common table. For several months Hitler declined to shake hands with Jodl, and on 30 January, 1943, he sent word that he was to be replaced. By a rare stroke of irony, Paulus, the man Hitler chose as Jodl's successor, the next day surrendered to the Russians at Stalingrad, a fitting comment to the end of this chapter in the history of Hitler's relations with his generals.

By the autumn of 1942 all Hitler's urging could not alter the fact that the German advance at Stalingrad, as well as in the Caucasus and North Africa, had been brought to a standstill. This was the end of Hitler's offensives. For the first time since he proclaimed Germany's rearmament in 1935, the initiative passed out of Hitler's hands, never to return.

On the night of 23 October, 1942, the British 8th Army under General Montgomery attacked the German lines at El Alamein and after twelve days' heavy fighting broke out into the desert beyond.

On the night of 7-8 November British and American troops landed along the coast of Morocco and Algeria, and within a few days occupied the whole of French North Africa as far as the Tunisian frontier.

On 19 and 20 November three Russian Army Groups under the command of Generals Vatutin, Rokossovsky and Eremenko attacked on a huge front north and south of Stalingrad and within five days succeeded in encircling twenty-two German divisions between the Volga and the Don.

Taken together, these three operations mark the turning-point in the war and the seizure of the initiative by the Allies. Henceforward Hitler was on the defensive.

Hitler's very success in halting a German retreat now proved a fatal legacy. His one idea was to hold fast. He telegraphed to Rommel: "The position requires that the El Alamein position be held to the last man. There is to be no retreat. . . . Victory or death!" When Rommel flew back to Germany at the end of November and told Hitler that Africa was lost, and the only course was to get the *Afrika Korps* out to fight in Italy, Hitler shouted at him that he was a defeatist and his troops cowards. Despite his categorical orders, however, neither Rommel nor anyone else could halt the Allies' advance.

The allied landings in French North Africa in November took Hitler completely by surprise. He immediately summoned Laval, as well as Ciano for a meeting at Munich. Hitler bluntly informed Laval that the Germans would occupy Tunisia at once, together with the rest of Unoccupied France. At last Mussolini had his way over France, but he was no longer in a position to derive much satisfaction from it.

After his long neglect of the Mediterranean Hitler began to pour troops and supplies into Tunisia in order at all costs to hold a bridgehead covering Tunis and Bizerta. In something of a panic Mussolini urged Hitler to come to terms with Russia, so that the greatest number of divisions could be moved to the Mediterranean and the west. These suggestions were ignored. Hitler was determined to hold Tunisia but he was equally determined not to give up anything elsewhere.

Meanwhile the Russians methodically tightened the net round the German Sixth Army at Stalingrad. The formula which had proved successful the previous winter was monotonously repeated: Stand and fight to the last man. Hitler refused to let von Paulus attempt to break the ring from the inside. No conceivable military purpose was served by holding the German troops in their positions, but Hitler's personal prestige as a leader was now engaged, and against that the lives of three hundred and thirty thousand men were nothing.

Towards the end of January, 1943, Paulus reported that the suffering of the troops, through cold, hunger and epidemics, was no longer bearable, and that to continue fighting in such conditions was beyond human strength. Hitler answered:

Capitulation is impossible. The 6th Army will do its historic duty at Stalingrad until the last man, in order to make possible the reconstruction of the Eastern Front.

Hitler did not hesitate to stoop to bribes: at the last moment he promoted Paulus to the rank of Field-Marshal in order to buy the loyalty of the commander whose troops he had deliberately condemned to death. To the Italian Ambassador he compared the German Army at Stalingrad with the Three Hundred at Thermopylae. They would show the world, he declared, the true spirit of National Socialist Germany and its loyalty to its Fuehrer.

The outcome was a far worse blow to Hitler's prestige than any order to withdraw could ever have been. On the night of 31 January, the Russians announced that they had completed the capture or annihilation of the remainder of the 6th Army and the 4th Panzer Army, adding that among the officers who had surrendered was Field-Marshal von Paulus himself, his Chief of Staff, General Schmidt, and the Commander of the II Army Corps, General von Seydlitz.

At noon on 1 February, the day after the Russian communiqué, Hitler held his usual military conference. Totally oblivious of his own responsibility for what had happened, the Fuehrer spared no thought for the men he had driven to death or captivity. He could think only of his commander's ingratitude and disloyalty.

> The man should have shot himself just as the old commanders who threw themselves on their swords when they saw their cause was lost. That goes without saying.
>
> What hurts me most, personally, is that I promoted him to Field-Marshal. I wanted to give him this final satisfaction. That's the last Field-Marshal I shall appoint in this war. You mustn't count your chickens before they are hatched. I don't understand that at all. So many people have to die, and then a man like that besmirches the heroism of so many others at the last minute. He could have freed himself from all sorrow and ascended into eternity and national immortality, but he prefers to go to Moscow. What kind of choice is that? It just doesn't make sense.

It was the comment of a supreme egotist, the complaint of a man who was to see in the sufferings and defeat of a nation only his own betrayal by a people unworthy of their Fuehrer.

In preparing to attack France Hitler had shown a brilliant understanding of how war could be waged with other than military weapons. But, although he repeatedly described the war with Russia as an ideological conflict and counted on a Russian uprising, the harsh policy he adopted in the east worked in the opposite direction.

There is evidence to show that when the German armies entered the Ukraine and the Baltic States they were looked upon as liberators. Ignoring all that might have been done to drive a wedge between the people and the Soviet Government, especially in the Ukraine, Hitler preferred to treat the inhabitants of Eastern Europe indiscriminately as Slave *Un termenschen,* fit only for slave labour. The spirit of German policy was expressed by Erich Koch, Gauleiter of East Prussia whom Hitler appointed Reich Commissioner for the Ukraine. Speaking to a German audience at Kiev on 5 March, 1943, Koch proclaimed: "We did not come here to serve out manna. We have come here to create the basis for victory. We are a master race, which must remember that the lowliest German worker is racially and biologically a thousand times more valuable than the population here."

Goebbels was quick-witted enough to see the opportunities that were being lost. In 1942, he tried to get Hitler to issue a proclamation promising the Russians greater freedom and some relief from the oppressive exactions of the Soviet Government. But Hitler, whose political interests had waned as he became absorbed in his new role of military genius, was set upon clear-cut victory in the field and remained indifferent to the possibility of winning support in the east.

Hitler's policy in Eastern Europe was no hasty improvisation: it was the calculated expression of a mind which could conceive of politics only in terms of domination and could understand the exercise of power soley in terms of the whip.

The proof of this is to be found in the records of a number of discussions between the Nazi leaders which go back at least to 1940, and in which Hitler explained his plans for the future not only of Russia but of the two other Slav countries of Poland and Czechoslovakia.

Hitler's ideas were perfectly clear.

The Poles [he declared] in direct contrast to our German workmen, are especially born for hard labour. We must give every possibility of advancement to our German workers; as to the Poles, there can be no question of improvement for them. On the contrary, it is necessary to keep the standard of life low in Poland, and it must not be permitted to rise. . . . The Government-General should be used by us merely as a source of unskilled labour. . . . It is indispensable to bear in mind that the Polish landlords must cease to exist, however cruel this may sound, they must be exterminated wherever they are. . . .

There should be one master only for the Poles—the Germans. Two masters, side by side, cannot and must not exist. Therefore all representatives of the Polish intelligentsia are to be exterminated. This, too, sounds cruel, but such is the law of life.

The Poles will also benefit from this, as we look after their health and see to it that they do not starve, but they must never be raised to a higher level, for then they will become anarchists and Communists. It will therefore be proper for the Poles to remain Roman Catholics: Polish priests will receive food from us and will, for that very reason, direct their little sheep along the path we favour. . . . If any priest acts differently, we shall make short work of him. The task of the priest is to keep the Poles quiet, stupid and dull-witted. This is entirely in our interests. Should the Poles rise to a higher level of development, they will cease to be that manpower of which we are in need. . . . The lowest German workman and the lowest German peasant must always stand economically ten per cent above any Pole.

Hitler was presented with a number of plans for the future of the Protectorate of Bohemia-Moravia. After deliberation he accepted one which provided for the settlement of an increased number of Germans in the Protectorate where they would assimilate that part of the Czech population which was of racial value.

The other half of the Czechs must be deprived of their power, eliminated and shipped out of the country by all sorts of methods. This applies particularly to the racially Mongoloid part and to the major part of the intellectual class.

These were the precedents for Hitler's policy in Russia, and they were faithfully followed. On 16 July, 1941, a month after the invasion of the Soviet Union, Hitler held a conference at his Fuehrer Headquarters which was attended by Goering, Rosenberg, Bormann, Keitel and Lammers, the head of the Reich Chancery. Rosenberg's attempts to plead for a friendly policy towards the Ukrainian people had no effect; the note which Hitler struck was in a wholly different key. Under cover of military occupation of the areas seized, plans for a permanent settlement were to be introduced. "Nobody," he warned his audience, "must be able to recognize that it initiates a final settlement, but this need not prevent our taking all necessary measures—shooting, re-settling, etc.—and we shall take them."

The first need was to exploit the occupied eastern territories for the strengthening and relief of the German war economy. This had been foreseen in the economic directives drawn up before the invasion, and was continually reaffirmed by Goering and others. In a conference on 6 August, 1942, Goering, as Plenipotentiary for the Four-Year Plan, told the commissioners for the occupied regions: "It used to be called plundering. But today things have become more genteel. In spite of that, I intend to plunder and to do it thoroughly."

As the bombing of German industry and the losses of manpower and equipment began to exert a greater strain on the German economy, so the demands on the eastern territories mounted. These demands were not limited to raw materials, food and machinery, but extended to manpower as well. Russia, like Poland and the other occupied countries in the west, France, Belgium and Holland, was turned into a vast labour camp to provide the human material which German industry and agriculture needed. The organization of this new slave traffic was in the hands of Sauckel, and the brutality of the methods by which men, women and children were rounded up, shipped to Germany and forced to work, often under unspeakable conditions, beggars description.

Hitler's policy in the eastern occupied territories, however, was only in part determined by Germany's immediate economic needs. As he explained in the conference of 16 July, 1941, under cover of the occupation he was determined to lay the basis of a final settlement in the lands between the Vistula and the Urals. Colonies of settlers from Germany and from the German minorities in other countries (*Volksdeutsche*) were to be established in Poland and European Russia, each settlement being linked by a network of military roads and protected by S.S. garrisons one of whose tasks was to keep the native population in permanent subjection. Part of this native population was to provide slave labour for the industries and agriculture of the new German Empire, and was to remain in a status of total inferiority, without rights and treated literally as a sub-human race at the arbitrary disposal of their overlords. The surplus—including all those of education, property and position who might provide a nucleus of leadership—was to be exterminated to make room for the new colonists, or left to die of starvation. The task of carrying out this nightmarish programme was the special privilege of Himmler and the S.S.

Hitler had appointed Himmler as Trustee for the Consolidation of German Nationhood on 7 October, 1939. His tasks were defined as the elimination of such alien groups as represented a danger to the Reich and the German Folk Community, and the formation of new German settlements from returning German citizens and racial Germans abroad. To carry out these duties Himmler set up special departments and outlined his programme in speeches which give an authoritative picture of Hitler's plans for the future.

The most interesting of these speeches is one which Himmler made on 4 October, 1943.

One basic principle must be the absolute rule for the S.S. men: we must be honest, decent, loyal and comradely to members of our own blood and nobody else. What happens to a Russian and a Czech does not interest me in the slightest. What the nations can offer in the way of good blood of our type we will take, if necessary, by kidnapping their children and raising them here with us. Whether nations live in prosperity or starve to death interests me only in so far as we need them as slaves for our *Kultur*: otherwise it is of no interest to me. Whether ten thousand Russian females fall down from exhaustion while digging an anti-tank ditch interests me only in so far as the anti-tank ditch for Germany is finished. We shall never be rough and heartless when it is not necessary, that is clear. We Germans, who are the only people in the world who have a decent attitude towards animals, will also assume a decent attitude towards these human animals. But it is a crime against our own blood to worry about them and give them ideals, thus causing our sons and grandsons to have a more difficult time with them. When somebody comes to me and says:"I cannot dig the anti-tank ditch with women and children, it is inhuman, for it would kill them," then I have to say: "You are the murderer of your own blood, because if the anti-tank ditch is not dug German soldiers will die, and they are the sons of German mothers. They are our own blood. . . . " Our concern, our duty is our people and our blood. We can be indifferent to everything else. I wish the S.S. to adopt this attitude to the problem of all foreign, non-Germanic peoples, especially Russians.

In passing Himmler mentioned the extermination of the Jews:

Most of *you* know what it means when a hundred corpses are lying side by side, or five hundred or one thousand. To have stuck it out, and at the same time—apart from exceptions caused by human weakness—to have remained decent fellows, that is what has made us hard. This is a page of glory in our history which has never been written and is never to be written . . . We had the moral right, we had the duty to our people to destroy this people [the Jews] which wanted to destroy us.

Among the particular duties of the S.S. was that of organizing the concentration camps. At the outbreak of war there were six such camps in Germany, with a prisoner population of 21,000. According to the S.S. official records, by 1942 this had risen to 44,700 in the original camps, while nine additional camps had been constructed. In a circular letter of

28 December, 1942, an official of the S.S. Main Office complained that out of 136,870 new arrivals in concentration camps between June and November 70,610 were already dead: this, he pointed out, seriously reduced the numbers available for armaments work in the concentration camp factories.

The work of guarding the concentration camps and carrying out the brutal sentences of flogging, torture and execution which were everyday occurrences was alloted to the S.S. Death's Head Units (*Totenkopfverbände*). In a speech which he delivered to S.S. leaders at Metz in April, 1941, Himmler described such work as "fighting the sub-humanity (*Untermenschentum*). This will not be a boring guard duty, but, if the officers handle it right, it will be the best indoctrination on inferior beings and the sub-human races."

More terrible even than the concentration camps were the extermination camps. According to the official German figures, at Mauthausen in Austria, close on two million people, mainly Jews, were exterminated between 1941 and 1945.

Lest these figures should appear incredible, it is worth while adding an extract from the affidavit of Rudolf Hoess, the Commandant of the Auschwitz Camp in Poland. In his affidavit he says:

> I estimate that at least two and a half million victims were executed and exterminated at Auschwitz by gassing and burning and that at least another half million succumbed to starvation and disease, making a total of about three million dead. This figure represents about seventy to eighty per cent of all persons sent to Auschwitz as prisoners, the remainder having been selected and used for slave labour in the concentration-camp industries. . . .
>
> The "final solution" of the Jewish question meant the complete extermination of all Jews in Europe. I was ordered to establish extermination facilities at Auschwitz in June, 1941. At that time there were already three other extermination camps in the Government-General: Belzek, Treblinka and Wolzek. I visited Treblinka to find out how they carried out their extermination. The Camp Commandant told me that he had liquidated eighty thousand in the course of one half year. He was principally concerned with liquidating all the Jews from the Warsaw ghetto. He used monoxide gas and I did not think that his methods were very efficient. So at Auschwitz I used Cyclon B, which was a crystallized prussic acid dropped into the death chamber. It took from three to fifteen minutes to kill the people in the chamber, according to climatic conditions. We knew when the people were dead because their screaming stopped. We usually waited about half an hour before we opened the doors and removed the bodies. After the bodies were removed, our special commandos took off the rings and extracted the gold from the teeth of the corpses. Another im-

provement that we made over Treblinka was that we built our gas-chambers to accommodate two thousand people at one time. . . .

When the invasion of Russia began Hitler and Himmler recruited four special units known as *Einsatzkommandos* to carry out the extermination of the Jewish population and also of Communist functionaries. Otto Ohlendorf, the Chief of the Security Police (SD), who commanded *Einsatzgruppe D* in southern Russia for a year, estimated that ninety thousand men, women and children were liquidated by his formation during that period. At first the victims were made to dig mass trenches into which they were thrown after execution by shooting: the scenes described of terrified children and distracted mothers are without pity. In the spring of 1942, however, the efficient Main Office in Berlin began to supply gas vans for mobile extermination. Another formation, *Einsatzgruppe A*, in northern Russia, killed a hundred and thirty-five thousand Jews and Communists in its first four months of operations.

It has been widely denied in Germany since the war that any but a handful of Germans at the head of the S.S. knew of the scope or savagery of these measures against the Jews. One man certainly knew. For one man they were the logical realization of views which he had held since his twenties, the necessary preliminary to the plans he had formed for the resettlement of Europe. That man was Adolf Hitler.

Himmler organized the extermination of the Jews, but the man in whose mind so grotesque a plan had been conceived was Hitler. Without Hitler's authority, Himmler, a man solely of subordinate virtues, would never have dared to act on his own. This was the subject of those secret talks "*unter vier Augen*" between the Fuehrer and the *Reichsfuehrer S.S.* at which no one else (save occasionally Bormann) was allowed to be present and of which no records survive. There are few more ghastly pages in history than this attempt to eliminate a whole race, the consequence of the "discovery" made by a young down-and-out in a Vienna slum in the 1900s that the Jews were the authors of everything that he most hated in the world.

It is all too easy to dismiss such a conception as the fantasy of a diseased brain: it is well to remember, however, that in the sinister sites of Auschwitz and Mauthausen, and the well-kept records of the S.S., there are the proofs of how near the fantastic came to being realized.

CHAPTER THIRTEEN

TWO JULYS

1943-1944

The immediate consequences of the Stalingrad disaster did not lead to a collapse of the German front in the east. When the winter fighting came to an end the German line was still deep in Russian territory. It was not until the late summer of 1943 that the Russians renewed their attacks. By that time Hitler was faced with an even graver situation in Italy.

Hitler's rapid decision to seize Tunisia in November, 1942, proved effective in balking the Allies of victory before the end of that year. The news from Italy, however, made him anxious: the Duce was ill, dislike of the Germans was widespread, and the one ambition of the Italian people was to get out of the war as soon as possible. When Ciano left the Foreign Ministry to become Ambassador to the Vatican, the Germans were sure that he had gone there to negotiate a separate peace.

Something must clearly be done to stiffen his failing ally, and at the end of February, 1943, Hitler sent Ribbentrop on a visit to Rome with a long personal letter to the Duce. He insisted that the war in the east must go on until the Russian giant was destroyed: until that was accomplished Europe would never know peace. The rest of the letter was taken up with an encouraging survey of the war situation, in which Hitler stressed the success of the U-boats.

Ribbentrop's visit was followed by Hitler's agreement to allow the Italian workmen in Germany to return home—a considerable concession at a time when Sauckel was mobilizing the labour resources of the rest of Europe to work for Germany. But Mussolini, ageing, sick and disillusioned, was fast losing control of the situation. Mass strikes in Turin and Milan, with the slogans "Peace and Liberty," were a pointer to the impending collapse of the régime. All that Mussolini could think of was a renewed appeal to Hitler to make a separate peace with Russia. Hitler's reply was to press Mussolini to come to Salzburg, where they met in the middle of April.

Mussolini promised his lieutenants that this time he would stand up to Hitler: he was determined to urge peace with Russia, and the withdrawal of the German armies from abroad to defend their homeland. But, face to face with the dynamic Fuehrer, he succumbed and sat silent while Hitler talked.

On this occasion Hitler overrated his powers as a faith-healer. Mussolini returned to Rome leaving unsaid all he had meant to tell the Fuehrer, but at heart already a defeated man, no longer able to convince himself of the part he had to play. His despair was soon justified. On 7 May Tunis and Bizerta were captured by the Allies and within a week the entire Axis forces in Africa, which Hitler, against Rommel's advice, had built up to more than two hundred and fifty thousand men, were taken prisoner with all their equipment.

It was obvious that the Allies would attempt a landing on the northern shores of the Mediterranean—and equally obvious that, with the loss of the troops in Tunisia, Hitler and Mussolini would be hard pressed to prevent them. Co-operation between the Italian and German Armed Forces was increasingly strained. Report after report from German officers in Italy left Hitler in no doubt of the danger of the situation, but he feared to take drastic action lest this should drive the Italians into open revolt.

The allied attack came on 10 July, in Sicily, and the Allies at once made good their landings.

Nine days later Hitler summoned Mussolini to meet him at Feltre, in northern Italy. It was their thirteenth meeting, and in a last effort to put new life into the alliance, Hitler talked for three hours on end before lunch. There was one course open to them, he declared, to fight and go on fighting, on all fronts—in Russia as well as Italy—and with a fanatical will to conquer.

After lunch Hitler summoned up his energies for a second performance. Once again, as Ciano had so often noted, he talked, talked, talked; and once again the Duce sat silent to the end. He even failed to get a promise of reinforcements from the Germans.

Immediately after the Feltre meeting Italian discontent with the German alliance and with the Duce as its representative came to a head. The Fascist Grand Council met on the night of 24-25 July, and Mussolini had to listen to violent criticism of his conduct of the war. The following evening the Duce was dismissed by the King and placed under arrest. The veteran Marshal Badoglio formed a non-Fascist government; the Party itself was dissolved, and Fascist officials expelled from their posts. The new Government's authority was the Crown and the Army.

As soon as the news reached his headquarters Hitler summoned an immediate conference of all the Nazi leaders, together with Rommel, Doenitz and other military figures. The fact that a situation he feared had at last materialized relieved rather than depressed Hitler. Despite the strain, intensified by heavy fighting on the Eastern Front, he kept his head, showing not only determination and energy in dealing with the crisis, but considerable skill as well. This combined with the slowness of the Allies in taking advantage of the situation, enabled him to make a brilliant recovery.

In a conference with his generals between 9.30 and 10.15 on the evening of 25 July, only a few hours after Mussolini's dismissal, Hitler brushed aside Jodl's argument that they ought to wait for exact reports.

> Certainly, [he replied] but we have to plan ahead. Undoubtedly, in their treachery, they will proclaim that they will remain loyal to us; but this is treachery. Of course they won't remain loyal. . . . Although that so-and-so Marshal Badoglio declared immediately that the war would be continued, that won't make any difference. They have to say that. But we'll play the same game, while preparing everything to take over the whole area with one stroke, and capture all that riff-raff.

By the time Goebbels and the rest arrived on the 26th, Hitler had prepared four sets of plans, and the forces to carry them out were steadily being collected. The first, known by the code word *Eiche* ("Oak"), was a plan for the rescue of Mussolini; the second, *Student*, provided for the occupation of Rome and the restoration of the Fascist régime; the third, *Schwarz* ("Black"), covered the military occupation of Italy, and the fourth, *Achse* ("Axis"), dealt with measures for the capture or destruction of the Italian Fleet.

Hitler attached great importance to securing Mussolini in person to lead a restored Fascist government. While Goering and Ribbentrop supported Hitler, Goebbels, in his diary, described Hitler as "over-optimistic about the Duce and the possibilities of a Fascist come-back." Doenitz, Rommel and Jodl thought the same and said so. "These are matters which a soldier cannot comprehend," was Hitler's retort. "Only a man with political insight can see clearly."

The practical question was one of timing. Hitler, Goering and Goebbels wanted to act at once: the King, Crown Prince and Badoglio's Government should be seized and brought to Germany, while Mussolini was restored to power in Rome. Rommel (whom Hitler had appointed Commander-in-Chief in Italy) and the other soldiers wanted to wait until the situation became clearer. They feared that precipitate action would drive Badoglio, whom they hoped to keep on their side, into the arms of the Allies; they were highly sceptical about the authority of Mussolini or the popularity of a revived Fascist régime.

Hitler continued to defer final orders from day to day, much to his advantage. For Hitler was right in supposing that Badoglio would at once begin negotiations for a separate peace, but until he could reach agreement with the Allies he had to keep up the pretence of co-operation with the Germans. At the end of the six weeks which the Allies allowed to elapse between Mussolini's fall (25 July) and the publication of the armistice with the Badoglio Government (8 September) Hitler had increased the German forces in Italy and was in a very much stronger position.

The announcement of the Italian armistice again took Hitler by surprise. He was away at Zaporozhe in the Ukraine, dealing with the situation on the southern sector of the front, and arrived back at his headquarters shortly before the news came in. The Italians kept up appearances to the last moment and succeeded completely in deceiving the Germans. There was only time to send the code-word for action to Kesselring, who was in command in southern Italy; thereafter, communications became difficult and information scarce. But by 10 September, the German forces, some sixteen divisions, now proceeded to disarm the much more numerous Italian formations and to seize the key positions, including control of Rome, without meeting any serious resistance. The King and Badoglio fled from the capital, and within a matter of hours the Germans were masters of the greater part of the country.

Simultaneously with the announcement of the armistice, the Fifth and Eighth Armies had landed on the Italian mainland and begun to fight their way north. To Kesselring's relief, however, the Allies landed much farther south than he had dared to hope, at Salerno, to the south of Naples. Hitler agreed to recast his plans and allow Kesselring to fight on the Winter Line drawn across the peninsula not far to the north of Naples. This left more than two-thirds of Italy, including the industrial north, in German hands, and it was not until June, 1944, that the Allies succeeded in reaching Rome.

After his fall Mussolini was moved by the Badoglio Government from one place to another until he was finally taken to a small hotel at the Gran Sasso, high up in the Abruzzi Mountains. Hitler took a close personal interest in Mussolini's movements, and once he had been located a spectacular rescue from the air was planned. On 12 September this was carried out with success by an S.S. detachment under the command of Otto Skorzeny, and Mussolini was brought to the Fuehrer's Headquarters at Rastenburg.

The first meeting between the two men was cordial, but a rapid disenchantment followed. Hitler's plan was to re-establish the Fascist régime in Italy. A small number of former Fascist leaders had reached Germany and were already at work. But to be successful the new Fascist Republic must have Mussolini at its head. The Duce, however, was now a shrunken, ageing man without political ambition, whose real wish was to be allowed to go home to the Romagna. Under Hitler's urging—and scarcely veiled threats—he agreed to play the part, but it was without enthusiasm and, as it soon appeared, only with the help of vigorous prompting from the producer.

On 15 September Mussolini's restoration to the leadership of Fascism was proclaimed, and the new Italian Social Republic came into being. Its "Government" followed a squalid and undistinguished career until the end of the war in Italy, despised by the Germans and hated by the Italians.

As for Mussolini himself, the last phase of his life was the most degrading of all. In November he was obliged to hand over Ciano to the Germans, and he shut himself up with his mistress, refusing to see his daughter Edda. But Hitler exacted the full humiliation. In January, 1944, Ciano was shot by a Fascist firing squad acting under the nominal authority of his father-in-law. The fascination which Hitler had once exerted over Mussolini was turned to hatred.

However, taken with the German success in occuping the greater part of Italy and holding the Allies well south of Rome, the restoration of Mussolini could be presented as a triumphant ending to the crisis which had threatened in the summer to leave the southern frontiers of the Reich directly exposed to allied attack.

Moreover, the Germans not only secured most of Italy, but also took over the Italian zones of occupation in the Balkans, in Yugoslavia, Albania and Greece, where Hitler had for some time been apprehensive of a British landing. Considering the course of events in the Mediterranean theatre since El Alamein and the landings in North-west Africa, Hitler might well congratulate himself at the end of 1943 on the effective way in which, by energy, determination and luck, he had retrieved a disastrous situation.

Even so, however slow might be the allied advance, all that Kesselring could do was to fight a skilful rearguard action. If this was true of Italy, the prospect elsewhere was still darker.

In the east, after throwing back the Russians in March, 1943, in July the Germans launched a new offensive against their lines round Kursk, carrying it out with unusually large tank forces. After heavy and costly fighting the Russians not only succeeded in bringing the German attack to a halt, but on 12 July themselves opened an offensive (for the first time in the summer) farther north. Gradually their attacks spread along the whole front. On 4 August they retook Orel, and on 23 August Kharkov. On 25 September they recaptured Smolensk, from which both Napoleon and Hitler had directed their invasions of Russia.

However hard the Germans fought, they were borne back by the sheer weight of the attack. No sooner had one thrust been sealed-off than fighting would flare up on another sector. The sole result of Hitler's inflexible orders to stand and fight, without giving a yard, was to double the German losses. As the year ended the Red Army was steadily pushing the Germans back to the Polish and Rumanian frontiers.

The Russian advances, especially in the south, had political as well as military repercussions. As the Red Army drew nearer to their frontiers, fear began to spread among the satellite states, Rumania, Hungary and Slovakia, whose loyalty to the Axis had been badly shaken by events in Italy. Hitler, already worried about the Balkans and the possibility of landings there, watched Turkey too with anxiety.

It was for these political as much as for military reasons that he obstinately refused to give up the Crimea at the cost of losing well over a hundred thousand men, mostly Rumanian troops. When Field-Marshal von Weichs and Admiral Doenitz urged him to evacuate the German garrisons in the Aegean and on Crete, he could "not order the proposed evacuation of the islands on account of the political repercussions that would necessarily follow. The attitude of our allies in the south-east, and also of Turkey, is determined exclusively by their confidence in our strength. . . . To avoid such a blow to our prestige, we may even have to accept the eventual loss of the troops and material."

In the west, in 1943, Hitler replaced Raeder as Commander-in-Chief of the Navy with Doenitz, the Navy's U-boat specialist, but as the Allies strengthened their defences against submarine attack, the figures for U-boat losses began to rise, and at the end of May Doenitz was driven to withdraw all his vessels from the North Atlantic.

Hitler was no longer blind to the importance of the Battle of the Atlantic, but he lacked the resources to support it. He might promise Doenitz increased production of U-boats, but it could only be at the expense of other equally urgent needs. Although the U-boat crews returned to the convoy routes in September, by the end of 1943 the Battle of the Atlantic was lost.

During the year the American day-bombers joined the

R.A.F. in keeping up an almost continuous offensive against targets in Germany and Western Europe. In July Hamburg was devastated by a series of attacks, while between mid-November, 1943 and mid-February, 1944, the R.A.F. dropped twenty-two thousand tons of high-explosive on Berlin.

Hitler was beside himself with fury at the failure of Goering and the Luftwaffe to fend off the attacks or to satisfy his demand for reprisals on Britain. He was indifferent to the loss of life; what worried him most was the effect on German war production.

In 1938 and 1939 Hitler had been warned by Schacht and others that Germany had not the economic resources to wage another major war. By 1943 the accuracy of these warnings was obvious. Scarcely a single issue was discussed at Hitler's conferences which was not affected by Germany's increasing shortage of everything—shortage of manpower, of raw materials, of transport, of oil, of food, of steel, of armaments and planes. Even if the German people could withstand the strain of the air war, the effect on war production was such that it must in the end place Germany in a position of permanent inferiority.

Thus, if the last months of 1942 mark the turning-point of the war, 1943 may be taken as the year of Germany's defeat.

> Towards the end of 1943 at the latest [writes General Halder, once Chief of Staff to the German Army] it had become unmistakably clear that the war had been lost. . . . By the sacrifice of German blood and at the cost of exposing the homeland to the enemy Air Forces, the war could still be kept going for a little longer. But were the results to be gained by such a course worth the sacrifice?

The man with whom alone rested the answer to this question was now in his fifty-fifth year. The strain imposed upon him by the war, particularly since the winter of 1941-1942, had begun to leave its mark. During the course of 1943 Hitler began to suffer from a trembling of his left arm and left leg, which became steadily more pronounced and refused to yield to any treatment. In an effort to control this tremor, Hitler would brace his foot against some object and hold his left hand with his right. At the same time he began to drag his left foot, as though he were lame. Professor de Crinis, of the Charité Hospital in Berlin, believed that these were the symptoms of Parkinson's disease (*Paralysis agitans*), but he never had the opportunity of examining Hitler, and other specialists believed that they had an hysterical origin like the stomach-cramps from which he suffered.

To meet the demands which he made upon himself between

1930 and 1943 Hitler must have had an iron constitution. He was inclined to fuss about his health, believing that he had a weak heart and complaining of pains in his stomach and occasional bouts of giddiness. But his doctors found nothing wrong with his heart or his stomach, and until 1943 he actually suffered very little from ill-health.

Under the stress of war, however, Hitler began to take increasing quantities of drugs to stimulate his flagging energies. Since 1936 he had kept as his personal physician in constant attendance on him a Professor Morell, a quack doctor who had once practised as a specialist in venereal disease in Berlin. Morell, who was introduced to Hitler by the photographer Hoffmann, won Hitler's confidence by curing him of eczema of the leg, and used his position to make a fortune by manufacturing patent medicines under the Fuehrer's patronage. He is described by Mr. Trevor-Roper after the war as "a gross but deflated old man, of cringing manners, inarticulate speech and the hygienic habits of a pig." Even in Hitler's circle Morell added a touch of the grotesque, and Hitler himself never trusted Morell, trying constantly to trip him up and threatening him with ejection or worse. He evidently resented his dependence upon him, but the fact of this dependence was incontestable. At every meal Hitler took a considerable number of tablets prepared by Morell and had frequent injections as well every day during the last two years of his life.

When Dr. Giesing examined Hitler after the attempted assassination in July, 1944, he found that, to relieve the pains in his stomach, Morell had been giving him for two years at least a drug known as Dr. Koester's Antigas Pills which was compounded of strychnine and belladonna. Giesing believed that Hitler was being slowly poisoned by these pills and that this accounted both for the intensification of the pains and for the progressive discoloration of Hitler's skin. The only result, however, of telling Hitler was the dismissal of his other doctors, who supported Giesing, and the end of Dr. Giesing's own visits to the Fuehrer's Headquarters. During the last two years of the Third Reich, not only Hitler but practically all the other members of his entourage kept themselves going on the drugs obligingly dispensed by Dr. Morell.

To the strain of responsibility and the evil effects of Morell's ministrations must be added the effects of the life Hitler was now leading. From the summer of 1941 Hitler made his permanent headquarters at *Wolfsschanze,* in East Prussia. Under the threat of air-raids Hitler moved to one of the massive concrete bunkers embedded in the ground, and made his home in a suite of two or three small rooms with bare, undecorated concrete walls and the simplest wooden furniture.

The austerity of Hitler's life at his headquarters matched the bleakness of the surroundings. General Jodl, who spent much time there, described it as "a mixture of cloister and concentration camp. There were numerous wire fences and much barbed-wire. There were far-flung outposts on the roads leading to it, and in the middle was the so-called Security Zone No. 1. Apart from reports on the military situation, very little news from the outer world penetrated this holy of holies."

The main event of each day was the Fuehrer's Conference at noon. To describe these as conferences is actually to misrepresent their character: they were a series of reports on the military situation, in which decisions were taken solely by the Fuehrer. A certain number of officers were nearly always present: Generals Keitel and Jodl, from the Fuehrer's own Supreme Command of the Armed Forces; the Chief of Staff of the Army; the Chief of Staff of the Air Force, or his deputy; the representative of the Commander-in-Chief of the Navy; the permanent representatives of Himmler (*S.S. Gruppenfuehrer* Fegelien) and of Ribbentrop (Ambassador Hewel). Other commanders or ministers would attend intermittently: sometimes Goering or Speer would be there, or the Commander-in-Chief of the Navy, less frequently Himmler. Each of these officers was accompanied by his adjutants, who carried the maps to be spread out on the big centre table, or the memoranda and diagrams to be presented. As each report was made—Eastern Front, Italy, air war and so on—Hitler would announce his decision, and the officers concerned would leave the room to send off the necessary instructions. There was no general discussion of the situation as a whole: only the Fuehrer was allowed to concern himself with the over-all picture.

Another, more restricted military conference sometimes followed late in the evening, and there were frequent private meetings between Hitler and his chief lieutenants, Himmler, Bormann, the powerful head of the Party Chancery, or Goebbels on a flying visit from Berlin.

Hitler rose late, breakfasted alone, and after the noon conference took lunch, often with some of the visitors to the conference, at any time between 2 and 5 p.m. Usually he rested in the late afternoon, resuming his talks at six or seven o'clock. Dinner might be served at any time between 8 p.m. and midnight. There followed further discussions and his day ended with tea in the company of his secretaries—possibly

Morell and Julius Schaub, his adjutant, as well—at four o'clock in the morning.

Apart from a short walk with his Alsatian bitch, Blondi, which had been given him by Bormann to raise his spirits after Stalingrad and to which he became very attached, Hitler took no exercise and enjoyed no form of relaxation. As the war went on he dropped the habit of seeing films after dinner, apart from news-reels. Up to the time of Stalingrad, he sometimes spent an evening listening to gramophone records, Beethoven, Wagner or Wolf's *Lieder*. After Stalingrad, however, he would hear no more music, and his sole occupation as they drank their tea in the early hours of the morning was to recall the past, his youth in Vienna and the years of struggle. This was interspersed with reflections on history, on the destiny of man, religion and other large subjects. Soon, his secretary complains, his remarks became as familiar as the records; they knew exactly what he would say and kept awake only with the greatest difficulty. On no account was the war or anything connected with it permitted as a subject of discussion during the tea-hour. For similar reasons Hitler finally ate alone with his secretaries, who were under strict instructions not to mention the war.

The dominant impression derived from accounts of life at the Fuehrer's Headquarters in 1943 and 1944 is one of intense boredom, punctuated by excitement like that caused by Mussolini's fall and by Hitler's outbursts of rage, usually directed against the generals.

Hitler's ostensible reason for shutting himself up in this way was the demands made on him by the war. But there was a deeper psychological compulsion at work. Here he lived in a private world of his own, from which the ugly and awkward facts of Germany's situation were excluded. He refused to visit any of the bombed towns, just as he refused to read reports which contradicted the picture he wanted to form. The power of Martin Bormann, Hitler's personal secretary, was built up on the skill with which he pandered to this weakness, carefully keeping back unpleasant information and defeating the attempts of those who tried to make Hitler aware of the gravity of the situation.

As the allied armies began to press in on Germany in the course of 1944, some of the Nazi leaders began to look around for ways to disappear or make private deals with the enemy. This, if inglorious, may be regarded as a normal human reaction to such a situation. Hitler's was wholly different. He was fighting for something more than his power or his skin; he was fighting to preserve intact that image he had created of himself as one of Hegel's "World Historical Individuals." The unforgivable sin was to fail, as Mussolini had failed, to rise to the measure of events. Hitler's faith was crystallized in the belief that if only he could survive the buffetings of the waves breaking over him he would be saved by some miraculous intervention and still triumph over his enemies. Everything depended upon the will to hold out.

This belief in turn depended upon the fundamental belief which he never abandoned to the end of his life—that he was a man chosen by Providence to act as the agent of the World Historical Process. Every incident in his life was used to support the truth of this assertion: the number of times he had escaped attempts at assassination, which he placed at seven, culminating in his extraordinary escape from serious injury on 20 July, 1944; or the fact that the Russians had not broken through in the winter of 1941-1942. Anything, however trivial, which went right in the last two years of the war served Hitler as further evidence that he had only to trust in Providence and all would be well.

There were other, more material factors on which Hitler based his hopes of a dramatic reversal of the war in his favour. In his speech of 8 November, 1942, after declaring that he would never lay down his arms until five past twelve, Hitler referred to the new secret weapons which Germany was building and promised the Allies an answer to their bombing raids "which will strike them dumb." The weapons he had in mind were the V1, the flying bomb, and the V2, the rocket. To these must be added the new jet fighter-planes, with which the Luftwaffe was to sweep the enemy from the skies, and new types of U-boats, with which the Navy was to cut the Allies' supply lines.

The secret weapons actually existed, and, in the case of the V1 and V2, were to play some part in the final stages of the war. But the hopes which Hitler and Goebbels placed upon them ignored the almost insuperable difficulties of mass-production under the allied air-attacks, they expected of them not merely increased losses for the enemy, but a transformation of the strategic situation, a miracle which would set at naught rational calculations of manpower, economic resources and military strength. This was a hope to which Hitler clung until the very end, it was his unfailing answer to every objection, yet it was a hope built upon the slenderest foundation, and the secret weapons, too—at least as they figured in Hitler's mind—soon belonged more to the realm of fantasy than that of fact.

More substantial, it may now appear, was the parallel set of hopes which he built up of a split between the partners in the Grand Alliance. No one, looking back at German anti-Bolshevik propaganda from the era of the Cold War, can fail to be struck by the aptness of much of the argument.

"It is no longer a question," Hitler declared in his broadcast of 30 January, 1944, "whether the present war will maintain the old Balance of Power or re-establish it, but of who will predominate in Europe at the end of this struggle—the European family of nations, represented by its strongest State, Germany, or the Bolshevik colossus. . . . There can only be one victor in this war, either Germany or the Soviet Union. Germany's victory means the preservation of Europe: Soviet Russia's means its destruction."

The speciousness of such an argument in the mouth of Hitler, the man who had signed the Nazi-Soviet Pact in 1939 and who did more than any other to destroy Europe, does not alter the fact that subsequent events have shown how precarious was the basis of the wartime alliance between the Western Powers and the U.S.S.R. German propaganda, constantly repeating the theme of the Bolshevik threat to European civilization, was quick to pick on any hint of friction between the Allies, and Goebbels as well as Ribbentrop urged Hitler to follow this up with diplomatic action to split the alliance.

One difficulty was to decide which of the Allies, Great Britain and the U.S.A., or the U.S.S.R., was more likely to listen to German overtures for a separate peace. Precisely the same question, it is worth noting, divided German opposition circles in their discussions of how to get rid of Hitler and end the war.

Hitler preferred negotiations with Stalin, and expected more of them than from an approach to Mr. Churchill, whom he described as "guided by hatred and not by reason." But he gave the same answer to Goebbels as he gave to Ribbentrop: nothing could be achieved by negotiation until a decisive success had been won in the east. Only then would the Russians be in the right frame of mind to consider the terms Hitler was determined to exact. As this condition continued to elude Hitler the proposal lapsed.

But all these hopes—the secret weapons and the break-up of the Grand Alliance—were subsidiary to the central pillar of Hitler's faith, the belief in himself, in his destiny and consequent ability to master any crisis. To the "historic" image of the Fuehrer, Hitler was prepared to sacrifice the German Army, the German nation, and in the end himself. From this course he never deviated: the only question was whether the German Army and the German nation were prepared to let him.

Little in the way of dissuading Hitler, still less of opposing him, could be expected from the other Nazi leaders. Goering, still Hitler's successor, Reichsmarshal, Commander-in-Chief of the Air Force, Minister for Air, Plenipotentiary for the Four-Year Plan, Chairman of the Council of Ministers for the Defence of the Reich, Minister President of Prussia, President of the Reichstag and holder of a score of other offices, had steadily lost authority since the beginning of the war. In 1933-1934 he was unquestionably the second man in Germany; by 1942, sloth, vanity and his love of luxury had undermined not only his political authority but his native ability. He took his ease at Karinhall, hunting and feasting, amassing a fabulous collection of pictures, jewels, and *objets d'art* for which the cities of Europe were laid under tribute, and amusing himself by designing still more fantastic clothes to fit his different offices and changing moods. When he appeared in Rome or at the Fuehrer's H.Q. in a new white or sky-blue uniform, surrounded by a retinue of *aides de camp* and carrying his bejewelled Marshal's baton, he still blustered loudly and claimed a privileged position. But it was a hollow show, with nothing behind to support it.

The failure of the Air Force finally discredited the Reichsmarshal in Hitler's eyes. There were angry scenes between the two men, Hitler accusing the Luftwaffe of cowardice as well as incompetence, and blaming Goering for letting himself be taken in by the Air Force generals. Some personal feeling for Goering remained until the end, but Hitler had no longer any confidence in him, and Goering kept out of his way.

The last of the original leadership, Joseph Goebbels, was both able and tough. A genius as a propagandist, he claimed that no one since Le Bon had understood the mind of the masses as well as he—forgetting Hitler for the moment. But his cynical intelligence and caustic tongue did not make him popular in the Party.

As early as 1942 Goebbels began to campaign for a more drastic mobilization of Germany's resources. This was a clever line to adopt when, as Goebbels was quick to see, many people in responsible positions were beginning to hedge. Goebbels was the man, not Hitler or Goering, who visited the bombed cities in the Rhineland, and who won high praise for his conduct as Gauleiter of Berlin during the heavy bombing of the capital. He was one of the few men with whom Hitler could still exchange ideas, and he was Hitler's choice for the office of Reich Chancellor in the Government he bequeathed to Admiral Doenitz.

Goebbels saw well enough the disaster which threatened

Germany, and in 1943 and 1944 tried to persuade Hitler to consider a compromise peace. When this came to nothing he was too intelligent to suppose that there was any future for himself apart from Hitler, and instead of turning against the Fuehrer he began to out-Herod Herod in his demands for still more drastic measures. It was Goebbels who, in 1945, proposed that Germany should denounce the Geneva Convention and shoot captured airmen out of hand, and who persuaded Hitler not to leave Berlin. The strong nihilist streak in his character was attracted by the idea of fighting on to the end, however hopeless the position, and he was the one member of the original group who joined Hitler in the Berlin bunker and, disdaining capture, killed his wife, children and himself when Hitler committed suicide.

Of those who became prominent after 1933 only three are worth more than cursory mention, Himmler, Bormann and Speer. Himmler's rise dated from 1934; in the following ten years he acquired sole power over the whole complex structure of the police state. As Minister of the Interior, Himmler controlled the Secret Police, the Security Service (SD) and the Criminal Police. As *Reichsfuehrer S.S.* he commanded the political *corp d'élite* of the régime and, in the *Waffen* (Armed) *S.S.* possessed a rival army to the Reichswehr, numbering half a million men by the summer of 1944. Through the concentration camps, which he also controlled, he organized his own labour corps, which was set to work in factories run by the S.S. In the east he was in charge of all plans for the resettlement of the conquered territories. Himmler's *Reichs Sicherheitshauptamt* (the Reich Security Main Office), in effect, administered the embryonic S.S. State of the future, jealously defending its prerogatives and ceaselessly intriguing to extend them.

In 1944 the functions of military counter intelligence were turned over to Himmler, who established a unified Intelligence Service. After the unsuccessful plot of July, 1944, he became Commander-in-Chief of the Reserve Army, took over all prisoner-of-war camps from the Armed Forces and, before the end of the year, assumed the active command of an Army Group at the front.

Here was a concentration of power which even Hitler could not ignore. In 1943, an approach was made to Himmler by two members of the anti-Hitler opposition, in the hope of persuading him to take independent action. Himmler was the last man of whom any such action could be expected, for two very good reasons.

He lacked the initiative to strike out a line for himself,

particularly if it meant any conflict with the Fuehrer, or to understand the gravity of Germany's position and conceive of alternative courses.

Moreover—the second reason—Himmler unquestioningly believed in the doctrines of Nazism, with a single-minded faith. A racist crank, he was passionately interested in all sides of *völkisch* and Aryan "culture," from astrology and the measurement of skulls to the interpretation of runes and prehistoric archaeology. To Himmler the Nazi *Weltanschauung* was the literal, revealed truth, and his humourless pedantry, which rivalled that of Rosenberg, bored and irritated Hitler.

This was poor material out of which to make the leader of an opposition, and only in the last days of the collapse was Himmler brought, with the utmost difficulty, to admit the possibility of acting on his own initiative to end the war.

The last of the great feudatories of the Nazi Court to carve out his demesne was Martin Bormann. Succeeding to Hess's position as Head of the Party Chancery, early in 1942, he was able to secure a directive laying down that he alone was to handle the Party's share in all legislation; jobs for Party members in the State administration, and all contacts between the various ministries and the Party.

This could be made into a powerful position, and Bormann was indefatigable in working to enlarge his claims. His agents were the Gauleiters, who were directly responsible to him. In December, 1942, the Gauleiters, now Reich Defence Commissioners as well, gained an effective control over the whole of the civilian war effort. After Himmler became Minister of the Interior in 1943 a clash between the two empires of the S.S. and the Party was inevitable. To the surprise of most people, Bormann not only held his own against the powerful *Reichsfuehrer S.S.* but by the end of 1944 had gained a lead in the struggle for power.

While both men controlled powerful organizations, Bormann grasped the importance of making himself indispensable to Hitler. In constant attendance on him, he succeeded in drawing most of the threads of internal administration into his hands. Hitler, preoccupied with the war, was glad enough to be relieved of the administrative burden and in April, 1943, Bormann was officially recognized as Secretary to the Fuehrer. It was Bormann who decided whom the Fuehrer should and should not. see, what he should or should not read, was present at nearly every interview and drafted the Fuehrer's instructions. The importance of this position can scarcely be overestimated, for, as Weizäcker says: "Ministerial skill in the Third Reich consisted in making the most of a favourable hour or minute when Hitler made a decision, this often taking the form of a remark thrown out casually, which then went its way as an 'Order of the Fuehre'."

In this way Bormann, a brutal and much hated man, acquired immense power which he exercised not in his own right, but solely in the name of Hitler. For him, as with Himmler the road to power lay through acquiring Hitler's favour, and Bormann's voice, like that of Goebbels, was always raised in advocacy of more extreme measures.

As for the others, Ribbentrop still occupied the post of Foreign Minister, but had ceased to be taken seriously by Hitler or anyone else. Ley, when he was sober, ran anxiously from one group to another, trying to curry favour.

Until the last few days of Hitler's life when Himmler and Goering made their last-minute attempts to negotiate with the Allies—and were promptly expelled from the Party—Hitler's hold over his Party remained intact. Had it not been for Hitler not one of them—with the possible exception of Goebbels and Goering—would ever have risen from obscurity. Their power was derivative, their light reflected. If nothing else, the common crimes in which they had shared bound them together. But there was something more than fear.

> They were all under his spell, blindly obedient to him, and with no will of their own—whatever the medical term for this phenomenon may be. I noticed during my activities as architect, that to be in his presence for any length of time made me tired, exhausted and void. Capacity for independent work was paralysed.

The man who gave this account—Albert Speer—is perhaps the most interesting case of them all, precisely because he is so different.

Speer only came into prominence in the spring of 1942, when Hitler suddenly nominated him as Minister for Armaments Production, but his rise in the next two years was rapid. By August, 1944, he was responsible for the whole of German war economy, with fourteen million workers under his direction. It was Speer who, by a remarkable feat of organization, patched up the bombed communications and factories, and somehow or other maintained the bare minimum of transport and production.

Speer was not unaffected by the spell Hitler was still able to cast over those near him, but he stood apart from the contest for power which absorbed the energies of men like Bormann. He was interested far more in the job he had to do than in the power it brought him. Illness kept him away from the Fuehrer's Headquarters from February to June, 1944, but on his return he became disquieted at the price for which Germany prolonged the war and—more disquieting still— realized that Hitler was determined to destroy Germany rather than admit defeat.

Having arrived at this conclusion, Speer early in 1945, planned to kill Hitler and the men around him by introducing poison-gas into the ventilation system of his underground bunker. The plan had to be abandoned for technical reasons. Although Speer continued his efforts to thwart Hitler's orders he never again attempted to remove the author of the policy he opposed. The reason is interesting. Speer did not lack the courage to make a second attempt, but, as he admitted later, in his own conflict of loyalties he could not rid himself of the belief that Hitler was, as he claimed to be, the only leader who could hold the German people together, that he was, in von Brauchitsch's phrase, Germany's destiny, and that Germany could not escape her destiny.

Here, in the self-confessed failure of the one man among the Nazi leaders who retained the intellectual independence to see clearly the course on which Hitler was set and the integrity to reject it, is the clearest possible illustration of the hold which Hitler kept until the end over the régime he had established and the Party he had created.

If little had ever been expected of the Party by those Germans who saw in Hitler the evil genius of their country, much had been hoped of the Army. So far the Army had disappointed those hopes. However great their misgivings (at least in retrospect), however little the enthusiasm they felt for "the Corporal" and his régime, the generals obeyed his orders, fought his battles for him and accepted the titles, the decorations and the gifts he bestowed on them.

After the invasion of Russia it was Hitler, not the generals, who took the offensive. Again and again he reversed the decisions of his senior commanders, ignored their advice, upbraided them as cowards, forced them to carry out orders they believed to be impossible to execute, and dismissed them when they failed, while the generals submitted to treatment such as no previous German ruler had ever dared to inflict on the Army.

Hitler's criticism of the German Officer Corps was directed against its "negative" attitude towards the National Socialist revolution. In practice, the revolutionary spirit meant willingness to carry out Hitler's orders without hesitation, the spirit Paulus so lamentably lacked at Stalingrad by his failure to prolong a useless resistance until the last man was dead. The generals who retained office were the compliant, the ambitious who concealed their doubts, or rough-and-ready soldiers who went up to the front, drove their men to the limit and did not worry about the strategic situation.

As the war went on Hitler came to rely more and more on the *Waffen S.S.* divisions, who were provided with the best equipment, given priority in recruitment and reserved for the most spectacular operations. The growth of this rival S.S. Army was a particular grievance with the Regular Army officers. Knowing this, Hitler delighted to praise the S.S. troops and to give their exploits special mention in his communiqués. Thus he kept his promise of 1934 that there should only be one bearer of arms in the State—the Army.

After the fall of Mussolini, Hitler congratulated himself upon having no monarchy in Germany which could be used to turn him out of office. The thorough process of Nazification to which he had subjected the institutions of Germany, from the Reichstag to the Law Courts, from the trade unions to the universities, had destroyed, he believed, the basis for an organized opposition. However two institutions in Germany still retained some independence.

The first was the Churches. Among the most courageous demonstrations of opposition during the war were the sermons preached by the Catholic Bishop of Münster and the Protestant pastor, Dr. Niemoeller. Nazi zealots like Bormann regarded the Churches with a venomous hostility. Neither the Catholic nor the Evangelical Churches however, as institutions, felt able to assume open oppostion to the régime. Yet without the support of some institution, the Opposition appeared hopeless individuals pitting their strength against the organized power of the State. It was natural, therefore, that they should continue to look with expectation to the Army, the only other institution in Germany which still possessed a measure of independent authority, if its leaders could be persuaded to assert it, and the only institution which commanded the armed force needed to overthrow the régime.

From the collapse of the plot to overthrow the Government in 1938, discussion of the possibility of renewing the attempt continued among a small group of conspirators. Among those who remained active were two older men generally regarded as the leaders of the conspiracy, General Ludwig Beck, the former Chief of Staff of the Army, and Dr. Karl Goerdeler, a former *Oberbürgermeister* of Leipzig. With them may be mentioned, as other senior members, the former Ambassador to Rome, Ulrich von Hassell; the Prussian Minister of Finance, Johannes Popitz; and Field-Marshal von Witzleben. Under the benevolent patronage of Admiral

Canaris, the head of the O.K.W.'s Counter-Intelligence (the *Abwehr*), General Oster, his chief assistant, collected a small group of men around him.

The *Abwehr* provided admirable cover for the attempts of the conspirators to make contacts abroad. A second valuable focus for illegal activity was provided by General Olbricht, Chief of Staff of the Reserve Army, while, on the Eastern Front, a resistance cell was formed by General Henning von Tresckow, attached to the Staff of the Central Army Group.

A summary list of names cannot pretend to include all those who played a part in the conspiracy, or even all those who lost their lives in it. But the thirty-eight-year-old Graf Helmuth von Moltke, leader of the Kreisau Circle, who died for his beliefs with great courage, was strongly opposed to any active steps to get rid of Hitler. Not all the Kreisau circle, however, agreed with Moltke's views, and after his arrest (in January, 1944) some members of the group became more directly involved in the conspiracy.

There is some danger, in talking of the "German Opposition," of giving altogether too sharp a picture of what was essentially a number of small, loosely connected groups, fluctuating in membership, with no common organization and no common purpose other than their hostility to the existing régime. To diversity of motives must be added considerable divergence of aims. It would, indeed, be difficult to imagine a greater contrast than that between von Moltke, with his quietist views, at one end of the scale, and the radical von Stauffenberg, who became the ringleader in the conspiracy, at the other.

From the point of view of Hitler their activities were only important in so far as they led to action. Yet the bomb explosion of 20 July, 1944, was not the only attempt made to kill Hitler in these years.

After Stalingrad it was agreed among the little circle of Army officers who would have to bear the responsibility for any action that only after Hitler had been killed would it be possible to persuade the Army commanders to move. General von Tresckow and Fabian von Schlabrendorff on 13 March, 1943, after Hitler's visit to H.Q. of the Central Army Group, succeeded in placing a time-bomb on the plane which carried him back to East Prussia. By the devil's own luck—a not inappropriate phrase—the bomb failed to explode. With remarkable coolness, Schlabrendorff flew at once to the Fuehrer's Headquarters, recovered the bomb before it had been discovered—it had been hidden in a package of two bottles of brandy to be delivered to a friend—and took it to pieces on the train to Berlin. Had the attempt succeeded,

General Olbricht and General Oster had prepared plans for a seizure of power by the military authorities in Berlin, Cologne, Munich and Vienna.

As many as six more attempts on Hitler's life were planned in the later months of 1943, but all for one reason or another came to nothing. In the meantime Himmler's police agents, although singularly inefficient in tracking down the conspiracy, were beginning to get uncomfortably close. Too many threads led back to the *Abwehr,* which the rival S.S. Intelligence Service was eager to suppress, and in December, 1943, General Oster, the key figure in the *Abwehr,* was removed from office.

Fortunately, just as the *Abwehr* circle was being broken up, in the summer of 1943, General Olbricht, the Chief of Staff of the Reserve Army, found a new recruit in Colonel Graf von Stauffenberg, a distinguished young officer who had been badly wounded in North Africa and assigned to staff duties with the Reserve Army in Berlin. Stauffenberg, a man of strong will and personality, rapidly assumed a leading part in the conspiracy. By 1943, much wider support was to be found in the Army, in the hope of making a compromise peace which would save Germany from the further disasters that Hitler's continuation in power promised. Stauffenberg drew up detailed plans for a military *coup,* which he hoped to carry out with the aid of sympathizers at the Fuehrer's headquarters, in Berlin and in the German Army in the west. The essential preliminary was the assassination of Hitler: this task Stauffenberg reserved for himself, despite the handicap of having lost his right hand, two fingers of his other hand and the sight of one eye.

The conspirators were now working against time in a double sense. Further arrests were made early in 1944, including that of von Moltke, and in the summer of 1944 Himmler told Admiral Canaris, now deprived of his office as head of the Counter Intelligence, that he knew a revolt was being planned in Army circles and would strike when the moment came. It was equally obvious that if the Opposition was to realize its hopes of a compromise peace it was of the greatest possible importance to overthrow Hitler's Government before the allied invasion of western Europe took place.

Personal differences, inevitable under the strain of the conditions in which they worked, and differences of opinion, especially on the issue of an approach to Russia versus an approach to the Western Powers, added to the conspirators' difficulties.

On 6 June the Allies launched their invasion of Normandy, and the need to act became urgent. At the beginning of July, two of the conspirators were arrested following an attempt, which Stauffenberg had urged, to make contact with underground German Communists. On 17 July a warrant was issued for the arrest of Goerdeler. The plot was now in danger of being wrecked by further arrests within a matter of hours.

Stauffenberg had already made two attempts to carry out the assassination of Hitler. On 11 July he attended a conference at Berchtesgaden with a time-bomb concealed in his brief-case, but in the absence of Himmler and Goering he decided to wait until there was a better chance of killing all the leaders at one blow. A second chance came on 15 July when he was again summoned to the Fuehrer's Headquarters in East Prussia, but Hitler was called away. At a meeting with Beck the following day Stauffenberg agreed that whatever happened the attempt must be made on the next occasion. Four days later, on 20 July, he flew to East Prussia determined that his third chance should be decisive.

For Hitler the first six months of 1944 had brought nothing but an intensification of all the familiar problems. In January the Russians freed Leningrad from its German besiegers; and by the end of June large sections of the German front ceased to exist. The German divisions Hitler insisted on holding in the Baltic States were threatend with encirclement, while the Russians were already thrusting towards East Prussia, the first German territory to be threatened with invasion. On 20 July Hitler was at the height of one of the worst crises he had had to face on the Eastern Front, now several hundred miles nearer to Germany since July, 1943.

During the same six months the allied air forces continued to bomb German cities and communications with monotonous regularity and in March the Americans made their first day raid on Berlin. In Italy Kesselring was forced to retreat. The Allies entered Rome, the first European capital to fall to them, on 4 June.

Two days later at dawn the British and Americans began the long-awaited assault from the west. In preparation for the invasion, Hitler had recalled Rundstedt to act as Commander-in-Chief in the west. Considerable effort had been expended in building defences along the western coastline of Europe, but the Atlantic Wall was less strong and much less complete than German propaganda represented it to be. In June, 1944, sixty German divisions were available to hold a front which extended from Holland to the south of France; few were of first-rate quality, and only eleven of them were armoured formations. These were barely adequate forces with which to hold the west, especially in view of their dispersal and allied air supremacy.

German Intelligence was badly at fault in forecasting the date, place and strength of the invasion. Hitler rightly guessed that Normandy would be the part of the coast chosen by the Allies—against the advice of Rundstedt and other generals. Hitler, however, also believed, as did Rommel, that a second landing would take place in the narrower part of the Channel, where the sites for the V1s were situated, and the elaborate deception planned by the British was accepted at face value. As a result powerful German forces—the Fifteenth Army, numbering fifteen divisions—were stationed north of the Seine and held there, on Hitler's orders, when their intervention in the fighting in Normandy might have had great effect.

The actual landing in the early hours of 6 June caught the Germans unawares. Rommel was on his way to see Hitler at Berchtesgaden. Hitler's insistence that major decisions must all be referred to him imposed further delays, and once the bridgehead had been made good, Hitler refused to give his commanders a free hand, constantly intervened to dictate orders out of keeping with the situation at the front, and persisted in believing that the Allies could still be thrown back into the sea. Relations between Hitler and the generals on the spot rapidly became strained, and on 17 June he summoned both Rundstedt and Rommel for a conference at Margival, near Soissons.

General Speidel describes him as "worn and sleepless, playing nervously with his spectacles and an array of coloured pencils which he held between his fingers. He was the only one who sat, hunched upon a stool, while the Field-Marshals stood."

The Fuehrer was in a bitter mood. The fact that the allied landings had succeeded he ascribed to the incompetence of the defence. When Rommel answered with an account of the difficulties of the situation, which were only increased by Hitler's rigid insistence on defending every foot of territory, Hitler went off into a monologue on the subject of the V-weapons which, he declared, would be decisive. Hitler talked of "masses of jet-fighters" which would shatter the allied air superiority, described the military situation in Italy and on the Russian front as stabilized, and lost himself in a cloud of words prophesying the imminent collapse of Britain under the V-bombs. When Rommel finally urged him to consider ending the war in view of the desperate situation in which Germany found herself, Hitler retorted: "Don't you worry about the future course of the war. Look to your own invasion front."

At lunch, Speidel reports, Hitler ate his plate of rice and

vegetables only after it had been tasted for him. Two armed
S.S. men stood behind his chair throughout and a selection
of pills and medicines was ranged before him. The same night
Hitler left again for Berchtesgaden without going near the
front: one of his own V-bombs which exploded near his
headquarters hastened his departure.

Further efforts to make Hitler realize that the attempt to
defeat the landings had already failed proved no more successful. After a visit to Berchtesgaden at the end of June,
when the two Field-Marshals again tried to persuade Hitler to
give them a free hand in the west and to end the war,
Rundstedt was relieved of his command. Hitler offered his
place to Field-Marshal von Kluge. But Kluge was no more
able than Rundstedt or Rommel to stem the allied advance,
and by 20 July, although he still refused to recognize the
fact, Hitler, for the first time, was being made to realize
the meaning of "war on two fronts."

Hitler returned to his Headquarters in East Prussia in the
middle of July. Mussolini was due to visit him there on the
20th, and for that reason the conference had been moved
to 12.30 p.m. It was a hot summer day and the conference
was held not in the Fuehrer's concrete bunker (which was
being repaired) but in a wooden hut in which there was a
large room suitable for such meetings. This accidental change
of place saved Hitler's life. For the force of the explosion
confined within thick concrete walls must have killed everyone in the room, while the thin wooden walls of the hut
provided no such resistance.

Stauffenberg flew from Berlin during the morning and was
expected to report on the creation of new front-line divisions from the Reserve Army, to which he had become Chief
of Staff. He brought his papers with him in a brief-case in
which he had concealed the bomb fitted with a device for exploding it a few minutes after the mechanism had been
started. The conference was already proceeding with a report on the East Front when Keitel took Stauffenberg in and
presented him to Hitler. Twenty-four men were grouped
round a large, heavy, wooden table on which were spread
out a number of maps. Himmler, Goering and Ribbentrop
were not present. The Fuehrer himself was constantly leaning
over the table to look at the maps, with Keitel and Jodl on his
left. Stauffenberg took up a place near Hitler on his right,
next to a Colonel Brandt. He placed his brief-case under the
table, having started the fuse before he came in, and then
left the room on the excuse of a telephone call to Berlin. He
had been gone only a minute or two when, at ten minutes

to one, a loud explosion shattered the room, blowing out the walls and the roof, and setting fire to the debris which crashed down on those inside.

In the smoke and confusion, with guards rushing up and the injured men inside crying for help, Hitler staggered out of the door. One of his trouser legs had been blown off; he was covered in dust, and he had sustained a number of injuries. His hair was scorched, his right arm hung stiff and useless, one of his legs had been burned, a falling beam had bruised his back, and both ear-drums were found to be damaged by the explosion. But he was alive. Those who had been at the end of the table where Stauffenberg placed the brief-case were either dead or badly wounded. Hitler had been protected, partly by the table-top over which he was leaning at the time, and partly by the heavy wooden partition which supported the table and against which Stauffenberg's brief-case had been pushed before the bomb exploded.

Although badly shaken Hitler was curiously calm, and in the early afternoon he appeared on the platform of the Headquarters station to receive Mussolini. Apart from a stiff right arm, he bore no traces of his experience and the account which he gave to Mussolini was marked by its restraint.

As soon as they reached *Wolfsschanze* Hitler took Mussolini to look at the wrecked conference room. Then, as he began to re-enact the scene, his voice became more excited. "After my miraculous escape from death today I am more than ever convinced that it is my fate to bring our enterprise to a successful conclusion." Nodding, Mussolini could only agree: ". . . This was a sign from Heaven."

In this exalted mood Hitler went to his quarters for tea. Goering, Ribbentrop and Doenitz had joined Keitel and Jodl, and sharp recriminations began over the responsibility for the war. Hitler sat quietly with Mussolini until someone mentioned the Roehm "plot" of 1934. Suddenly leaping to his feet in a fury, Hitler began to scream that he would be revenged on them all, that he had been chosen by Providence to make history and that those who thwarted him would be destroyed. This went on for half an hour. When he had exhausted his rage Hitler relapsed into silence, sucking an occasional pastille and letting the protestations of loyalty and a new quarrel between Goering and Ribbentrop pass over his head.

In the confusion after the bomb had exploded Stauffenberg had succeeded in flying back to Berlin. Some time passed before anyone at the Fuehrer's headquarters realized what had happened—at first Hitler thought the bomb had been dropped from an aeroplane—and it was longer still before it was known that the attempted assassination had been followed by an attempted *putsch* in Berlin.

There, in the capital, a little group of the conspirators had gathered in General Olbricht's office at the General Staff Building in the Bendlerstrasse. Among the group were General Beck, who was to act as Regent (*Reichsverweser*) of Germany; Field-Marshal von Witzleben, who was to assume the Command-in-Chief of the Armed Forces; General Hoeppner, stripped of his rank by Hitler in the winter of 1941, now to take over the command of the Reserve Army; and General Olbricht, who was to become Minister of War. Their plan was to announce, immediately after Hitler's death, that a group of the remaining Nazi leaders was trying to seize power with the aid of the S.S. in order to stab the Army in the back. To prevent this—so the announcement ran—a state of emergency had been declared, Beck and Witzleben had taken over power in the name of the Army, and ordered the subordination of the entire State administration, the S.S., the police and the Party to the Commanders-in-Chief of the Army, both at home and in the occupied countries. In Berlin plans had been concerted to bring in troops from barracks outside the city to secure the Gestapo headquarters and the radio station, and disarm the S.S.

Everything depended upon two conditions, the assassination of Hitler, and the destruction of the elaborate communications centre at the Fuehrer's Headquarters, to be carried out by General Fellgiebel, the Chief Signals Officer there, as soon as the bomb exploded.

The first of these conditions had already been invalidated, but this was not known to Stauffenberg, who left the Fuehrer's Headquarters convinced that no one could have survived. Reaching Rangsdorf airfield, outside Berlin, in the middle of the afternoon, he sent a message to this effect to the Bendlerstrasse, and by four o'clock the orders for action were beginning to go out. By the time it became known that Hitler was not dead it was too late to draw back.

Almost as disastrous as the failure of the assassination was Fellgiebel's failure to destroy the communications centre. For, as soon as it was realized there what was happening, Keitel began to send out messages to all commands denying that Hitler was dead, countermanding the instructions issued from Berlin and directing all commanding officers to ignore orders not countersigned by himself or by Himmler, Commander-in-Chief of the Reserve Army and in charge of the security of the Reich.

In the capital the Berlin Guard Battalion under Major

Remer had been ordered in from Döberitz to occupy the Government quarter. But a Lieutenant Hagen, attached to the regiment as a National Socialist Political Officer, persuaded Remer to let him seek confirmation of Hitler's death from Goebbels. As a result Remer, instead of arresting Goebbels, was put through by telephone from Goebbels' office to East Prussia, spoke to the Fuehrer himself and (after being promoted to Colonel on the spot) was ordered to suppress the *putsch*.

In the Bendlerstrasse the situation of the conspirators was already hopeless. Once it was known that Hitler was not dead—they had unfortunately failed to capture the Berlin radio station as well as the Army's communications network—fear of Hitler's revenge, and eagerness to re-insure, became the dominant motives in the minds of that large number of officers who waited to see if the *putsch* was successful before committing themselves.

In the evening a group of officers loyal to Hitler broke out of custody, released General Fromm (whose office as Commander-in-Chief of the Reserve Army had been taken over by Hoeppner) and disarmed the conspirators. Fromm's own behaviour had been equivocal and he was now only too anxious to display his zealous devotion by getting rid of those who might incriminate him. Fromm ordered Stauffenberg, Olbricht and two other officers to be shot in the courtyard, where the executions were carried out by the light from the headlamps of an armoured car. Beck was allowed the choice of suicide. Fromm was only prevented from executing the rest by the arrival of Kaltenbrunner, Himmler's chief lieutenant, who was far more interested in discovering what could be learned from the survivors than in shooting them out of hand. Himmler, reaching Berlin from East Prussia, set up his headquarters at Goebbels' house, and the first examinations were carried out that night. The man-hunt had begun.

Only in Paris were the conspirators successful. There they had been able to count on a number of staunch supporters, headed by General Heinrich von Stülpnagel, the Military Governor of France, and General Speidel, the Chief of Staff to Army Group B. As soon as he received the code word from Berlin Stülpnagel carried out the orders to arrest the S.S. and Security Service (SD), and the Army was rapidly in complete command of the situation. But here, too, the conspirators were dogged by the same ill-luck that had pursued them throughout the day.

In the spring of 1944 Field-Marshal Rommel had also reached the conclusion that, if Germany was to be saved, Hitler must be got rid of, and he was brought into contact

with the group round Beck and Goerdeler. Rommel was opposed to an assassination of Hitler on the grounds that they
must avoid making a martyr of him. He proposed instead
that Hitler should be seized and tried before a German court.
He accepted the leadership of Beck and Goerdeler, however,
was willing to take over command of the Army or Armed
Forces—his popularity would have been a considerable asset
—and proposed to initiate negotiations with General Eisenhower on his own authority, on the basis of a German withdrawal from the occupied territories in the west in return
for the suspension of the allied air-raids on Germany. In
the east the fighting was to be continued, with the German
forces defending a line running from Memel to the mouth of
the Danube.

On 15 July, Rommel sent Hitler an urgent memorandum
in which he forecast an allied break-through in two or
three weeks. ". . . The troops are fighting heroically everywhere, but the unequal struggle is nearing its end. I must beg
you to draw the conclusions without delay. I feel it my duty
as Commander-in-Chief of the Army Group to state this clearly."

After sending the memorandum by teleprinter, Rommel
told his Chief of Staff that if Hitler refused this last chance, he
was resolved to act. On 17 July, however, while returning
from the front, Rommel's car was attacked by British fighters and the Field-Marshal severely injured. Thus, on 20 July,
Rommel was lying unconscious in hospital, and the command-in-chief in the west, was in the hands of Field-Marshal
von Kluge, a horse of another colour. Kluge had been approached by the conspirators as long ago as 1942, and he
had endorsed the view expressed in Rommel's memorandum
to Hitler. But when the attempt on Hitler's life failed, he
refused to consider independent action in the west. Without
the support of the commander in the field, Stülpnagel could
do nothing: he had created an opportunity which there
was no one to exploit. So, by dawn on the 21st, the *putsch*
had collapsed in Paris as well as in Berlin, and Stülpnagel
was summoned home to report. Now it was Hitler's turn to
act, and his revenge was unsparing.

Half an hour after midnight of the 21-20 July all German
radio stations relayed the shaken but still recognizable voice
of the Fuehrer speaking from East Prussia.

If I speak to you today [he began] it is first in order that you
should hear my voice and should know that I am unhurt and
well, and secondly that you should know of a crime unparal-
leled in German history. A very small clique of ambitious,

irresponsible and at the same time senseless and stupid officers had formed a plot to eliminate me and the High Command of the Armed Forces.

I am convinced that with the uncovering of this tiny clique of traitors and saboteurs there has at long last been created in the rear that atmosphere which the fighting front needs. . . .

This time we shall get even with them in the way to which we National Socialists are accustomed.

Hitler's threats were rarely idle. No complete figure can be given for the number of those executed after 20 July, although a list of 4,980 specific names has been compiled. Many thousands of others were sent to concentration camps. The investigations and executions of the *Gestapo* and S.D. went on without interruption until the last days of the war. The first trial, held on 7 August, resulted in the immediate condemnation of Field-Marshal von Witzleben, Generals Hoeppner, Hase and Stieff, together with four other officers, and they were put to death with great cruelty, by slow hanging, on 8 August. The executions were filmed from beginning to end for Hitler to see the same evening in the Reich Chancellery.

Hitler and Himmler used the opportunity to imprison or kill many who had only the flimsiest connection, or none at all, with the conspiracy, but who were suspected of a lack of enthusiasm for the régime. Among others sent to concentration camps were Dr. Schacht and General Halder, both of whom had been living in retirement. Few who had ever shown a trace of independence of mind could feel safe.

By the autumn evidence had been collected to rouse Hitler's suspicions of Rommel. In October, Rommel received a brief message from the Fuehrer offering him the choice between suicide and trial before the People's Court. For the sake of his family, Rommel chose the former. The cause of his death was announced as heart failure, due to the effects of his accident, and the Fuehrer accorded him a State funeral at which he was personally represented by Field-Marshal von Rundstedt. "His heart," declared the funeral oration, which Rundstedt was called upon to read, "belonged to the Fuehrer."

To the defeatism, cowardice and conservatism which—as Hitler convinced himself—had balked him of victory, the generals had now added the crime of treason. Had Hitler been free to give full rein to his anger, he would have made a clean sweep and imprisoned or shot every general within sight. But however reluctant he was to concede it, he still needed the Officer Corps to win the war for him. Nor would his own prestige allow him to admit that the Army no longer had complete faith in his leadership. Therefore, elaborate measures were taken to conceal the split between the Army and its commander-in-chief. In a broadcast, Goebbels described the plot as having been crushed by the Army itself.

The Order of the Day issued by the new Chief of Staff of the Army, General Guderian, on 23 July, followed the same line and the next day Bormann issued a directive to the Party ordering that there should be no general incrimination of the Army and a Court of Honour expelled the guilty officers from the Army and handed them over, as civilians, to the People's Court.

But in fact the humiliation of the Army was complete. The generals had now to accept the *Waffen S.S.* as equal partners with the Army, Navy and Air Force. On 24 July the Nazi salute was made compulsory "as a sign of the Army's unshakeable allegiance to the Fuehrer and of the closest unity between Army and Party." On the 29th General Guderian issued a further order which insisted that henceforth every General Staff Officer must actively co-operate in the indoctrination of the Army with National Socialist beliefs and publicly announce that he accepted this view of his duties. National Socialist Political Officers were appointed to all military headquarters in imitation of a Russian practice which was abandoned by the Soviet Government during the war.

Despite the measures taken to ensure loyalty, and the purge of the Officer Corps, Hitler's distrust of the Army was now unconcealed. This was bound to affect the desperate effort which had to be made to contain the enemy. There was little enough hope of doing that in any case; there was less still when the Commander-in-Chief's attitude towards his own commanders was one of invincible suspicion and vindictive spite.

CHAPTER FOURTEEN

THE EMPEROR WITHOUT HIS CLOTHES

Hitler was forced to commit all his reserves in order to hold any line in the east, but he stubbornly refused to withdraw his troops from the Baltic States, which had no bearing on the main battle for the approaches to Germany. Hitler's reasons for this refusal were the possible effect on Sweden (with the all-important iron-ore supplies), and the loss of the Baltic training grounds for the new U-boats. He argued that Schoerner was engaging Russian divisions which would otherwise be used on more vital fronts. The Russians, however, were not short of manpower, while the Germans were. Guderian protested in vain. Hitler was still trying to hold with much-reduced forces a line longer than that through which the Russians had already broken. The man who had proclaimed mobility the key to success now rejected it in favour of the utmost rigidity.

The Russian break-through in Poland was followed by an American break-through in France. On 28 July the Americans captured Coutances, by the 31st they were into Brittany. The German left flank collapsed. Patton's Third Army striking eastwards for Le Mans, and the threat of encirclement at Falaise, were the plainest indication that the time had come for an immediate German withdrawal behind the Seine. Hitler, remote in his East Prussian headquarters, and ignorant of the massive superiority of the allied forces, refused to consider such a course. Kluge was ordered to counter-attack at once. The S.S. generals at the front were the loudest in their protests against the folly of gambling the remaining armoured divisions on an attack which seemed almost certain to fail. Kluge's only reply was that these were Hitler's orders and that the Fuehrer would tolerate no argument.

When the operation failed Hitler ordered the attack to be renewed. To General Warlimont, who had visited the front, Hitler remarked: "Success only failed to come because Kluge did not want to be successful." On 15 August, when Kluge, at the front, was out of touch with his headquarters for twelve hours, Hitler leaped to the conclusion that the Field-Marshal was trying to negotiate a surrender. The next day he summoned Model from the east and ordered him to take over Kluge's command. On his way back to Germany Kluge committed suicide: he closed a long letter of self-defence to Hitler with the advice to end the war.

Model, now called on to rescue the German Army in France as he had already done in Poland, was one of the few generals whom Hitler trusted and allowed to argue with him. A rough character, with nothing of the stiff military caste conventions, Model had identified his fortunes with Hitler's. But no one could prevent the collapse in France.

While Patton struck out for the east and Paris was liberated, the German Army was streaming back across the Seine in headlong retreat. In the circumstances Model did well to preserve anything from the rout. On 29 August, he reported that out of the sixteen infantry divisions which he had got back over the Seine he could raise men to form four, but was only able to equip them with small arms. Another seven infantry divisions had been totally destroyed, while of some two thousand three hundred tanks and assault guns only a few over a hundred crossed the Seine. These were the fruits of Hitler's direction of the battle.

France was lost. It was now a question of whether the Rhine could be held. On the evening of 11 September an American patrol crossed the German frontier: five years after the Polish campaign, the war had reached German soil.

In a conference with three of his generals on the afternoon of 31 August Hitler made it clear that, whatever the cost to Germany, he was determined to maintain the struggle.

If necessary [he declared] we'll fight on the Rhine. It doesn't make any difference. Under all circumstances we will continue this battle until, as Frederick the Great said, one of our damned enemies gets too tired to fight any more. We'll fight until we get a peace which secures the life of the German nation for the next fifty or hundred years and which, above all, does not besmirch our honour a second time, as happened in 1918. . . . Things could have turned out differently. If my life had been ended (i.e. on 20 July) I think I can say that for me personally it would only have been a release from worry, sleepless nights and great nervous suffering. It is only a fraction of a second, and then one is freed from everything, and has one's quiet and eternal peace. Just the same, I am grateful to Destiny for letting me live, because I believe . . .

In this mood, compounded of inflexible determination and self-pity, Hitler called on the German people for one more effort, and for the last time they responded. They no longer saw, or even heard, the man whose orders they obeyed, but the image of the Fuehrer still carried conviction, and conviction was power reinforced by fear.

It was to fear that Goebbels now openly appealed: the news of the Morgenthau Plan, which provided for the dismemberment of Germany, and her conversion into an agricultural and pastoral country, appeared to offer proof that Goebbels was right when he declared that the Allies intended the extermination of a considerable proportion of the German people and the enslavement of the rest. The fact that the American Secretary of the Treasury, Henry Morgenthau, Jrn. was a Jew was not missed. The grim picture which Goebbels had been drawing of the German people's fate under a Russian occupation was now supplemented by the prospect of an equally terrible revenge at the hands of the Western Allies. With the Red Army on the threshold of East Prussia, and the British and Americans on the Rhine, the argument had a new urgency. To add point to it, Himmler announced that the families of deserters would be summarily shot.

The Allies' plan was to burst into Germany before winter, but bad luck, bad weather, difficulties of supply and differences of opinion combined to defeat their hopes. To these must be added the unexpected recovery of the German Army. Field-Marshal von Rundstedt, whom Hitler had recalled to be Commander-in-Chief in the west at the beginning of September, had few illusions about the future, yet the measures taken by him and by Model, won for Hitler the breathing space of the winter before the Allies could bring their full weight to bear in the battle for Western Germany.

Hitler used this respite to build up new forces with which to fill the gaps left by the summer's fighting. In the west alone 1944 had cost him the loss of a million men. On 24 August Goebbels announced a total mobilization which went far further than any previous measures. With this last reserve of manpower Hitler hoped not only to re-form the divisions which had been broken up on both the Western and Eastern Fronts, but to create twenty to twenty-five new *Volksgrenadier* divisions, eight to ten thousand men strong, under Himmler's direction. This was partly bluff, for units which had been reduced to the fighting value of no more than a battalion were retained as divisions in the German Order of Battle. Rather than use the men available to rebuild these to full strength, or break them up completely, Hitler set up new divisions and retained the old formations at a half or a quarter of their strength. In this way he could keep up the illusion that he was still able to increase his forces to meet the crisis. As a final measure Hitler called up every ablebodied man between the ages of sixteen and sixty to form a *Volkssturm*, or Home Guard, placed under the orders of Himmler.

It was Hitler's own decision that kept the very considerable force of some seven and a half million men holding hopeless positions in the Baltic States, the Balkans and Scandinavia, instead of concentrating for the defence of the Reich itself. He refused to abandon hope of reversing the situation by a dramatic stroke. Thus Western Holland must be held to allow the V2s to be directed against London; Hungary and Croatia for the bauxite supplies necessary for the jet-aircraft; the Baltic coast and the naval bases in Norway for the new U-boats.

Thanks to Speer, armaments production had not yet been crippled by bombing. The German aircraft factories and those producing other arms showed a remarkable ability to maintain, and even to increase, the rate of production.

The greatest material difficulty, however, was the desperate shortage of oil and petrol, due to the systematic bombing of the synthetic oil plants, refineries and communications. By the end of September the Luftwaffe had five weeks' supply of fuel. Moreover, Speer maintained arms production only by drawing heavily on supplies of raw materials which could scarcely be replaced. Germany made a remarkable recovery, but it was the last reserves of men, materials and morale on which Hitler was now drawing; if he squandered these there was nothing left.

Everything turned upon the use which Hitler proposed to make of the forces which he had scraped together. The momentary calm on all fronts encouraged his illusions. But the real weakness of the German position was shown by the success of the Red Army's autumn offensive in the Balkans.

For the Russians, having forced Hitler to throw in all his reserves on the Centre Front in the summer, now reaped their advantage in the south. On 20 August a new offensive opened with the invasion of Rumania and continued to the end of the year. In the first few days Rumania capitulated, and the Russians were able to occupy the oilfields. On 8 September the Red Army began the occupation of Bulgaria, and the loss of Germany's two Balkan satellites was accompanied by the withdrawal of Finland from the war. In October the British freed Athens, and the Russians reached Belgrade, where they joined with Tito. By December the Germans were besieged in Budapest, less than a hundred and fifty miles from Vienna.

Hitler did not ignore the danger from the south-east, and succeeded in prolonging the battle for the Hungarian capital into February, 1945. But Hitler had already made up his mind that the new and reformed divisions were to go to the west. At the same time the panzer divisions already in the west were re-equipped, and over two-thirds of the Luftwaffe's planes deployed in their support.

In deciding for the west against the east, Hitler was not thinking in terms of defence of the German frontiers; he thought solely of an offensive which would take the Allies by surprise, enable him to recapture the initiative and so gain time for the development of the new weapons and of the split between the members of the Grand Alliance. If the basis of this calculation was slender, it was natural for Hitler to think along these lines. For him at least the only choice lay between victory or death. His one chance was to stake what was left on the gamble of attack. In the west distances were shorter, less fuel would be needed, and strategic objectives of importance were closer than in the open plains of the east. Nor did he believe the Americans and British were as tough opponents as the Russians. The British, he soon convinced himself, were at the end of their resources, while the Americans were liable to lose heart if events ceased to go favourably.

Accordingly, Hitler and Jodl set to work to plan a counter-offensive in the west for the end of November. The object was the recapture of Antwerp by a drive through the Ardennes and across the Meuse, cutting Eisenhower's forces in two and trapping the British Army in the angle formed by the Meuse and the Rhine as they turn westwards towards the sea. Letting his imagination race ahead, Hitler was soon talking of a break-through comparable with that of 1940 and leading to a new Dunkirk from which this time the British Army would not escape.

The idea was excellent. The last thing the allied commanders expected was a German attack. The Ardennes sector was the weakest point in their front, and the loss of Antwerp would have been a major blow at the air supply lines. But the idea bore no relation to the stage the war had reached in the winter of 1944-1945. The permanent disparity between the resources of Germany in 1944 and those of the three most powerful States in the world could not be redressed by a single blow. The utmost Hitler could hope to inflict was a set-back, not a defeat, and in the process he ran the heavy risk of throwing away his last reserves.

The attempt of the men in command to persuade Hitler to accept more limited objectives proved unsuccessful, and is well illustrated by his rebuke to Guderian, when the latter ventured that he was leaving the Eastern Front dangerously weak.

> There's no need for you to try to teach me [Hitler shouted back] I've been commanding the German Army in the field for five years, and during that time I've had more practical experience than any "gentleman" of the General Staff could ever hope to have. I've studied Clausewitz and Moltke and read all the Schlieffen papers. I'm more in the picture than you are.

The final plans were sent to Rundstedt with every detail down to the times of the artillery bombardment, and with the warning in Hitler's own handwriting: "Not to be altered." In order to keep even tighter control Hitler moved his headquarters to Bad Nauheim, behind the Western Front.

Four days before the attack was due to begin, Hitler summoned all the commanders to a conference. After being stripped of their weapons and brief-cases, they were led between a double row of S.S. troops into a deep bunker. When Hitler appeared, he is described as looking old and broken. He made a long, rambling two-hour speech, during which S.S. guards behind every chair watched every movement that was made.

Much of what Hitler said was a justification of his career and of the war. He laid particular stress on the incongruity of the alliance with which Germany was faced.

> Ultra-Capitalist states on the one hand; ultra-Marxist states on the other. On the one hand, a dying empire, Britain; on the other, a colony bent upon inheritance, the United States. . . . America tries to become England's heir; Russia tries to gain the Balkans, the narrow seas, Iran and the Persian Gulf; England tries to hold her possessions and to strengthen herself in the Mediterranean. . . . Even now these States are at loggerheads, and he who, like a spider sitting in the middle of his web, can watch developments, observes how these antagonisms grow stronger and stronger from hour to hour. If now we can deliver a few more heavy blows, then at any moment this artificially bolstered common front may collapse with a gigantic clap of thunder. . . . Wars are finally decided by one side or the other recognizing that they cannot be won. We must allow no moment to pass without showing the enemy that, whatever he does, he can never reckon on a capitulation. Never! Never!

With this exhortation Hitler dismissed the soldiers, and at dawn on 16 December the attack was launched.

Hitler achieved the satisfaction of taking his opponents by surprise, and in the first few days the German Army made considerable gains which the Press puffed up into one of the greatest victories of the war. Yet never were the Germans within sight of Antwerp. As soon as the Allies had recovered their balance the Germans were thrown back on the defensive, fighting hard to hold the gains they had made. By Christmas it was evident that they would be well advised to break off the battle and withdraw.

Hitler furiously rejected any such suggestion. Twice Guderian, who was responsible for the east, visited Hitler and tried to persuade him to transfer troops as there were ominous signs of a new Russian offensive. Hitler rejected Guderian's reports. The Russians he declared, were bluffing. "It's the greatest imposture since Genghis Khan." After reinforcements had been sent to Budapest, the reserves for a front of seven hundred and fifty miles in the east totalled twelve and a half divisions. Yet Hitler refused to write off the Ardennes offensive. Not only was Model ordered to reach the Meuse, but a new attack was to be launched into northern Alsace.

As a preliminary Hitler again assembled the commanders. He depicted the results of the fighting in the most exaggerated terms—"a transformation of the entire situation such as no one would have believed possible a fortnight ago." He would not listen to the argument that they were not yet ready.

I have been in this business for eleven years, and during those eleven years I have never heard anybody report that everything was completely ready. Our situation is not different from that of the Russians in 1941 and 1942, when, despite their most unfavourable situation, they manoeuvred us slowly back by single offensive blows along the extended front on which we had passed over to the defensive.

Once again the German attack fell short—this time Strasbourg—while Model's second attempt to break through the Ardennes was no more successful than the first. On 8 January Hitler reluctantly agreed to the withdrawal of the armour on the Ardennes front. It was a tacit admission that he had failed. He continued to claim that he had inflicted a heavy defeat on the enemy, but the figures do not bear him out. The First and Third U.S. Armies fighting in the Ardennes lost 8,400 killed, with 67,000 wounded and missing. The total German casualties were around 120,000, in addition to the loss of 600 tanks and assault guns and over 1,600 planes. Most important of all, while the Americans easily made good their losses, Hitler's were irreplaceable. The consequences of his unsuccessful gamble in the west, when added to the policy of "no withdrawal" on every front, were not long in appearing.

When Guderian tried to point out the dangers to Hitler at a conference on 9 January he was met with an hysterical outburst of rage. "He had," says Guderian, "a special picture of the world, and every fact had to be fitted into that fancied picture. As he believed, so the world must be: but, in fact, it was a picture of another world."

Reality, however, was to prove stronger than fantasy. On 12 January, the Red Army opened its offensive and the German defences went down like matchwood before a hundred and eighty Russian divisions attacking from the Baltic to the Carpathians. By the end of the month Zhukov was within a hundred miles of the German capital, and the Berlin Home Guard was being sent to hold the line of the Oder.

During the late summer and autumn Hitler's health became worse and he was frequently confined to his bed. The most serious effect of the bomb explosion had been the damage to his ears. After a period of rest these healed. But the effects of being shut up in his bunker without exercise or relaxation—not to speak of the effects of Morell's drugs—could only be cured if he was prepared to take a holiday. His doctors urged him to, but he refused. So long as he remained in East Prussia, he declared, it would be held, but if he left it would fall to the Russians.

In the middle of September, however, he had to return to bed. Apart from continual headaches and stomach cramps, he was troubled by his throat. Professor von Eicken, who had removed a polyp on his vocal cords in 1935, operated to remove another in October; he had also to treat him for a sinus infection. For a time Hitler's voice was unrecognizable. His secretary, who visited him while he was laid up in September, came away with the impression that he had reached the limit of his strength. Lying on a camp-bed between the naked concrete walls, he appeared to have lost all desire to live.

Yet by one more effort of will Hitler recovered sufficiently to get up and resume work. The attempt of the doctors who were called in to destroy Hitler's faith in Morell recoiled. Brandt, who had been his personal surgeon for twelve years, was abruptly dismissed and Hitler only waited for an opportunity to have him imprisoned and condemned to death a few months later. Morell's position remained unchallenged, while he continued to provide the drugs and injections on which the Fuehrer was now wholly dependent.

Although Hitler was able to leave his bed, all those who saw him agree in their description of him as an old man, with an ashen complexion, shuffling gait, shaking hands and leg. This was his state of health when he moved into the Reich Chancellery.

The vast pile which Hitler had built to overawe his tributaries was now surrounded by ruins. Jagged holes had appeared in the Chancellery's walls; the windows were boarded up; the rich furnishings removed—except from Hitler's own quarters. For, by some odd chance, the wing in which Hitler had his rooms was still undamaged. During air-raids Hitler moved to the massive shelter built in the Chancellery garden. He took no risks, and on one occasion at least, showed undisguised anxiety at the possibility of being trapped underground.

Hitler rarely moved out of the Chancellery building, and in the last month lived almost entirely in the deep shelter. One of the few visits he paid was in January, when he drove out to Goebbels' home and took tea with his wife and family. It was the first visit he had paid them for five years, an indication of Goebbels' return to favour. Hitler was accompanied by six S.S. officers, his adjutant, and a servant carrying the Fuehrer's own vacuumflask and a bag of cakes. They spent the afternoon reviving memories and discussing the plans for rebuilding Berlin. When Hitler left, Frau Goebbels expressed her satisfaction with the remark: "He wouldn't have gone to the Goerings."

Two other descriptions of Hitler at this time have been given by the young orderly to Guderian and by one of Hitler's secretaries.

Captain Gerhard Boldt had never met Hitler before February, 1945, when Guderian took him to a conference in the Chancellery. The military guard, which was still stationed outside the entrance, presented arms as the Chief of Staff drove up; inside, however, they were subjected to a thorough examination by the S.S. guards and obliged to hand over their revolvers and cases. In the ante-room they found sandwiches and drinks laid out on the sideboard, though the air of hospitality was again tempered by the presence of S.S. officers with tommy-guns in front of Hitler's study.

When the group was finally allowed to enter, Hitler met them in the centre of the room. Boldt was the last to be introduced. He noticed that Hitler's handshake was weak and soft.

> His head was slightly wobbling. His left arm hung slackly and his hand trembled a good deal. There was an indescribable flickering glow in his eyes, creating a fearsome and wholly unnatural effect. His face and the parts around his eyes gave the impression of total exhaustion. All his movements were those of a senile man.

The first to report was Jodl, who described the fronts for which the O.K.W. was responsible. Boldt was impressed by the practised way in which he slipped in brief references to the withdrawal of divisions under cover of colourful accounts of individual actions.

At the end of the conference, on Guderian's insistence, Admiral Doenitz raised the question of evacuating by sea the half-million men cut off in the Baltic States. Hitler rose from his desk and took a few paces up and down the room before shouting: "I have said once before, a withdrawal of these forces is out of the question. I cannot give up the material and I have to take Sweden into consideration." The most he would concede was the evacuation of a single division.

With that Hitler dismissed his officers, keeping only Bormann in attendance. The rest trooped out into the ante-room, and orderlies brought in drinks and cigars. The conference had lasted nearly three hours and it was dark when Boldt drove back with the Chief of Staff through the deserted streets to the Army's H.Q. at Zossen. The day's work, however, was not over. Later they were summoned to a further conference in the Chancellery shelter at 1 a.m.

This time they met in a small underground room, less than twenty feet square. A single bench, a table and a desk-chair were the only furniture. Guderian made a strong plea for the withdrawal of troops from all fronts to form a concentration in Pomerania and so relieve the pressure from the east. Hitler allowed him to speak without interruption; only his hands clenched nervously together showed his feelings. When Guderian finished a long silence followed, punctuated by the noise of exploding time-bombs. Then Hitler slowly stood up, staring into space, and took a few shuffling steps forward. Without a word he signalled to them to go; once again only Bormann remained behind.

This was Hitler at his clumsiest: unable to answer Guderian, he fell back on the oldest of his tricks—or was he sincere in seeing himself as the genius surrounded by pygmies who failed to rise to the level of his vision?

The second picture comes from the middle of March. His secretary, who was lunching alone with him, was kept waiting until three o'clock. Hitler was in an angry mood, kissed her hand in perfunctory fashion, and at once began to complain that he could trust no one. Now his personal adjutant, Albrecht Bormann (brother of Martin), had failed to carry out his express orders about strengthening the shelter.

I am lied to on all sides [he continued], I can rely on no one, they all betray me, the whole business makes me sick. If I had not got my faithful Morell I should be absolutely knocked out—and those idiot doctors wanted to get rid of him. What would become of me without Morell was a question they didn't ask. If anything happens to me Germany will be left without a leader. I have no successor. The first, Hess, is mad; the second, Goering, has lost the sympathy of the people, and the third, Himmler, would be rejected by the Party.

In any case, he added, Himmler was unacceptable because of his lack of artistic feeling. The question of a successor preoccupied him. After telling his secretary not to talk rubbish, he apologized for bringing political problems to the table. When he finished he stood for a few minutes lost in thought and then turned to go with the parting words: "Rack your brains again and tell me who my successor is to be. This is the question that I keep on asking myself without ever getting an answer."

As the façade of power crumbled Hitler reverted to his origins; there is a close resemblance between the early Hitler of the Vienna days and the Hitler of 1944-1945. The crude hatred, contempt and resentment which were the deepest forces in his character appeared undisguised. They found expression in the increasing vulgarity of his language. It was the authentic voice of the gutter again.

The man who had made it his first principle never to trust anyone now complained bitterly that there was no one he could trust. Only Eva Braun and Blondi were faithful to him, he declared, quoting Frederick the Great's remark: "Now I know men, I prefer dogs."

His rages became more violent and more frequent. On one occasion Guderian's aide-de-camp felt so alarmed that he pulled the general back for fear that Hitler might make a physical attack on him. On another occasion Guderian had an argument with him which lasted two hours.

> His fists raised, his cheeks flushed with rage, his whole body trembling, the man stood there in front of me, beside himself with fury and having lost all self-control. After each outburst of rage Hitler would stride up and down the carpet-edge, then suddenly stop immediately before me and hurl his next accusation in my face. He was almost screaming, his eyes seemed about to pop out of his head and the veins stood out on his temples.

When he found, however, that Guderian was not to be shifted from his opinion, Hitler suddenly gave way, and added, with his most charming smile: "Now please continue with the conference. Today the General Staff has won a battle."

Years before, Hermann Rauschning, describing Nazism as the St. Vitus's Dance of the twentieth century, had diagnosed its essential element of nihilism. In his conversations with Hitler during the years 1932-1934 he records many remarks that betray this underlying passion for destruction.

In talking to Rauschning, Hitler frequently became intoxicated with the prospect of a revolutionary upheaval which would destroy the entire European social order. Earlier in 1934, when Rauschning asked him what would happen if Britain, France and Russia made an alliance against Germany, Hitler replied: "That would be the end. But even if we could not conquer them, we should drag half the world into destruction with us, and leave no one to triumph over Germany. There will not be another 1918. We shall not surrender."

This was the stage Hitler had now reached, and he was

as good as his word. Goebbels shared Hitler's mood, and Nazi propaganda in the final phase has a marked note of exultation in the climax of destruction with which the war in Europe ended. But Hitler's determination to drag Europe down with him was not limited to propaganda. It was most clearly expressed in his insistence on war to the bitter end and in his demands for a "scorched earth" policy in Germany. Speer did his best to dissuade Hitler on the grounds that the German people must still go on living even if the régime were to be overthrown. Within four to eight weeks, he wrote, Germany's final collapse was certain. Destroying Germany's remaining resources to deny them to the enemy could not affect the war. The overriding obligation of Germany's rulers, without regard to their own fate, was to ensure that the German people should be left with some possibility of reconstructing their lives.

Hitler was adamant. On 19 March he issued categorical and detailed orders for the destruction of all communications, rolling-stock, lorries, bridges, dams, factories and supplies in the path of the enemy. Sending for Speer, he told him:

> If the war is to be lost, the nation also will perish. This fate is inevitable. There is no need to consider the basis even of a most primitive existence any longer. On the contrary, it is better to destroy even that, and to destroy it ourselves. The nation has proved itself weak, and the future belongs solely to the stronger Eastern nation. Besides, those who remain after the battle are of little value; for the good have fallen.

Hitler never wavered. In these senseless orders to destroy everything and to shoot those who failed to comply with his directive he found some relief for the frustrated anger which possessed him, and it was only thanks to the devotion of Speer that these orders were not fully carried out. But, as General Halder remarks, this mood was something more than the product of impotent rage. "Even at the height of his power there was for him no Germany, there were no German troops for whom he felt himself responsible; for him there was—at first subconsciously, but in his last years fully consciously—only one greatness, a greatness which dominated his life and to which his evil genius sacrificed everything—his own Ego."

In order to keep alive the will to go on fighting, Hitler made desperate efforts to conceal the hopelessness of the situation. At the words: "The war is lost," in Speer's memorandum, he refused to read another line and locked it away in his safe.

Hitler turned for comfort to Frederick the Great, who, when Prussia was invaded by half a dozen armies and all hope seemed gone, won his greatest victories and routed his foes. He kept Graff's portrait of Frederick hanging above his desk and told Guderian: "When bad news threatens to crush my spirit I derive fresh courage from the contemplation of this picture. Look at those strong, blue eyes, that wide brow. What a head!"

His private conversation in the early hours of the morning, however, was increasingly pessimistic. Before the war he had condemned suicide, arguing that if only a man would hold on something would happen to justify his faith. Now he espoused Schopenhauer's view that life was not worth living if it brought only disillusionment. He was depressed by his own ill-health. "If a man is no more than a living wreck, why prolong life? No one can halt the decay of his physical powers."

His secretary records that his conversation became entirely self-centred and was marked by the monotonous repetition of the same stories. His intellectual appetite for such large subjects as the course of world history, religion and the future of science had gone; even his memory began to fail him. His talk was confined to anecdotes about his dog or his diet, interspersed with complaints about the stupidity and wickedness of the world.

These early morning sessions grew later and later. Hitler frequently continued interviews and conferences well after midnight and often did not go to bed till dawn. He cut down his sleep to three hours, rising again about noon, strolling round the garden in the afternoon and usually taking a brief nap in the evening.

Yet to those in daily contact with him the sorcerer's magic was not yet exhausted. In March, 1945, Forster, the Gauleiter of Danzig, came to Berlin determined to make Hitler realize the desperate situation of his city. This time, he told the secretaries they could count on him to tell the brutal truth. But when Forster came out of his interview he was a changed man.

The Fuehrer has promised me new divisions for Danzig [he declared]. I was not at all clear where he would find them, but he has explained to me that he means to save Danzig and that there is no further room for doubt.

Sustained by these promises, Forster returned to continue the fight.

Forster, it is worth remembering, had known Hitler for many years, yet he was still susceptible to his charm and conviction. The same is true of the other old Party members —Goebbels, Goering, Himmler, Bormann, Ribbentrop—every one of whom clung to the hope that the man to whom they owed everything would yet find a way out.

Himmler was the most obvious heir to Hitler. But Himmler in accepting the active command of an Army Group, made the mistake of removing himself from the Fuehrer's court; while his failure to halt the Russian advance much reduced his standing. In the last six months of the Third Reich it was Bormann who was the rising power at the Fuehrer's Headquarters.

For Bormann, content to appear solely as the devoted servant of the Fuehrer, took care never to leave Hitler's side. He adjusted his way of life in order to go to bed and rise at the same time as Hitler, and he strengthened his control over access to him. Bormann was still not powerful enough to keep out Himmler, Speer and Goebbels. But Himmler came little to headquarters now, and Bormann soon made sure of Himmler's permanent representative with Hitler, Hermann Fegelein. He took every opportunity to undermine Hitler's confidence in Speer, while with Goebbels he concluded a tacit alliance. They joined in advocating extreme measures and constituted the leaders of a radical group, the other members of which were Fegelein, Ley and General Burgdorf, the Fuehrer's chief military adjutant, who had presented Rommel with Hitler's message and the phial of poison in October, 1944.

In the middle of these rivalries Hitler's own position remained unchallenged. No more striking testimony to Hitler's hold over those around him can be imagined that the interest they still showed in the unreal question of who was to succeed him.

As day succeeded day in the isolated world of the Chancellery garden shelter, the news grew steadily worse. Between 12 January, the day on which the Russians opened their offensive in Poland, and 12 April, the day on which the U.S. Ninth Army crossed the Elbe, the Allies inflicted a total defeat upon the German Army. On the 13th the Russians captured Vienna, and on the 16th they broke the defence line on the Oder. The way to Berlin was open, and it was now only a question of time before the armies advancing from the west met those coming from the east and cut Germany in two.

Hitler had lost all control over events, and by April he had the greatest difficulty in discovering what was happening. Once the operations in the Ardennes had failed all sense of purpose was lost. The discussions of the military situation in the early months of 1945 are rambling, confused and futile. Hours were wasted in discussion of questions of detail and local operations, interrupted by reminiscences and re-criminations. Hitler no longer showed any grasp of the situation. His orders became wilder and more contradictory, his decisions more arbitrary. By his refusal to let his commanders make their stand behind the Rhine, and his insistence that they must fight to the west of the river, he flung away a score of divisions needlessly.

Hilter had long scorned the belief that war can be waged without resort to terrorism. In February, 1945, Goebbels proposed that the High Command should denounce the international conventions, shoot all captured enemy airmen and use the new poison gases, *Tabun* and *Sarin*. Characteristically, the argument that most attracted Hitler was the effect this would have on the German soldier.

> If I make it clear that I show no consideration for prisoners but treat them without any consideration for their rights, regard-less of reprisals, then quite a few (Germans) will think twice before they desert.

Only with the greatest difficulty was he restrained from taking this desperate and irresponsible step.

Without bothering to investigate the facts he ordered the dismissal, degradation and even execution of officers who, after fighting against overwhelming forces, were forced to give ground. Even the *Waffen S.S.* was not exempt from his vicious temper. When Sepp Dietrich, once the leader of his personal bodyguard, was driven back into Vienna, Hitler radioed:

> The Fuehrer believes that the troops have not fought as the situation demanded and orders that the S.S. Divisions *Adolf Hitler, Das Reich, Totenkopf,* and *Hohenstsuffen,* be stripped of their arm-bands.

When Dietrich received this he summoned his divisional commanders and exclaimed: "There's your reward for all that you've done these past five years." Rather than carry out the order, he cabled back, he would shoot himself.

Hitler still tried to buoy himself up with the belief that the new weapons, would work a miracle. But gradually these hopes too faded.

The last hope of all was a split in the Grand Alliance. At his conference on 27 January Hitler suddenly asked:

> Do you think that, deep down inside, the English are enthusias-tic about the Russian developments?
> Goering: They certainly didn't plan that we hold them off while the Russians conquer all of Germany. If this goes on we will get a telegram in a few days. . . .

Jodl: They have always regarded the Russians with suspicion.

Hitler: I have ordered that a report be placed into their hands that the Russians are organizing two hundred thousand of our men, led by German officers and completely infected with Communism, who will then be marched into Germany. . . . That will make them feel as if someone had stuck a needle into them.

Goering: They entered the war to prevent us from going into the east, not to have the east come to the Atlantic.

Hitler's political instinct was still keen, but time was against him. Churchill, Roosevelt and Stalin, meeting at Yalta in February, contrived an agreement which, however impermanent, outlasted Hitler. The demand for unconditional surrender was reaffirmed, and the allied armies never paused in their advance.

The level to which the hopes of the German leaders were now reduced is well illustrated by their reception of the news of Roosevelt's death. The story is recounted by Schwerin von Krosigk, Hitler's egregious Finance Minister, and confirmed by other eye-witnesses.

A few days before the 12th, Goebbels, in order to comfort the Fuehrer, had read him the passage in Carlyle's *History of Frederick the Great*.

How the great king himself did not see any way out and did not know what to do; how all his generals and ministers were convinced that he was finished; how the enemy already looked upon Prussia as vanquished; how the future appeared entirely dark, and how in his last letter to the Minister Graf Finckenstein he set himself a time limit: if there was no change by 15 February he would give up and take poison. "Brave king!" Carlyle writes, "wait but a little while, and the days of your suffering will be over. Behind the clouds the sun of your good fortune is already rising and soon will show itself to you." On 12 February the Czarina died; the Miracle of the House of Brandenburg had come to pass. The Fuehrer, Goebbels said, had tears in his eyes.

Thereupon Goebbels sent for the horoscopes of the Fuehrer and of the Weimar Republic, both of which, he claimed, had been astonishingly right about the war and now predicted a great success for Germany in the latter half of April, followed by peace in August.

Goebbels was so taken with this historical parallel that on 12 April he tried to convince General Busse and his Staff that:

for reasons of Historical Necessity and Justice a change of fortune must occur now just as it did in the Seven Years War with the Miracle of the House of Brandenburg. One of the officers present asked somewhat sceptically which Czarina was to die this time. To this Goebbels replied that he did not know either, but that Fate held all sorts of possibilities in her hands. He then went back home and received the news of Roosevelt's death. Immediately he telephoned to Busse and said: "The Czarina is dead." Busse told him that this made a great impression on his soldiers; now they saw another chance.

In his excitement Goebbels called for champagne and rang up Hitler:

"My Fuehrer, I congratulate you! Roosevelt is dead. It is written in the stars that the second half of April will be the turning-point for us. This is Friday, 13 April. It is the turning-point."

Goebbels' mood was fully shared by Hitler, but the sense of relief did not last long. When reports from the front showed that Roosevelt's death had not affected the enemy's operations, Goebbels remarked disconsolately: "Perhaps Fate has again been cruel and made fools of us."

In the middle of April the Nazi Empire which had once stretched to the Caucasus and the Atlantic was reduced to a narrow corridor in the heart of Germany little more than a hundred miles wide. Hitler had reached the end of the road.

Shortly after Hitler's hopes had been raised and dashed by Roosevelt's death, Eva Braun arrived unexpectedly in Berlin and, defying Hitler's orders, announced her intention of staying with him to the end. For some time Goebbels had been urging Hitler to remain in Berlin and make an ending worthy of an admirer of Wagner's *Goetterdaemerung*. Goebbels scorned any suggestion that by leaving the capital he might allow the two million people still living there to escape the horrors of a pitched battle in the streets. "If a single white flag is hoisted in Berlin," he declared, "I shall not hesitate to have the whole street blown up."

None the less Hitler's mind was not yet made up. Preparations were in train for the Government to move to the "National Redoubt" in the heart of the Bavarian Alps, round Berchtesgaden, where the Fuehrer was expected to make his last stand. Various ministries and commands had already been transferred to the Redoubt area, and the time had come when Hitler himself must follow if he was still to get through the narrow corridor left between the Russian and American armies.

Hitler's original plan was to leave for the south on 20 April, his fifty-sixth birthday, but at the conference on the 20th, following the reception and congratulations, he still hesitated. For the last time, all the Nazi hierachs were present —Goering, Himmler, Goebbels, Ribbentrop, Bormann, Speer —together with the chiefs of the three Services. Their advice was in favour of his leaving Berlin. The most Hitler would agree to, however, was the establishment of Northern and Southern Commands, in case Germany should be cut in two by the allied advance. There and then he appointed Admiral Doenitz to assume the full responsibility in the north, but, although Kesselring was nominated for the Southern Command, Hitler left open the possibility that he might move to the south and take the direction of the war there into his own hands.

On the 21st Hitler ordered an all-out attack on the Russians besieging Berlin. Every man was to be thrown in, and any commander who withheld forces was to be shot. The direction of the attack Hitler confided to an S.S. General, Steiner, and he built the most exaggerated hopes on its success. It was the disappointment of these hopes which led him finally to refuse to leave the capital.

For Steiner's attack was never launched. The withdrawal of troops to provide the forces necessary allowed the Russians to break through the defences in the north, and Hitler's plan foundered in confusion. Throughout the morning a series of telephone calls from the Bunker failed to elicit any news of what was happening. By three o'clock in the afternoon there was still no news.

The storm burst during the conference, which lasted for three hours and left everyone who took part in it shaken and exhausted. In a universal gesture of denunciation Hitler cursed them all for their cowardice, treachery and incompetence. The end had come, he declared. There was nothing left but to die. He would meet his end there, in Berlin; those who wished could go to the south, but he would never move. From this resolution he was not to be swayed.

All the grandiloquent talk of dying in Berlin cannot disguise the fact that this petulant decision was a gross dereliction of his duty to the troops still fighting under his command and an action wholly at variance with the most elementary military tradition.

Jodl later described the unavailing efforts to persuade Hitler to change his mind.

Hitler declared that he had decided to stay in Berlin, lead its defence and then at the last moment shoot himself. For physical reasons he was unable to take part in the fighting personally, nor did he wish to, for he could not run the risk of falling into enemy hands. We all attempted to bring him over from this decision and even offered to move troops from the west to fight in the east. His answer was that everything was falling to pieces anyway, and that he could do no more: that should be left to the Reichsmarshal (Goering). When someone remarked that no soldier would fight for the Reichsmarshal, Hitler retorted: "What do you mean, fight? There's precious little more fighting to be done and, if it comes to negotiating, the Reichsmarshal can do better than I can." The latest development of the situation had made the deepest impression on him, he spoke all the time of treachery and failure, of corruption in the leadership and in the ranks. Even the S.S. now told him lies.

His decision to stay in the capital was irrevocable; as a logical consequence he began to burn his papers and invited Goebbels, the advocate of a "world-historical end," to join him in the Fuehrerbunker.

The setting in which Hitler played out the last scene was well suited to the end of so strange a history. The Chancellery air-raid shelter, in which the events of 22 April had taken place, was buried fifty feet beneath the ground, and built in two storeys covered with a massive canopy of reinforced concrete. The lower of the storeys formed the Fuehrerbunker. It was divided into eighteen small rooms grouped on either side of a central passageway. Half of this passage was closed by a partition and used for the daily conferences. A suite of six rooms was set aside for Hitler and Eva Braun. Eva had a bed-sitting-room, a bathroom and a dressing room; Hitler a bedroom and a study, the sole decoration in which was a portrait of Frederick the Great. A map-room used for small conferences, a telephone exchange, a power-house and guard rooms took up most of the rest of the space, but there were two rooms for Goebbels (formerly occupied by Morell) and two for Stumpfegger, Brandt's successor as Hitler's surgeon. Frau Goebbels, who insisted on remaining with her husband, together with her five children, occupied four rooms on the floor above, where the kitchen, servants' quarters and dining-hall were also to be found. Other shelters near-by housed Bormann, his staff and the various Service officers.

The physical atmosphere of the bunker was oppressive, but this was nothing compared to the pressure of the psychological atmosphere. The incessant air-raids, the knowledge that the Russians were now in the city, nervous exhaustion, fear and despair produced a tension bordering on hysteria, which was heightened by propinquity to a man whose changes of mood affected the lives of all those in the shelter.

Such sleep as Hitler got appears to have been between eight and eleven o'clock in the morning. As soon as the midmorning air attacks began, Hitler got up and dressed. He had a horror of being caught either lying down or undressed.

Much of the time was still taken up with conferences. The midday or afternoon conference was matched by a second after midnight which sometimes lasted till dawn. The evening meal was served between 9 and 10 p.m., and Hitler liked to drag it out in order not to be left alone during a night air-raid. Sometimes he would receive his secretaries at six in the morning, after a late-night conference. He would make an effort to stand up and greet them, but rapidly sank back exhausted on to the sofa. The early-morning meal was the one he most enjoyed, and he would eat greedily of chocolate and cakes, playing with Blondi and the puppies which she produced in March. To one of these puppies Hitler gave his own nickname, Wolf, and brought it up without anyone's help. He would lie with it on his lap, stroking it and repeating its name until the meal was over and he tried to get some sleep.

Between 20 and 24 April a considerable number of Hitler's entourage—including Goering and Morell—left for the south. In the last week of his life Hitler shared the cramped accommodation of the Fuehrerbunker with Eva Braun; the Goebbels and their children; his surgeon; his valet; and his S.S. adjutant; his two remaining secretaries; his vegetarian cook, and Goebbels' adjutant. Frequent visitors to the Fuehrerbunker from the neighbouring shelters were Bormann; General Krebs, who had succeeded Guderian as the Army's Chief of Staff; General Krebs, who had succeeded Guderian as the Army's Chief of Staff; General Burgdorf, Hitler's chief military adjutant; Artur Axmann, the leader of the Hitler Youth (a thousand of whom took part in the defence of Berlin), and a crowd of *aides-de-camp*, adjutants, liaison officers and S.S. guards.

On Monday, 23 April having at last come to a decision, Hitler was in a calmer frame of mind. Speer, who flew back from Hamburg to say farewell, made a full confession of the steps he had taken to thwart Hitler's orders for scorching the German earth. Hitler undoubtedly had a genuine affection for Speer, but it is surprising that Speer was neither arrested nor shot, but allowed to go free. Now that Hitler had abandoned the attempt to flog himself and those around him into keeping up the pretence he was resigned to facing death as a release from the difficulties which overwhelmed him. He repeated to Speer what he had told Jodl and Keitel the day before, that he would shoot himself in the bunker and have his body burned to avoid its falling into the hands of the enemy. This was stated quietly and firmly, as a matter no longer open to discussion.

While it is true that Hitler never varied this decision, his moods remained as unstable as ever, anger rapidly succeeding to resignation, and in turn yielding to the brief revival of hope. This is well illustrated by the incident of Goering's dismissal, of which Speer was also a witness before he left the bunker for good on the 24th.

When Goering flew to the south he left behind as his representative General Koller, the Chief of Staff of the Air Force. On 23 April Koller appeared at the Obersalzberg and reported the decisions of the fateful conference in the bunker the day before. Believing that Hitler had abandoned the direction of the war, and interpreting literally his remark that "if it comes to negotiating the Reichsmarshal can do better than I can," Goering assumed that he was now the Fuehrer's successor, as he had been designated by the decree of June, 1941. He wirelessed to Hitler for confirmation. The message, sent on 23rd read as follows:

My Fuehrer,
   In view of your decision to remain at your post in the fortress of Berlin, do you agree that I take over, at once, the total leadership of the Reich, with full freedom of action at home and abroad, as your deputy, in accordance with your decree of 29 June, 1941? If no reply is received by ten o'clock tonight I shall take it for granted that you have lost your freedom of action, and shall consider the conditions of your decree as fulfilled, and shall act for the best interests of our country and our people. You know what I feel for you in the gravest hour of my life. Words fail me to express myself. May God protect you, and speed you quickly here in spite of all.

                    Your loyal
                              Hermann Goering.

When Goering's message reached the bunker it did not take long for Bormann to represent it as an ultimatum. Speer, who was present, reports that Hitler became unusually excited, denouncing Goering as corrupt, a failure and a drug addict, but adding: "He can negotiate the capitulation all the same. It does not matter anyway who does it."

The addition is revealing. Hitler was clearly angry at Goering—the habits of tyranny are not easily broken—he agreed to Bormann's suggestion that Goering should be arrested for high treason—yet "it does not matter anyway." As Speer pointed out at Nuremberg, all Hitler's contempt for the German people was contained in the off-hand way in which he made this remark.

To try to make too much sense out of what Hitler said would be to misread both the extraordinary circumstances and his state of mind. Those who saw him at this time and who were not so infected by the atmosphere of the bunker as to share his mood regarded him as closer than ever to that shadowy line which divides the sane from the insane. He spoke entirely on the impulse of the moment, and moods of comparative lucidity, such as that in which Speer had talked to him on the 23rd, were interspersed with wild accusations, wilder hopes and half-crazed ramblings.

Hitler found it more difficult than ever to grasp that this was the end. Conferences continued until the morning of the day on which he committed suicide, and as late as the evening of the 29th Hitler was demanding news of General Wenck's Army which he had ordered to relieve Berlin. On the 24th he sent an urgent summons for Colonel General Ritter von Greim, in command of Air Fleet 6, to fly from Munich to Berlin. Greim made the hazardous journey, with the help of a young woman test-pilot, Hanna Reitsch, at the cost of a severe wound in his foot. When Greim arrived it was to find that Hitler had insisted on this simply in order to inform him that he was promoting him to be Commander-in-Chief of the Luftwaffe in succession to Goering. The only result of Hitler's action was to imprison the new Commander-in-Chief in the bunker for three days and to cripple him with a wounded foot.

The scene when Hitler greeted Greim was marked by the theatricality of Hitler's behaviour. Hanna Reitsch describes the tears in his eyes as he referred to Goering's treachery:

His head sagged, his face was deathly pallid, and the uncontrolled shaking of his hands made the message (from Goering) flutter wildly as he handed it to Greim.

The Fuehrer's face remained deathly earnest as Greim read. Then every muscle in it began to twitch and his breath came in explosive puffs; only with effort did he gain sufficient control to shout: "An ultimatum! A crass ultimatum! Now nothing remains. Nothing is spared to me. No allegiances are kept, no honour lived up to, no disappointments that I have not had, no betrayals that I have not experienced—and now this above all else. Nothing remains. Every wrong has already been done me."

Later that night Hitler sent for Hanna Reitsch and gave her a vial of poison. "Hanna, you belong to those who will die with me. Each of us has a vial of poison such as this. I do not wish that one of us falls into the hands of the Russians alive, nor do I wish our bodies to be found by them." At the end of a highly emotional interview Hitler reassured her: "But, my Hanna, I still have hope. The army of General Wenck is moving up from the south. He must and will drive the Russians back long enough to save our people. Then we will fall back to hold again."

Hitler's resentment found expression in constant accusations of treachery, which were echoed by Goebbels and the others. Hanna Reitsch describes Eva Braun as "raving about all the ungrateful swine who had deserted their Fuehrer and should be destroyed. It appeared that the only good Germans were those who were caught in the bunker and that all the others were traitors because they were not there to die with him." Eva regarded her own fate with equanimity. She had no desire to survive Hitler, and spent much of her time changing her clothes and caring for her appearance in order to keep up his spirits. Her perpetual complaint was: "Poor, poor Adolf, deserted by everyone, betrayed by all. Better that ten thousand others die than that he should be lost to Germany."

On the night of the 26th the Russians began to shell the Chancellery, and the bunker shook as the massive masonry split and crashed into the courtyard and garden. Resistance could scarcely last much longer. The Russians were now less than a mile away.

The climax came on the night of Saturday-Sunday, 28-29 April. Between nine and ten o'clock on the Saturday evening Hitler was talking to Ritter von Greim when a message was sent in to him which determined him to end at last the career which had begun twenty-seven years before, at the end of another lost war. It consisted of a brief Reuter report that Himmler had been in touch with the Swedish Count Bernadotte for the purpose of negotiating peace terms.

Since the beginning of 1945 Himmler had been secretly urged by Walter Schellenberg, the youngest of his S.S. generals, to open negotiations with the Western Powers on his own initiative, and when Court Bernadotte visited Berlin in February to discuss the release of Norwegian and Danish prisoners, Schellenberg arranged for Himmler to meet him. At that stage the reluctant *Reichsfuehrer S.S.*, much troubled by his loyalty to Hitler, had been unwilling to commit himself. But following the dramatic conference of 22 April while Hitler was raging at the disloyalty of Goering, Himmler accompanied Schellenberg to Lübeck for another meeting with Count Bernadotte at the Swedish Consulate. Hitler, he told Bernadotte, was quite possibly dead; if not, he certainly would be soon.

In the situation that has now arisen [Himmler continued] I consider my hands free. I admit that Germany is defeated. In order to save as great a part of Germany as possible from a Russian invasion I am willing to capitulate on the Western Front in order to enable the Western Allies to advance rapidly towards the east. But I am not prepared to capitulate on the Eastern Front.

Bernadotte agreed to forward a proposal, although he warned the two Germans that he did not believe there was the least chance that Britain and the U.S.A. would agree to a separate peace.

On 27 April, Bernadotte returned with the news that the Western Allies insisted on unconditional surrender. This was a heavy blow, especially to Schellenberg. But worse was to follow: on the 28th the fact that Himmler had been taking part in such negotiations was reported from London and New York. Himmler was now to discover, as Goering had before him, that it was unwise to discount Hitler before he was really dead.

Hitler was beside himself at the news. Goering had at least asked permission first before beginning negotiations; Himmler, in whose loyalty he had placed unlimited faith, had said nothing. That Himmler should betray him was the bitterest blow of all, and it served to crystallize the decision to commit suicide. This final decision followed the pattern of all the others: a period of hesitation, then a sudden resolution from which he was not to be moved. Throughout the week Hitler spoke constantly of taking his own life, and on the night of the 27th—if Hanna Reitsch's report is to be believed—he held a conference at which the plans for a mass suicide were carefully rehearsed and everyone made little speeches swearing allegiance to the Fuehrer and Germany. But still he waited and hoped—until the night of the 28th. That was the night of decisions.

Shortly after he received the news Hitler disappeared behind closed doors with Goebbels and Bormann. Hitler's first thought was revenge, and Bormann had at least the satisfaction of removing Himmler as well as Goering before the Third Reich crumbled into dust.

Himmler's representative with the Fuehrer, Fegelein, had already been arrested after it had been discovered that he had slipped quietly out of the bunker with the apparent intention of making a discreet escape. The fact that he was married to Eva Braun's sister was no protection. He was now subjected to a close examination and then taken into the courtyard to be shot. Himmler was more difficult to reach, but Hitler ordered Greim and Hanna Reitsch to make an attempt to get out of Berlin by plane and entrusted them with the order to arrest Himmler at all costs. "A traitor must never succeed me as Fuehrer," Hitler shouted in a trembling voice. "You must go out to insure that he will not."

Greim and Hanna Reitsch left between midnight and 1 a.m. on the morning of Sunday, 29 April, and Hitler now turned to more personal matters. Now that he had decided to end his life, the argument he had always used against marriage—that it would interfere with his career—no longer carried weight. So, between 1 a.m. and 3 a.m. on the 29th, Hitler married Eva Braun. The ceremony was hurriedly carried out by one of Goebbels' staff, a Gau Inspector, who was brought into the shelter for the purpose. Goebbels and Bormann were present as witnesses and signed the register after the bride and bridegroom. Eva began to write her maiden name of Braun, but struck out the initial B and corrected her signature to "Eva Hitler, *née* Braun." Afterwards the bridal party returned to their private suite, where a few friends—Bormann, Goebbels and his wife, Hitler's two secretaries, his adjutants and his cook—came in to drink champagne and to talk nostalgically.

The celebration went on while Hitler retired to the adjoining room with his secretary, Frau Junge. There, in the early hours of 29 April, he dictated his will and his political testament. Both documents are of such interest as to justify quotation at length.

Facing death and the destruction of the régime he had created, this man who had exacted the sacrifice of millions of lives rather than admit defeat was still recognizably the old Hitler. From first to last there is not a word of regret, nor a suggestion of remorse. The fault is that of others, above all the Jews, for even now the old hatred is unappeased. Word for word, Hitler's final address to the German nation could be taken from almost any of his early speeches of the 1920s or from the pages of *Mein Kampf*. His mind remained as tightly closed as it had been on the day when he wrote: "During these years in Vienna a view of life and a definite outlook on the world took shape in my mind. These became the granite basis of my conduct. Since then I have extended that foundation very little, I have changed nothing in it."

The second part of the Testament contains Hitler's provision for the succession. He began by expelling Goering and Himmler from the Party and from all offices of State. He accused them of causing immeasurable harm to Germany. As his successor he appointed Admiral Doenitz President of the

Reich, Minister of War, and Supreme Commander of the Armed Forces—and promptly proceeded to nominate his Government for him. Goebbels and Bormann had their reward, the first as the new Chancellor, the second as Party Minister and after other officers had been nominated, he returned once more to the earliest of his obsessions: "Above all I charge the leaders of the nation and those under them to scrupulous observance of the laws of race and to merciless opposition to the universal poisoner of all peoples, international Jewry."

The Testament was signed at four o'clock in the morning of Sunday, 29 April, and witnessed by Goebbels and Bormann for the Party, by Burgdorf and Krebs as representatives of the Army. At the same time Hitler signed his will. This was a shorter and more personal document:

> Although I did not consider that I could take the responsibility during the years of struggle of contracting a marriage, I have now decided, before the end of my life, to take as my wife the woman who, after many years of faithful friendship, of her own free will entered this town, when it was already besieged, in order to share my fate. At her own desire she goes to death with me as my wife. This will compensate us for what we have both lost through my work in the service of my people.
>
> What I possess belongs—in so far as it has any value—to the Party, or, if this no longer exists, to the State. Should the State too be destroyed, no further decision on my part is necessary.
>
> My pictures, in the collection which I have bought in the course of years, have never been collected for private purposes, but only for the establishment of a gallery in my home-town of Linz on the Danube.
>
> It is my heartfelt wish that this bequest should be duly executed.
>
> As my executor I nominate my most faithful Party comrade, Martin Bormann. He is given full legal authority to make all decisions. He is permitted to hand to my relatives anything which has a sentimental value or is necessary for the maintenance of a modest standard of life (*"eines kleinen buergerlichen Lebens"*); especially for my wife's mother and my faithful fellow-workers who are well known to him. The chief of these are my former secretaries, Frau Winter, etc., who have for many years helped me by their work.
>
> I myself and my wife choose to die in order to escape the disgrace of deposition or capitulation. It is our wish to be burned immediately in the place where I have carried out the greater part of my daily work in the course of my twelve years' service to my people.

Hitler's choice of Doenitz as his successor is surprising. Since Doenitz had replaced Raeder as Commander-in-Chief, however, Hitler had come to look upon the Navy with different eyes. He attached the greatest importance to the U-boat campaign, and contrasted the "National Socialist spirit" of the Navy under Doenitz with what he regarded as the treachery of the Army and Air Force. To command the Armed Forces—which in effect, meant to negotiate a surrender—someone else, preferably a serving officer, must become head of the State and Minister for War. Goebbels was thus to succeed Hitler as Chancellor, but Doenitz was to become head of the State and Supreme Commander. By choosing an officer from the Navy, rather than from the Army, Hitler offered a last deliberate insult to the military caste on whom he laid the blame for losing the war.

Hitler knew very well that the war was lost, but, in his political testament he made a clumsy attempt to save something for the future. As a legacy however, it was singularly unimpressive. Nothing remained but the stale and unconvincing slogans of the beer-hall agitator of the 1920s.

Characteristically, Hitler's last message contained at least one striking lie. His death was anything but a hero's end; by committing suicide he deliberately abandoned his responsibilities and took a way out which in earlier years he had strongly condemned as a coward's. It is worth noting that when General Weidling, the Commandant of Berlin, discovered that Hitler had committed suicide shortly after refusing the garrison permission to fight its way out of the city, he was so disgusted that he at once released his soldiers from their oaths. None the less the fiction was maintained in the official announcement, and Doenitz, in his broadcast of 1 May, declared that the Fuehrer had died fighting at the head of his troops.

In the course of Sunday, the 29th, arrangements were made to send copies of the Fuehrer's Political Testament out of the bunker, and three men were selected to make their way as best they could to Admiral Doenitz's and Field-Marshal Schoerner's headquarters.

The war had been begun by the Jews, it had been lost by the generals. In neither case was the responsibility Hitler's and his last word of all was to reaffirm his original purpose:

> The efforts and sacrifice of the German people in this war have been so great that I cannot believe they have been in vain. The aim must still be to win territory in the east for the German people.

During the 29th, while the messengers were setting out from the bunker, the news arrived that the Duce, together with Clara Petacci, had been caught by the Partisans and shot.

Their bodies were taken to Milan and hung in the Piazzale Loreto. The news can only have confirmed Hitler in the decision he had taken about his own end. Even when dead he was determined not to be put on show.

He now began to make systematic preparations for taking his life. He had his Alsatian bitch, Blondi, destroyed, and in the early hours of Monday, 30 April, assembled his staff in the passage in order to say farewell. Walking along the line, he shook each man and woman silently by the hand. Shortly afterwards Bormann sent out a telegram to Doenitz, instructing him to proceed "at once and mercilessly" against all traitors.

On the morning of the 30th Hitler was given the latest reports on the situation in Berlin. The Russians had occupied the Tiergarten and reached the Potsdamer Platz, only a block or two away from the Chancellery. Hitler received the news without excitement, and took lunch at two o'clock in the afternoon in the company of his two secretaries and his cook. Eva Hitler remained in her room and Hitler behaved as if nothing unusual were happening.

In the course of the early afternoon Erich Kempka, Hitler's chauffeur, was ordered to send two hundred litres of petrol to the Chancellery Garden.

Meanwhile, Hitler went to fetch his wife, and for the second time they said farewell to Goebbels, Bormann and the others. Hitler than returned to the Fuehrer's suite with Eva and closed the door. A few minutes passed while those outside stood waiting in the passage. Then a single shot rang out.

After a brief pause the little group outside opened the door. Hitler was lying on the sofa, which was soaked in blood: he had shot himself through the mouth. On his right-hand side lay Eva Braun, also dead: she had swallowed poison. The time was half past three on the afternoon of Monday, 30 April, 1945, ten days after Hitler's fifty-sixth birthday.

Hitler's instructions for the disposal of their bodies had been explicit, and they were carried out to the letter. Hitler's own body, wrapped in a blanket, was carried to the garden by two S.S. men. The head was concealed, but the black trousers and black shoes which he wore with his uniform jacket hung down beneath the covering. Eva's body was picked up by Bormann, who handed it to Kempka. They made their way up the stairs accompanied by Goebbels, Guensche and Burgdorf. The doors leading into the garden had been locked and the bodies were laid in a shallow depression of sandy soil close to the porch. Picking up the five cans of petrol, one after another, Guensche, Hitler's S.S. adjutant, poured the contents over the two corpses and set fire to them with a lighted rag.

A sheet of flame leapt up, and the watchers withdrew to the shelter of the porch. A heavy Russian bombardment was in progress and shells continually burst on the Chancellery. Silently they stood to attention, and for the last time gave the Hitler salute; then turned and disappeared into the shelter.

In the deserted garden, the two bodies burned steadily side by side. It was twelve years and three months to the day since Hitler had walked out of the President's room, Chancellor of the German Reich.

The rest of the story is briefly told. Bormann at once informed Doenitz by radio that Hitler had nominated him as his successor, but he concealed the fact of Hitler's death for another twenty-four hours. During the interval, on the night of 30 April, Goebbels and Bormann made an unsuccessful effort to negotiate with the Russians. The Russian reply was "unconditional surrender." Then, but only then, Bormann sent a further cable to Doenitz, reporting Hitler's death. The news was broadcast on the evening of 1 May to the solemn setting of music from Wagner and Bruckner's Seventh Symphony: the impression left was that of a hero's death, fighting to the last against Bolshevism.

An attempt at a mass escape by the men and women crowded into the network of bunkers round the Chancellery was made on the night of 1-2 May, and a considerable number succeeded in making their way out of Berlin. Among them was Martin Bormann: whether he was killed at the time or got away has never been established. Goebbels did not join them. On the evening of 1 May, after giving poison to his children, Goebbels shot his wife and himself in the Chancellery Garden. The bodies were set fire to by Goebbels' adjutant, but the job was badly done, and the charred remains were found next day by the Russians. After Goebbels' death the Fuehrerbunker was set on fire.

In the following week Doenitz attempted to negotiate terms of surrender with the Western Allies, but his reply was uncompromising. The German Army in Italy had already capitulated and the British and Americans refused to be drawn by Doenitz's clumsy efforts to secure a separate peace. On 4 May Admiral von Friedeburg signed an armistice providing for the surrender of the German forces in North-west Europe, and early on the morning of the 7th General Jodl and Friedeburg put their signatures to an unconditional surrender of all the German forces presented to them jointly by the representatives of the U.S.A., Great Britain, the U.S.S.R. and France at Rheims.

The Third Reich had outlasted its founder by just one week.

EPILOGUE

In this age of Unenlightened Despotism Hitler has had more than a few rivals, yet he remains, so far, the most remarkable of those who have used modern techniques to apply the classic formulas of tyranny.

Before the war it was common to hear Hitler described as the pawn of the sinister interests who held real power in Germany, of the Junkers or the Army, of heavy industry or high finance. This view does not survive examination of the evidence. Hitler acknowledged no masters, and by 1938 at least he exercised arbitrary rule over Germany to a degree rarely, if ever, equalled in a modern industrialized State.

At the same time, from the re-militarization of the Rhineland to the invasion of Russia he won a series of successes in diplomacy and war which established an hegemony over the continent of Europe comparable with that of Napoleon at the height of his fame. While these could not have been won without a people and an Army willing to serve him, it was Hitler who provided the indispensable leadership, the flair for grasping opportunities, the boldness in using them. In retrospect his mistakes appear obvious, and it is easy to be complacent about the inevitability of his defeat; but it took the combined efforts of the three most powerful nations in the world to break his hold on Europe.

Luck and the disunity of his opponents account for much of Hitler's success—as it will of Napoleon's—but not for all. He began as a man without a name and without support other than that which he acquired for himself, not even a citizen of the country he aspired to rule. To achieve what he did Hitler needed—and possessed—talents out of the ordinary which amounted to political genius, however evil its fruits.

His abilities have been sufficiently described in the preceding pages: his mastery of the irrational factors in politics, his insight into the weaknesses of his opponents, his gift for simplification, his sense of timing, his willingness to take risks. An opportunist entirely without principle, he showed considerable consistency and an astonishing power of will in pursuing his aims. Cynical in the exploitation of his histrionic gifts, he retained an unshaken belief in himself as a creature of destiny.

The fact that his career ended in failure, and that his defeat was pre-eminently due to his own mistakes, does not by itself detract from Hitler's claim to greatness. The flaw lies deeper. For these remarkable powers were combined with an ugly and strident egotism, a moral and intellectual cretinism. The passions which ruled Hitler's mind were ignoble: hatred, resentment, the lust to dominate, and, where he could not dominate, to destroy. His career did not exalt but debased the human condition, and his twelve years' dictatorship was barren of all ideas save one—the further extension of his own power and that of the nation with which he had identified himself. Even power he conceived of in the crudest terms: an endless vista of military roads, S.S. garrisons and concentration camps stretching across Europe and Asia.

The great revolutions of the past, whatever their ultimate fate, have been identified with the release of certain powerful ideas: individual conscience, liberty, equality, national freedom, social justice. National Socialism produced nothing. Hitler constantly exalted force over the power of ideas and delighted to prove that men were governed by cupidity, fear and their baser passions. The sole theme of the Nazi revolution was domination, dressed up as the doctrine of race, and, failing that, a vindictive destructiveness, Rauschning's *Revolution des Nihilismus.*

It is this emptiness, this lack of anything to justify the suffering he caused rather than his own monstrous and ungovernable will which makes Hitler both so repellent and so barren a figure. Hitler will have his place in history, but it will be alongside Attila the Hun, the barbarian king who boasted "in a saying," Gibbon writes, "worthy of his ferocious pride, that the grass never grew on the spot where his horse had stood."

The view has often been expressed that Hitler could only have come to power in Germany, and it is true—without falling into the same error of racialism as the Nazis—that there were certain features of German historical development, quite apart from the effects of the Defeat and the Depression, which favoured the rise of such a movement.

This is not to accuse the Germans of Original Sin, or to ignore the other sides of German life which were only grossly caricatured by the Nazis. But Nazism was not some terrible accident which fell upon the German people. It was rooted in their history, and while it is true that a majority of the

German people never voted for Hitler, it is also true that thirteen millions did. Both facts need to be remembered.

From this point of view Hitler's career may be described as a *reductio ad absurdum* of the most powerful political tradition in Germany since the Unification. This is what nationalism, militarism, authoritarianism, the worship of success and force, the exaltation of the State and *realpolitik* lead to, if they are projected to their logical conclusion.

There are Germans who will reject such a view. They argue that what was wrong with Hitler was that he lacked the necessary skill, that he was a bungler. It only he had listened to the generals—or Schacht—or the career diplomats —if only he had not attacked Russia, and so on. They refuse to see that it was the ends themselves, not simply the means, which were wrong: the pursuit of unlimited power, the scorn for justice or any restraint on power; the exaltation of will over reason and conscience; the assertion of an arrogant supremacy, the contempt for others' rights. As at least one German historian, Professor Meinecke, has recognized, the catastrophe to which Hitler led Germany points to the need to re-examine the aims as well as the methods of German policy as far back as Bismarck.

The Germans, however, were not the only people who preferred in the 1930s not to know what was happening and refused to call evil things by their true names. The British and French at Munich; the Italians, Germany's partner in the Pact of Steel; the Poles, who stabbed the Czechs in the back over Teschen; the Russians, who signed the Nazi-Soviet Pact to partition Poland, all thought they could buy Hitler off, or use him to their own selfish advantage. They did not succeed, any more than the German Right or the German Army. In the bitterness of war and occupation they were forced to learn the truth of the words of John Donne which Ernest Hemingway set at the beginning of his novel of the Spanish Civil War:

> No man is an Iland, intire of it selfe; every man is a peece of the Continent, a part of the maine; If a clod bee washed away by the Sea, Europe is the lesse, as well as if a Promontorie were, as well as if a Mannor of thy friends or of thine own were; Any man's death diminishes me, because I am involved in Mankinde; And therefore never send to know for whom the bell tolls; It tolls for thee.

Hitler, indeed, was a European, no less than a German phenomenon. The conditions and the state of mind which he exploited, the *malaise* of which he was the symptom, were not confined to one country, although they were more strongly marked in Germany than anywhere else. Hitler's idiom was German, but the thoughts and emotions to which he gave expression have a more universal currency.

Hitler recognized this relationship with Europe perfectly clearly. He was in revolt against "the System" not just in Germany but in Europe, against that liberal bourgeois order, symbolized for him in the Vienna which had once rejected him. To destroy this was his mission, the mission in which he never ceased to believe; and in this, the most deeply felt of his purposes, he did not fail. Europe may rise again, but the old Europe of the years between 1789, the year of the French Revolution, and 1939, the year of Hitler's War, has gone for ever—and the last figure in its history is that of Adolf Hitler, the architect of its ruin. *"Si monumentum requiris, circumspice"*—"If you seek his monument, look around."

BANTAM CLASSICS

NOVELS

(continued on next page)

DRAMA

FOUR GREAT COMEDIES OF THE RESTORATION AND EIGHTEENTH CENTURY..... ......FC2*50¢
Introduction by Brooks Atkinson
    THE COUNTRY WIFE by William Wycherley
    THE WAY OF THE WORLD by William Congreve
    SHE STOOPS TO CONQUER by Oliver Goldsmith
    THE SCHOOL FOR SCANDAL by Richard Brinsley Sheridan

FOUR GREAT PLAYS BY CHEKHOV...........FC5*50¢
Anton Chekhov
    THE SEA GULL • UNCLE VANYA
    THREE SISTERS • THE CHERRY ORCHARD

CYRANO DE BERGERAC....................AC19*35¢
Edmond Rostrand (Translated by Brian Hooker)

FOUR GREAT PLAYS BY IBSEN.............FC23*50¢
Henrik Ibsen (Introduction by John Gassner)
    A DOLL'S HOUSE • GHOSTS
    AN ENEMY OF THE PEOPLE • THE WILD DUCK

THE CRUCIBLE ....AC31*35¢
Arthur Miller (Introduction by Richard Watts, Jr.)

COLLECTIONS

THE COMPLETE SHORT STORIES OF MARK TWAIN ....SC3*75¢
Charles Neider (Ed.)

FIFTY GREAT SHORT STORIES.................FC29*50¢
Milton Crane (Ed.)

RASHOMON AND OTHER STORIES...........AC42*35¢
Ryunosuke Akutagawa (Introduction by Osamu Shimizu)

BIOGRAPHY

HENRY THE EIGHTH..........................FC9*50¢
Francis Hackett

CLEOPATRA ....FC27*50¢
Emil Ludwig

UP FROM SLAVERY ....FC37*50¢
Booker T. Washington

NON-FICTION

THE VOYAGE OF THE BEAGLE.............FC11*50¢
Charles Darwin

ONLY YESTERDAY ....FC15*50¢
Frederick Lewis Allen

TWO YEARS BEFORE THE MAST...........FC20*50¢
Richard Henry Dana (Introduction by Mark Van Doren)

MARRIAGE AND MORALS....................FC32*50¢
Bertrand Russell

HIROSHIMA ....AC26*35¢
John Hersey

Look for Bantam Classics at local newsstands and bookstores. If your dealer does not carry these books, they may be ordered by sending the price of the book plus 10¢ postage and handling charge for each copy to: Dept. BC; Bantam Books, Inc.; 657 W. Chicago Ave.; Chicago 10, Ill. (On orders for 5 or more books there is no postage charge.) Sorry no C.O.D.'s. Send check or money order. No currency please. Allow three weeks for delivery.